NEWCOMER'S HANDBOOK®

Country

GU*i*DE

CHINA

2nd Edition

FIRST BOOKS®

PORTLAND • OREGON
WWW.FIRSTBOOKS.COM

© 2012 by Firstbooks.com, Inc. All rights reserved.

Newcomer's Handbook Country Guide for China, 2nd Edition

Newcomer's Handbook® and First Books® are registered trademarks of First Books.

Reproduction of the contents of this book in any form whatsoever is not permissible without written permission from the publishers, First Books®, 6750 SW Franklin Street, Suite A, Portland, OR 97223-2542, 503-968-6777., www.firstbooks.com.

First Books® is not legally responsible for any change in the value of any enterprises by reason of their inclusion or exclusion from this work. Contents are based on information believed to be accurate at the time of publication.

First Books® has not accepted payment from any firms or organizations for inclusion in this book.

Authors: Navjot Singh

Editor: Linda Franklin
Publisher: Jeremy Solomon
Interior Layout and Composition: Masha Shubin
Photographs © Navjot Singh
Cover photos: © Navjot Singh, unless otherwise noted.
West Lake pagoda photo @ Linda Franklin

Paperback:
ISBN-13: 978-1-937090-44-9 | ISBN-10: 1-937090-44-2
ePub:
ISBN-13: 978-1-937090-45-6 | ISBN-10: 1-937090-45-0
Kindle:
ISBN-13: 978-1-937090-46-3 | ISBN-10: 1-937090-46-9

Printed in the U.S.A.
All paper is acid free and meets all ANSI standards for archival quality paper.

1 3 5 7 9 10 8 6 4 2

CONTENTS

INTRODUCTION

HE INITIAL MISCONCEPTIONS THAT MANY PEOPLE HAVE OF CHINA ARE of people dressed in traditional Chinese costumes, busy streets filled with bicycles, men wearing pointy straw hats while pulling tricycles with their hands, men with shaved foreheads and long ponytails, and women with long silky hair wearing beautiful dresses. In reality it's not quite as you would have imagined! These days, a first-time visitor to China would be somewhat disappointed to know that most of these ancient stereotypical traditions of Chinese culture are to be seen in museums, Hollywood movies, or Chinese soap operas shown on state-owned television channels.

New arrivals into the country will also be taken aback at how surprisingly modern China has become. Though still years behind other Asian developing countries such as Singapore, Japan, or South Korea in terms of infrastructure and cultural outlook, it is, however, catching up rapidly with Western economies.

My interests with China grow each time I even think about the country. It's almost as if the country's culture itself has become part of my life and DNA. The concept of writing a unique travel guide to the "Middle Kingdom" initially started off with an informal meeting with the Director of the China National Tourist Office (CNTO) in London.

A developing country that is no longer just the most populous in the world, 21st-century China is firmly placed on a fast track to being the largest trading power on the globe and among the top three world economies. Many economic pundits are predicting that China's economy is set to overtake that of the USA by around 2050 and will continue to dominate the global economic scene. Above all else, moving away from the economic and political topics, China is also a very beautiful and romantic country.

Whatever differences China has had with its rivals in the past, these days no country wants to make enemies with her because the whole world is now enmeshed with China, politically and economically, as never before. Proof of this exists through the country's major cities, where foreign investment thrives on a massive scale. Two things strike a first-time visitor to China, the first being the massive population density and the other the amount of construction going on. "It looks like a huge building site" was what I thought when I first arrived here (and it still does and will continue to do so for a number of years), and at one time it was reported that roughly 60% of the world's cranes were in Shanghai alone! China is not just urbanizing, it is globalizing. Little more than a generation ago, this was a country where Red Guards in Mao suits chanted anti-imperialist slogans. Today, young people with money dress much like their counterparts in Hong Kong, New York, London, or Paris.

The People's Republic of China (along with Vietnam, North Korea, Laos, and Cuba) is one of the five remaining Communist states in the world. Before the early 1980s there was no advertising on the streets or in other forms of media, there were very few cars on the roads (if you had a car you were considered a millionaire or even a billionaire!), and everyone wore navy blue Mao suits with Mao caps (including children and women).

The Great Wall is one of the world's greatest wonders.

So what do we have now? A country that has an endless hunger for modern cars, planes, trains, advertising, and fashion. China is a country of extremes. The world's most populous nation; the world's fastest-growing major economy; the world's biggest exporter. It has the world's longest sea bridge, the world's fastest train, and is the world's biggest market for cars. The list goes on and on. And its record-breaking ways look like they are set to continue for a while yet. The country's big cities dazzle when night falls. Multi-colored illuminations light up everything from the housing blocks that rise up on the hillsides to the giant city center replicas of the Empire State Building. Motorway crash barriers glow pink, blue, green, and purple. This is the scene all around the country.

Take that last point. In the mid-1980s the country only produced a few thousand cars and hardly anyone actually owned one. Now, it is the world's largest producer of cars and the world's largest consumer. Last year, 18 million vehicles were sold, dwarfing the 12.7 million sold in the US. And this sudden explosion has meant a massive rise in one thing: traffic.

There are too many cars on the streets, too many planes (and too many airlines), people are wearing the latest designer clothes, an increasing number of Chinese people go on holiday abroad, and there is an abundance of advertising everywhere, marketing everything ranging from the latest electronic goods to the latest coffee being offered at Starbucks (yes, coffee being sold in China—no longer mission impossible!). Modernism and traditionalism, communism and capitalism— all seem to be living comfortably side by side. It's amazing how the Chinese have achieved this as it certainly is not an easy mix to deal with. The Chinese people are proud to be making history by contributing to the economic growth, and this emerging market has become a role model and a prime example for other developing nations to look up to.

The country's hosting of the Beijing Olympics in 2008 made the future for this country look even better in terms of attracting direct foreign investment from a variety of industry sectors. Because of this attraction in various industries, China has at the same time drawn a considerable number of expatriates who have made China their second home. On October 1, 2009, China celebrated 60 years of Communist rule with an extravagant military display laid across Tiananmen Square. No country in history has seen such rapid economic growth in its culture, infrastructure, and environment in such a short period of time as China has. The objective of this book is not to be a tourist guide but instead to provide an insight into Chinese life and a guide for expats who are planning on relocating to China for a job, for marriage, or for whatever other purposes that they may have.

A number of changes have occurred since the first edition of this book, namely with the increase of infrastructure in all the major cities. For example, there are more expats in China now than before the Olympics, every major city has a metro line network, and there are more buildings going up all the time. For most other countries normally the skyline and a city's infrastructure changes every decade or so, but for China this rapid change is happening almost every few months! For me it has been a privilege to witness the immense beauty and growth of this country at first hand and I hope that anyone who is coming to China for the first time to start a new life as an expat (for business or pleasure) will enjoy the benefits of living in this stunning nation, as I have done. I wish you a very pleasant stay in China and hope this book provides you with a smooth welcome.

QUICK FACTS ABOUT CHINA (中国, ZHONG GUO)

Official Name	Zhōnghuá Rénmín Gònghéguó (People's Republic of China, 中国人民共和国) Not to be confused with the "Republic of China," as this is the official name of Taiwan.
Capital City	Beijing (北京)
Largest City	Shanghai (上海) (also China's financial capital)
Government	Socialist Republic. Communist Party members choose the leader and other think tanks. No general elections. The country operates on a one-government, two-systems policy where Hong Kong and Macau are designated as the Special Administrative Regions (S.A.R.), each one having a governor to oversee the day-to-day running, while all the important decisions are made by Beijing.
Leader of the P.R.C. (President)	Hu Jintao (AKA Chairman Hu Jintao) is the President of the People's Republic of China. At the time of writing Vice President Xi Jinping was tipped to be the next President of China, and is the party General Secretary.
Premier	Premier Wen Jiabao
Establishment	People's Republic declared on October 1, 1949
Area	9,596,960 square km (3,705,405 square miles) China is officially the third largest country in the world by area.
Population	(2010) 1,353,311,000 Officially the world's largest population. Although the figures vary slightly, some 20–25% of the world's population consists of Chinese people.
Special Economic Trade Zones	Shenzhen, Dalian, Xiamen, Hainan Island, and Shantou

	Han (Approx. 91.9%). The rest are minority groups made up of: Yao, Zhuang, Hui, Manchu, and She. There are officially 55 ethnc minorities listed in China, plus smaller tribal minorities within the rural areas.
Density	140/km² (53rd), 363/sq mi
GDP (PPP)	2010 Total: $11,316 trillion, Second in the world. Per Capita: $8,394, 90th
GDP (nominal)	2010 Total: $6.988 trillion (2nd in the world) Per capita: $5,184 (90th in the world)
Growth Rate (Overall)	For the past few years, China has seen a healthy growth rate of around 10% annually. At present, this is higher than any other country in the world.
Currency	Renminbi, 人民币 (RMB, ¥), commonly called yuan Symbol: CNY Approx. 11 yuan is equal to £1 GBP Approx. 7 yuan is equal to 1 US$ Approx. 10 yuan is equal to 1 Euro
Average Salary	Average salaries used to be very low in China, normally as little as 4,000 yuan per annum for some professions. The last 10 years have seen a steady rise in salaries for both farmers and city professionals. The current average salary for a degree-holding professional with 5 years' experience is around 6,000 yuan per month.
Major Ports	Tianjin, Shanghai, Guangzhou, Hong Kong (S.A.R), and Qingdao (Tsingtao)
Official languages	Chinese Pǔtōnghuà—普通话, also known as Mandarin, 中文. There are seven main Chinese languages and at least another 56 minority languages.
Official Airline	Air China (IATA Code: CA) HQ: Beijing Capital Airport
Official Airport	Beijing Capital International Airport

Official Bank	People's Bank of China (Zhong guo ren min yin hang, 中国人民银行)
Time Zone	Beijing time is officially used, +8 Hours GMT (+7 Hours GMT during the summer). The country extends over five time zones; however the Beijing time is used exclusively.
Border Countries	(From East to West, anti-clockwise): North Korea (DPRK), Mongolia, Russia, Kazakhstan, Kyrgyzstan, Turkmenistan, Uzbekistan, Pakistan, India, Nepal, Bhutan, Burma, Laos, and Vietnam
International Internet Domain	.cn (In July 2010 there were just over a staggering 420 million internet users and this number is estimated to increase even more.)
International Calling Code	00 86
Water Coverage	2.85% of the Earth's supply
Rivers	China's major rivers are the Yangtze, Yellow River, Heilongjiang River, Pearl River, and the Huaihe River. The Yangtze River is the third longest in the world, and the longest river in China, with a total length of approximately 6,350 km. The river snakes its way across major cities such as Shanghai, Nanjing, Wuhan, and Chongqing.
Food & Agriculture	Rice and noodles are the staple foods, while soya, cow's milk, and various lentils are available throughout in abundance. China has become a country that can support its own people and be able to support people in the poorest of nations around the world. Remarkably only 15–20% of the land is arable. Self-sufficient food.
Top 10 Trade Partners	Australia, Britain, Russia, India, France, Germany, Italy, Japan, United States, South Korea
Electricity	China uses 220v/50Hz. Wall sockets have two or three pin connectors. It would be useful to have a travel voltage adapter.
Age Structure	0–15 Years: 27.1% 15–65 Years: 68.5% 65 Years and above: 4.4% (2009 Figures)

Life Expectancy	72 (Male); 77 (Female) (2012 estimates)
Religion	Majority of Chinese people do not believe in god (atheist). Taoism, Confucianism, and Buddhism are practiced by many, while there are minorities consisting of Muslims, Jews, Catholics, and Protestants.
Products	Rice, potatoes, corn, sorghum, millet, wheat, sugar cane, peanuts, soybeans, sesame, tea; silk cocoons, ambary hemp, jute; sun-cured tobacco; bananas, oranges, lychees, pineapples, longans, and other tropical and subtropical fruits; rubber, oil palm, sisal hemp; coffee, cocoa, lemongrass, pepper; oyster, abalone, pearl, sea horse, and other sea products; timber wolfram, tin, antimony, bismuth, molybdenum, copper, lead, zinc, oil shale, salt, sulphur.

CHAPTER 1

CHINA: A BRIEF HISTORY

Ancient China	Neolithic 12000–2000 B.C.	
	Xia 2100–1800 B.C.	
	Shang 1700–1027 B.C.	
	Western Zhou 1027–771 B.C.	
	Eastern Zhou 770–221 B.C.	770–476 B.C.—Spring and Autumn period
		475–221 B.C.—Warring States period
Early Imperial China	Qin 221–207 B.C.	
	Western Han 206 B.C.–A.D. 9	
	Hsing (Wang Mang interregnum) A.D. 9–25	
	Eastern Han A.D. 25–220	
	Three Kingdoms A.D. 220–265	
	Western Chin A.D. 265–316	
	Eastern Chin A.D. 317–420	
	Southern and Northern Dynasties A.D. 420–588	Southern Dynasties 420–478—Song 479–501—Qi 502–556—Liang 557–588—Chen
		Northern Dynasties 386–533—Northern Wei 534–549—Eastern Wei 535–557—Western Wei 550–577—Northern Qi 557–588—Northern Zhou
	Sui A.D. 580–618	

Early Imperial China cont.	T'ang A.D. 618–907	
	Five Dynasties A.D. 907–960	907–923—Later Liang 923–936—Later Tang 936–946—Later Jin 947–950—Later Han 951–960—Later Zhou
	Ten Kingdoms A.D. 907–979	
	Song A.D. 960–1279	960–1125—Northern Song 1127–1279—Southern Song
	Liao A.D. 916–1125	
	Western Xia A.D. 1038–1227	
	Jin A.D. 1115–1234	
Later Imperial China	Yuan A.D. 1279–1368	
	Ming A.D. 1368–1644	
	Qing A.D. 1644–1911	

HISTORY

Given China's history of over five thousand years, it's no surprise that there is a lot of culture and heritage waiting to be absorbed in this vast land. It's not easy to describe the rich history of China in just a few pages, and so instead I will provide a brief outline. "Zhōnghuá Rénmín Gònghéguó" is the official Chinese name of the People's Republic of China (not to be confused with the Republic of China, which is the official name of Taiwan). However, in everyday usage, it is referred to as "Zhong Guo" (meaning "Middle Kingdom"). This name is thought to have been invented by previous civilizations to describe the central importance of China.

One of the proudest and most industrious people I have ever met, the Chinese people strongly believe that China is the future and it's the place to be in. The roots of this hard-working culture and pride lie in the history of the Chinese. Many inventions and concepts originated in China. Chinese science, transmitted to Europe, Africa, and the Middle East in waves, laid the foundations for many of the constituents of the modern world. Indeed, the Chinese are known worldwide for much that we in the West take for granted without noticing that they are in actual fact "Made in China."

Approximately 3500 years ago the Chinese were heavily involved in the trade of silk and carving jade (both silk and jade are of high importance to the culture even today) as well as growing wheat and rice. Fireworks (namely gunpowder), paper, and the noodle (including pasta, spaghetti, which, according to many historians, Marco Polo took back to Europe from China) were invented in China. The crossbow, used in Europe and the Middle East, was also invented in China.

*The gateway of the Forbidden City facing opposite
Tiananmen Square in the capital city, Beijing.*

The Chinese were also famous for recording events in a written language of thousands of characters. The first known dynasty was the Xia Dynasty (historians estimate that before the Xia was the Neolithic, from about 12000 to 2000 B.C.). The Xia ruled from about 2100 to 1800 B.C. By 1027 B.C. (during the reign of the Shang Dynasty) a full written language had been developed along with the first Chinese calendar being introduced. Next came the period of the Western and Eastern Zhou (or pronounced Chou) Dynasty (1027–221 B.C.). This period saw the introduction of money, formal laws, metals (including iron) and the philosophy of Confucianism. The idea of Confucianism led to the idea of a "Mandate of Heaven" (known as Ti'en Ming), in which the Heavens tended to give the rulers a mandate to impose laws on the people. Ultimately this led to the Chinese addressing their Emperors as the "Son of Heaven." Since that period, this concept remained very much alive in Chinese culture, right up to the death of Chairman Mao Zedong in 1976. The "Mandate of Heaven" had various beliefs such as that natural disasters are caused by disapproval by the rulers of Heaven. Such was the superstition among the rulers that the "Mandate of Heaven" started to go hand in hand with the Taoist belief. This book won't delve any deeper into the concept of the Taoist belief because there is so much of it to write about and it goes beyond our scope.

During the period between 481 and 221 B.C. the Zhou Empire broke up into smaller kingdoms; this period was known as the "Warring States Period." Even today, historians refer to the Zhou Empire as the golden age in Chinese history and the Chinese are very much proud of this era as it established the firm foundations for the China that we witness today.

The Qin Dynasty (221–207 B.C., pronounced "Chin") had successfully defeated its enemies and united the empire in 221 B.C. The Qin Dynasty favored numerous construction projects instead of agriculture. These projects included the partial construction of the Great Wall, a monumental man-made structure, claimed to be visible from space by the naked eye, which has effectively become one of the iconic attractions of China. The consequent famine resulting from the lack of concentration in agriculture assisted in the upsurge of a farmer's revolt, which eventually ended with the fall of the Qin Dynasty.

Subsequent to the Qin's rule came the four-hundred-year reign of the Western and Eastern Han dynasties (206 B.C. until A.D. 220) which orchestrated an increase in relationships with cultures in central Asia. This allowed China to exchange its silk for precious minerals such as gold, all along the famous Silk Road that runs through the Northwest of China and into some countries in Central Asia.

During this period, Buddhism from India was established for the first time in China. Despite the Han Dynasty only ruling for approximately four hundred years, its influence on the Chinese people was vital, and even today the native Chinese are known as the "Han," while the alternative word used for Mandarin is "Hanyu" (pronounced "Han U").

The Han Dynasty's demise put the country into almost four hundred years of civil war, brought on by an uprising and social divide that split the country into three territories. Not long after that, the Sui Dynasty (A.D. 580–618) came into power, which formed a new government by reuniting China. The Sui Dynasty gave way to the Tang Dynasty (A.D. 618–907). The Tang dynasty had its government seat based in the capital of Shaanxi province, Xi'an (then known as Chang'An). The Tang Dynasty did not last long either, as it experienced war and an economic decline that led to a period of approximately 50 years of no rule until the arrival of the Song Dynasty in A.D. 960.

The introduction of the Song Dynasty paved the way for trade with most foreign countries, especially in Africa and the Middle East, to flourish. Towards the conclusion of the Song Dynasty's ruling years came an explorer from the West called Marco Polo. His travels in China lasted almost two decades and during that time, some historians claim that some trade secrets were taken back to Europe, such as noodles—hence the introduction of pasta in Italy! Despite all of this there was a considerable amount of instability and threat looming in northern China. Genghis Khan, emperor of the Mongol Empire, which had already taken control of Russia and Central Asia, took over China in 1279, therein ending the rule of the Song Dynasty.

The grandson of Genghis Khan, Kublai Khan, took control of Beijing and declared the city to be the capital of the Mongol Empire. The Mongols did not last long and were eventually succeeded by the Ming Dynasty in 1368. It was during the reign of the Ming Dynasty that the first foreigners to arrive by sea into China, the Portuguese, reached the southern city of Guangzhou, in 1516. Around this time the Portuguese started making Macau a home away from home. The British, Spanish, and the Dutch followed in subsequent years. The Ming Dynasty, instead of focusing on all these foreign visitors that were coming into southern China, was deeply embedded in preventing any threats from other advances such as Mongolian highwaymen and Japanese pirates in northern China, evidently a very difficult dilemma for the emperors to deal with.

The Ming Dynasty was eventually succeeded by the Qing administration in 1644. Between this time and the early 1800s, there is a lot to write about; however the next interesting era in Chinese history didn't arrive until the early 1800s when the British started selling smuggled Indian-grown opium to the Chinese, in return for tea and silk. This smuggling of opium started to cause widespread addiction throughout the country, naturally disturbing the Qing government.

In return for the opium, the British demanded that the payment be made in silver. However with finances running short and the opium trade blossoming, the Qing emperors were not able to meet the demands of the British and therefore confiscated all the opium from Guangdong province. This provided a perfect setting for a conflict between the British and the Qing government and hence resulted in the commencement of the Opium Wars. There were two major Opium Wars, with the first one taking place between 1839 and 1842, in which the British attacked Guangzhou and Nanjing. During the course of these Opium Wars the Chinese were forced to open up six ports (including Hong Kong and Shanghai) for trade purposes with Europe. The second Opium War started in 1856 and was prosecuted by the British and the French against the Qing Dynasty for four years.

Towards the beginning of the 19th century, the powerhouses of Britain, Germany, Russia, and France made separate attempts to colonize China, with Shanghai bearing the brunt of the impact. None of these attempts was successful, and following an open door policy led by America, colonial partition was eventually vetoed. Because of this experience, the Chinese know what it is like to be under colonial rule, which may provide enough evidence to counter any suggestion from economic think tanks who believe that the Communist Party wants to colonize the African continent in this day and age.

During and after the Opium Wars, peasants were angered with the liberties that foreigners were taking at China's cost. The Boxers or "Anti-western society of the harmonious fist" (direct translation from their Chinese name), as they were known, were formed by peasants, starting in Shandong province. They put into practice a principle called the "Boxer Rebellion," which cemented their nationalistic viewpoint that all foreigners should be expelled from China. The bloodbath that followed included the deaths of many foreigners and destruction of any infrastructure that they brought with them into China, such as churches, ships, train lines, and even their homes. This did not last long and eventually the Boxers were defeated by foreign armed forces. This brought further bad news for the Qing dynasty, which became powerless overnight.

Dr. Sun Yat Sen (also known as Sun Zhongshan) was the leader of the National People's Party (known as the Guomindang), who with his revolutionary leadership in 1911 tried to bring democracy to China. He was partly responsible for the overthrowing of the Qing dynasty and the expulsion of foreigners from China. Victory was gained in 1912 for the revolutionists and Dr. Sun Yat Sen proudly declared the birth of the People's Republic of China. A new flag was introduced and Dr. Sun Yat Sen became an overnight hero throughout China, and was subsequently better known as the father of modern China. Even today, most cities have parks, roads, educational establishments, shopping centers, hospitals and lakes named after him. Even the city of his birth, Zhongshan in Guangdong province, bears the great man's name.

Meanwhile the Japanese had taken the German colonized port of Qingdao in the aftermath of World War I and were advancing further into Shandong province.

In 1921 the Chinese Communist Party was founded and in the same year Dr. Sun Yat Sen was elected the leader of the National People's Party, the Guomindang. In the years ahead, the Communist Party and the Guomindang Party worked together on many issues ranging from agriculture, which won them the support from the peasants, to the economy. After Dr. Sun Yat Sen's death in 1925, his brother-in-law Chiang Kai-Shek (Jiang Jieshe) took over the nationalist party. Instead of working together with the Communists, Chiang Kai-Shek fell out with them and there was a period of civil unrest from 1926 onwards.

Around the same time, the Japanese took control of Shanghai in 1937, followed by Beijing and Nanjing (including the Nanjing massacre), and eventually made inroads into Guangzhou. These were understandably painful times for the Chinese as they bore the aggression by the Japanese. According to many Chinese history books, bodies, some horribly mutilated by the Japanese samurai, lay scattered in major cities such as Shanghai or Nanjing, and people were starving to death, naturally engendering even until today strong feelings against the Japanese in many Chinese people. With the most modern days, relations between the two nations are getting somewhat better given the fact that most Chinese people today drive Japanese-manufactured cars and indulge in Japanese food.

Led by Mao Zedong, almost 81,000 Communists responded to the military campaign from the nationalists by taking part in the famous "Long March" that started off in southeast China and made its way to the northwest of the country, stretching a distance of just over 3,000 miles. By the time the marchers reached its final point at Yan'an in Shaanxi province, only about 11% of the troops had survived the journey. Coming from an affluent farmer's family, Mao had belief and trust in peasants, miners, and laborers. He in return won their support, admiration, and trust.

While all of this was going on in the south, the Japanese were attacking major northern cities, especially Shanghai, where many foreigners became trapped in unfortunate events. Quite a number of movies have portrayed these events in China's history, the most famous of which is the Hollywood movie *Empire of the Sun*, directed by Steven Spielberg, which illustrates how foreigners coped during the Japanese occupation of Shanghai.

After the Japanese finally surrendered in 1945, a civil war erupted between the Nationalists and the Communists the following year, and in 1949 the Red Army (later known as the People's Liberation Army or PLA, as they are known today) led by Mao Zedong defeated the nationalists in Nanjing. Chiang Kai-Shek withdrew to Taiwan (then known as Formosa Island) along with two million other refugees.

This finally led Chairman Mao Zedong to stand in Tiananmen Square in front of thousands of people and officially declare October 1, 1949, as a national day. The People's Republic of China was confirmed as a Communist state and China was officially born!

Subsequent to the declaration, China enjoyed her first few years as a sovereign republic and the early 1950s seemed to be prosperous for her people. Then with the economy improving, Mao Zedong introduced the principle of the "Great Leap Forward" in 1958, a five-year ambitious plan to accelerate the Chinese economy to bring it to par with most developed countries. This did not materialize as the Communist Party wanted it to; with natural disasters causing widespread damage to the economy in 1959, things did not go quite as planned. During the 1959–1961 period China sadly bore the brunt of the world's worst famine, leading to the deaths of twenty to forty million people.

China's economy spiraled down, bringing about massive protests in 1966 from students who denounced their educational establishment acministrations, an era that Chairman Mao echoed as the "Great Cultural Revolution" began. Under Mao's teachings, many of Beijing's students organized themselves into a political private army called the "Red Guards." The Red Guards were up in force against party opponents, at times almost taking the country to the brink of another civil war.

China was effectively separated from the world as all Western philosophies were neglected. Mao consistently encouraged the Chinese people to take notice of the farmers and those not so well off. His famous slogan "the poorer the better" was something that people looked up to during the Cultural Revolution. China, in those days, was in a state of chaos that led to academics being publicly humiliated and tortured. The only books available to read were *The Quotations of Chairman Mao* or the *Little Red Book of Thoughts*, as it was known, or other minor Communist propaganda material. Many of the ideologies of the Chinese Communist Party were taken from the Soviet Communist Party.

It was observed as somewhat of an opportunity to rekindle relations with the West when President Nixon paid a visit to Beijing in 1972 and went on a diplomatic tour of the Great Wall with Chairman Mao. In a way this thawed the period in which political brutality loomed over China.

Chairman Mao died on September 9, 1976. His portrait was placed on the top of the main gateway of the Forbidden City facing Tiananmen Square in Beijing, where his body is on public display at the mausoleum.

A view of central Beijing as seen from the top of Jingshen park.

Towards the end of the Cultural Revolution, Deng Xiao Ping took control of daily duties within the Communist Party in 1977, and started leading the country a few years after Mao's death. With Deng Xiao Ping at the helm, the future became brighter. Deng actively encouraged foreign trade and opened Special Economic Zones (SEZ) across the east coast of the country, such as Shenzhen and Dalian, where an open door policy was inaugurated. As opposed to Chairman Mao's slogan of "the poorer the better," Deng's slogan of "to get rich is glorious" is certainly being put to good practice in the current climate. Economic and political ties with the world started to improve; a prime example of this was the first China-Russia summit in Beijing since 1959, in May of 1989. Foreign investment increased and China's economy since 1979 has seen a doubling in figures every eight years.

PRESENT SITUATION

The twenty-first century has already witnessed some remarkable events in China's history such as its entry into the World Trade Organization (WTO) in December 2001, which has enabled its economy to move forward at a rocketing pace. With rapid urbanization, a technological revolution could mean that manual jobs may be short lived. Thirty years ago the existence of foreign brands was unthinkable, along with the prospects for foreigners to open their private stores, as everything used to be state controlled. All of that is changing now, and for these reasons, an increasingly high number of expatriates are coming to live and work in China. The UK, USA, and many European countries are investing heavily in China's experiment with capitalism.

People are no longer starving, general standards of living are improving along with an increase in life expectancy, electric power cuts are rare, people have clean water in almost all of the major cities, infrastructure is one of the best in the Asia Pacific region, and Chinese people have an abundance of food and minerals. You might be amazed at how much rice people throw away these days and how they take things for granted, just as people do in the developed world. Mao would have been shocked to see all of this!

Higher standards of living in China are driving inflation high in Europe and the USA. It's having a direct impact on things such as food and fuel prices that have been steadily increasing. This is especially true in the Western world, where there is a huge demand for cereals and dairy products.

The Temple of Heaven, known as Tiantan, in Beijing was constructed between 1406 to 1420 during the reign of the Yongle Emperor.

CHINA AND THE WORLD

In recent years the current Chinese government has made a number of attempts to sustain friendships with neighboring countries as well as with countries which in the past China may have had some differences with. There has been interest in building a stronger partnership with developing countries such as India, Korea, and many countries in the African continent. Ever since the foundations of the Communist Party in 1921, there have been continuous relationships with Russia as well as with all the major European countries. Germany, France, Italy, Australia, Pakistan, and the USA are among some of China's many trading partners. China continues to enjoy being a member of the UN Security Council since November 1971.

CHINA AND THE AFRICAN CONTINENT

An African friend told me that there is a saying along the lines of "Without Chairman Mao there would be no China," "Without Deng Xiao Ping there would be no modern China," and "Without modern China, there would be no twenty-first century Africa." Cities such as Guangzhou and Shanghai have a large number of expats from the African continent. China is the third largest investor in Africa, with annual trade reaching over $29 billion in the 2009 financial year. There has been an increase in both passenger and cargo flights between Chinese cities and such important African hubs as Nairobi (Kenya), Addis Ababa (Ethiopia), Johannesburg (South Africa), and Lagos (Nigeria). It sounds like a weird combination, but the China-Africa bonding is in actual fact working quite well, even better than expected, as pointed out by some think tanks in the West. And the West is taking notice of this.

Although China has been open to traders from the African continent for thousands of years, China's presence and relationship with Africa has become stronger only since the late twentieth century. Following on from the success of the first China-Africa Forum in Beijing in 2006, when Hu Jintao announced a record $5 billion support for the China-Africa development fund, the China-Africa Corporation Forum business summit in South Africa in October 2009 further enhanced the goals of the Sino-African relationship. The summit between the 21st and 23rd of October established a blueprint for cooperation and engagement for businesses seeking partnerships across industries in their respective countries. At the end of 2009, annual trade between China and Africa was worth more than $100 billion (£63 billion). China's trade relations with Africa are strengthening while much of the developed world languishes in economic doldrums. China was Africa's third-largest export market, behind Europe and the United States, and it trailed only Europe as a source of imports. China-Africa trade in 2013 is expected to reach US$200 billion. That is far ahead of US-Africa trade and fast catching up with Europe-Africa trade. Some forecasts suggest the number will double to $300 billion by 2015. From January to September 2011, Africa's trade with China was $122.2 billion.

The scale and pace of investment by Chinese companies across the African continent is picking up, with South African financial services group Standard Bank alone responsible for advising Chinese companies on recent deals worth more than 10 billion yuan.

Two large deals were concluded in 2011, namely the US$1.3-billion sale of mining company Metorex to Jinchuan and the sale of a 25% stake in black economic empowerment (BEE) investment holding company Shanduka to China Investment Corporation for R2-billion.

An example of the economic friendship between China and Africa is clearly illustrated in Ethiopia. The country's capital Addis Ababa is quickly expanding, mostly thanks to Chinese hands—and money. The Asian giant is hungry for resources to fuel its expanding economy—and many African nations are determined to feed it in order to trade their way to prosperity. At the 2012 Davos summit, Stephen King, group economist at HSBC, predicted a return to the world economy of 1,000 years ago—with the center of world trade centered on China, India, Indonesia, and the east coast of Africa.

Such generous offerings of aid to the African continent by China have been greeted with open arms by some African governments because infrastructure, construction, and other aid come with hardly any of the governance and human rights strings that usually accompany Western contributors. One-third of China's oil supplies come from the African continent, mainly from Angola. Investments of Chinese companies in the energy sector have reached high levels in recent years. In some cases, like in Nigeria and Angola, oil and gas exploration and production deals reached more than $2 billion.

China is providing tremendous assistance in the building of a modern twenty-first century Africa. China has by far the largest number of professionals based on the African continent compared with any other country, from Chinese doctors helping to treat AIDS victims to engineers building the much-needed infrastructure in some of the poorer regions. Amazingly, food (rice, wheat, and fruit) is provided to many African countries through international charities by China, a country that was classed as part of the Third World only 30 years ago. In return Africa offers vast reserves of coal, oil, and gas to China, and many African nationals who speak fluent Mandarin are attending Chinese universities or working for Chinese companies.

The relationship is so cemented that some economic analysts have also commented that perhaps China wants to colonize Africa, a rumor consistently denied by the Communist government. Whatever the facts, China could be the nation that assists in bringing most countries in Africa in line with other newly industrialized countries in the developing world. Clearly, for the moment, wooed by Beijing's hands-on approach, African countries are willing to fill whatever needs China may have. Paul Kagame, the Rwandan president, commented in October 2009 that the Chinese bring what Africa needs: investment and money for governments and companies. His words have been echoed by China's gifts to modern-day Africa that include the construction of a gleaming new conference center at the headquarters of the African Union in Addis Ababa costing $150 million (£75 million)—a symbol of Beijing's commitment to African development, as put by one Chinese official.

CHINA AND INDIA

Prior to the latter parts of the 20th century, Asia's two largest neighbors, India and China, were, with all due respect, not close in any economic or political ways. Relations have been improving since the early 21st century following four decades of hostility over a border dispute that resulted in a short war in 1962. India still claims that China occupies 14,670 square miles (38,000 hectares) of territory, while Beijing claims the entire northeastern state of Arunachal Pradesh. Thankfully, with the change of times, these two giants of Asia have established friendship years (2006, 2007, and 2012), joint military exercises, and exchange visits by political figures as well as captains of industry. Economic and political ties have been boosted since the 2006 visit by President Hu to India, when promising trade agreements were signed, including an annual forecasted trade figure of $12 billion by 2010 between the two countries. Both India and China's growing economic heft and developing-country status could make them allies in setting prices for natural resources, partners at trade forums, and big buyers of each other's goods. In the 3rd quarter of 2009 it was established that China had become India's largest trade partner. Bilateral trade rose 40% to $85 billion in the second quarter of 2011 from the year earlier, according to Chinese government statistics. India is expected to reach US$100 billion dollar trade with China by 2015.

In 2006 Air China commenced services to India with a direct flight from Beijing to New Delhi (with a stop in Kathmandu), while Air India, India's flag carrier, started operations from both Beijing and Shanghai for the first time in history. Air links continued to increase when in June 2009 China Eastern Airlines increased its flight services between Kunming and Kolkata, capital of eastern India's West Bengal state and home to the largest Chinese community in India, from four to seven flights weekly.

Another area in which these two Asian powerhouses are burgeoning is technology. Both China and India are major players in the international consumer marketplace, and the transition of both countries to all-digital information and entertainment networks is now fueling significant domestic demand for the latest electronic products, such as set-top boxes, which can bring the luxuries of satellite TV to the heart of even a rural village. With the world's attention firmly focused on India and China, the future can only get better and more interesting for these two nations. At the time of writing there were an estimated 25,000 Indian expats resident in China (and an equal number based in Hong Kong).

CHINA AND JAPAN

Despite great efforts by both the Chinese and Japanese governments in recent years to put their past troubles behind them and look forward to the future with confidence, some Chinese still have negative feelings towards the Japanese. On a positive note, there is a large amount of trade between the two nations, especially in the food and automotive manufacturing industries. When I asked one friend why there are Japanese restaurants everywhere in China and why Chinese people drive Japanese manufactured cars, all this despite the fact that most Chinese have uncomfortable feelings towards the people from the land of the rising sun, his reply was, to my surprise: "In China we have a saying: Will you drop a stone into the well when someone is drowning? or Do you try to provide them with a rope to pull them?" He went on to confirm that the "Chinese don't think at times of difficulty that you should wash your hands and walk away in an old friendship, and in China friendship is a tradition." It goes without saying that this is very much true in all aspects of Chinese culture. China and Japan are respectively the world's second—and third-largest economies. Just some of the many Japanese companies that have a presence in China include Nissan, Toyota, Kawasaki, Mitsubishi, Canon, and Panasonic.

Japan's total trade with China rose 17.9% year-on-year to $163.2 billion in the first half of 2011, making China Japan's top two-way trade partner. China was also the biggest destination for Japanese exports in 2011. As of October 2011, the number of Japanese nationals living in China (excluding Hong Kong and Macau) is 158,282, the third largest group of Japanese people outside of Japan after Brazil and the United States, according to a report by the Japanese Ministry of Foreign Affairs. Major cities in China where large numbers of Japanese people reside include Suzhou, Shanghai, Beijing, Dalian, Guangzhou, and Hangzhou. There are countless daily flight connections between many Chinese and Japanese cities, hence forging strong relationships between the two countries.

CHINA AND BRITAIN

Ever since Captain John Weddell arrived in Macau on June 27, 1637, to forge trade links between Britain and China, these two countries have had a roller coaster historical ride of good times and bad times (the Opium Wars and World War II). On August 29, 1842, the Treaty of Nanking was signed to officially end the 1st Opium War. It included the cession of Hong Kong Island to the British, and opening of five treaty ports to international trade. Henceforth, Hong Kong was governed by the British until July 1, 1997. It was a cautious period in history for both countries. It is said that in 1982, during negotiations with the former British Prime Minister Margaret Thatcher about the return of Hong Kong, Deng Xiao Ping bluntly told her that China could simply invade Hong Kong if it wanted to. Rather to the shock of many, it was eventually revealed in 2007 that such plans indeed existed. Nowadays, however, Britain has had a long-standing positive relationship with China over many issues, including political, economic, and cultural. Trade and partnership has blossomed in the past few years. On June 26, 2011, the Chinese PM Wen Jia Bao visited London in order to plan trade worth billions of pounds between the two countries. There are also a myriad number of Chinese students that are studying in UK universities, which automatically brings investment into the UK.

As of October 2011, there were around 36,000 registered British people living in mainland China, and over 3 million British people registered living in Hong Kong. UK-China trade reached $64 billion in 2010, and in the same year both countries agreed to increase the value of bilateral trade by 2015 to $100 billion per year. A significant amount of UK-China trade goes via Hong Kong rather than directly. From January to July 2011 the value of UK re-exports to China reached HK$5,350,211, an increase of 10.1% over 2010. Many British companies, including GSK, Pearson Education (Wall Street Institute, Longman Education), Unilever, Tesco, and B&Q, have set up business in China. An athletic connection between the two countries was strengthened when after the conclusion of the Beijing 2008 Olympics, the Olympic torch was passed officially to the next city, London, host of the 2012 Olympic games.

One area where Britain can forge better links with China is through air travel. At the time of writing, the only Chinese cities to which you can fly non-stop to from the UK are Beijing, Shanghai, and Hong Kong. British airlines have not been able to tap into the second tier cities such as Chongqing, Chengdu, Xi'an, Guangzhou, or even Xiamen. Perhaps this will change as the number of British expats in China increases.

CHINA AND AMERICA

Most analysts characterize present Sino-American relations as being complex and multi-faceted. The United States and the People's Republic of China are usually neither allies nor enemies; the US government and military establishment do not regard the Chinese as an adversary, but as a competitor in some areas and a partner in others. As of 2011, the United States had the world's largest economy and China the second largest, though many in the US believe that China "is the world's leading economic power." China has the world's largest population and the United States has the third largest. The two countries are the two largest consumers of motor vehicles and oil, and the two greatest emitters of greenhouse gases. At the time of writing (2012), there were an estimated 66,000 US expats living and working in mainland China (and an equal number living in Hong Kong). A lot of American companies present in China are heavily involved in a two-way America-China investment (it's a win-win situation for both countries' economies). Some of the famed companies include Yum Restaurants (Pizza Hut, KFC), McDonalds, Boeing, Walt Disney Inc., JW Marriott Hotel Group, GAP, Timken, and Caterpillar. There are non-stop connections between Beijing, Shanghai, and Hong Kong and major American cities.

THE FUTURE FOR CHINA?

After the revolution in 1949, the Taiwanese government announced that mainland China would withdraw as a GATT (General Agreement on Tariffs and Trade) member, even though the Beijing central government never officially accepted this decision in public and in 1986, to the surprise of the international community, China rejoined GATT. During that time, China was one of the original members of the GATT. In 1994 the GATT was transformed into the WTO (World Trade Organization), and the entry of China into the WTO has been extremely significant in the country's modern economic history.

The advantages the WTO has brought to China include direct decision-making based on straightforward cost considerations by foreign investors and businesses as well as factors such as tax, land use fees, labor, and insurance. It's not just the "cheaper operative and distributive costs" that have contributed to the attractiveness of setting up businesses on the mainland; the logistics of distribution in China also mean that companies find it easier to set up production manufacturing plants in the major cities.

With the inaugural manned space flight in October 2003, captained by China's first astronaut Yang Liwei, and the future manufacturing of world-class semiconductor technology taking place in China, the next 15–20 years definitely belong to this country. It is effectively an exciting time to be in China and a privilege for those who are able to witness its immense growth. For example in the nine years that I have lived in China, I have seen more changes than I have seen in thirty-two years in the UK. Most expats comment that whenever they return to Europe or the States, the skyline and infrastructure do not change much, while in China the skyline and even your local road will most likely change in a very short period of time.

In the Chinese government's roadmap for the next ten years, a large proportion of the funds are for the improvement of newer cities (such as Shenzhen, Suzhou, Qingdao, Dalian, and Zhuhai) as well as the financial and infrastructural improvement of the country's agricultural industry. Foreign Direct Investment is also on the increase. In 2012, China launched a 50 billion yuan ($7.93 billion) fund in Shanghai to aid overseas acquisitions by Chinese companies as part of efforts to promote international use of the yuan and build the commercial hub into a global financial center.

The government-backed fund, Sailing Capital International, has a fundraising target of 50 billion yuan and has already raised 12 billion yuan, the Shanghai government said on its website. It will eventually expand total funds available for investment to more than 150 billion yuan through leverages such as setting up subsidiary funds or issuing bonds, it said.

The fund will back Chinese companies' overseas expansion through loans and equity investment, with the yuan as the preferred currency for pricing, transaction, and settlement in cross-border investments.

In the aftermath of the 2007–2008 global financial crisis, China has been stepping up efforts to promote international use of the yuan in a bid to reduce reliance on the US dollar, and has also been encouraging domestic companies to acquire crisis-hit foreign companies.

According to a recently published blueprint, Shanghai, which is aiming to become a global money hub by 2020, is looking to double assets under management in the city to about 30 trillion yuan by 2015 ($1 = 6.3016 Chinese yuan). It will be interesting to see how long this economic boom will continue.

CHAPTER 2

THE EXPAT CITIES

HINA IS THE WORLD'S FOURTH LARGEST COUNTRY BY LAND AREA, AND topographically the country is 35% mountains, 27% high plateau, 17% basin or desert, 8% hilly areas and 13% plains. Surprisingly, only 11% of the country is agriculturally useful. China is officially the world's most populous country, with approximately 1.3 billion people (2012 figures). It goes without saying that unlike in the past, when almost everyone lived under strict Communist standards of living, nowadays there is a widening gap between the extremely rich and the poor, and they live side-by-side in the major cities. This chapter will describe some of the largest and best-known cities in greater China: Beijing, Guangzhou, Hong Kong, Macau, Shanghai, and Shenzhen; and it will also focus on cities where there is a large expat community (Suzhou, Hangzhou, Nanjing, Zhuhai, and Qingdao). I have included these extra cities because of their vital economic importance as emerging cities where foreigners are coming to live and work (especially those expats working in the oil, gas, and telecom industries). It's important for newly arrived expats to any city in China to find housing, and get settled as quickly as possible. Moving to a city is often a stressful experience and the aim of this guide is to alleviate some of those stresses.

The sixth national census bulletin, announced by China's National Bureau of Statistics (NBS), shows that towards the end of 2010 there were 1,020,145 expats from around the world living in China, including 234,829 people Hong Kong Special Administrative Region (SAR) residents living in the Chinese Mainland, 21,201 from Macau SAR, 170,283 people from Taiwan, and 593,832 from other countries. The figures showed that there were 71,493 Americans, 19,990 Canadians, 15,087 French, 14,446 Germans, 13,286 Australians, 120,750 Koreans, 66,159 Japanese, 15,051 Indians, and less than 9,000 British people living in mainland China.

By the end of 2010, Guangdong had the largest number of expatriate people in China (316,138), followed by Shanghai (208,602), Beijing (107,445), and Jiangsu (64,177).

BEIJING

Beijing (or "Peking" as foreigners used to pronounce it) is the capital city of the People's Republic of China. History tells us that before Beijing was made a capital city by the Mongol Emperor Kublai Khan in the early 13th century, Xi'an and Nanjing had also been capital cities of China. In 1421 the third Ming Emperor moved his government from Nanjing to Beijing and he became the city's main architect, establishing Beijing as we know it today. The number of expats staying in Beijing for longer than six months at the end of October 2011 was roughly 115,000. Among that total, there were 40,000 workers, 30,000 students, 30,000 foreigners who not on a work or study visa and over 15,000 diplomats and their relatives. Per the China government policy, foreigners need to account for at least 10% of the population before Beijing can call itself an international city. The latest data released by the Beijing statistical bureau at the end of 2011 showed the population of Beijing as 16.5 million, which means the number of foreigners represents 0.6%.

A fine view of the Qianmen area of Beijing.

According to the municipal exit and entry administration, the majority of foreigners in Beijing are from South Korea, followed by the United States, and about one third are aged between 21 and 30 years. Foreign expats are most likely to live in Chaoyang district, where there are numerous restaurants and bars, or Haidian district near the universities.

GEOGRAPHY

The city, with a population of approximately 20 million people, lies in northern China surrounded by the provinces of Hebei and Tianjin. The most striking thing any first-time visitor notices about Beijing is how symmetrical the city is, laid out in an east-west and north-south design. It must be one of the world's most carefully planned and laid-out cities. Everything from parks and roads to buildings is laid out as mirror images on either side. Unlike the other cities in China, it is a city that is becoming modern at a dizzying pace while keeping intact its ancient historical features—there are areas of Beijing where people still live as they would have done hundreds if not thousands of years ago. For example the ancient way of traveling in China using bicycles is still largely practiced throughout the metropolis; however, these days the cycle lanes run side by side with multiple-lane carriageways that are flooded with vehicles of all shapes and sizes. Then there are the historic buildings lying side by side with large concrete blocks that have high shining glass, making Beijing look similar to any Western metropolis.

Beijing is divided into 16 urban and suburban districts and two rural counties. It currently has six ring roads, and more are under consideration. The first ring road is not officially defined and is around the Forbidden City. The second, third, fourth, and fifth are multi-lane motorways. Anywhere outside the fourth ring road is considered to be the suburbs. Beijing's "Silicon Valley" is located in the northeastern areas of Shangdi and Qi Er Xi, where the likes of IBM/Lenovo, P&G, and many others have their China HQ offices. China's most prestigious seat of learning is also located around here, including Beijing and Tsinghua universities (around the Wu Dao Kou area).

CLIMATE

Winters are freezing with temperatures well below 0°C (32°F), while the summers are very hot. Beijing's climate is defined as one of "continental monsoon." The four seasons are distinctly recognizable with a temperate spring, rainy summer, clear autumn, and a cold, snowy winter. The best time to be in Beijing is during the spring and autumn, especially during the months of April, May, September, and October. Autumn is generally considered the best time to visit Beijing because the skies are clear and the weather is comfortable. The average temperature throughout the year is approximately 15°C (59° F). The coldest month is January, with an average temperature of approximately –5°C (23°F) and the hottest month is July at an average temperature of approx. 28°C (82.5°F). Unfortunately, spring and autumn are shorter than summer and winter. Although winter is quite cold, indoor heating is widely available so the temperatures should not prevent you from traveling to Beijing.

TRANSPORTATION

BUSES

Beijing has a numbered bus system, from which you can distinguish the type of bus operating. Buses that are numbered in the 200s are used for night service. Buses that are numbered in the 800s are air conditioned and comfortable to travel in while the rest of Beijing's buses are older, more crowded, and shabbier than public transport in other cities. It is not uncommon to see a bus jam-packed at, say, 6 a.m. on a Sunday. There are four well established bus terminals in the capital.

Beijing houses some of the finest architectural marvels in the world. Here is seen the futuristic CCTV building.

1. **Deshengmen bus station** is located within walking distance from either Gulou or Jishuitan subway stations. Deshengmen serves routes to the north of the capital, including an express service to the Badaling Great Wall.

2. **Dongzhimen bus station** is located close to the subway station that bears the same name. It is close to the expat area and Sanlitun, where most of the embassies are to be found.

3. **Majuan bus station** is located on Guanqumenwei Dajie in the southeast of the city and serves for most long distance destinations to the east and south of the city.

4. **Yongdongmen bus station** is located in the south of the city next to the train station that bears the same name. There are plenty of long-distance

buses available to various destinations within Hebei province and to Tianjin and connections by rail to other cities in China.

AIR

The capital's only passenger airport, Beijing Capital International Airport (BCIA), is located approximately 28 km to the northeast of the city center and is the home base of the national airline, Air China. The airport has undergone some refurbishment with new runways and terminal buildings. On average every year, over 60 international and domestic airlines use the airport. In 2009 Beijing airport handled more than 55 million passengers. Terminal 3 of the BCIA is currently the second largest airport passenger terminal building of the world. Its title as the world's largest was taken over by Dubai Airport's Terminal 3 (which has over 1,300,000 m^2) on October 14, 2008.

TAXI

Taxis are ubiquitous, metered and available 24 hours a day. The base rate at the time of writing is 10 yuan (approx. $1.50) between 6:00 a.m. and 11:00 p.m. for the first mile. Bear in mind that taxis are not allowed to drop off or pick up passengers on the roads surrounding Tiananmen Square.

METRO

Since the last edition of this book was written, Beijing has welcomed 13 more metro lines in operation which includes an above-ground train line (line 13). The two oldest lines are Line 1 and Line 2. Line 2 runs in a circular pattern around the city. It has connections with Line 13 at Xizhimen (to the northwest of the city) and Dongzhimen (to the northeast of the city). Line 1 runs in an east-west direction across the city center between Pingyuoyuan and Sihui Dong station. The metro operates between 5.30 a.m. and 11 p.m. seven days a week. Tickets for using the metro are priced at 2 yuan per single journey, irrespective of how many stops you make and can be used if you change lines (this includes Line 13 as well). The Airport Express charges 25 yuan for a one-way ticket (again, irrespective of how many stops are taken). Since the Beijing 2008 Olympics, an electronic pre-paid card system was introduced for passengers to purchase the tickets (prior to 2003 paper tickets were used). All but two of Beijing metro's 15 lines were built within the past decade. The most recent additions, Line 9, along with sections of Lines 8, 15 and Fangshan, entered into operation on December 31, 2011. Despite the rapid expansion, the existing network cannot adequately meet the city's mass transit needs and extensive expansion plans call for 19 lines and over 703 km (437 mi) of track in operation by 2015 and 1,000 km (620 mi) by 2020. The network is set to reach 420 km (260 mi) by the end of spring in 2013.

The metro's first line opened in 1969, and the network now has 15 lines, 190 stations and 372 km (231 mi) of track in operation. It is the oldest metro system in mainland China. Among the world's metro systems, the Beijing metro ranks third in track length after the metros of Shanghai and London, and fourth in annual ridership after those of Tokyo, Seoul, and Moscow.

Unlike metro Lines 1 and 2 (the loop lines), which encircle the Tiananmen Square area, the traditional city center, the new lines reach all the major corners of the capital, including the outskirts of the city.

TRAIN

There are two main stations in Beijing: Beijing Zhan and Beijing Xi Zhan (Beijing West Station). The former is located in the city center while the latter is located just south of the Junshi Gowuguan subway. Beijing Xi Zhan was opened in 1996. It's more modern and larger in size than Beijing Zhan and sends trains to the north and west of the city. Beijing Zhan is used for destinations to the south and east of the city (such as Shanghai for example). Beijing Xi Zhan was classed as Asia's largest railway station, covering an area of over 510,000 square metres. However it only enjoyed this title for a short period as by 2010, Shanghai Hongqiao railway overtook it as Asia's largest railway station.

FOOD

Beijing is home to around 250 different types of cuisines to cater to all kinds of tastes. By the beginning of 2012, there were just over 8563 restaurants registered in the capital! The most famous foods are roasted duck, Beijing hot pot (boiled meat balls, slices of meat, and various vegetables), and dried fruit. Some of the tours operated by local companies to the Great Wall and the thirteen Ming Tombs may also include a visit to a duck factory (normally on the outskirts of the city), where you can purchase all kinds of duck meat products, such as freshly made roasted ducks, sweets made from duck meat, duck pies, preserved duck meat, and medicine derived from the organs of ducks.

These factories also have a "live" exhibition where you can see the end–to-end production of roasted ducks from behind a reinforced glass wall. On one side of the shop floor you have the ducks quacking away, while on the other side you will see the roasted end product! A famous Peking duck restaurant, and also one of the oldest, established in 1864, is the "Quanjude Roast Duck Restaurant" on 32

Qienmen Avenue (Qienmen Dajie). The huge, luxurious dining hall is filled with diners eager to try the dishes on offer in their most authentic setting.

The two major areas for shopping are Xidan and Wangfujing. Xidan is located to the west of Tiananmen Square and Wangfujing is located to the east of the square. Both have a myriad of shops and restaurants, some offering the usual gifts, while others offer more unusual items such as a cushion that contains self-heating crystals (once a button is pressed a chemical reaction causes the crystals to heat up and turn the hard bag of crystals into a soft hot cushion that can be used to keep warm at night), or you might like to try fried scorpions or freshly boiled beetles and worms in Wangfujing.

Breakfast on the go!

China's biggest indoor shopping mall, known as the Lufthansa Shopping Center, is located in Beijing. As well as shops and restaurants, the mall houses corporate and government offices (including airlines) as well as a large multi-story car park. Solana Park is nearby and also presents one of the most brightly lit shopping streets in Beijing. Located right next to Solana Park is Lucky Street, hosting a myriad of restaurants serving various international cuisines. This is the area where you will also find a lot of diplomatic residences.

PLACES TO SEE

Beijing's rich history and presence as the seat of government and education in China make it a natural destination that is also full of great tourist attractions.

While Beijing does not offer the kind of buzz and rave that Shanghai may have in store for the young and trendy, you are sure to find numerous bars and clubs where you can bop away until the early hours of the morning. KTV (karaoke) is an equally popular way to while away those evenings after a long day at work. There are places for all ages and all kinds of people. Even more so after the Olympic games in 2008, Beijing has attracted an increasing number of tourists and business people.

Beijing Opera is a traditional form of Chinese theatre that consists of artists telling a story using a variety of methods, including singing folk songs, acrobatics, dancing and miming. Beijing opera has four main types of characters: *Sheng* (Male Roles), *Dan* (Female Roles), *Chou* (Comedy Roles), and *Jing* (Painted face males). All the roles can be played by both males and females, and require a mixture of experience, talent, and years of practice. One of the most talented and famous Beijing Opera actors was Méi Lánfāng (1894–1961), who was acclaimed for playing the *Dan* role. Born into a family of Beijing Opera performers and with a career spanning an impressive 50 years, Méi was the first artist to spread Beijing Opera outside of China.

Lao She Teahouse, located in Building 3, Qianmen Xidajie, Tiananmen Square, one of the most famous and oldest in Beijing, features all kinds of Chinese tea and also a performance of Beijing Opera, acrobatics, magic, and Beijing folk music. Beijing tea houses not only are places to appreciate fine Chinese tea but to also put forward a show for Chinese culture through Beijing Opera, or by folk music. It can also be a place where you can just relax and while away your time after a long day. The Lao She Teahouse is one of the best and provides snacks and food as well. The Lao She Teahouse is a good reflection of Beijing tea culture and is truly worth a thoughtful observer's eye.

Li Yuan Theatre at the 1/F, Qianmen Jianguo Hotel, No. 175 Yong'an Lu, comprises Beijing Opera, acrobatics, cross-talk, and story-telling. Li Yuan Theatre is the personification of and strongly represents Chinese culture. The theatrical performances here combine singing, dancing, music, art, and literature, which have evolved to entertain people in China and those from overseas. In a cross-talk, performers use diverse ways to make you giggle. They may tell jokes, imitate, show stunts or sing in embellished ways. The Li Yuan Theatre is very popular, hence very busy, so you may need to book in advance.

The **No. 52 Bar**, Sanlitun Beijie, is a popular place both for professional white collar workers as well as tourists who want to relax, have a drink and chat with friends or colleagues. The atmosphere is nice, good food is available (both Chinese and Western), and the music is suitable for everyone—although if you are after some specific type of music or bar, just take a walk in the Sanlitun bar area. The majority of the bars, restaurants, and clubs are located here.

Apart from Sanlitun, the **Hou Hai** area seems to be the next most happening place in the city. It is located in the region of a man-made lake at the north of Beihai Park. With a bright decoration of neon, the place is available for boating till midnight. It's also a popular place with young couples. Equally impressive are the Propaganda and Zub bars in **Wudaokou**, which has also become a popular hangout for tourists and foreign students alike (Tsinghua and Beijing Universities are located here), on the north side of Beijing.

Situated in the Xi'an nong Temple, in Xuanwu District, is the **Beijing Ancient Architecture Museum.** This is China's first themed museum that puts a heavy emphasis on the research, collection, study, and exhibition of the architecture of Beijing and its surrounding areas. The exhibitions of the Ancient Architecture Museum are mainly located in the Xi'an nong Temple. The temple was first constructed during the Ming Dynasty (1368–1644), and refurbished later in 1754 during the sovereignty of the Emperor Qianlong in the Qing Dynasty (1644–1911). The exhibition is displayed via numerous pictures, photos, and sophisticated working models, and the museum shows the technology, development, and achievement of Chinese ancient architecture from primitive times to the Qing Dynasty. The cost at the time of writing is 15 yuan and it is easily accessible by public transport.

SIGHTSEEING IN BEIJING

Highly recommended is the **Badaling Great Wall**. Allow over half a day to witness the wall at Badaling. A well-known Chinese saying goes that "He who has never been to the Great Wall is not a true man." If the bricks and rocks from the Great Wall were laid from end to end to form a wall one meter wide and five meters high, it could circle the earth at the equator nearly one and a half times. It is such a stunning and magically created architectural feat that anyone who comes to China should not miss it under any circumstances.

Tiananmen Square is the geographical center of Beijing and one of the largest city squares in the world, occupying an area of over 430,000 square meters (over 100 acres) and able to accommodate 10 million people at one time (although this has not been formally verified). The square is an architectural feast of striking and gorgeous flowers and the red national flag, which flutters in the wind. The raising of the national flag at sunrise and the lowering of the flag at sunset is something which should not be missed by visitors to Tiananmen Square. Tiananmen Square is a place that has this special magnetic attraction to it that will keep pulling your senses towards it again and again. North of Tiananmen Square is the **Forbidden City**, the world's largest palace complex, covering 74 hectares (approx. 183 acres). It is placed in the center of Beijing, and as you will notice with the rest of the parks and trees—everything is symmetrical. Moving away from the Forbidden City, Beijing offers other splendors, such as **Beihai Park** and **Tian Tan**, which dates back to the Ming Dynasty. The Tiantan Park (also Temple of Heaven) is one of the largest religious architectural complexes in the world and a masterpiece of the Chinese people created in ancient times. It covers an area of over 2,700,000 square meters, which is just under four times the area of the Forbidden City. The temple was built in 1420 during the Ming Dynasty (1368–1644), and was enlarged during the Qing

Dynasty (1644–1911). On a clear day, you can get some really nice panoramic views across the city, and looks towards the Forbidden City.

To the west of the city, there are two historical palaces, **Yi He Yuan** (Summer Palace) and **Yuan Ming Yuan** (The Old Palace). The Summer Palace is a place that can offer tranquility to those fed up with being in the rage of a Beijing traffic jam, and even for natives, it is a place to escape from the stresses of daily life for a few hours on the weekend. This is the beauty of China that attracts me most to it, it's just too romantic and beautiful—the kind of place where fairy tales and reality are bound to meet each other. A few km to the west of the Summer Palace are the **Xi'ang Shan Gong Yuan** (Fragrant Hills) and the **Beijing Botanical Gardens**, both best seen in the autumn when the leaves are red.

Take a half-day trip to go and explore the magnificent **Ming Tombs**, located 50 km northwest of the city. The concept of the Ming Tombs is impressive. A huge processional pathway lined with stone statues (the Sacred Way) leads to the tombs. The Ming Tombs are actually a tomb cluster of the Ming Dynasty (1368–1644), which includes the mausoleums of 13 emperors, seven tombs for concubines, and one grave for eunuchs. This massive garden of remembrance is world renowned because of the 13 emperors buried here. Located at the foot of Mount Yan and occupying a region of more than 120 square km (29,653 acres), it is an extremely spectacular place. It looks awfully magical, and one would find it hard to digest that so much energy and effort has been put to lay at rest the thirteen great Mind Emperors. The Ming Tombs were listed in the World Heritage List in 2003. Allow half a day to fully enjoy the Ming Tombs.

TOP TEN THINGS TO DO

1. The Great Wall at **Badaling** OR **Simatai** Great Wall—the former is normally jam-packed with tourists; the latter is a bit far away and quieter, but offers more history, as well as stunning views on a clear sunny day!

2. Visit the 91,000-seat **Beijing Olympic Stadium** (an engineering work of exceptional quality also known as the "Bird's Nest"); along with its neighboring buildings—the equally impressive 17,000-seat **Aquatics Center** (known as the "**Water Cube**" and used for the Swimming and indoor pool events) and **Digital Beijing** (the control and data center for the Games, scheduled to become a museum and exhibition center for digital design and technologies)—it has set an exhilarating example for the architectural world.

3. **Panjiayuan Market** is a popular haunt for antique hunters. Choose from paintings, pottery, old furniture, jade, and everything else Chinese!

4. A trip to Beijing is not complete without a visit to world famous **Quanjude Restaurant,** (www.qmquanjude.com.cn), on 32 Qianmen. If you love (or just want to try) fresh n' crispy Duck—just ask and you will not be disappointed!

5. **Yong He Gong (Lama Temple).** This is Beijing's biggest Buddhist temple.

6. Take a walk through the **Temple of Heaven Park.** The park opens from dawn until late daily, admission 35 yuan.

7. Take a relaxing Rickshaw ride or walk around the many **Hutongs** that surround the Forbidden City. It's best to ask before you take photographs of the locals, and make sure you don't get lost as the Hutongs are famous for having many turns. The longest Hutong is Dong Jiaomin Hutong, with a total of 6.5 km, lying between Chang'An Avenue and East Street.

8. In the evening or morning, take a stroll in **Tiananmen Square**, and to make it more special, you can watch the daily flag hoisting and lowering ceremonies at sunrise and sunset respectively.

9. Visit the **Summer Palace** (Yi Hi Yuan) and the **Old Palace** (Yuan Ming Yuan).

10. Visit **Xi'ang Shan Gong Yuan** and **Beijing Botanical Gardens**, located to the west of the city. A world away from the hustle and bustle of the city center.

SHOPPING

Beijing is a shopper's paradise throughout the year. Try the new **Sun Dong An Plaza**, Beijing's most modern shopping mall, which occupies a 20,439-square-meter site in Wangfujing, or try the old, yet equally lively **Beijing Department Store,** which has been in service since 1955 and is the first great, state-invested department store in the history of China. In Beijing, there is a huge selection of items from elsewhere in China and abroad. Many emporiums and selected tourist shopping centers have foreign currency exchange counters and accept major credit cards. Recommended here are the main areas for shopping in Beijing:

Wangfujing Street and its surroundings have quite a selection of shopping options. The 810-meter-long street is the only commercial pedestrian street in Beijing, but like the majority of shopping areas in China, expect it to be jampacked with people! There are two modern malls which offer everything you can imagine, from a self-heating cushion to keep you warm in the winter to a preserved Beijing Duck! One of the malls is "Sun Dong An," which is confusing because this is not its Chinese name, in actual fact its real Chinese name is "Xin Dong An." This one is the older of the two, positioned on the center crossroads of Wangfujing Street, approximately twelve minutes' walk to the north of the subway station. The Sun Dong An mall consists of six floors of shops, each floor specializing in different fashion categories; for example one floor may be for men and another for household goods and so on. The second of the two malls is situated close to the Wangfujing subway station and is called Oriental Plaza. In comparison to the Sun Dong An plaza, the Oriental Plaza only comprises two floors, but does stretch as long as the eye can see into the horizon. That's not exaggerating much; it does take about half an hour to walk from one side to another. Although that's assuming there is no shopping done as you can actually stay there as long as you wish! Close to the Oriental Plaza is located one of the largest book stores in Beijing, the six-story-high Wangfujing Book Store. Mostly catering for the Chinese reader, although there is a section selling foreign English titles, expect to pay international prices for these as they are imported. VISA, American Express and other international credit cards are accepted in the book store and many of the larger stores in both malls.

Known as the second Wangfujing, and slightly larger in area, the **Xidan Area** is equally frequented by native Beijing residents as well as tourists. The good news is that as a tourist you will be able to get a glimpse of what native Beijing people purchase, the kinds of food, the clothes and general household goods. It gives one an idea of how advanced and modern China has become. It is highly recommended that tourists buy plenty of preserved dried fruit and try one of the many local snack foods available. Its center is the Xidan Commercial Street which is about a mile long and located west of the Tiananmen Square. It is an integration of shopping malls and department stores, like the Grand Pacific Mall, Xidan Department Store, Zhongyou Department Store, and the Science-tech Plaza where you can purchase genuine high-quality electronic goods such as DVD players, digital cameras, MP4 players, and so on. Even in the department stores, you may have to haggle over a price to get the best deal.

The **Hong Qiao Market,** located in the south central area of Beijing, just to the east of the Temple of Heaven, is an indoor mall that consists of a seafood market on the ground floor and three floors offering all kinds of less expensive, yet genuine, electronic household products. You may find some international brands, but the vast majority are Chinese local "no brand name" brands. The prices are affordable, and the products are worth haggling for.

Compared with Beijing's history and the long-standing shopping malls that have been described above, the **Xiu Shui Jie Shopping** market is relatively new and was reopened for business in its shiny new five-story shopping mall in 2005, replacing the infamous original outdoor Xiu Shui market. In doing so, it has become Beijing's one-stop tourist shopping paradise after Wangfujing and Xidan. Located near the Yong'an Li subway station (on Line 1), the market is easy to get to, and to make it even easier for foreign visitors, the name is now written in English across the entrance as simply "Silk Street." If you don't have too much time for shopping in Beijing, this could be the only place you need to visit. The staffs are professional and fully trained to deal with foreign visitors; some can even speak very good English. There is also a small convenience store located on the ground floor. Compared with Europe or the Americas, the prices of the goods are ridiculously cheap, and compared with the rest of China, they are perhaps even cheaper, but still genuine. One thing is for sure, you can get a decent bargain on anything. Try some of the stall food snacks and savories on offer. You can shop and walk around while munching away on delicious Chinese savories.

Located from Dongdan (东单) to Dongsi (东四), near the Oriental Plaza, is **Silver Street**, which is a haven for all kinds of designer names and products, such as Gucci, Armani, and Yves Saint Laurent. Hence, it is known and widely appreciated as the "Nobles Street." In this street, you can find almost all the foreign name-brand stores, famous sporting goods shops, and numerous shops selling a variety of fashion dresses. The street is becoming a beehive for the well off and those with a taste for designer wear, Chinese or Western. Prices are less expensive compared to the Western world.

USEFUL BEIJING LINKS

- www.ebeijing.gov.cn Official government website for Beijing
- www.thebeijinger.com Monthly expat magazine for Beijing
- www.beijingpage.com Official directory of all things in Beijing
- www.beijingimpression.com Website for Beijing tours—in and around Beijing
- www.bjreview.com.cn Weekly news—online edition
- www.beijingtrip.com Tour operator—with tours in and around Beijing
- www.bjsubway.com The corporate website of Beijing subway
- www.bcia.com.cn Official website of Beijing Airport
- www.visitbeijing.com.cn Official Beijing Tourism Board

CHENGDU

In 2010, according to China's sixth population census, Chengdu, the capital city of Sichuan province in southwest China and home to the panda, ranked fourth (at 14 million people) out of all Chinese cities in terms of permanent resident population, after Chongqing (28.8462 million), Shanghai (23.0191 million), and Beijing (19.6120 million). It was also here in Chengdu that the world's first paper money was invented (Northern Song Dynasty, around A.D. 960). Yes, it was thanks to the Chinese that we use paper notes! Chengdu is a sub-provincial city. It has direct jurisdiction over 9 districts, 4 county-level cities, and 6 counties.

The largest among all sub-provincial cities, Chengdu is also one of the most important economic centers, transportation, and communication hubs in Western

China. According to the 2007 Public Appraisal for Best Chinese Cities for Invest-ment, Chengdu was chosen as one of the top ten cities to invest in out of a total of 280 urban centers in China. Chengdu is about 200 miles away from Chongqing.

Dating back to more than 4,000 years ago, when the prehistoric Bronze Age culture of Jinsha established itself in this region, Chengdu certainly has plenty to offer to the visitor. Along with the massive inflow of foreign investments in Chengdu, the expatriate population in Chengdu has been expanding quickly in recent years. At the end of 2011, nearly 23,000 foreigners from 125 countries and regions lived in the city, 21% of which worked in the foreign invested enterprises (FIEs). The native language in Chengdu is Sichuanese (Sichuanhua); however like elsewhere in China, everyone communicates and understands Mandarin Chinese.

GEOGRAPHY

Founded in 311 B.C., and occupying an area of 12,132 sq km (4,684 sq mi), Chengdu lies in the southwest of China at the western edge of the Sichuan Basin and sitting on the Chengdu Plain; the dominating terrain is plains. Neighboring prefectures are Deyang (NE), Ziyang (SE), Meishan (S), Ya'an (SW), and the Ngawa Tibetan and Qiang Autonomous Prefecture (N).

CLIMATE

Chengdu has a monsoon-influenced humid subtropical climate and is largely mild and humid throughout the year. It has four distinct seasons, with neither sweltering summers nor freezing winters. Its favorable climate contributed to the develop-ment of agriculture, making Chengdu a comfortable place for sustained human habitat. Winters usually average 5.6°C (42.1°F), and the summers are hot and humid, but not as bad as the hottest cities such as Wuhan, Nanjing, and Chongqing. Snow is rare but there are a few periods of frost each winter. July and August average around 25°C (77°F), with afternoon highs sometimes reaching 33°C (91°F); sus-tained heat as in some cities in Southeastern China is rare.

The humid weather may put some people off, especially if you are the kind of person that does not like to be covered with perspiration minutes after taking a shower! If you thought that the humid and sweltering hot weather of Guangdong was bad, try a week or two in Chengdu. No wonder why the pandas are adaptable to this climate! Extremes have ranged from −5.9°C (21°F) to 40.0°C (104.0°F). Mind you though, humid weather is actually good for the skin as it keeps it moist; hence many people in places with a high humidity end up looking young as they get old (and it saves you spending money on moisture creams!).

TRANSPORTATION

AIR

Chengdu is served by the Chengdu Shuangliu International Airport located 16 km southwest of downtown. In recent years it has been one of the busiest airports in Central and Western China and the sixth busiest airport nationwide, with a total of 17.25 million in terms of passenger traffic in 2008. At the time of writing, there were direct international flights by airlines like Etihad Airways, KLM, Thai Airways, Asiana Airways, Air AsiaX, and All Nippon Airways.

The Chengdu Airport has constructed a second runway, capable of landing an Airbus A380, the largest commercial airplane to date. Chengdu is the fourth city in China with double commercial runways, after Beijing, Shanghai, and Guangzhou. At the time of writing there was also a long-term plan to build a second airport in Jintang County with five runways. Upon completion, it will take less than 30 minutes to travel from Jintang to downtown Chengdu.

METRO

Chengdu Metro officially opened on October 1, 2010. At present there is only one line stretching for 18 km north-south. The line runs from Shenxian Lake (near northern railway station) to Century City (south Chengdu/Software Park). Four more lines are planned to open in the next few years (before 2015).

TAXI

In recent years, Chengdu has created hundreds of new taxi stands in its streets. The stands are approximately 2 meters (78.7 inches) high, with a green ginkgo leaf–shaped board on a blue Y-shaped support. The signs are written in both Chinese and English. At the time of writing, the taxi fare is 5 yuan for the first 3 km and 1.4 yuan per every succeeding km from 6:00 a.m. to 10:00 p.m. From 10:00 p.m. to 6:00 next morning, the taxi fee is 6 yuan for the first 3 km and 1.7 yuan per every succeeding km.

BUS

Chengdu has at least seven bus stations. The major ones for long distance travel are Chengdu Bus Station (Wugui Bridge Bus Station), New South Gate Bus Station, Ximen (West Gate) Bus Station, Dongmen (East Gate) Bus Station, and Gaosuntang

Bus Station. There is no need to book tickets in advance, as you can go to any of these stations and purchase a ticket on the day of travel. Chengdu's public bus services extend in all directions. You can get to most of places, especially sights inside the city, by bus. Common public buses charge 1 yuan, while buses with air-conditioning charge 2 yuan. Take small change as there are no conductors on many of the buses.

TRAIN

There are four railway stations in Chengdu, and which one you use depends on if you are going on a long-haul (Beijing, Shanghai) or short-haul journey. Among them the North Marshalling Station is the largest freight station in China. Chengdu East station is also used as one of the main stations for long-haul travel. Chengdu is a major railway junction city, and rail administrative center in southwestern China.

FOOD

People all over the world know that Sichuan cuisine is considered to be hot and exceedingly spicy! It's not just about that but there are three official kinds of Chengdu cuisine: Sichuan, hotpot, and snacks. There are over 5,000 restaurants serving everything from local cuisine to Western cuisines from all around the world.

SICHUAN CUISINE

Sichuan cuisine has developed over the centuries and is famous the world over. If you are in London or New York for example, you may come across a Chinese restaurant that says "Sichuan Style Chinese food!" Well, when you are in Chengdu, you will know what that really means, as Sichuan food only tastes good in Sichuan! Its distinctive flavors entice people throughout China (and the world over!). When you mention Sichuan cuisine to Chinese colleagues, be prepared for some hysterical laughter and smiles with the everlasting common question: Do you like spicy food? It is somewhat hilarious that Sichuan cuisine is in fact much spicier and hotter than Indian food or Mexican food, but the vast majority of Chinese people would still disagree with that comment. Sichuan cuisine is famous for piquancy, but its flavoring is complex as well as hot. Typical dishes include the following:

- Ma Po Tofu (bean curd with ground pork and chili oil): This is one of my favorites and is one of the most influential flavors of Sichuan cuisine, served in every Sichuan restaurant.

- Kung Pao Chicken (spicy diced chicken with peanuts): A specialty of Sichuan cuisine consisting of diced chicken, hot pepper, and peanuts. This dish is actually a firm favorite with many foreigners because of its nice chunky chicken cubes blended in with rice and spices. It's somewhat similar to some Western dishes.
- Fish Flavored Shredded Pork: though the dish is named "fish-flavored," but there is no fish meat or fish sauce inside the dish. (The spice mixture used was traditionally also used to flavor fish.) It has its own unique style of Sichuan cuisine with shredded pork, mushrooms, bamboo shoots, and carrots.

HOTPOT

When people think of Chengdu, they immediately think of hotpot. Introduced from Chongqing, Chengdu hotpot has its own style ranging from simple spicy to moderate, three or four kinds of spices, as well as fish head hotpot, medical herbs hotpot, and so on. Hotpot is not for the faint hearted as the food can be spicy to the max! If you sweat when indulging in hot food (like I do), then be prepared to drink lots of water or beer with any spicy hotpot dish.

PLACES TO SEE

Since 1963, the **Wolong Panda Reserve**, located around a 3-hour drive from the center of Chengdu to the east of Mount Qionglai, has been the largest and best-known panda reserves in the world. Occupying an area of around 494,200 acres, the Wolong National Natural Reserve was placed on the UNESCO list of acclaimed "Man and Biosphere Reserve Networks" in 1980. Sixty-seven captive pandas are among the 150 total numbers of pandas in the Wolong Panda Reserve, which is managed by the China Conservation and Research Center for the Giant Panda. Tourists can take pictures with the cuddly adult panda or even the mice-like panda babies. After the devastating earthquake on May 12, 2008, the Wolong National Natural Reserve suffered a lot of damage, making over fifty giant pandas living in captivity totally homeless. In order to save these state treasures, Wolong National Natural Reserve has, since May 15, 2008, carried out an evacuation plan. Twenty-seven giant pandas were transferred in batches to Chengdu, Suzhou, and Beijing, and the rest were moved to the splendid Bifeng Gorge Base of China Panda Protection and Research Center. Tourists can go to the Bifeng Gorge, located in Ya'an City, which is just over one hour by bus from Chengdu. The gorge is made up of two small gorges, which measure 4.3 miles and 3.7 miles long respectively. Standing between 2,297 to 6,467 feet high, the Bifeng Gorge is well known for the breathtaking views of diverse foliage, valleys, and waterfalls. Its original landscape attracts an increasingly high number of visitors annually to discover its wild attractiveness. The giant pandas that temporarily live in the base will return to the Wolong National Natural Reserve after its restoration, which is expected by the end of 2012. Pandas are national treasures and also goodwill ambassadors. Many Chengdu city center–based tour operators arrange tours, or alternatively you can ask for more information of a hotel concierge. There is an abundance of information in the many cafés, hotels and small tourist shops around Chengdu on how to best explore the panda reserves. Be sure to take your camera with you and enjoy the atmosphere!

Sanxing Dui Bowuguan is a contemporary designed, spiral-shaped museum that opened in 1997. The museum accommodates one of the most extraordinary collections of ancient sculptures, masks, and ritual bronzes in China! The vast majority of the artistically sophisticated collection was discovered in 1986, although their original date of production goes as far back as the 14th century B.C. Highlights include a charming ornament-bearing bronze holy tree supported by three kneeling guards and crowned with hawk-beaked birds. The piece most representative of the Sanxing Dui is an 8-foot standing bronze figure thought to be of a barefoot sorcerer. The bronze figure has a long forehead, oversize eyes, and ears shaped like butterfly wing—very unusual and bizarre. Many of the bronze heads that are shown in the museum actually are made up of pure gold. There are guides available in a number of languages including English and French. The official website of the museum: http://www.sxd.cn/

Apart from the panda, Sichuan province is highly acclaimed for the popular **Jiuzhaigou Valley**. It is said that if mythological fairylands existed on earth, then Jiuzhaigou Valley would be one of them; in fact it is in real life! Jiuzhaigou Valley is located in Nanping County, about 280 miles to the north of Chengdu City. Its name ("Nine Village Valley" comes from the nine villages of Tibetan origin along its length, and it has always been regarded as a holy mountain and watercourse by the Tibetan people. Adored by many Chinese, Indian and Hollywood film directors as a location for filming of historical periodical dramas, especially Chinese television period dramas, the area is made up of the three main valleys. These three valleys that make up Jiuzhaigou are the Shuzheng Valley, the Rize Valley and the Zechawa Valley; however there is much more beautiful scenery to enjoy surrounding these three valleys. Just some of the fascinating sights in Jiuzhaigou include the Panda Lake Waterfall, which has the longest drop in Jiuzhaigou Valley—ultimately freezing and transforming into beautiful crystal icicles during the winter; a gigantic Pearl "Beach" that is made up of greenery; the Bamboo Lake, which is dotted with lush greenery as well as a sea of bamboo shoots proving a magical backdrop for photographers; and the magical Swan Lake, which is not only populated by swans, but where in the winter the backdrop scenery transforms into something out of a fairytale. There are many other truly spectacular sights to be seen around the area that combine turquoise lakes, waterfalls, verdant forests, snow-covered mountains, and the folk customs of the Tibetan and Qiang peoples. Apart from the lakes, trees and many of the pathways, the main beauty spots are the twelve summits that make the Jiuzhaigou Valley into a wonderful piece of living art. There are 108 colorful lakes in the region, among which the most famous one is the Haizi. It is best to allow a full day or even more to enjoy the full extent of Jiuzhaigou. There are plenty of small hotels and restaurants scattered around the enormous park.

First constructed during the Tang Dynasty, **Qingyang Palace** on Yihuan Xi Lu at the junction of Xi Erduan Lu and Qing Yang Zheng Lu is the oldest Taoist temple in the city and one of the most renowned in the country. Six courtyards open out onto each other before one arrives at the sculptures of two goats, which represent one of the earthly incarnations of Lao Tzu (the legendary founder of Taoism). The best time to come to the temple is in the morning when you will be able to see worshipers offering fruits and incense sticks to the gods. The temple is also home to the "Two Immortals Monastery," the only such facility in southwest China, and an area in which nuns and monks worship. There is a small tea house on the premises along with a small shop selling refreshments.

Du Fu's Thatched Cottage (Du Fu Caotang) on Caotang Lu, off Yihuan Xi Lu, is named in recognition of the famous poet Du Fu (712–770) from the Tang Dynasty, whose poetry continues to be read today at many universities, colleges, and in theatres around the country. Du Fu was a Manchurian who came to Chengdu from Xi'an, and in time built a small hut overlooking the bamboo—and plum tree–lined Huanhua River. During the four years he spent here he wrote well over 240 poems. After his death the area became a garden of remembrance; a temple was added during the Northern Song Dynasty (960–1126). Some of Du Fu's calligraphy and poems are on display here. English-speaking guides are available, as are English translations of his poems. There is a small entrance charge.

THINGS TO DO

For nightlife and entertainment, Chengdu is well known throughout the country for its beautifully built tea houses. In actual fact, Chengdu considerably outnumbers Shanghai in the number of tea houses and bars—all of this despite having less than half the population. Surprising as it may seem, Sichuan's tea houses are ranked first in the world, while those of Chengdu rank first in Sichuan. Chengdu's inhabitants have had a long reputation in China for having a laid-back attitude and for knowing how to enjoy life—not just in tea houses but also by going to the Sichuan opera. Both tea houses and Sichuan opera play an important role in the lives of Chengdu natives; it's not just the passion but also a lifestyle, and a part of their culture. It's normal, say, on Friday evening for colleagues or friends to go to see the latest performance at one of the local theatres or to go and relax in one of the tea houses in town. So therefore these tea houses and theatres that show Sichuan opera are far more than places for drinking tea In the tea house, one may enjoy such genuine Chinese teas as jasmine, maofeng and zhuyeqing while chatting with friends or colleagues. Some people prefer to have their feet massaged while they are drinking tea.

Sichuan opera has a special place not just in Chengdu but also in neighboring Yunnan and Guizhou provinces as well. Sichuan opera is an important part of Chengdu culture because many myths and stories about the life and history of Sichuan Province are told through the performances. The Sichuan opera dates back to the Qing Dynasty (1644–1911), when it was provided as a combination of five operatic tunes introduced from other regions. Retaining the Sichuan dialect, the role of the chou (clown) covers a comparatively large part of the performance, and Sichuan opera often presents a charming witty atmosphere. Its varied performances, such as bianlian (changing faces), gundeng (rolling lamps), and tuhuo (spitting fire) are very popular; bianlian is famous even overseas for its mysterious techniques. The actors in Sichuan opera are presented with a challenge to quickly change their face mask in a split second without anyone noticing.

The famous "changing faces" can be seen in the **Sichuan Opera Theatre**, at 20 Zhuangyuan Street, and also in the **Shunxing Old Tea House**, located on the third floor of the Chengdu International Exhibition Center on 258 Shawan Road. There are three types of face changes in Sichuan opera: In the Wiping Mask routine the actor applies cosmetic paint in a certain position on his face; The Blowing Mask routine works with powder cosmetics, such as gold, silver, and ink powders; and lastly the Pulling Mask routine is the most challenging, where masks are painted on pieces of damask, cut out, hung with a silk thread, and then individually pasted lightly to the face.

Below are some of the finest tea houses and theatres that show Sichuan opera in Chengdu. For most of the tea houses there is no need to book in advance, and you don't really need to speak Chinese either because the staff will understand the reason why you are there; and most of the staff members at these tea houses are very professional and friendly. Even for the Sichuan opera performance there is really no need to book in advance, although during some national holidays they may be busy. So sit back, and enjoy the performance!

Yuelai Tea House, located on Huaxingzheng Street, provides free Sichuan opera performances from 14:00 to 16:00 every Tuesday and Saturday—this would be included in your entrance fee and the fee you pay for your tea drinking session. So this is another way to relax. By drinking your chosen Chinese tea, you can have your feet massaged, chat with your colleagues or friends, or just simply enjoy the performance. There are facilities for refreshments, shower, and toilets.

Heming Tea House, an outdoor tea house located inside Renmin Park, provides beautiful picturesque views and is quiet—except for the pleasant sound of the stringed Zheng being played in the background (not live). The tea house is open daily from 6 in the morning to around 8 in the evening. All the staff are dressed in traditional costumes.

Dabei Temple Tea House enjoys an excellent reputaticn for its history and surrounding ancient architecture. Antique and Chinese calligraphy and painting exchanges often take place here at the same time while you are drinking your tea.

There is quite a lot of activity going on at the **Jinli Recreational and Cultural Street**, which continues to reflect the old culture of the city and also has many entertainment centers, such as bars, KTV bars and small cafés with outdoor seating. In ancient times, Jinli Street in Chengdu was one of the busiest of commercial boulevards of the Kingdom of Shu, throughout the Three Kingdoms Period (220–280). It is consequently recognized as the "First Street of the Shu Kingdom." The music clubs that play live music, the theatres showing the opera, the KTV bars and the tea houses all reflect the local life—especially the nightlife, which is very much significant for the locals and foreigners alike. Although one can go there anytime, it is highly recommended that visitors go to the street in the evening—that's when the place really becomes lively with a lot of activity.

Situated in Jinhe Lu, **Renmin Park** is a typical Chinese park, where you can relax and rest far away from the hustle and bustle of everyday life. Renmin Park constitutes of a bonsai garden with small ponds and a small children's park. You can hire a paddle boat, usually in the shape of a large duck, and ride it for as long as you like in the lake, which is in the middle of the park. The best way to get a feel for the park is by strolling around it and soaking in its serene and peaceful atmosphere. The park has a resident tea house, which features some of the finest teas available in Chengdu. Take a camera with you as you'll have lots of fun by taking photos!

SHOPPING

The main hot spot for shopping in Chengdu is around Chunxi Road. The 70-year-old street is equivalent to Oxford Street in London, or Wangfujing in Beijing. Chunxi Road boasts one of the most typical and prosperous commercial pedestrian streets to be seen in Chengdu. Department stores, boutiques, modern cafés, and a spacious square that comes complete with live street music by local bands, will leave you with pleasant memories. There are also loads of restaurants featuring different world cuisines, and major shopping malls. Chengdu's main shopping centers converge at Chunxi Road, Zongfu Road, and the Luomashi area. Here you can shop for a huge range of things, with everything from souvenirs and street stall items to supermarket and department store goods on offer.

If you prefer to purchase some products for, say, a long train journey, or for long days when you'll be sightseeing around Chengdu, then the best place to go to is the huge Renmin Shangchang (People's Market) opposite the main railway station. It also has a bakery and a fast-food restaurant that serves a Chinese breakfast. Prices are inexpensive, the products are of high quality, and the food at the small restaurant is delicious. Try the breakfast wrap. which contains two whole boiled or fried eggs with some vegetables, all wrapped in a tortilla. Chengdu is well-known for the *Shu Brocade* and *Embroidery* created by the local people, and those in the surrounding villages. The Chinese are known for silkworm breeding and mulberry growing; therefore it is no surprise that with a history dating back to around 221 B.C., Chengdu's celebrated silk handicrafts and embroidery are well worth investigating. In addition, the local lacquerware is well known for its resistance to aging and corrosion, and for its exceptional polish.

Around the city center there are various markets that specialize in different kinds of gifts and products for tourists.

If you are interested in purchasing handicrafts, then head down to the **Chengdu Shu Brocade Factory** on 1 Caotang East Road; if you are interested in some bamboo-weaving arts and crafts, then head down to the 1st Section of Jie-fang Road. Products manufactured from bamboo are strong, of high quality and therefore last longer. After all, you are in Sichuan where the panda's main food is also bamboo! Products made out of bamboo are considered to be somewhat of a souvenir in Chengdu.

Finally for some souvenirs the best place to go is the **Song Xi'an Qiao Antique City** on 22 Huan Hua Bei Lu, near the Wu Hou Temple., considered China's second-largest antiques market. With more than 500 separate stalls selling everything from jade (real and fake), marble statues, and Buddha statues to wonderful watercolor paintings, you will be spoiled for choice as to what to buy, and more importantly how long to spend here because it's not a place where you can just go and shop for a product—you will need to take time and explore. Perhaps the most prized paintings for tourists are the hand-painted portraits that you can get for around 20 yuan. It may require you to stay still seated for around an hour, but it's worth it. Unlike other places where you can get similar portraits, this is different because the paintings are created with special paint and designed to blend in the background with something connected to Chinese culture and art.

CHONGQING

Founded in 316 B.C., and with over 30 million people, Chongqing is one of the most notable cities for history and culture in China, and serves as the economic center of the upstream Yangtze area. It is the major manufacturing center and a transportation hub for Southwest China, and also dubbed as China's fastest growing city (most people think it is Shanghai, but it's actually Chongqing!). Created as a municipality on March 14, 1997, and succeeding the sub-provincial city administration that was part of Sichuan Province, Chongqing has jurisdiction for over 19 districts, 15 counties, and 4 autonomous counties. With an area of 82,401 square km (31,815 sq mi), it is the largest direct-controlled municipality, larger even than one province and an autonomous region. Towards the end of 2010, Chongqing had a GDP of around 789.4 billion yuan, which amounts to a GDP per capita of 27,596 yuan.

The city has changed more quickly than most other cities in China. Most significantly, the Three Gorges Dam construction has finished in the past few years, and its most noticeable effect here is on the Yangtze River, which flows through the city. It is a fact that China's development is one of humanity's worst environmental disasters. According to the World Bank, 16 of the planet's 20 dirtiest cities are in China, and Chongqing is one of the worst. In past years the Yangtze River in Chongqing almost looked like a non-stop flow of thick chocolate-colored mud, very full in the summer months as the result of melting snow in Western Sichuan, and fairly dried up in the winter. The difference nowadays s that the Yangtze has changed to a rather glum grey color rather than the chocolatey color that it was before, is a bit more stable in its flow, and is much fuller in winter.

According to a July 2010 article from the official Xinhua news agency, the municipality has a population of 32.8 million, including 23.3 million farmers. The urban core itself has approximately 4 million residents. Set in the middle reaches of the Yangtze River, at its confluence with the Jialing River, Chongqing has long been the economic hub of western China. But after its government was given municipal control of surrounding territory the size of many countries, it has grown at a dizzying pace, becoming what is now the world's biggest municipality (more people than Singapore or New Zealand).

Infrastructure improvements have led to the arrival of numerous foreign direct investors (FDI) in industries ranging from auto to finance and retailing, such as Ford, Mazda, HSBC, Standard Chartered Bank, Citibank, Deutsche Bank, ANZ Bank, Scotiabank, Metro AG, and Carrefour, among other multinational corporations. According to the China National Bureau of Statistics, there were over 9,000 expats living and working in Chongqing towards the end of 2010.

GEOGRAPHY

If you take a map of China, you can easily see that Chongqing sits s ap bang in the middle of the country. Chongqing is surrounded by all sides by the following: Hubei (east), Hunan (southeast), Guizhou (south), Sichuan (west), and Shaanxi (north). Chongqing is the largest of the four direct-controlled municipalities of the People's Republic of China (the others are Beijing, Tianjin, and Shanghai). The boundaries of Chongqing municipality reach much farther into the city's hinterland than the boundaries of the other three provincial level cities.

Chongqing has numerous hills scattered across the downtown, somewhat reminiscent of San Francisco. Another feature of the culture of Chongqing is the renowned "stick" porters whose livelihoods depend on the hills around the city. These porters are known as part of the "stick army" because they earn their living by sherpa-ing all kinds of stuff using bamboo sticks with ropes on. Their charge depends on the weight, and distance.

Two elders in Chongqing.

CLIMATE

Chongqing has a monsoon-influenced humid subtropical climate, and for most of the year experiences very humid conditions. Known as one of the "Three Furnaces" of the Yangtze River, along with Wuhan and Nanjing, its summers are long and among the hottest and most humid in China, with highs of 33 to 34°C (91 to 93°F) in July and August in the urban area. The winters are slightly shorter than other parts of China and consist of average temperatures of around 7.8°C (46.0°F). The most annoying part of being in Chongqing is that it is very foggy for most part of the year. With an average of 100 days a year that are foggy, it is hence known as China's foggiest city (just make sure that you don't ride your bike in the fog!). In fact the fog is often augmented by the pollution into smog.

TRANSPORTATION

AIRPORT

Chongqing's main international airport, Chongqing Jiangbei International Airport, is situated in Yubei district, north of Chongqing city, provides links to all parts of

China, many Southeast Asian countries, Qatar (Qatar Airways started in November 2011), and Europe (to Helsinki operated by Finnair started in May 2012). In 2010, the airport reported close to 16 million people in passenger volume, which ranked it as the tenth in importance in China. Currently, it's the only airport in central and western China that has railway (light-rail) city transportation access under construction (CRT Line 3). Major airlines that operate from the airport include China Southern Airlines, Chongqing Airlines, Sichuan Airlines and Hainan Airlines' new China West Air, and Chongqing is a focus city of Air China. Therefore, it is very well connected with Star Alliance and Sky Team's international network. During the first half of 2011, Chongqing airport handled 8.87 million passengers, and surpassed Hangzhou Xiaoshan International Airport (8.48 million) to become the ninth busiest airport in terms of passenger traffic in mainland China.

METRO

Towards the end of 2011, there were two metro lines operating in Chongqing. The first is 14-km long CRT Line 1, a conventional subway, and the second is a 19-km long heavy monorail CRT Line 2 (through Phase II). Total track mileage is 35 km. Line 3, a new heavy monorail, connects the airport and the southern part of downtown. A new subway, Line 6, is currently in trials and is expected to open in the latter months of 2012. By 2050, there are plans in place for Chongqing to have 10 metro railway lines in operation, totaling 515 km, with over 260 stations, although more recent reports have now indicated as many as 19 metro lines are planned or proposed.

TAXI

The flat rate fare of most taxis in Chongqing is 8 yuan for the first 3 km (about 1.9 miles) and then the distance surcharge is about 2.1 yuan per kilometer. It usually costs passengers at least 75 yuan from the airport to downtown area in the day-time, but more than 100 yuan at night.

SHOPPING

Like most other big cities in China, Chongqing is all lit up n neon at night. The city at night is very spectacular. Nearly every building, road and bridge is lit up in many different colors giving it a wow factor! White Chongqing is not really known for being a beehive of tourists or shoppers, nevertheless it does house some interesting places where people can shop. Here are just a few of the many:

Jiefangbei is the main central business district and the center of economic development of Chongqing. It would be worthwhile to take a stroll on the Jiefangbei commercial pedestrian street in this well-known shopping area. A myriad of modern shopping malls and exclusive shops line the roadsides. Banks, theatres, KTV clubs, bookstores, hotels, bars and pubs are also quite easy to find. Some of the main buildings worth popping into include the Chongqing Department Store, the New Century Department Store, the Commercial Mansion, Friendship Shopping Center, and New Oriental Women Plaza. You won't find anyone hassling you to buy the goods, which allows you to stroll at a relaxed pace.

If you are into purchasing fresh produce or flowers, then head down to **Nan Bin Road,** located at the entrance of Huang Ge Du Park, where there is a lovely flower market. Though this market comes alive in the spring (Chinese New Year), and at major holidays, it is nevertheless worth paying a visit. The street started with one flower shop many years ago, and in time over 100 flower shops, handicrafts stores, and tea houses have lined both sides of the street.

Located on East Jiefang Road, **Chaotianmen Market** is considered to be one of the biggest markets in Chongqing. The market primarily sells wholesale garments (made in China of course!), and it is rumored that the goods traded in the market come from or are sold to more than 200 counties in Sichuan, Hubei, Jiangsu, and Hunan provinces. It's the closest thing to the real life Aladdin's cave, and you can find almost anything here. Shoppers can expect to find stylish clothes and very reasonable prices.

PLACES TO SEE

Because Chongqing was China's provisional capital for 10 years from 1937 to 1945, it the city was also known as one of the three headquarters of the Allies. One of the most amazing aspects of the city is that Chongqing has many historical World War II buildings or sites, probably more than Shanghai or Beijing.

Some of the places to see in and around Chongqing include the following:

Situated around 271 km from Chengdu on its west, and around 167 km from Chongqing on its east, the historic yet perfectly preserved **Dazu Rock Carvings** can be found at any of 75 protected sites located in the steep hillsides of Dazu County (i.e., within Chongqing municipality). Wander around the area to capture the series of religious statues and carvings showing aspects of Buddhism, Taoism, and Confucianism, all of which can be dated as far as back to the 7th century A.D. Hiring a taxi or a tour guide would be a wise option as the best parts to visit are situated a few miles apart from each other. Try Mount Baoding and Mount Beishan. Both of these giants have carvings that were made as early as A.D. 650, and some were created in the late 9th century (especially at Mount Beishan). Although they were opened to the public in 1961, a muddy track kept them reasonably unknown until 1975. It was only in 1980 that the carvings were opened to foreign visitors (before that only Chinese visitors could go there). The carvings were listed as a World Heritage Site in 1999.

Founded around 1,700 years ago, covering an area of some 1.2 square km, and located around 14 km to the west of Chongqing on the banks of the Jialing River, not far from its confluence with the mighty Yangtze River, is the ancient village of **Ciqikou**. The beauty of this village is that Ciqikou appears to be a town still in keeping with its history. It somewhat portrays an enlightening impression of what Chongqing would have been like in the distant past. Contrasting sharply with the boom of big Chinese cities, it is a respite from the hustle and bustle.

The one key reason why most people come to Chongqing is because it is a connecting port to the enormous **Yangtze River**, the mother of all the rivers in China. Sometimes the Yangtze is also known as Changjiang River in China. The Yangtze River passes through Yunnan Province, Sichuan Province, Hubei Province, Hunan Province, Jiangxi Province, Anhui Province, Jiangsu Province, and Shanghai City and eventually flows into the East China Sea. The whole drainage area of Yangtze River is more than 1,800,000 square km and it covers 25% of China's territory. The section of Yangtze River in-between Chongqing and Yichang is the most challenging for sailors to sail through because of its difficult physical terrain and complicated water conditions. The area is generally known as the Three Gorges area, comprising the spectacular Qutang Gorge, Wuxia Gorge, and the Xiling Gorge. The cruising trip takes around 4 days to complete, and it ends in Chongqing (or can also begin here). The Yangtze River Cruise will take you through the most beautiful parts of China, while giving you the opportunity to witness some of the natural wonders of the world. Throughout the cruise tourists can take various stops at towns and villages that lie along the river.

Initially built on a high piece of land between the Yangtze and Jialing Rivers and widely known for offering fantastic views across the whole of the city, **Eling Park** was one of the earliest private gardens to be built in Chongqing (in 1909). What makes it even more famous and interesting to see is that it became the home of Chiang Kai-Shek during the war against Japan. The site has been home to numerous embassies from around the world. In 1958 the site was proclaimed a public park by the government. They named it Eling or "Goose Neck" Park because of its narrow configuration in the shape of a duck's neck!. Home to many species, the park also houses a beautiful stone bridge with intricately carved railings in the design of rope (weird, but wonderful).

Located in the Yuzhong Region of Chongqing, and occupying an area of around 1.2 acres, is the beautiful **General Joseph W. Stilwell Museum.** The museum was opened in 1991 as a tribute memorial to the great American general Joseph W. Stilwell (1883–1946), the former chief commander of US forces in China-Burma-India (CBI) during World War II. In 1942, ranked as a major general, he was dispatched to CBI and was regarded as the best field commander in the entire United States Army. General Stilwell was a true friend of the Chinese people as well as being one of the very few Americans at the time who could converse fluently in Mandarin Chinese. It's worth a visit if you wish to understand the history and culture of Chongqing!

DALIAN

Surrounded on three sides by the sea, the gorgeous looking seaside city of Dalian lies on the southern tip of the Liaodong Peninsula. Dalian has in recent years become a city famous for hosting various events related to international trade and economic affairs, such as the 2006 World Trade Organization (WTO) meeting attended by global leaders. Because of this reason, sometimes Dalian is known as the "Hong Kong of Northern China." A pleasant destination for foreigners and locals alike, the city is a good sightseeing and recuperating spot. Dalian is well known for its long and open coastline, which gives way to a large number of outlying islands. This can clearly be observed and enjoyed along the 25-mile long Binhai Lu, which stretches southwest from downtown Dalian along the coastline. If you love surfing, or just relaxing on the beach, then Dalian is definitely the place for you. Much loved are the renowned picturesque spots of the Bangchuidao Scenic Area, the Laohutan Scenic Area, the Jinshitan Scenic Area, and the Xinghai Square. In addition to the spectacular cliffs and picturesque parks various places along the coastline are excellent for beach resort visitors and water sports lovers. Annual events include a fireworks festival for the Western New Year, the Dalian International Fashion Festival, the Locust Flower Festival, and an International Marathon race.

Shanghai used to be known as the "Paris of the East" during the 1930s; but that exquisite title has been taken over by Dalian, which boasts dozens of elegant squares, each with its own style.

Dalian has had its fair share of challenges and sad periods in history. After the Opium Wars, Dalian was plunged into conflict, with both Japan and Russia invading the city, first in 1894 and then in 1897. That changed the city's landscape, politically, economically, and culturally. Dalian became the victim of both Russian and Japanese colonial rule for decades. The Chinese government did not take over sovereignty of the port city of Lushun until 1955, when the hardest times in this city's history came to a firm conclusion. Needless to say, the city has, because of this historical connection, a strong affiliation with Japan and Russia. You will come across many authentic Russian and Japanese restaurants and places of interest, even statues in public parks, which will give you an idea of how much influence these two foreign cultures have had on Dalian.

Towards the conclusion of 2009, the city's resident population was over 6.1 million people. In 2009, Dalian realized its goal of achieving 441.8 billion yuan of GDP. The per capita GDP of the city was 71,833 yuan.

Dalian's main industries include machinery manufacturing, petrochemical, electronics, and shipbuilding, and Dalian is positioned to become an important center of IT and software, as well as financial and other services, in China. At the end of 2011, it is estimated there were around 5,000 expats living and working in Dalian, though these figures are sketchy.

GEOGRAPHY

Dalian is located west of the Yellow Sea and east of Bohai Sea roughly in the middle of the Liaodong peninsula at its narrowest neck or isthmus. With a coastline of 1,906 km (1,184 mi), it governs the entire Liaodong Peninsula and about 260 surrounding islands and reefs. It is known as one of China's open cities.

CLIMATE

Dalian has a monsoon-influenced humid continental climate (similar to what you expect in most northern cities) characterized by humid summers due to the East Asian monsoon, and cold, windy, dry winters that reflect the influence of the vast Siberian anticyclone. Except for winter, the city experiences a one-month seasonal lag due to its position on the Liaodong Peninsula. In the winter, average temperatures are around −3.9°C (25.0°F), and in the summer around 24.1°C (75.4°F). Its maritime location dictates that the mean diurnal temperature variation annually is small, at around 6°C (12°F). The winters can be bitterly cold, especially with wind chill and freezing humidity, so it is important to dress appropriately.

TRANSPORTATION

METRO

Dalian Metro is a rapid transit system in the city of Dalian, China. The system opened on May 1, 2003, making Dalian the fifth city in mainland China to have a subway after Beijing, Tianjin, Shanghai, and Guangzhou. At the time of writing the system currently consists of one full line and one branch line. The lowest fare, between two adjacent stations, is 1 yuan, while for every other station the fare is generally 2 yuan. So for example from Dalian station to the Golden Pebble Beach would be a total of 8 Yuan, and from Dalian station to Jiuli would cost a total of 7 yuan. The swipe-in IC card (Pearl Card) enables customers to get a small discount per journey as well as to accomplish various transportation and civic transactions.

TAXI

Taxis are ubiquitous in Dalian and flagging one down is rarely a problem except in the more remote parts of the city (where high car ownership exists or large numbers of residents would have trouble paying a taxi fare). At the time of writing, the rates start at 8 yuan (10.40 yuan after 10 p.m.) for the first 3 km and 2 yuan for each additional km.

BUS

The vast majority of people in Dalian use buses as the main form of public transport. The buses are frequent, safe, reliable, on time, and inexpensive to travel on. Roadside signs at the queues are available in Chinese and English. The good news is that most buses do have air conditioning, which can be a relief in extreme hot or cold weather. Services start early in the morning (anywhere from 4:30 a.m. to 8 a.m.), and usually finish around 10 p.m.

TRAM

Dalian is one of the few Chinese cities that have an existing tram line (most people think only Hong Kong has one!). This is all thanks to the colonial legacy from the years of Japanese occupation. It does add a bit of somewhat nostalgic flavor to the city, and makes it more appealing for tourists looking for something different. Nothing beats the picture of seeing a beautiful tram ascending a hilly street past colonial buildings. There are two main tram routes: 201 runs largely west-east from Xinggong Street near the Shahekou Railway Station to the Haizhiyun (Rhythm of the Sea) Park on the coast. Number 202 runs from the High Tech Zone (near Xiaoping Island) to the Jinhui shopping area where the #201 starts. The fare at the time of writing is 1 yuan.

AIR

Dalian's only airport is located in Ganjingzi District, about 10 km (6 mi) northwest of the city center. In 2010 the airport handled 10,703,640 passengers, making it the busiest airport in Northeast China and the 16th busiest nationwide. In September 2011, a new 71,000 square-meter terminal building was completed as part of the 2.2 billion yuan third-phase expansion project of the airport. International airlines using Dalian Airport include Aeroflot, Air Koryo, SAT Airlines, Korean Airlines,

Asiana Airlines, Japan Airlines, and All Nippon Airways. The airport is also a base for China Southern Airlines, China Eastern Airlines, and Dalian Airlines.

SEA

Dalian is linked by regular passenger ferry service to neighboring coastal cities, such as Tianjin and Yantai, as well as Incheon, South Korea. The ferries have excellent facilities such as an onboard restaurant and washroom. The boats are usually double decker and some of them can accommodate up to 200 people.

PLACES OF INTEREST

Though not really a touristy city, Dalian does attract its fair share of tourists from China, Russia, South Korea, and Japan. Most of these tourists are attracted to the beautiful beaches that Dalian offers. The following are also very popular destinations in Dalian:

A wonderful place for all ages is the amazing **Dalian Shengya Ocean World**, located at 608 Zhongshan Road in Shahekou District, inside Xinhai Park. This has the longest translucent underground sea channel in Asia. Visitors can stand on the moving passageway, which will take them slowly through the tunnel, bringing many forms of sea creatures closer, including different types of exotic fish, stingray, sharks and other sea life. There are over 300 different species in the main display area, with the approximate number of fish totaling more than 11,000. The most interesting part of the Ocean World is when trained divers go up close and personal to feed the sharks. There is an entrance fee, and some of the staff speak good English. Refreshment and washroom facilities are also available.

Covering an area of over 380,000 square km, which consists of 30,000 square km of decorated floors, 12,000 square km of greenery, and many sculptures, the "**Charm of the Sea Square**" is a magnificent example of fantastic Dalian architecture and splendour. What's more—there is no fee to go and see the place. In the center of the Square is a 19.9-meter-high sculpture commemorating the 100th anniversary of the founding of Dalian in September of 1899. Twenty-one flying seagulls symbolize the 21st century. The whole sculpture resembles a flying dragon, hence the name "Charm of the Sea." Standing 60 meters tall at the center of the square is a manmade waterfall, visible from a long distance. It's really is something special, even more so if you are a photographer.

Located around 5 miles away from the center of Dalian City, in the middle of Binhai, is **Dalian Laohutan Ocean Park**, one of the top five aquariums in Dalian. The park has four smaller "gardens" situated within its grounds: a coral garden with over 3500 corals that cover over 200 different species; a unique polar garden, showcasing polar bears and their habitats; a science education center; and an undersea marine animals' show area. The coral garden is a special protected park by the Dalian government. There is also an aviary featuring over hundred different types of birds, and a sculpture garden with granite animal statues. There is an admission charge for the Ocean Park. Restaurant and washroom facilities are available throughout the park.

The **Bangchuidao Scenic Area,** located in the east of the Binhai Road, is a well-known beach resort combining Bangchuidao Islet, the natural lido, and the splendid Bangchuidao Hotel. The area is completely surrounded by lush greenery. The relatively small Bangchuidao Islet located around 650 meters from the seashore is shaped like a Bangchui (wooden club) used by the local Chinese people as a washing tool, hence its name. Finally the eminent Bangchuidao Hotel is situated here.

On the southwestern side of Dalian City bordering Xinghai Bay you can find **Xinghai Park**. Just under half a mile long, the lush green park features abundant trees and flowers as well as a golden sand beach. Although it is not that far from the hustle and bustle of the city center, it is remarkably quiet here. On the sea facing side, visitors can take a swim in the clear and clean waters. The beach is well managed, safe to swim in and the water is neither too deep nor subject to other than modest waves. Some of the beach guards speak English. The park itself has many attractions inside, such as the Sun Asia Ocean World, where you can watch many of creatures that live in the sea. This aquarium is the first in China to have an underwater tunnel from which you can view the marine life at close range, as well as the world's first underwater pyramid, city, and flying saucer. The museum also includes a fine collection of fossils from all over the world.

THINGS TO DO

You will be spoiled for choice on the 62-square-kilometer **Dalian Golden Pebble Beach**. Its four tourist centers are the Green center, Blue center, Silver center, and Color center. Occupying an area of around 18 square km, **the Green Center** contains the lavish Golden Pebble Golf Club, a member of both the American Golf Association and the World Tourism Association. There is an admission fee to get into the club, which is open from March to November. The **Blue Center** provides a boating experience with visitors being able to go to Qinyi Lake and take as long as they like to enjoy rowing their boat (or paddling if they have a "duck shaped" paddling boat for example). There are more than 60 pleasure boats. The **Silver Center consists of a** hunting club, an Italian bar, displays of Russian wooden houses and some Chinese farmyards. This experience is for those who want to just while away the time and relax over some good food, and take in the surrounding sights. Finally the **Color Center** is a garden that features the growth, display and sale of flowers and plants from around the world. It is the largest of its kind in Northeast China.

There is a charge for this garden. It is recommended that visitors bring their camera to this attraction to get most from their experience.

Constructed to honor the companionship of China with the former Soviet Union, the **Youhao Square** features a large eye-catching crystal ball, which is illuminated at night. The five hands holding the ball are meant to symbolize the camaraderie of people from the five continents of the world. The ball comes alive in the evening, when the color lights inside the crystal ball make it a worthwhile stunning view—it is popular with photographers. There is no admission fee. Quite a number of stalls sell refreshments, and there are various restaurants around the area.

You can either take a taxi or the "old-style buggy" which has regular service from the Railway Station to the **Haizhiyun (Melody of Sea) Square,** located in the northeastern section of Binhai Lu, the most scenic coastal area of the city. The square features a group of artistic sculptures resembling soaring seagulls and a mythical flying dragon. The man-made waterfall built in the middle of the square includes various totem sculptures presenting the harmony of human and nature. There is a small admission charge (10 yuan at the time of writing).

SHOPPING

Dalian still has many ancient style streets with small shops and hawkers selling all kinds of goods ranging from street food to even pet parrots. Lying side by side with these old streets are newly built department stores equal in quality and class to what you may find in any European country. With so many new infrastructural developments going on in Dalian in recent years, especially around the turn of the 21st century, Dalian has become a focal point for foreign business people from overseas. Large-scale shopping malls and supermarkets including MYCALL (Japan), Parkson (Malaysia), Carrefour (France), Walmart (US), and Tesco (UK) have been constructed in recent years. It's no longer mission impossible to sell foreign foods and services to the Chinese, although it goes without saying that people expect Chinese goods to be sold to the West instead! Dalian has something for everyone, and you will surely experience this when you see and travel around the numerous shopping centers in the city. Below are a few recommended stores:

Just as you come out from the railway station you will see the Qingniwan area. Just like Beijing's Wangfujing or Shanghai's Nanjing Xi Lu, the Qingniwan area is a major commercial attraction of the city—more popular with tourists than the locals because the price and range of the goods available here are catered for the tourist industry. The goods are inexpensive and the quality is high. Take plenty of empty bags with you!

Just around 100 feet from the north of Zhongshan Square and east to Shengli (Victory) Square you will come across a fabulous street known as the Tianjin Walking Street. Tianjin? We are in Dalian, of course, but the street has many features which are reminiscent of Tianjin. And of course you will find a Tianjin Street, Beijing Street, or Zhongshan Street in almost all of China's major cities—it's a historical connection more than a local cultural one. Tianjin Walking Street has a history of more than 200 years, and started off as a poultry market. Nowadays there's not much bloodbath on the road, but more glamor, fashion and young rich Chinese people spending whatever they can on whatever they can. The shopping street has a labyrinth of shops and stalls. In recent years, the government has invested the time, money, and effort to convert the whole area into an elaborate European style shopping area housed in a large number of skyscrapers. Friendship Shopping City (see below), a high-end shopping building, is on this street. Prices range from 10 yuan to 5,000 yuan! It purely depends on your taste, budget, and choice.

Xi'an Lu in the western part of the city is slightly smaller than Tianjin Walking Street, but it is also very popular and still considered extravagant by many. This is a popular alternative for locals with many supermarkets including Carrefour, Parkson, Walmart and other domestic retail outlets.

The Friendship Shopping City at No. 8 Renmin Lu (at the intersection with Zhongshan Square) has a special place in the hearts of the people of Dalian because it used to be popular during the 1920s and 1930s, especially frequented by government officials who wanted to do their shopping there. In actual fact, its name somewhat resembles its size and ambience—it really does feel like a city inside. It has now developed into a large six-story shopping center, along with two basement floors, as well as an area for car parking.

Shengli Square Shopping Center on No. 28 Shengli, inside the Shengli (Victory) Square busy shopping area, has a varied assortment of fashionable womanswear and menswear, as well as a whole floor dedicated to children's products, sports-wear and men's suits. It is a must for shopping lovers. Prices are reasonable and the quality of the products is impeccable.

GUANGZHOU

Guangzhou, the capital of Guangdong province, is the industrial hub of southern China. It is sometimes referred to as Canton by westerners. For many travelers Guangzhou is still the first real taste of China once they cross the border from Hong Kong. (Shenzhen is a modern city with no real history that does not feel like China because of its close proximity to Hong Kong and its ubiquitous high-rise glass build-ings.) First impressions of Guangzhou are that it is teeming, noisy, and polluted. The last is obvious with the smell of overflowing drains in most neighborhoods.

Guangzhou is famous for its great food and its biannual (April and October) trade fair, known as the Canton fair. The Canton fair is by far the biggest and most popular of the trade fairs that take place in China. It's just a huge market where traders from around the world come to Guangzhou to find a good deal for all kinds of "Made in China" goods. Imagine a city where it feels like you are living in the ancient past with night-time bazaars and trade markets, where you can buy almost anything that tickles your fancy, and at the same time that city tries to keep pace with life in 21st century China; that's Guangzhou. The city hosted the 16th Asian Games in 2010, attracting global publicity in the process.

According to the Guangzhou government statistics, the permanent foreign expat residents in Guangzhou total over 50,000, which is likely to increase in the coming years. It has been estimated that by 2015 the number will exceed 250,000, which would make Guangzhou second to none among provincial capitals in terms of permanent foreign expats. Over 30,000 foreign citizens applied for a visa in Guangzhou in 2011, and over 25,000 for resident permits. Involving over 180 countries, the temporary foreign residence registrations reached nearly 900,000, among which about 40,000 foreign expats live in apartments or Chinese citizens' residences. The foreign expats in Guangzhou's apartments total up to 15,000, accounting for nearly half of the total, and foreigners living in Chinese citizens' residences exceed 8,000, accounting for nearly 26% of the total. The total population of Guangzhou is 12.7 million people.

Guangzhou is also famous for being the hometown of overseas Chinese in China and a metropolis with the largest number of overseas Chinese. According to statistics, the population of overseas Chinese, compatriots from Hong Kong and Macau, returned overseas Chinese, and their relatives is around 3.5 million in Guangzhou, including 1.06 million overseas Chinese, and 877,200 compatriots from Hong Kong and Macau, who previously had spread into many countries and regions of the world. In 2011 the GDP of Guangzhou reached 1238 billion yuan, and the GDP per capita reached 13,000 yuan. The economic strength of Guangzhou has ranked third among all major cities of China for 22 consecutive years.

GEOGRAPHY AND HISTORY

Guangzhou is located on the Pearl River (Zhu Jiang) Delta and lies 45 km upriver from Humen (also called Bocca Tigris on older maps). The city has a magnificent history dating back to approximately 214 B.C., when, according to historians, the city may have been founded. The original name of the metropolis was Panyu (named by the Qin Emperor, Qin Shi Huangdi), and Guangzhou first appeared sometime between the years 222 and 280. Towards the conclusion of the Han dynasty, the city's name was changed to Jiaozhou. In 226, the eastern part of Jiaozhou became Guangzhou, and ever since then Panyu has been called Guangzhou. Guangzhou has been a trade center ever since the Tang Dynasty (618–906).

In the period of the Five Dynasties, Guangzhou was firmly placed as the capital city of southern China (or Han as it was known), and it was still the biggest foreign trade port and commercial city in China. This was especially true from 1757 to 1842, when Guangzhou was used as a major center for trading in China, as in those days it was the only port opened for foreigners for trade. The initial securing of the trade monopoly by the Portuguese in the 15th century was later broken by the British in the latter part of the 17th century, while in the 18th century the French and Dutch followed suit into the city. However it was only during the Tang dynasty that Guangzhou became a world-famous port.

French and British forces occupied Guangzhou during 1856 following a political uproar. Later the island of Shameen (now known as the expat area of Shamian) was acquired for business and residential purposes rather than colonial quarters (much of the architecture can still be seen today).

During the nationalist uprising, Guangzhou was the residence of many revolutionaries, including the popular Dr. Sun Yat Sen in 1911. From Guangzhou the Nationalist armies of Chiang Kai-Shek marched northwards in the 1920s to establish a government in Nanjing. In 1927, Guangzhou was briefly the seat of one of the earliest Communist movements in China. The fall of Guangzhou to the Communist armies in late October of 1949 signaled the Communist takeover of the whole country.

Since then, Guangzhou has been built up as an industrial center and a modern port for Southern China. Amongst the locals, Guangzhou's famous nickname is "Yangcheng," which means "City of the Ram," and this name comes from an enchanting myth. It is said that over two thousand years ago, five immortals rode five rams with rice stalks in their mouths and they literally flew to Guangzhou. These immortals gave the rice to peasants and prayed that they would be blessed with harvests. The immortals flew away and left the five rams behind, now turned into stones. The stone structure of the Five Rams is one of the symbolic attractions of the city, and can be seen in Yeuxiu Park.

Since April 2005, Guangzhou restructured its administrative division. Now there are ten districts under Guangzhou's jurisdiction, namely, Yuexiu, Haizhu, Liwan, Tianhe, Baiyun, Huangpu, Huadu, Panyu, Nansha, and Luogang, and two county-level cities, Conghua and Zengcheng. So, in a nutshell, there are 6 urban districts, 4 suburban districts, and 2 sub-cities.

CLIMATE

For the majority of the year Guangzhou has a tropical climate with a relative humidity between 70 and 90%—very unpleasant if you don't enjoy getting sweaty all the time! One key cause of this is that the Tropic of Cancer runs not many miles to the north of the city, making life very uncomfortable even at night-time during the summer months. For a short period of time in July the sun is straight over the city, which makes the congested and polluted streets even worse. The climate is subtropical-tropical, humid, and monsoonal, with the rainy season from April to September and occasional typhoons from May to November. Thankfully the majority of offices and homes have air conditioning.

TRANSPORTATION

BUS

Guangzhou has numerous bus connections operating all around the city during the day and a few at night-time. Bus fares are 1 yuan for buses that have no air conditioning (i.e., those that are noisy, have uncomfortable seats that look like wooden park benches, and no PA system to inform you which stop is approaching) and 2 yuan for those with air conditioning (i.e., those that have TVs showing adverts or music videos, have plastic seats, and have an automated PA system that informs you which stop is approaching next). The majority of buses in Guangzhou are modern and clean but normally overcrowded.

Guangzhou has quite a number of bus stations. There is a bus station located at Guangzhou Dong Zhan (Guangzhou East Station), with buses operating to almost all destinations around the city as well as surrounding towns and villages.

The city's main bus station for long-distance travel is located near the Guangzhou Train Station on Huanshi Xi Lu at the Provincial Bus Station. Not far across the road is the Liuhua Bus Station, which also caters to long-distance buses.

The third main coach station for medium- to long-distance coach operations is located in Tianhe (opposite the Tianhe Stadium and adjacent to the tallest building in Guangzhou—the CITIC Plaza). Buses within Guangdong province also operate from here (to Shenzhen, Zhongshan, Dongguan, and Foshan).

AIR

Guangzhou has one major international airport. Situated 32 km northwest of the city center, near the Pearl Delta, Guangzhou Baiyun International Airport offers connections to major Asian, African, and European cities as well as many domestic flights. China Southern Airlines has its HQ and base at Baiyun Airport with flights within China and internationally. With its opening in 2004, the airport is one of the most contemporary in Asia. The airport is large enough to accommodate wide-bodied jets such as the latest Boeing 777-200LR, Airbus A340-500, and the Boeing 747-400, and even the super jumbo Airbus A380. In 2011, Guangzhou Baiyun International Airport was the second busiest airport in mainland China in terms of passenger traffic, with 95,435,472 people handled. Guangzhou connects to over 90 international and over 100 domestic destinations.

TAXI

Taxis are ubiquitous, metered, and available 24 hours a day. The base rate at the time of writing is 7 yuan (approx. $1) 24 hours a day, plus a fuel charge of 1 yuan that is added to the final bill.

TRAIN

Guangzhou has two main train stations, Guangzhou Train Station (Guangzhou Zhen) and Guangzhou East Train Station (Guangzhou Dong Zhan). The former is extremely chaotic and is the focal point for connecting Guangzhou with the rest of China, whereas the latter is used for more local routes. The most frequently operated route out from Guangzhou East Train Station is the Guangzhou to Shenzhen line. Trains run every 20/25 minutes with some trains stopping in Dongguan or Shi Long; the trip takes just over one hour. The one-way fare at the time of writing is 80 yuan. The Beijing-Guangzhou railway is the trunk line from the south to the north built in 1957, with a total length of 2,324 km. As well as being the longest, it is also the busiest railway line in China, with a strategic importance. Tibet railroad from Guangzhou to Lhasa was opened on October 1, 2006. The first passenger train from Guangzhou to Sanya started operating on April 17, 2007. The Wuhan to Guangzhou high-speed railway was put into operation formally in 2009.

METRO

Guangzhou has an extensive metro system with eight lines operating at the time of writing. Line 1 operates from Guangzhou East Station in Tianhe District through to the ferry terminal at Nanhai (Pingzhou). As of February 2012, Guangzhou Metro has eight lines in operation, namely Line 1, Line 2, Line 3, Line 4, Line 5, Line 8, Guangfo Line, and Zhujiang New Town APM. A major portion of the metro system services the urban areas of the city, while Lines 2, 3 and 4 also reach into the suburban areas in Huadu, Baiyun District, Panyu and Nansha; Guangfo Line connects Guangzhou and Foshan and is the first intercity underground metro line in the country. Daily service hours start at 6:00 a.m. and end at midnight, and ridership averages 4.39 million. Having delivered 1.64 billion rides in 2011, Guangzhou Metro is the sixth busiest metro system in the world.

Guangzhou Metro operates 144 stations, including 14 interchange stations, and 236 km of tracks. Massive expansion of the metro network has been planned for the decade of 2011–2020. Two new lines, Line 6 and Line 9, and the extension of Guangfo Line are already under construction and expected to be completed before 2015. Total operational capacity is scheduled to exceed 600 km by 2020.

The intersection between Line 3 and Line 1 at Zhujiang New Town and at Tian He stadium is the busiest all day. The network covers much of the city center and is growing rapidly outward. The fare ranges from 2 to 12 yuan. Most of the signs and announcements are also available in English. Tickets can be bought from vending machines in the stations. Bills from 5 to 10 yuan or coins from 0.5 to 1 yuan are accepted at these machines.

You can break up your big bills at the customer service counters. The ticket is a small plastic token, which you swipe over the blue reader at the gate to enter the platform, and at the exit where you insert the token into the slot like a vending machine. Multi-Pass and Yang-Cheng-Tong are also accepted and can be purchased at the customer service counter. Most of these machines do not accept old or torn notes. You can exchange old or torn notes for coins at the customer service counter. Tell the officer at the counter where you want to go and he or she will return your note with the requisite fare in coins and the rest in notes.

Metro stations can be identified by a large logo consisting of a Red "Y" made up of two lines on a yellow or white background. Costs for single trips range from 1 yuan up to 6 yuan depending on the length of the journey.

Below is shown the official logo for the Guangzhou metro:

YANG CHENG TONG CARD

Yang Cheng Tong Card is a contactless smartcard that can be used on the metro and the public buses in Guangzhou. It is similar in function to the Octopus Card in Hong Kong or the Oyster Card in London where customers can top-up as much money they like into the card and use it without the worry of using coins. Yang Cheng Tong Card offers a 5% discount for each journey on the metro for the first 15 journeys of the month, and 40% off for all other journeys after the 15th journey up to the end of the month. At the beginning of the following month, customers must start at the 5% discount again.

SEA

Guangzhou has a small ferry terminal located in the southwest of the city. The Nanhai port (Pingzhou) has twice-daily service to Hong Kong Central. It takes about two hours and costs approximately 170 yuan for a single trip. To get to the ferry terminal you can either take a taxi or the metro (Line 1). The latter is preferred because it is cheap and quick. In April 2007, Guangzhou launched a water-bus service, easing the pressure on road transport during the rush hour, though this can also get busy as well. There are areas in Guangzhou that are busy all the time and in a country like China it is difficult to find a place where there are not so many crowds.

FOOD

Guangzhou offers a considerable amount of choice when it comes to trying local and international restaurants. In that Guangzhou offers over 9,000 restaurants featuring every type of cuisine under the sun and also is the provincial capital of Guangdong, it is no surprise that the food is one of the strengths of this fantastic city. Because of the presence of various consulates and international companies, Guangzhou has a myriad of choice for international cuisines including Turkish, Ethiopian, Middle Eastern (Egyptian tea house!), and European. As an expat you will be spoiled for choices as new food may be enjoyed every day and for a very reasonable price too.

PLACES TO SEE

Situated on what was the original site of Zhongshan University in Guangzhou, the **Guangdong Provincial Museum** on 215 Wenming Road (on the corner of Yuexiu Road) consists of two separate buildings. One of the buildings is the Lu Xun memorial hall containing an exhibition of objects related to Lu Xun as well as to some other intellectuals connected with his work. The second, newer building contains several distinctive exhibitions which would be of interest to those who want to know more about Guangzhou, and indeed Guangdong Province's history as well. You will find here a remarkable historical exhibition of "Chaozhou wood carving" including many elaborately carved wood objects along with explanations of their historical and cultural significance. Perhaps one of the most interesting parts of the exhibition is upstairs where you can find many objects such as kitchen tools and other general household and lifestyle objects used by the locals in prehistoric Guangzhou. The exhibition in the new museum is displayed in both English and Mandarin, while the exhibitions in the building that used to house Zhongshan University are in Mandarin. There is a small admission charge. Photography is forbidden in most of the museum.

Located at Zhongshan 7th Road, the famous **Chen Ancestral Temple** is also known as the Chen Clan Academy. It is an important unit for the conservation of local antiques belonging to the Chen family who lived in 72 different parts of Guangdong province. It was constructed in the 12th year of the reign of Emperor Guangxu (1894). The home has been transformed into a museum, and now is largely known as the Folk Craftwork Museum. It is recommended to take plenty of photos, and spend around an hour at least to see the sights of the place. There are numerous rooms, halls and beautiful gardens. Every room, every wal , every pathway and every garden has some kind of strong connection with Guangzhou's rich history. There is also a souvenir shop as well as a snack shop. A small entrance fee applies to enter the garden.

The Sun Yat-Sen (Zhongshan) Memorial Hall in Guangzhou.

A key influential figure in China's revolution during the 1910s was Dr. Sun Zhongshan (Yat Sen), after whom many parks, roads and universities are named. More commonly the great democratic nationalist is also known as the father of modern China. The city of his birth also bears his name, "Zhongshan." In 1929 the famous Chinese architect, Mr. Lu Yanzhi, ordered the commencement of the construction of the **Sun Yat Sen Memorial Hall**, to commemorate the contributions of Sun Zhongshan. It is a memorial construction donated by the people of Guangzhou and by the overseas Chinese and listed as one of the most important cultural relics in Guangdong Province. Sun Yet Sun Memorial Hall, located on Dongfeng Road Middle in downtown Guangzhou, is an octagonal structure 49 meters high, with a floor space of 3,700 square meters. Renovated and restored in 1998, today the memorial hall plays host to many national and international live orchestra, opera and music concerts. There is a small entrance fee. The beautiful gardens surrounding the hall provide a place for peace and tranquility away from the hustle and bustle of the city center.

Initially built in the third year of the Datong (A.D. 537), during the Liang Dynasty, the **Six Banyan Monastery** (Liu Rong Si) was originally known as the Baozhuangyan Temple. The Six Banyan Monastery is located on Liurong Road, with the nearest metro station being "Liu Rong." Even today, the temple is still an active monastery for Buddhists. As you enter the temple, be sure to take some incense sticks, available for around 3 yuan, because right at the entrance there is a large prayer bowl full of fruit and a heap containing many incense sticks left by worshipers and visitors alike. At the back end of the temple complex is a small courtyard that displays photos showing the history of the temple, and of Buddhism. There are descriptions in Mandarin and English. The pagoda in the middle of the temple is the highest in all of Guangzhou, ten stories high. However, because the temple today is surrounded by high-rise buildings, the view from the top is not as exciting as it used to be. You can nevertheless, get a good picture of the temple complex from the top of the pagoda.

Yuexiu Park (Yuexiu Gong Yuan) is the premier landscaped park in Guangzhou, situated towards the east of the city center, and surrounded on all sides by major roads; the park has four main entrances. There is a small entrance fee, and on average it would take a visitor around two hours to experience the full sights and smells of the park, which includes a lake containing duck-shaped paddling boats, a pagoda, an ancestral home turned into a museum, and the famous statue of the Five Rams. The statue of the Five Rams is the official symbol of Guangzhou city, and you can see it upfront on a small hill as you turn left after entering the main opening of the park on Jiefeng Lu. There is also the attractive Tower Looking at the Sea (Zhen Hai Lou), which is a museum about the history of Guangzhou. On a hot and humid day take plenty of water with you. There are many hawkers selling ice creams and cold drinks all throughout the park. The maximum you will need to spend is around 5 yuan for a drink or ice cream.

THINGS TO DO

Apart from going to Yuexiu Park, a trip to Guangzhou would not be complete without going to the peak of **Baiyun Shan Gong Yuan (White Cloud Mountain Park)**. This refers to the mountain range located around 8 km to the northwest of Guangzhou and made up of around 30 peaks, with an area of 28 sq. km. The highest peak, the Moxing Ridge (Star-scraping Ridge) stands in the center of Baiyun Mountain, measuring 382 meters in height, and, on a clear day, provides beautiful panoramic views of the city of Guangzhou. While the park provides the local people an oasis for weekends and national holidays, it is also of great interest for people from around China and the world. There are some stunning views of downtown Guangzhou from the peak. A cable car takes people to the peak, and near to the peak there are lots of beautiful temples and a small lake. Baiyun Mountain is a park with natural hills and waters, and an ideal sightseeing place and summer resort, with a development history of over 1,000 years. Allow at least half a day to experience the park in full.

If you want to see Guangzhou as it used to look and feel like in the 18th and early 19th century, then head to the beautiful **Shamian Island**, which is still very much a residential area for expats. History informs us that from the 18th century to the middle of the 19th century, the foreigners who lived and traded in Guangzhou resided in a row of houses known as the "Thirteen Factories" in close proximity to the present Shamian. The three streets that run east-west on the island, formerly named Canal Street, Central Avenue (a beautiful tree-lined boulevard), and Front Avenue were renamed Shamian North Road (Shamian Beijie), Shamian Main Street (Shamian Dajie), and Shamian South Road (Shamian Nanjie). The five north-south streets are named Shamian 1 Street to Shamian 5 Street. The French Catholic church, Our Lady of Lourdes, has been restored and stands on the main boulevard. Located at the French end of the island, it was completed in 1892. The area still has that ambience of peace and quiet. In the middle of all of the colonial buildings, there is also a Starbucks café, which somewhat reminds you that you are in the 21st century Shamian! The nearest metro station is the Huangsha Station, which is within a short walking distance across the river.

Located on the affluent Ersha Island is the fabulous **Xinghai Concert Hall** on 33 Qing Bo Lu. The building structure is unmistakable with its distinctive architecture resembling the sail of a boat! The venue is the premier location for music concerts, opera and theatrical shows by (mostly) international artists, although Chinese artists perform here also. The venue is named after Xi'an Xinghai, a renowned Chinese composer, who was born and grew up in Guangzhou. The Hall consists of three parts, a Symphony Hall with 1500 seats for concerts and orchestras, a Chamber Music Hall, and a Music Material Room. More information about events at the Concert Hall can be found at this website: www.concerthall.com.cn

Lian Hua Shan (in Panyu), also known as Lotus Hill Park, is located on the outskirts of Panyu, around a 30-minute bus or taxi ride from Tian He Bus Station. The park contains a fine pagoda which offers some stunning views of the surroundings from its top floor. The overall cultural conservation in the park reaches back to over 2,000 years and includes the well-preserved Ancient Site of Stone Quarry, the Lotus Pagoda built in the Wanli reign of the Ming Dynasty, the Lotus Wall built in the Kangxi reign of the Qing Dynasty, and the newly built 40.88-meter tall bronze Kwan-yin/Guanyin statue, said to be the highest outdoor Guanyin statue in the world. During Chinese New Year, expect to hear deafening firecrackers and loud traditional Chinese music being played in the background. There is a small admission charge to enter the park, and visitors are encouraged to take some incense sticks with them. There is also a Buddhist temple, which offers delicious vegetarian food.

Built in 1983 and covering an area of around 11,000 m², the **Huanghuagang Theatre** on 96 Xianlie Lu in Yuexiu district derives its name from the nearby Huang-huagang Park. The Huanghuagang Theatre has a seating capacity of just over 1,700 and is fully equipped with modern acoustical and light equipment and central air-conditioning. There are regular shows here, most of which are packed to full capacity. Russian Opera, Cantonese Opera, and Beijing Opera shows prove very popular with the crowds. It's a place where people can go after a long day at work, and just relax to watch a show along with their family and friends. Normally it is not required to book seats in advance, however if you are curious, there is no harm in just going and seeing what events are happening while you are in Guangzhou. Whatever the show, you will enjoy it because it is something different and something unique to Guangzhou.

SHOPPING

In southern China, after Hong Kong, most people (even native Hong Kong people) come to Guangzhou for shopping. Your best bargains are going to be found in the local and traditional street markets around Beijing Lu, so start there if you like to poke around. If you're good at bargaining, you will be spoiled for choice around the Beijing Lu area. Here you can get some great deals, and can purchase just about everything from watches and jewelry to designer clothes. Although beware that some shops may sell fake goods. In China, it is sometimes very difficult to distinguish between a genuine and fake item (even the leather on clothes may look, smell and feel real!). The area becomes lively in the evening and is bustling right into the night. The best way to bargain is to say *"Pian e Dian"* while waving your hand downwards to indicate "Please bring down the price." Just like most cities in China, Guangzhou has an assorted blend of shops to submerge into, from enormous air-conditioned malls to humid and crowded open air bazaars. If you are in the right place you will find good quality products (some locally manufactured), much cheaper than in Hong Kong. Hence the reason why most people from surrounding cities, such as Shenzhen, Hong Kong, and Dongguan, come to Guangzhou on the weekend to do bargain hunting.

    Beijing Lu is the place to do shopping, eating, and people watching. It ranks first among pedestrian streets in Guangzhou, and has urbanized its own business model of "Xiguan (usually means western Guangzhou) Culture." With a long history, Beijing Pedestrian Street has gathered many old and new famous brands such as the Greenery Café Restaurant, which is part of a chain of restaurants. The one on Beijing Lu is special because it contains the fuselage of a former China Southern Airlines de Havilland aircraft transferred into a dining room. The business class seats are used as seating for the diners, while the original windows, flooring, and interior lighting are used. Even the original cockpit of the plane is placed at the front. Although a bit dark inside, it nevertheless provides a romantic dining experience. At both entrances to the street, there is a glass-covered section of the original Beijing Lu dating back to the Tang Dynasty, perfectly preserved in all its beauty.

    Apart from Beijing Lu, there is the large "**Tee Mall**" Shopping center in Tian He, located opposite the Citic Plaza (the tallest building in Guangzhou) in Tian He district. The Tee Mall is one of the largest indoor shopping malls in Southeast Asia. The prices may be higher than the Beijing Lu shops; however, the majority of the goods are genuine and of high quality. Also many people from Hong Kong and Macau come here to do shopping because the designer goods are a bit cheaper here. The nearest metro station is either Tiyu Xilu on Line 3 or Tianhe Sports Center on Line 1.

Shangxiajiu Pedestrian Street is located at the junction of Shangjiu Road and Xiajiu Road. Not quite as extravagant as Beijing Lu, it is nevertheless does have a strong ambience that echoes the cultural and historical aspects of Guangzhou's shopping scenery. Aimed at predominantly locals as well as tourists, the shopping mall boasts colorful clothes, mostly Chinese labels, and an abundance of antique dealers selling jade and all other bric-a-brac items. Prices are nexpensive, and the vast majority of the products are exported from or imported to Guangzhou for wholesale. It's very close to the modern Liwan Plaza (Li Wan Guangchang). Here you will find a labyrinth of shops selling all things that are "Made in China."

Nanshan Tea Market on Shiwei Dadao Zhong is located on the outskirts of Guangzhou, in a small town called Fangcun. This is one place in Guangzhou where you can purchase all types of high quality Chinese tea ranging from Jasmine tea to the more ancient HuangSha tea. The sidewalks of Shiwei Zhong Lu Central are stacked high with sacks, boxes, and urns of loose tea, filling the air with the scent of oolong, jasmine, dried chrysanthemum, and many more types. Even though the vast majority of the shops are catering for the retail trade, these shops sell everything from bulk tea to teapots, tea sets, serving utensils, and furniture. Around the area is also a fish market, as well as a bird market—both to keep the birds as pets, and also for some game meat.

Yide Lu is a famous street in Guangzhou specializing in providing dried fish and dried meat, generally more of the former than the latter. It is one of the oldest streets, perhaps second oldest in Guangzhou to Beijing Lu. Hundreds of wholesale booths line the road, vending items like dried scallop, cuttlefish, abalone, fish maw, shark's fin, and sea cucumber. These dried marine products come from all over the world, from places as near as Shandong Province to countries as remote as Brazil, Canada, and even neighboring South Korea. Five percent of the goods are used locally, and 95% are sold to markets and restaurants in other parts of the country; annual turnover has reached four billion yuan. The preserved fish and meat is of a high quality, inexpensive, and good for anyone's health. In actual fact some people use the ingredients from this dried fish market as part of a recipe for traditional Chinese medicine.

USEFUL LINKS

- www.gzmtr.com Guangzhou metro official website
- www.guangzhou.gov.cn Guangzhou official website
- www.gz.gov.cn Guangzhou (Government) official website

- www.lifeofguangzhou.com Guangzhou Daily Newspaper
- www.baiyunairport.com Official website of Guangzhou Baiyun Airport

China Foreign Trade Center
China Foreign Trade Center (Group)
   117 Liuhua Road
   Guangzhou, P. R. China
   Telephone: +86 (0)20 2608 8888
   Website: www.cftc.org.cn
   Website: www.cantonfair.org.cn

HANGZHOU

Hangzhou is the capital city of Zhejiang province and has previously served as one of the eight ancient capital cities of China. Right through its long history, the city has benefited from its position as the last remaining stop on the Grand Canal, the main corridor for providing grains and produce to the north of the country.

With a population of around 8.7 million people, Hangzhou has in time become a very popular tourist destination. In 2011, the GDP was 701.2 billion yuan, with a GDP per capita of 80,000 yuan. Although not big, it has a concentration of more than 45 picturesque spots and places of interest—plenty to keep you occupied during your stay here. The 6-square-km West Lake is the pride of this provincial capital city, and most sites of interest are around it. Unlike the man-made lakes of other cities, where earth is dug and piled up to make hills, the West Lake is natural, and its sights are delightful, no matter what the season. Scholars and poets have left a legacy of rhapsodic poetry and prose after visits to the lake, and some settled, or stayed on to live a hermit's life here. There are so many scenic spots around the West Lake that the view changes at every step. It was once said that its scenery is poetic, picturesque, and ethereal. A picture taken from any angle resembles a beautiful landscape painting.

If you love flowers then you will be glad to know that Hangzhou is the place of origin of the sweet osmanthus and the fragranced camphor trees, which can be found in abundance. The Sweet Osmanthus is Hangzhou's city flower, and is used as a key symbol to represent the city. The West Lake is one of the five largest places in China where you can see the sweet osmanthus at first hand. It's heaven for landscape photographers. The native residents of Hangzhou, like those of Zhejiang Province, speak a Wu dialect. However, the Wu dialect varies throughout the area where it is spoken; hence Hangzhou's dialect differs from that spoken in parts of southern Zhejiang and southern Jiangsu.

Tea is an important part of Hangzhou's economy and culture. Hangzhou is best known for originating Longjing, a famous variety of green tea. There are many types of Longjing tea, the most famous being Xi Hu (West Lake) Long Jing. Jing is grown near Xi Hu (West Lake) in Hangzhou, hence its name. Further, Hangzhou is also known for its artistic creations, such as silk, umbrellas, and Chinese hand-held folding fans.

GEOGRAPHY

Only a 45-minute ride on the train from Shanghai, Hangzhou is located in northern Zhejiang province, eastern China, at the southern end of the Grand Canal of China. The prefecture-level region of Hangzhou extends west to the border with the hill-country Anhui Province, and east to the flat-land near Hangzhou Bay. The city center is built around the eastern and northern sides of the West Lake, just north of the Qiantang River.

CLIMATE

Hangzhou's humid subtropical climate has four distinctive seasons, characterized by long, very hot, humid summers, and short, chilly, cloudy, and dry winters (with occasional snow). The winters can be cold at an average of around 4.3°C (39.7°F) in January, while the summers are the other extreme with an average temperature of around 28.4°C (83.1°F) in July. These temperature extremes present real estate developers a challenge in providing the best of both central heating and air conditioning.

TRANSPORTATION
AIR

Hangzhou Xiaoshan International Airport is located 17 miles from Hangzhou city center and also serves as an alternative airport in case Shanghai Pudong Airport is not operational. The airport is a major gateway to the rest of China, and does have a few direct international flights to destinations in southeast Asia. In 2008, the airport handled over 12.5 million passengers and was officially the 8th busiest airport in China.

The airport is well connected to the city center with buses running shuttle services every 15 minutes. An alternative route to Hangzhou is to first fly into Shanghai's Pudong airport, and then take the bus to Hangzhou using the Shanghai-

Hangzhou-Ningbo Expressway, about a 2.5-hour trip (at the time of writing it is 80 yuan one-way).

BUS

There are four bus stations in Hangzhou: East Bus Station on no. 215, Genshan East Road; South Bus Station located on no. 407, Qiutao Road; West Bus Station situated on no. 89, Tianmushan Road, and North Bus Station on no. 758, Moganshan Road. Every bus station is unique for different destinations. So as an example, at the time of writing, if you wanted to go to Shanghai, then the best station to go to is East Bus Station; for Huangshan it's best to leave from the West Bus Station; for Nanjing it's the North Station and for Ningbo it will be the South Station. These are just rough indications. More accurate information can be obtained from either of these bus stations. It is best to take a Chinese-speaking friend with you, or even better if you can converse in Mandarin yourself.

There are a total of 278 public bus lines in Hangzhou. In addition, visitors also have the option of taking special tourism buses, the lake bus lines, or the night bus lines.

TRAIN

Hangzhou train station is on the main line from Shanghai. There are (at the time of writing) eight daily trains running between Shanghai and Hangzhou. The journey only takes around 1 hour and 10 minutes. Hangzhou is also well connected to other cities such as Suzhou, Nanjing, and to the south of the country as well.

METRO

Hangzhou's metro system is currently under construction, with the first metro line (Line 1) destined to be opened in October 2012. The first line will connect downtown Hangzhou to the suburbs. Altogether there are plans for 8 lines with a length of 278 km to be in operation within the next 5 years.

PLACES TO SEE

Just as the Great Wall of China is famous in Beijing, the **West Lake** is the most well-known attraction in Hangzhou. The lake region occupies an area of over 60 square km and is surrounded by beautiful green and mountain scenery and culturally significant sites. What makes it extra special is that the lake is encircled on three sides by mountains while the banks of the lake are delightfully landscaped with trees and flowers. The beauty of this is that in each of the four seasons the West Lake provides a different colorful experience, with autumn's red and orange leaves, summer's lotus blossoms, spring's budding willows, and winter's plum flowers.

WEST LAKE SITES

Ten celebrated sites of the **West Lake** are well-known throughout China and have been attracting visitors to Hangzhou for many years. Because of their vital importance in the history and culture of Hangzhou, I have decided to include them in this book.

THE SU CAUSEWAY

The 3-km-long Su Causeway crosses the West Lake from Nanping Hill to Qixia Hill. It was named after Su Dongpo, a renowned poet, writer, and statesman in the Song Dynasty, who is said to have created the foundations of the causeway's construction by using mud dredged from the West Lake. Well worth visiting especially in the spring or winter because of the beautiful colors it projects in those seasons.

LOTUS IN THE BREEZE

During the Song Dynasty reign, the crooked courtyard used to be a distillery placed on the shores of the West Lake. During this time in history, there were many lotuses located near the distillery. Legend tells us that in the summer, when the lotus flowers were in bloom, the warm summer breeze would blow their superb fragrances across the area. Perhaps not so surprising then that sitting by the banks of the West Lake sipping alcohol and enjoying the fragrant lotus blossoms is a favorite part of summer for the locals!

NANPING HILL

Located on the southern bank of the West Lake, Nanping Hill is just over 100 meters high but over 1,000 meters wide. It was here in A.D. 954 that an emperor from the Five Dynasties Period built Jingci Temple. Every evening at 8 p.m. (sometimes 9 p.m.), the bells of the Nanping Hill temple ring, with echoes being heard all around the town.

THREE POOLS REFLECTING THE MOON

The name of this place derives from three islands—small stone pagodas—that appear to be floating in the middle of the West Lake near the central island. These three pagodas are known as the "Three Pools mirroring in the moon" and can be found on the back of the 1-yuan note. There is a pavilion situated on an island adjacent to the pagodas from which, under the right conditions, you should be able to enjoy a picture-perfect reflection of the moon.

SUNSET GLOW AT LEIFENG PAGODA

A wonderful place to take advantage of the sunrise and sunset if you like photography. Like many other pagodas in China, this one also has a special significance in Hangzhou's history. According to romantic legend, a girl was magically changed into a White Snake and imprisoned **underneath the Leifeng Pagoda.** The pagoda itself was actually first built in A.D. 976 and reconstructed in 2001. Visitors can find the detailed story of the pagoda at the attraction itself.

TWIN PEAKS PIERCING THE CLOUDS

The two mountains known as the "Southern Mountain" and the "Northern Mountain" face each other on two banks of the West Lake. When the mist and clouds surround the mountains, the peaks stick out above the clouds, creating an enchanting vista.

BIRDS SINGING IN THE WILLOWS

As you take a stroll along the bank of the West Lake, you will see hundreds of willows that are also highly popular with orioles, which like to congregate in large numbers in the trees. After a long day spent walking in the West Lake area there is nothing better than to sit on its banks, admire the beauty facing you, drink some local Dragon Well Tea, and, of course, listen to the singing of the orioles!

FLOWERS AND FISH—A GREAT COMBINATION

During the Song Dynasty era, a minister constructed a home for himself in the West Lake area and decided to decorate it with flowers and a fish pond. In subsequent decades and centuries, countless persons were drawn to the beauty spot to take in the delights of the fragrant flowers and beautiful fish. The area has become a fine-looking large park that is still filled with flowers and goldfish.

AUTUMN MOON OVER THE CALM LAKE

This particular attraction is not actually a site but rather a unique event best observed during some Chinese festivals, such as the mid-autumn festival or the Lunar Festival—periods when the full moon is present in the sky. It has become a legacy that has adorned many Chinese poems for thousands of years in which poets vividly express their feelings and the experience gained while observing the view of the moon reflected in the West Lake.

MELTING SNOW AT THE BROKEN BRIDGE

The West Lake is adorned with many ancient bridges; most of them are small ones with little significance. Of all these ancient bridges in the West Lake, the **Broken Bridge** is the most well known. There is a simple concept behind the name of this bridge: During winter, when you look at the bridge from the West Lake, the bridge appears to be broken because the heavy snow on the bridge blends in with the white snow in the background. You may be surprised but yes, Hangzhou does experience occasional snow as well as quite cold weather in the winter.

OTHER WEST LAKE AREA SITES

Zhejiang Province is a major producer of Chinese tea, and over 16,000 tons of tea leaves are supplied from here each year. Over 8% of this tea comes from the West Lake region. Arguably considered to be the national tea of China, the **LongJing (Dragon Well Tea)** is famous not only for its delicate flavor, but for the various myths that surround its existence in Chinese culture. The original Dragon Well tea came from the slopes of the "Lion Peak Mountain" in **West Lake.** It is not cheap to purchase because its manufacture is complicated and highly time consuming. Due to its renowned name and reputation it is now cultivated throughout China. Dragon Well Tea was blessed with its name by Emperor Qianlong of the Qing Dynasty who discovered its qualities when he frequently visited a small village (name unknown) located on Phoenix Mountain in Hangzhou. There are also stories informing us that ever since A.D. 221–280 residents of this village believed that a dragon living in a local "well" had enough power to control the weather of the area. Because of this reason citizens from all around the province would travel to this well to pray for rain during the harvest season. It has also been said that Emperor Qianlong made a point of visiting the village to have a cup of the local tea. During one of his visits to the village, Emperor Qianlong is said to have collected the tea leaves and taken them back to his ill mother, the Empress Dowager, who remarkably recovered by drinking that tea. Delighted by his mother's rapid recovery upon drinking that tea, Emperor Qianlong designated eighteen of the village's tea farms as producers of the "Imperial Tea." This firmly cemented Dragon Well Tea's reputation, and the tea trees that are still alive have turned the village into a major tourist destination for tea lovers.

With a history spanning more than 1,700 years, **Lingyin Temple** (also referred to as "Yunlin Temple") is a famous Buddhist temple situated at the north of West Lake between the **Feilai Peak** and the **Beigao Peak.** Nestled in a location of tall trees and high mountains, Lingyin Temple is a quiet and pleasant attraction within the Jiangnan area. There are three main halls in Lingyin Temple, starting with the middle lane running straight to the temple's gate, the Tianwang Dian (facing the main hall of the temple) and the Yaoshi Dian, which faces the hill gate. As you look up from the middle lane, you will see the smiling Buddha staring straight at you.

CHINA SILK MUSEUM

If you are looking for real authentic Chinese silk, then it goes without saying that Hangzhou is the place to come to. Quite close to the West Lake, the China Silk Museum proudly boasts of being one of the biggest silk museums in the world. You can find out about the rich history of silk, hear some stories, and of course, see a small live production of silk material (yes there are silk worms on display in the museum). There is also a great area that shows the success that Hangzhou has achieved by producing and selling silk. Souvenirs can be purchased in the museum shop.

PAGODA OF SIX HARMONIES

Located just over 2 miles from the south of West Lake, as you climb to the peak of Yuelin Shan (which means Moon Mountain), you are bound to come across the highly impressive Pagoda of Six Harmonies, whose Chinese name is Liuhe Shan. It is not easy to climb to the top but once you are there you are provided with breathtaking views of the Qiantang River and the surrounding areas. The pagoda used to be decorated lavishly with old style oil lanterns employed to light up the windows, hence becoming a lighthouse for ships navigating in the river. The scene was supposed to be magical once the mist settles on the surface of the river, so the lighthouse seemed something out of a story. These days, every year on the 18th day of the 8th lunar month the Qiantang Reversal is celebrated. Crowds gather around the pagoda to get a good view of the event. On Qiantang Reversal, the flow of the river naturally reverses itself, in the process creating large waves that delight its observers. The park also includes an exhibit of around 100 miniature pagodas, representing every Chinese style.

THINGS TO DO

TEA HOUSES

Hangzhou's many tea houses should keep you busy. As you are walking past one tea house, it is very difficult to avoid going in and not trying the tea on offer, and then when you leave that tea house you come across another one and again it seems very rude not to try their tea as well! I am not sure what the exact attraction is, whether it be the friendly hosts of the tea houses, or the colorful architecture of the buildings that act as a physiological magnet, or even the aroma of the tea that pulls you into the shop, while your mind attentively says, "Hmmm…I want to try that tea!" But in Hangzhou, they still keep the ancient style. One of the most popular and famous tea houses is on Qiwang Road. It is said a famous minister in the Song Dynasty retired here, while the surroundings of this tea house are full of buildings deriving from the 1920s, some British and French colonial style architecture. The tea houses are special because they connect the tea, its history, its taste, and its aroma with the culture of the Song Dynasty.

ENJOYING THE WEST LAKE AT NIGHT

The West Lake at night is perfectly beautiful. The Hubin Road is the best place to combine visiting the West Lake with a shopping trip. A lot of stores here sell famous brand items, and due to the fashionable and new architecture, the area wins a lot of international prizes. In addition, a music fountain up against the beautiful West Lake provides a water, light, and musical show at night. It is a romantic experience to walk in the whole area.

BARS AND COFFEE SHOPS

Hangzhou has something for everyone. If you want to while away the evening sipping away a cup of freshly made tea or coffee, and chatting to friends—head down to the main bar street known as Nanshan Road. The bars are beautiful, small in size yet full of life, and above all else they are romantic. Many young people love them simply because they provide a place to enjoy the evening in a quiet place away from the hustle and bustle. The best aspect of some of these bars is that you can easily book yourself a curtained section of the restaurant, which would normally be dimly lighted in various colors with probably a candle on the table. That's the ideal setting which most couples prefer and Hangzhou knows how to cater to those individuals. Tourists on a honeymoon to China will also enjoy this setting. You won't find it in

Freshly made local cuisine in Hangzhou – served with a smile!

many places in Europe; that I can guarantee you. The way the coffee is served is unique as well. This is special considering that coffee is a new concept in China. Usually, the coffee beans are ground right in front of you and then boiled in the coffeepot. It can't get any fresher than this, and it retains the original aroma and sweetness of the coffee bean.

OTHER ATTRACTIONS

Occupying an area of over 330,000 square meters, Hangzhou's main theme park is one of the biggest in the whole of Asia (soon to be outsized by the one in Shanghai). The **Hangzhou Future World** at 186 Zhouzhijiang Road is divided into six parts: Merry Land, Romantic Qthletics, Brightly Lit Ceremony, Huaying Road, The Dreaming Central Square, and the Holiday Mansions Center. Each one of these areas provides a thrilling experience for people of all ages, whether they are single, married, young couple or senior citizens, the place is a fun day out for the whole family. There is also an indoor pleasure ground that occupies over 18,500 square meters and is the major spot of "future world" to expand in the coming years. There is a magical Disney style castle as well as a Gothic church, 36 meters high, situated on the top of a mountain.

The **Yuanyuan Minsu Theatre** on 69 Shuguang Lu Yue is a must-see attraction for those who want to see authentic Hangzhou opera performances. The opera performances take place on a daily basis in the morning, afternoon, and evening. All of the performances are free of charge, so take your cup of tea or other local savories and enjoy the show!

SHOPPING AND OTHER ACTIVITIES

Silk is a highly valuable commodity in Hangzhou. Satin is also very popular and Hangzhou is renowned for producing this material. Throughout its long history, a variety of Hangzhou silks and satins have been sold all over the world. As mentioned earlier in this chapter, the Silk Museum will provide you with a fascinating insight into how Hangzhou become to be known as the Silk capital of China and Far East Asia in general.

Now the best place to purchase the material is at Hangzhou Silk City. Located at No. 253 Xinhua Road (at the intersection of Fengqi Road, Tiyuchang Road, and Xinhua Road), Hangzhou Silk City is the principal silk wholesale and retail market in China with more than 675 silk enterprises dealing in a broad selection of pure silk fabrics, garments, handicraft articles, scarves, and ties. This is one place in Hangzhou where you will find eagle-eyed shoppers from all around the world. Whether they have come to Hangzhou Silk City for business or their own personal purchase, people are sure to find every kind of silk material in this place. Prices are reasonable, and quality is genuine.

I would highly recommend people to go and shop in **Wushan Road** (Wushan Lu) if they want something that is not necessarily catered for the tourist, but that is more adapted to what the locals would purchase for their home decor. Now this would be something special to purchase because you are going to get reasonably priced (not tourist-priced) goods that you may not find back in your home country. There are some wonderful artifacts that one can dig through such as genuine paintings and calligraphy, antiques, and antique furniture. One has to bear in mind that there are genuine and fake antiques, about which your tourist guide or local Chinese friend may be able to advise you. If you are an expert, then of course you will already be well aware of what's fake and what's not A set of genuine silk pajamas on one stall may sell for twenty yuan, but on another it may be bought for forty yuan. A certain trick that always works for me when bargaining with Hangzhou vendors is usually to offer a price slightly higher than half that quoted. In that way you can always negotiate your way to the best price, and you are in the ultimate control of what you want to haggle over!

The three-thousand-meter-long Yanan Road is considered to be the best commercial street in Hangzhou, most probably comparable to, say, Shanghai's Nanjing Xi Road. The street is full of high-rise buildings and department stores. On the south side of the road, visitors can find the provincial government's Great Hall of the People, the Hangzhou Cultural Center, the Victory Theatre (used for orchestras and opera performances), International Mansion, Hangzhou Department Store, Hangzhou Grand Hotel, and the Haifeng Western Restaurant. While on the north end, you may be interested in Wulin Square, the new center of culture and commerce where towers and skyscrapers are springing up on a regular basis. The main attractions on this side of the road are the Zhejiang Provincial Exhibition Hall, Hangzhou Shopping Center, Hangzhou Theatre, and the Zhejiang Provincial Science and Technology Museum.

One of the few streets in Hangzhou where you can still find material such as the street pavement stones laid out untouched since the Song, Ming, and Qing dynasties is Qinghefang Street. As you stroll on this street, you realize that you are actually walking on a bit of Hangzhou history, having been reassured that once in history, Emperors and Chinese Imperial rulers walked on these roads. There are also quite a lot of antique buildings and local crafts, such as s lk parasols, brocades, noted Zhang Xiaoquan scissors, and Hangzhou fans.

Ranging from just your "normal" high street ready-made suits and clothes, right through to large numbers of tubes of various materials, the Si Ji Ching clothes market located on 10-39 Hanghai Road, is the place where many clothes retailers from high street shops come and get their stocks. Textiles are a booming business in this province, one that is growing at a dizzying pace. As a tourist you might like to purchase the material here at a much cheaper price and then get your clothes tailored whether back home in your country or by a specialist tailor in downtown

Hangzhou. Many visitors buy silk and other materials from the clothes market and then get made-to-measure silk pajamas or three-piece suits in Hangzhou.

The majority of the materials are catered for the Chinese fashion shops, so people not into Chinese fashion may have a harder time finding clothes to their taste here. On the whole you can purchase just about anything and everything in this market—the majority of the goods are genuine because they are exported outside of China.

Pay a visit to Xixi National Wetland Park. It's the first and only national wetland park in China. The park lies at the southern tip of the longest and oldest canal in the world, the Hangzhou-Beijing canal (also known as "The Grand Canal of China"), the 10.64 square kilometer (26,300 acres) park features copious ecological resources, beautiful natural scenes, and a rich cultural heritage of many millennia. It is densely populated with six main watercourses, among which scatter thousands of ponds, lakes, and swamps. With a history of more than 1,800 years the park also happens to be the original site of Chinese South Opera. It's common to see birds such as the kingfisher, green headed duck, and the beautiful silver pheasant.

NANJING

Nanjing, sometimes known as Nanking, is the capital city of Jiangsu Province. The city is famous for cultural and historical reasons. Nanjing means The South Capital, as opposed to Beijing,, which means The Northern Capital. Nanjing has been declared China's capital repeatedly during several historical periods.

Located in the lower Yangtze River drainage basin and Yangtze River Delta economic zone, Nanjing has always been one of China's most important cities. Apart from having been the capital of China for six dynasties and of the Republic of China, Nanjing has also served as a national hub of education, research, transportation, and tourism throughout history. With an urban population of over five million, it is also the second largest commercial center in the East China region, after Shanghai.

CLIMATE

Average low temperatures in January are at around –2°C (28°F), while average high temperatures in July run about 32°C (90°F).

HOW TO GET TO AND AROUND NANJING

AIR

Nanjing has one major international airport, Lukou International Airport, which directly serves 85 national and international routes. In 2008, the airport handled almost 9 million passengers. It was ranked 13th among 126 civil airports in China in terms of yearly passenger transport, and 10th for yearly cargo transport. The airport is well connected to the city center by a 29-km highway, and is also linked to various intercity highways, making it accessible to passengers from the surrounding cities. Daily frequent flights are operated to high-profile destinations including Shanghai, Beijing, and Guangzhou.

RAIL

Nanjing has three railway stations, with Nanjing Railway Station being the main one used for long-distance routes, while both Nanjing West Railway Station and Nanjing South Railway Station are used for shorter routes around the region. When the expansion of Nanjing South Railway Station was completed in June of 2011, it officially became the largest railway station in Asia.

BUS

One of the most complex bus systems in China is in operation in Nanjing. Five bus companies operate over 365 routes on a daily basis.

TAXI

Like everywhere else in China, you can grab any available taxi at the side of the street corner whenever you want it. Always be careful to take a colored official city taxi, unless your hotel arranges a private one for you.

METRO

Nanjing currently has two Metro Lines in operation. Line 1 started service on in May 2005, and Line 2 began service in early part of 2006. Nanjing city has ambition plans to expand its metro system to complete a 655-km long Metro and light-rail system by 2050. This will eventually take the pressure off the numerous buses operating in the city.

Line 1 is 46.2 km long and has 31 stations. It runs mainly in a north-south direction. The line starts at Maigaoqiao station in the north, heading southwards until it splits at Andemen station, from where the main line heads westwards towards Olympic Sports Center station, while the branch line continues southwards to China Pharmaceutical University station.

Line 2 is 40.8 km long and has 26 stations. It runs mainly in an east-west direction, from Youfangqiao station in the southwest to Jingtianlu station in the northeast. A west extension line which will go across the Yangtze River is currently under construction. This line will be approximately 14.4 km in length with 8 stations. Construction started on the building of Line 3 in January 2010. When finished, this new line, with a north-south orientation, will be approximately 40.2 km in length and have 28 stations.

PLACES TO SEE

NANJING MASSACRE MEMORIAL HALL (DATUSHA JINIANGUAN)

I would recommend that any visitor to Nanjing come to this place first before going to any of the other attractions. It will give you an idea of the importance of Nanjing's place in global history. Located at No. 418 Waidajie Street in the Shuimen area, this is the principal memorial dedicated to the 1937 massacre perpetrated by invading Japanese troops that claimed in excess of 300,000 victims. Memorial services are held on December 13 every year. In the heat of August 1937, the Japanese Army occupied Shanghai after they encountered physically powerful confrontation from the Chinese army. After the fervent battle in the outer edge of the city, the Japanese Army broke all the way through the resistance of the Chinese army, and Nanjing, then the capital of China, fell into the hands of Japanese invaders on December 13, 1937. It was without a doubt the worst time in Chinese history as a large-scale massacre took place. Over 300,000 unharmed and innocent Nanjing inhabitants along with Chinese Prisoners of War were brutally slaughtered by the Japanese. The Nanjing Memorial Hall was first constructed in 1985 at one of several memorial sites of the Nanjing Massacre, Jiangdong Gate. The building was extended in 1995, and it allowed people from all around the world, including descendants of those who were murdered, to pay their respects in the most humble way. The magnificent Memorial Hall and its surroundings produced an atmosphere of commiseration, somberness and reflection. The memorial comprises three major areas for visitors to see: the outdoor exhibits; the sheltered skeletal remains of victims;

and an exhibition hall of historical documents related to the events leading to and after the massacre. There are statues and sculptures; the bones of massacre victims now exhibited in a coffin-shaped display hall were excavated from Jiangdongmen in 1985; and the tomb-like exhibition hall, half underground, contains more than thousand items related to the tragedy.

NANJING MUSEUM (NANJING BOWUGUAN)

The Nanjing Museum is located inside the Zhongshan Gate of Nanjing City. Presently the Museum is home to around 400,000 objects in its collections, among which are some of the rarest and fine art preserved in China, including ancient genuine Chinese porcelain. One of the most precious inclusions is the only complete set of jade suits sewed with silver thread in China, which are renowned throughout the world. The calligraphy and contemporary paintings compilations are also very unusual. Around a quarter of the 400,000 objects that have legitimately entered the collections come from the Ming and Qing dynasties. Among these collections, the most treasured are the Wu Men painting schools known as Yangzhou painting school and Jinling painting school, as well as a small number of works created during the Song and Yuan dynasties. A considerable number of works by the contemporary Chinese painter Fu Baoshi (1904–1965), and Chen Zhifo (1896–1962) are also displayed here.

ANCIENT CITY WALL

The capital of Jiangsu Province is surrounded by stunning mountain terrain and the Yangtze River. A man-made wall encircles the whole city as well—similar to what people may see in cities such as Xi'an.

The wall was first engineered to protect the city from its enemies by the first emperor of the Ming Dynasty, Emperor Zhu Yuan Zhang. Because Nanjing served as the capital for over six dynasties, it was vital that the city be protected from outside attacks. Just like a castle has a deep moat to protect its boundaries from outsiders, so the Emperor decided to protect the whole city with a powerful and solid structure that would sustain any sort of attack.

The ancient wall, which stands at 33.7 km long and has varying heights between 14 and 21 meters, took over 21 years to build (1365–1387) and used over 210,000 people to move over 7 million cubic meters of earth and place thousands of stones and bricks. The Ancient City Wall or Ming City Wall stands today as one of the longest surviving city walls in the world. It provides a great testimony to Chinese architecture and science.

CONFUCIUS TEMPLE

The Confucius Temple (known as Fuzimiao), dates back to the Song Dynasty. Constructed along the banks of the Qinhuai River, Fuzimiao faces an enormous 110-meter-long stone wall to the south. The place comes alive during between the 1st and the 18th days of the lunar calendar year for the Lantern Fair. It's a time in Nanjing when local souvenir shops, restaurants, and street hawkers assemble here to attract clients to purchase their goods. The Fuzimiao structural design consists of the Confucius Temple, Xuegong Palace, and the Gongyuan (place of imperial examinations), which forms an important part of the Qinhuai River scenery. In the Gongyuan itself, the Mingyuan building is a splendid piece of architectural success provided by the Qing Dynasty for eyes to feast on. Observing the temple, you will realize that just like all the other amazing magical structures which the Chinese built, the Confucius is also totally built using non-mechanical ways.

CHONGTIANGONG PALACE

Chongtiangong Palace (Known as Zhishan in Chinese), lies on Yeshan Hill in the southwest of Nanjing. The Chongtiangong Palace is said to be the most well-con-served cluster of prehistoric buildings in the south of the Yangtze River. Chinese legend tells us that because Fu Chai, the emperor of Wu State, used to cast swords here in the summer and autumn months, he ended up setting a trend for future Emperors to build their temples and palaces in this place. The name "Chongtian-gong" (meaning worshiping the Son of Heaven) is given by Taizu Zhuyuan Zhang, from the Ming Dynasty. In those days, the emperors used to worship their ances-tors in this palace. Towards the conclusion of the Qing Dynasty, the Chongtiangong Palace was reconstructed as Jiangning, a school used to educate underprivileged children in the area.

Like most structures in China, the architectural design of the current struc-tures is nothing short of a grand scale and they are built symmetrically on either side of the axis. Although the Chongtiangong Palace is now transformed into the Municipal Museum, as you stroll through its vast rooms, it makes you think that you are walking on a piece of something which has a great historical significance.

THINGS TO DO

Nanjing's equivalent of Shanghai's Xintiandi District is the **1912 District**, quite appropriately named after the year 1912. The area is full of small shops that sell everything from paintings, Chinese tea, designer goods, and even some upmarket designer clothes. Most shops are nicely decorated with the traditional Chinese red lanterns and other lavish Chinese decorations. This is one place in Nanjing where history and modernism rub shoulders with each other side by side. The location is great—right downtown just west of the Presidential Palace. There is an underground parking area for cars and extensive outdoor parking for bikes and motorcycles on the north side of the complex.

Purple Mountain (Zijin Mountain) accommodates the tomb of the first Ming Dynasty emperor and his consorts, the mausoleum of Dr. Sun Yat Sen (leader of the 1911 revolution), and the tomb of Sun Quan from the Three Kingdoms period. It would be wise to leave at least half a day for this so that you can explore the mountain and neighboring region. Like in most places in China, the park has a shuttle train made up of small buggies, where each buggy can hold about four people. You can ride this "train" to and from the entrance to the bottom of the park—prices are included in the entrance ticket.

Xuanwu Hu, one of Nanjing's lakes has several islands in the middle all linked by causeways. Activities in the surrounding park include visiting an amusement park for kids and a small zoo, as well as renting paddle boats. The natural beauty of this lake, plus the man-made traditional Chinese structures, make it a top Nanjing destination.

No visit to Nanjing is complete without watching a performance of Chinese kun ju opera performed at the Jiangnan Theatre on Yanling Xiang 5. Fans of traditional Beijing Opera would be thrilled to know that regular performances are shown at the People's Theatre on Yanggongjing 25. Performances usually begin at 7:30 p.m. and last around two hours. It is common for people to head down to the restaurants after the theatre performance, or to the many bars in town. In China, eating in a restaurant is a lively and long affair where you are not meant to rush your food, and should take time to chat to friends and enjoy the food, so it makes sense for people to go after the theatre show has finished; otherwise if they go at, say, 6 p.m., they will not have much time to enjoy the dinner before the performance begins at 7.30 p.m. Shops around the theatre sell pot noodles and other convenience food for the really hungry audience members.

SHOPPING

I would kick off my shopping trip by first going to **Xinjiekou** in Nanjing's fashion district. This is where you will find all the Western and Chinese high street names, designer or national brands—you will find whatever tickles your fancy here in Xinjiekou. It would be safe to say that Xinjiekou is the closest thing Nanjing has to, say, London's Oxford Street. If you love the fun of being in a bustling place, then Xinjiwkou is the right place for you. Plenty of lively happenings are going on from street clowns entertaining children to the newly upper class of China purchasing the latest

Gucci, Versace or DKNY. If you like Chinese porcelain, a couple of shops do sell genuine and rare Chinese porcelain; however, of course, be aware of fake ones too.

If you want something that would not do too much damage to your pocket, the next place to try would be the trendy Hunan Road (Hunan Lu). This popular night market flanked by Zhongshan Bei Lu and Zhongyang Lu is attractive, clean, and less busy than Xinjiekou. This is one place where you can purchase English books at the Phoenix International Bookstore—expect to pay similar prices as in the West (or even higher) because the books are imported. A decent collection of restaurants, including the now ubiquitous KFC and McDonald's, are well placed in Hunan Road. As you walk past the shops, expect to hear loud techno Chinese music and young shop attendants clapping their hands in rhythm to welcome you into the shop!

Jinying Yishu Zhongxin Hualang (Golden Eagle Art Center) is officially Nanjing's largest fine art gallery. Conveniently situated at Hanzhong Lu 89, 11th floor, the gallery has a huge compilation of traditional Chinese ink paintings, calligraphy, and contemporary oil paintings. Nanjing Yunjun Yanjiusuo (Brocade Research Institute) at Chating Dong Lu 240 (open 8:30am-4:30pm) sells cloud dragon brocade, which was once retained entirely for use by emperors. Prices are seriously expensive, but so is the quality of the paintings on offer.

For lovers of handicrafts and art décor, head down to the Nanjing Gongyi Meishu Dalou Gouwu Zhongxin at Beijing Dong Lu 31. Here you can explore two entire floors of moderately luxurious handicrafts from all over China. Ornaments for purchase include exquisite jade, silk embroidery, fans, lacquer ware, and jewelry.

Finally if you like clothes, silk, and general tourist-related goods, then find your way to the **area around the Confucius Temple** in the south of the city. A Chinese "Aladdin's Cave" may be the best way to describe this place because essentially it is full of small alleyways snaking their way like a maze, with some even having shops squeezed into walls. It is a fun environment, full of noise, color and culture. The only thing you won't find here is monkeys or any other exotic animals hovering around…it's not quite like something out of your average ancient Chinese movie but it may be the closest you will get to it! It's best that you come prepared to bargain and haggle as you won't buy everything at the first site you see it. The streets outside the temple area grant more shopping opportunities, as does the underground mall. There are also plenty of tea shops and traditional Chinese costume shops.

QINGDAO

Qingdao is best known in the West as the city where the Chinese beer "Tsingtao" is brewed. It's a major city_located on the southern coastline of the Shandong Peninsula, in east China's Shandong province. The city is often dubbed "Eastern

Switzerland," and is one of China's most important port cities. It borders Yantai to the northeast, Weifang to the west and Rizhao to the southwest. Lying transversely by the Shandong Peninsula at the same time as looking out to the Yellow Sea, Qingdao in the present day is not just a major seaport, naval base, and industrial center, but a major center of tourism as well. In Chinese the name Qingd⊠o stands for "Green Island"; perhaps uniquely in reality the city stands perfectly by its name. Qingdao is administrated at the sub-provincial level and just prior to the Beijing 2008 Olympics it was decorated with the title of "China's 9th-most livable city" (*China Daily*).

For most of the 20th century until 1949, Qingdao was a colony of Germany or Japan, which explains why you will see a lot of German and Japanese influenced architecture. This architectural remnant of the colonial period today beautifies this seaside city, which is full of red terracotta-tiled roofs, green trees, blue sea, and azure sky.

In cooperation with the Beijing Olympic Games 2008, Qingdao was proud to host the Sailing Competition. This without a doubt gave Qingdao an excellent platform for the outside world to explore because prior to the 2008 Beijing Olympics many people had not even heard about Qiangdao. They probably drank the Tsingtao beer, but were not aware that it was indeed Qingdao where the brewery is for this famous Chinese export product! This great event brought a great opportunity for this delightful city to construct its brilliant future. Of course just as if you were to go to Dublin and not try even half a pint of the Guinness beer, it would be totally pointless to come all the way to Qingdao and not try the famous Tsingtao beer and enjoy the museum in the brewery. Qingdao offers food with characteristic flavors, particularly seafood. The city is so close to the ocean that the catch is fresh, so one should not waste the opportunity to enjoy the delicious seafood of Qingdao.

You will also notice that there is a large Korean expat community in Qingdao, both from North and South Korea. This has been visible since the first Korean companies began doing commerce in Qingdao in the early 1980s. Since that time thousands of Korean people have moved to live and work here, which makes Qingdao the city with the most Korea investment enterprises in China. It provides a perfect reason to go and enjoy an authentic Korean meal in North China!

Qingdao Municipal Government now hosts and sponsors the Qingdao International Beer Festival, the Qingdao International Sea Festival, Beach Culture Festival, the Sea Affection Festival, and the Summer of Qingdao Festival. These are all must-see events to truly experience Qiangdao at its best.

CLIMATE

Average low temperatures in January run around –3°C (27°F), while average high temperatures in August are around 28°C (82°F).

HOW TO GET TO AND AROUND QINGDAO

AIR

Qingdao Liuting International Airport is located 30 km to the north of the city. The airport serves as the main corridor to the rest of China and the world, with over 15 international and over 80 domestic routes in operation. An expansion enabled the airport to become the 15th busiest airport in the country, with over 11 million passengers by 2010. Passengers can take metered taxis, which will cost around 100 yuan to the city center. There is an hourly service of the airport bus, which cost 15 yuan at the time of writing.

RAIL

Qingdao is served by two major railway stations, Qingdao and Sifang Railway Station. In the years leading up to the 2008 Summer Olympics, the Qingdao station underwent a significant restoration program in order to accommodate the increased passenger traffic for the Olympic period and afterwards. When you set your eyes upon the new station, you might for a moment feel that you are in Germany (because the restored building reflects the original German renaissance design from its 1899 opening). Both the Qingdao and Sifang stations serve destinations all around China.

SEA

Although mainly a cargo seaport, which makes Qingdao one of China's largest seaports, with an annual cargo handling capacity of over 80 million tons, Qingdao does have some passenger ferry services. There are regular services from Qingdao to Japanese and Korean destinations. The *Orient Ferry* connects Qingdao with Shimonoseki, Japan, and there are two ferry lines connecting Qingdao with South Korea. The *New Golden Bridge II* operates between Qingdao and Incheon, while the *Blue Sea Ferry* operates between Qingdao and Gunsan.

TAXI AND BUS

Metered taxis operate all throughout the city 24 hours a day. All you need to do is give a hand signal. The starting fare at the time of writing was 7 yuan for the first 4 km and then 1.2 yuan per kilometer. Over 4500 buses operate in the city alone, probably more than the taxis. However if you are a tourist, it would be highly recommended that you take the taxi. Most drivers can speak some English, but take a note with your destination written in Chinese if you can, or a Chinese-speaking friend.

PLACES TO SEE

Qingdao International Beer Festival began in 1991 when the Tsingtao Brewery first applied for permission for a Beer Festival and received approval with the great support from the Qingdao municipal administration. Since then the government has continued to sponsor the event. The first festival was opened on June 23, 1991, and has been held annually ever since. The festival integrates tourism, culture, sports, business, and trading activities. After many years of operation, the Qingdao International Beer Festival has become a well-known brand name and enjoys an extensive reputation both nationally and internationally. Past festivals have featured artistic parades, "Beer Carnival" games, beer tasting, drinking contests, music, food, and interactive performances, as well as merchandise stalls for various breweries. Your local travel agent or the China National Tourist Office would be able to provide further details about this very popular event. There is a small fee for attending the event.

Overlooking the enormous Yellow Sea, the **National Mount Lao Scenic Area** includes the rugged and the sculpted terrain of Mount Laoshan. It holds both a natural and religious significance. Centerpieced as China's highest coastal peak, at over 1,100 meters above sea level, the Mount Lao mountain range attracts numerous visitors every year as tourism continues to grow in China. There is an entrance fee for visitors. It is highly recommended that you allow around two hours to fully absorb the beauty of the surrounding area. There are some basic essential facilities such as a toilet and a snack shop for refreshments. On a hot day it is recommended that you wear a hat and sun block to prevent sunburn.

Shilaoren (translated into "Old Stone Man") is considered Qingdao's, if not China's, most impressive tourist beach. Shilaoren is named after the well-known rock structure that, according to local legend, is an old fishermen waiting for his daughter's return from the sea. That legend has in time turned this beach into a place of interest for tourists as well as a beach. Shilaoren Beach is an ideal location adjacent to several other Qingdao attractions including the Ocean Entertainment Center, several golf courses, Qingdao Dolphinarium, Qingdao International Exhibition Center, and Qingdao Cultural Exhibition Center. Like other beach resorts in China, the Shilaoren can get ridiculously crowded during popular days. There is a small charge for some parts of the beach, which are naturally cleaner.

Nothing in China compares to the sheer size and spectacle of Qingdao's 440-meter **Zhan Qiao Pier.** The pier is situated at the southern shore of Qingdao off Zhongshan Road, stretching far into the sea. In the distance an octagonal pavilion known as the "Billowing Back and Forth Tower" (Huilan Ge), can be clearly seen at the end of the pier. The pier, first constructed in 1891, has been extended a few times in its lifespan. The tower was constructed in 1930. Most government officials and the local tourism board have labeled the Zhan Qiao Pier as the official symbol of Qingdao. The next time you drink a Tsingtao Beer, you may notice a logo that shows a pier in the sea. That pier is the Zhan Qiao Pier. At the time of writing there is a small charge to go onto the pier (around 3 yuan).

Ba Da Guan is a key visitor attraction close to the coast. It consists of eight roads named after eight great military castles from ancient times. Along the streets are many traditional colonial style European houses built when Qingdao was a German dependency (1897–1914). Its ambience is unlike any other place in China, with large, grassy lawns, wide streets, and minimal traffic. Ba Da Guan is bordered on both sides by beach resorts, the "Number 1 Beach" on its west side, and "the number 3 Beach" on the east.

THINGS TO DO

The **Qingdao Brewery** has to be one of the highlights of any tour to China, and not just Qingdao. For die-hard beer lovers, this will probably be your first stop in the city, while even for people who do not have a liking for beer, it is definitely one of the best parts of any tour to Qingdao. It is officially China's largest brewery. Founded in 1903 by German settlers, it claims roughly around a fifth of the domestic market share. The beer is, of course, locally produced in Qingdao (and more recently in other breweries owned by the company as well), but the name of the beer uses the old École Française d'Extrême-Orient transliteration. The beer's present-day logo displays an image of Zhan Qiao (see above). There is an entrance fee, you will get a sample bottle or cup of the beer itself, and there is a souvenir shop that sells everything related to "Qingdao Beer"! Everyone knows the directions to the brewery, even if they don't speak English, you can just mention "Qīngdǎo píjiǔchǎng" to any Taxi Driver and they'll take you there!

Situated on the southern side of Zhanshan (literally meaning "deep mountain"), facing the sea is the beautiful **Zhanshan Temple.** This monastery was constructed in 1945 and is a dynamic and fully functional Buddhist sanctuary. Apart from the Olympic Mascot Bell Tower, located on the right-hand side of the Temple grounds, the residual buildings are to be found neatly placed in a rectangular format. As you enter the Temple, you will come across one of the many Buddhist scripture shops. Here, incense sticks and other Buddhist supplies are available for purchase—it is recommended that you purchase them prior to going into the Temple itself, hence the shop is firmly placed at the entrance. Adjacent to the scripture shop is a Bell Tower (Zhonglou) with the first of many statues of Buddha. Once you are on top of this tower, you will be presented with panoramic views of the immediate surrounding area; however, there is an additional fee of 10 yuan (at the time of writing) to see that view—it's worth it if you have a camera with you!

On the western side of No. 1 Bathing Beach is the inspiring **Lu Xun Gongyuan.** Built in 1929, Lu Xun Park (Lu Xun Gongyuan) looks towards the rocky coastline of Huiquan Bay. Its name was given in 1950 in honor of the distinguished Chinese writer and commentator, Lu Xun. The park is well respected and known to be the largest sandy beach in Asia. There is a small charge to enter the park. There is a sea of various colored flowers, all of which are pretty to take photos of or with!

Quite near to the Lu Xun Gongyuan is the **No. 1 Bathing Beach** on Huiquan Bay. Also known as the "Huiquan Bathing Beach,, this beach is noted for its clear and clean waters, mild waves, and the soft sand. The beautiful scenery with its European style atmosphere can easily compare to, say, Hawaii or closer to home, Sanya on Hainan Island. The beach was first built in 1901 by the Germans after they took control of Qingdao. At that time, it was a renowned place of leisure in all of Asia but it was only open to non-Chinese people. In 1984 and 2003, the local government carried out much renovation and expanded the place on a large scale. On a hot summer's day, it can get exceedingly crowded, but the atmosphere is great nonetheless.

The **Small Qingdao Island** lies to the southeast of the Zhan Bridge inside Qingdao Bay. It is a significant resort of vital importance to the Qingdao Coastal Scenic Area. If you want to just get away from it all, then it is a great place to enjoy the beautiful views of the sea and to soak up an island atmosphere. At one time Small Qingdao Island was an isolated island situated about 720 meters off shore but in the 1940s a seawall was built connecting it to the mainland.

Guanhaishan Park (Guanhaishan gongyuan) is tiny but charming. Conveniently situated close to 15 Guanhai Er Lu, this was the original place where the German high officials would practice their golf swing while looking down over the rest of the city. They would make their plans to expand the city from this viewpoint. The beauty of it all is that now tourists can take a stroll on the same bit of ground and admire the rich history and culture that has been left for many generations to come and admire here.

SHOPPING

The **Qingdao Art and Craft Store** on 212 Zhongshan Lu is one of the largest antique shops in Qingdao, with four floors containing nothing but Chinese porcelain, scroll paintings, silk, gold, jade, and other stones. You can find here a myriad of products that are of a high quality and priced much less expensively than in Europe or America. However, on the whole, like anywhere else, be very careful to distinguish which product is genuine and which will break on the flight back to your home. On the whole the art and craft store caters to all kinds of tastes, including products for children such as miniature souvenirs.

Located on 169 Zhongshan Lu, the **Ju Bao Zhai Art Shop** offers not only a selection of porcelain, metal, and stoneware, but also genuine art paintings, handcrafted wall decorations to hang in your kitchen or bathroom, and beautifully decorated carpets to display on your living room floor or atthe entrance to your home. Prices are reasonable and you will feel like taking everything if you are really up for it. So make sure you have enough space to take all your shopping with you!

Qingdao's nightlife is usually over a little earlier than that in some other coastal cities in China. However, one place where you are bound to find quite a lot of activity late into the evening is the city's Night Market. It should really be known as the evening market because it usually starts to close down by around 11 every night. You can join the night market on Yan'an Er Lu and Taidong Street. Here you can purchase all kinds of goods, everything from sailor uniforms to even cute small pet dogs and parrots. The place does become lively at times, especially if there is a national festival or local event going on in town. Restaurants, some with outdoor seating, line both Yan'an Er Lu and Taidong Street.

At 65 Xingyang Road is Qiangdao's oldest shopping mall, the Qingdao Laoshan Department Store. Dating back to more than 50 years, this enormous mall stretches over several floors and is a great place to pick up any essentials that you might need, or simply a souvenir of your visit. Prices are within reason, and this is one of the places in Qingdao where you will not find any fake items. As soon as you enter it, you may begin shopping to your heart's content!

One of the top five shopping malls in the city, located at 9 Shandong Street, right in the heart of downtown Qingdao, is the superb Haixin Plaza. Unlike other stores in Qingdao, the Haixin Plaza is a contemporary department store, which opened its doors in only 1997. The store has become popular with tourists because it sells both internationally branded products as well Chinese goods that can serve as souvenirs to tourists. In the process the store therefore has become quite accepted. With five floors, an excellent restaurant, and plenty of reasonably priced goods, you can easily spend many hours in this one shop alone.

SHANGHAI

Formerly a fishing and textiles village, Shanghai gained international magnitude in the late 19th century due to its favorable port location. The city was one of the first in China that opened to foreign trade by the 1842 Treaty of Nanking. This enabled the city to thrive as a multinational center of trade between China and the West by the 1930s. Divided into two parts by the Huangpu River into Puxi (west of the Huangpu) and Pudong (to the east of the Huangpu), 21st-century Shanghai has developed into a dynamic financial, fashion, architectural, and artistic capital of China and has in recent years also become a trademark city as well as a branding image for this country.

Shanghai, which means "over the sea" in Chinese, has been known, from time immemorial, as the "Pearl of the East." However, since the turn of the 21st century, China's contemporary art and fashion market bubble has boomed so much after becoming the hottest thing in the art world that this fascinating metropolis full of skyscrapers has been dubbed the "New York of the East." The city has been churning out some of the most sought after fashion designers. Twenty-first century Shanghai is still a burgeoning honey pot for global businesses and tourists alike—though these days it is more contemporary art collectors and budding architects that are rushing to the city. While maintaining its role as a gateway to nearby artistic and historical towns such as Hangzhou and Suzhou, both of which are centers of China's cultural and heritage significance, Shanghai itself has a wealth of heritage experiences as well as contemporary art and rich cultural offerings. For those who love to explore their gastronomical interests, Shanghai is heaven for fine fusion dining, as well as a spectacular destination for avid shopaholics. No trip is complete without a visit to the art galleries on Taikang Lu in the southern part of the French Concession (Luwan District), and Moganshan Lu just south of the Suzhou Creek in the northern part of town (Putuo District). Both roads are beehives for resident artists and fashion designers, located in a series of industrial warehouses that have been converted to galleries and artists' studios where much of Shanghai's burgeoning art scene has started to coalesce in the last few years. They are a must-visit if you like contemporary art, fashion and photography. Various former warehouses and factories along Suzhou Creek, such as Wu Wei Road (ShanghaiART) and Jumen Road (Galerie Dumonteil), are also being converted into galleries.

Downtown Shanghai on a sunny day.

In recent years Shanghai has become well known for its architectural inspiration. Shanghai has always been a cosmopolitan city, and the metropolis certainly does not disappoint. As one stands in People's Square, one almost feels dwarfed in a playground full of various weird and wonderful-looking tall skyscrapers. Shanghai has a rich assortment of buildings and structures of diverse architectural styles. Native Shanghainese have a passion for art, design and traditional Oriental, as well as, colonial heritage, which neatly blends in the ethos of Feng Shui. Evidence of this is everywhere—ranging from splendid boutique hotels, such as the **Mansion Shanghai** on 82 Xin Le Rd (inspiration of French architect Lafayette in 1932), and the **88 Xintiandi** (designed by Boston-based Wood and Zapata Inc.), right through to the 11,528 m^2 architecturally distinctive **Shanghai Grand Theater**, opened in 1998 and designed by French architect Jean-Marie Charpentier (Of "ARTE Charpentier" fame in Paris during 1969).

The Bund (known as Waitan) used to be recognized as the "the face" of British Colonial Shanghai, reflecting the strong power of the Empire with its twenty-two buildings—all with a strong Victorian architectural element, and the most notable reminders of this are the neoclassic **HSBC building** and the flamboyant **Peace Hotel,** where the architects delicately combined Western and Eastern elements. Glimpses of Shanghai's special relationship with Russia are still evident through the architectural style of the **Sino-Soviet Friendship Hall,** which reflects an exclusive chapter in Shanghai's history. The majority of the buildings with this Soviet neoclassical architecture were erected during the period from the founding of the People's Republic in 1949 until the Sino-Soviet split in the late 1960s. Few buildings like this have survived anywhere in the world.

For those in search of the true taste of authentic Shanghainese architecture, the **Shikumen** (石库门) residences are a must see ("Shikumen" literally means "stone storage door"). These are two- or three-story townhouses, neatly placed in between high rise contemporary buildings dotted around the city. The Shikumen are a perfect cultural blend of Chinese and Western architecture. All of the Shikumen have their front courtyards protected by a high brick wall and connected symmetrically by straight alleyways, known as a *Lòngtang* (弄堂). Residents have the luxury to grow their own vegetables in their own courtyard—plenty of fresh air and room for sunshine to enter the household—it feels more like being in the ancient China. The entrance to each alley is usually furnished with a 1920s style stone arch. It's the perfect example of how traditional dwellings coexist with new skyscrapers.

The new Shanghai and the future of this city are evident when one wanders across to the other side of the Huang Pu into Pudong district. Most of the attention for this growth leading to the Shanghai 2010 Expo was focused on the previously undeveloped Pudong (East Shanghai) area, which is now the site of the world's tallest buildings. The expansion of the Shanghai skyline here is spearheaded by the fabulous **World Financial Center** at 492 meters, which is also home to the second highest hotel in the world, the **Park Hyatt Shanghai** (occupying floors 79 to 93 of the building). This has to be quite possibly the most remarkable piece of architectural development to date. Located next to the World Financial Center is the **Jin Mao Tower**, where one can be treated to some dazzling views of a metropolis crackling with energy. Frequently noted as the world's finest skyscraper since the

Chrysler Building, Jin Mao blends a wonderful pagoda-shaped building with the complex inside art deco to produce a stunning contemporary structure. It does not end here. A third skyscraper, the **Shanghai Tower**, is destined to become the second tallest building in the world at 632 meters when it's completed in 2014. The affluent air around **Pudong** (known as Lujiazui) reflects the nature of Shanghai's elite, who roam on many evenings to wine and dine, while admiring the architectural success that this city continues to enjoy.

Puxi is famous for "The Bund," its riverfront lined with elegant buildings deriving from colonial style architecture. The alleyways of Shanghai retain a unique historical feel. There are plans for a Disneyland and a Universal Studios Theme Park to be developed in Shanghai sometime in the near future (around 2015).

In recent years, Shanghai's status as a cultural (as well as financial) city has grown from strength to strength. Shanghai has also been a pioneer city in terms of "introducing" modernism and perhaps even somewhat a flavor of Western culture to its inhabitants. Pudong's transformation from uninhabited marsh land to teeming metropolis in only a couple of decades has been just as spectacular as the transformation of Shenzhen, the city in the south of China.

Since the early 21st century, the city has hosted major international sports events such as the Shanghai Grand Masters (Tennis), the annual Shanghai Formula One Grand Prix (since October 2005), annual Snooker world championships, and major international golf tournaments held annually—all of these firmly putting Shanghai on the sports map. One of China's biggest soccer (football) stadiums, seating up to 80,000 people, is in Shanghai.

All around the metropolis there are remnants of Shanghai's colonial past that blend in side by side with Western styled Chinese architecture, ranging from hotels to ancestral residences with strong historical implications. More significantly this is the place for anyone who wants to show their new art and architectural works. So much so that even nightclubs have been inspired to decorate their

The Jin Mao Tower and the IFC Tower behind it are the pillars of the new Pudong area in Shanghai.

interiors using the latest art handpicked from Moganshan Lu! If ever there was a city that wanted to embellish the walls of its skyscrapers and had the financial resources to do so, Shanghai is it. Little wonder then that the art scene in Shanghai is growing at a dizzying pace and the city is well on its way to becoming the country's most interesting and provocative contemporary art center.

Shanghai's oyster beds remain among the world's most fertile grounds for pearls, of both the saltwater and freshwater variety—these proving to be the vital ingredients for contemporary art and fashion items.

In 2010 73 million visitors attended the World Expo in Shanghai, which straddles the tributary of the mighty Yangtze River. The futuristic side of the river is called Pudong, and the older side is known as the Bund. The changes to the city in the last two decades have been enormous. If I were you, I would make a point of coming here and enjoying the sights and smells of this city. Have lunch at the Long Bar at the Waldorf Astoria, a drink at Flair at The Ritz-Carlton Shanghai, Pudong, and dinner at the Peninsula Hotel. Then bask in 3,000 years of history in the city that is spearheading China's incredible growth.

GEOGRAPHY

The name Shanghai stands for "over the sea" and is classed as a province itself, known as Shanghai Shi Province. It's flanked by Jiangsu Province to the west/northwest and Zhejiang Province to the west/southwest. The eastern side of Shanghai is surrounded by Hangzhou Bay to the south and by the mouth of the Yangtze River (which flows into the East China Sea) to the northeast.

Central Shanghai is densely populated despite covering an area of only approximately 15 km^2. It is amazing to observe just how much of the Pudong area has grown in the few years since the beginning of the 21st century.

CLIMATE

Winters are very cold, but not as cold as up in the northern cities such as Beijing or Dalian, while the summers are hot and humid. The best time to visit Shanghai is either around April and May when the weather is neither too cold nor too hot, or between August and September when again the weather is mildly cold as it creeps towards the freezing Shanghai winter. During this "mildly cold" weather, it is neither as hot as mid-summer or exactly cool, but just appropriate for late summer/early autumn. Which means you can still wear your shorts and T-shirt on some days!

TRANSPORTATION

BUSES AND COACHES

Shanghai has numerous bus connections operating all around the city during the day and a few at night-time. Most buses run from early in the morning (around 5 a.m.) to 11 p.m. For long-distance travel there is a bus station located on Heinan Bei Lu about 1.5 km north of Suzhou Creek. The bus station is within walking distance of the "Baoshan Jie" Metro stop. The Shanghai Tour Bus Lines depart from Shanghai Stadium to destinations mostly in the suburban districts.

AIR

Shanghai has two major international airports, HongQiao and Pudong. Pudong is the new international airport located 45 km to the east of the city beside the East China Sea, while HongQiao, located 15 km west of the city, is much smaller and older. HongQiao is mostly used for domestic flights. Pudong is also the base and HQ of China Eastern Airlines. Over 50 worldwide airlines use the airport, with an annual average passenger capacity of 28 million (2011 figures).

TAXI

The minimum fare is 11 yuan (US$1.38), which covers the first 3 km, and then 2 yuan are charged for every additional kilometer. After 10 km, the fare jumps 50%—to 3 yuan for every additional kilometer.

TRAIN

Shanghai has two train stations. Shanghai station, north of the Suzhou Creek, has several routes connecting with other Chinese cities. Shanghai West station is situated remotely to the northwest of the city.

METRO

Shanghai has one of China's largest metro systems with twelve metro lines running across the city. Line 1 operates from Xinzhuang to Gongfu Xincun, Line 2 from Zhongshan Park to Zhangjiang High-Tech District, Line 3 from Jiangwan Town to Shanghai South Railway Station, Line 5 from Xinzhuang to Minhang Development

District. Shanghai metro is very clean, safe and an efficient way to get around China's largest city. All signage has station names in Chinese AND English. Once you are onboard the indicator shows the previous stations in red, and the last one in amber, and the next station in green. The arrows indicate stations with connections to other lines.

Shanghai traffic can be chaotic any time of the day, not just during the peak rush hour.

Ticket prices range between 3 and 5 yuan depending on the length of your journey. The metro starts operation at 5.30 or 6.30 a.m., depending on which line, with last trains from each terminus leaving between 10.20 p.m. and 11.00 p.m.

Ten new metro lines were built between 2005 and 2012, stretching almost 389 km. The entire length of the Shanghai metro system reached around 500 km by 2012, among which 400 km were in use before the 2010 Expo. Below is shown the logo for Shanghai metro.

Public Transit cards are available in any metro station at the service center (usually found in the middle of the first level underground of the metro station). You will pay a 20-yuan deposit when acquiring the card. You can then give the attendant at the service center money to put on the card, which will be deducted each time that you use the subway or the bus. You need to lay the card on the sensor pad found at entrance turnstiles before proceeding through the gate and also when you exit through the turnstile at your destination. You can add money to your Public Transit system or buy a single ride at machines in metro stations. In the upper right hand corner of the screen, touch the "English" button and follow the instructions on the screen.

THE MAGLEV

An air-conditioned and high-tech transrapid link, known as the Maglev, operates between downtown Shanghai (Longyang Road metro station) and Pudong Airport. The Maglev is the fastest train in the world, capable of accommodating speeds of up to 400 km/h. Because of the relatively short distance, however, it travels at approximately 320 km/h for the 7-minute journey. It uses the technology of a raised magnetic track that allows the trains to effectively "hover" at high speeds. Inside the train it feels no different than sitting inside a plane and is considerably more comfortable.

A one-way ticket costs 50 yuan. If you show your flight ticket for that day, you will benefit from a 10-yuan discount. However, you can buy only one discounted train ticket per flight ticket.

Operation from Longyang Road station runs at 15-minute intervals, starting at 7 a.m. and ending at 9 p.m. The operation from Pudong runs at the same intervals, from 7:02 a.m. to 9:02 p.m.

THINGS TO SEE AND DO

Shanghai's most happening place has to be around the **Xintiandi district**. Apart from the fruit sellers and other street hawkers, the old paved lanes are crammed with small gift shops and many of the bars have live music, both Western and Chinese. Whenever darkness falls, Xintiandi will be bright and a l the lights will start to work. The wonderful Xintiandi nightlife supersedes its busy day life. If you have ever wondered what happened to 1920s Shanghai, or even the phrase "Paris of the East," then the closest feeling you may get to that is by taking an evening stroll down the Xintiandi District. There is a lot of live activity happening at night-time, snaking through Xintiandi as if time had turned back to the old Shanghai-ancient building (not high), aged flagging, the red brick wall, and the massive black gate. Most of the city's bars and clubs are located here.

Pujiang Cruise (from South Bund to Yangpu Bridge): Shanghai's famous Bund waterfront has been mentioned in many Hollywood movies and other media representations have laid accolades to the scenic waterfront. I would highly recommend not taking a sightseeing boat ride during the daytime for two reasons:

(1) it's too hot and hazy during the day; and (2) the views at night-time are much better. A Huangpu River Cruise is one of the best ways to see both old and new Shanghai. Many boats have restaurants on board that serve Chinese savories and green tea or beer.

The Bund (Wai Tan): The 1½-mile long road in front of the Huangpu River across from the Pudong area (opposite the tall TVB Pearl Tower) is known as the Bund. Here you will have plenty of fun digesting the sights and smells whether it is day or night. There is plenty to see and do. The long line of colonial buildings that used to house banks and insurance corporations are now replaced by lavish hotels, shopping malls, and local corporate offices. The promenade can get exceptionally crowded during national holidays or in the evenings.

Shanghai Grand Theatre is very hard to miss with its distinctive white arc roof with four corners pointing to the air. It houses two show halls, including a classical open-air odeum and air garden. The theatre is located to the northeast of the People's Square. With an area of 72,000 square meters with 10 stories (divided into 2 basement floors, 6 floors, and top 2 floors), Shanghai Grand Theatre was designed by the French architect Jean-Marie Charpentier. It was intended to be the paramount theatre in China and the biggest in Asia, as well as being one of the most advanced in the world. There are three playhouses: the main house (with 1800 seats), the medium house (with 600 seats), and the small house (with 200 seats). Its looks and feels good on the inside, just as it equally looks good from the outside. Website: www.shgtheatre.com

Located on 701 Fu Zhou Road in Huangpu District, the **Tian Chan Yi Fu Theatre** is the oldest and chief Peking Opera center in Shanghai. Built in 1925, it derives from the Tian Chan Theatre in 1916, which had a longer history. If you are keen to watch Peking Opera in Shanghai, I would highly recommend that you go to the Yi Fu Theatre. From 1989, the Yi Fu Theatre has been under the jurisdiction of Shanghai Peking Opera Theatre. At its prime, the theatre had Peking Opera performances shown well over 300 times. Not expensive and well worth a visit. Website: www.tianchan.com

57 Maoming Road is an address with which most people are familiar because it is the location of the Lyceum Theatre, one of the oldest theatres in Shanghai (founded in 1866). It once served as the get-together place for consuls and celebs from all circles. This classic European-style theatre hosts performances including Chinese operas, dramas, acrobatics & circus, children & family theatres, ballet and so on. The transportation there is very convenient as it is at the crossing of two famous roads in Shanghai—Maoming Road and Changle Road. Many famous hotels are located next to this theatre, such as the Garden Hotel Shanghai, Jinjiang Hotel, and the Jinjiang Tower.

TOP TEN

I have compiled a list of the top ten things to see in Shanghai. There are not in any particular order or preference. My recommendation would be to choose a focal point on the map and make your way around the various attractions. Two days are sufficient for a taste of all ten attractions.

1. **Shanghai Pearl Oriental TV Tower**—The Shanghainese consider the Oriental Pearl Television Tower (Dongfang Minzhu) to be equivalent to the Eiffel Tower. It is made up of eleven steel spheres of different sizes that are supposed to represent pearls (as in Shanghai, Pearl of the Orient), with the top "pearl" offering a revolving restaurant that provides (on a clear day) a superb 360-degree view.

2. **Moganshan Road Art District**—The place where you can find exhibitions of everything from contemporary sculpture and oil paintings to old Art Deco furniture.

3. **Xintiandi** (pronounced Shin tea-en dee)—the latest entertainment area of Shanghai. If you want to know what Shanghai may have felt like in the 1930s, then Xintiandi (see above) is probably the closest you will get to experiencing it.

4. **Shanghai Museum** is home to some of the famous house paintings, sculptures, ceramics, calligraphy, jade, Ming and Qing dynasty furniture and coins. The collection of bronzes is among the best in the world

5. **Dong Tai Road**—located near the old Hong Qiao Airport, it's a shopping oasis for Chinese antiques lovers. Dong Tai is stretched over two buildings and has many shops with vendors selling vintage products, furniture, and bric-a-brac.

6. **Jin Mao Tower (88 Floors)** and the **Shanghai World Financial Center** (**101 floors**)—two of the tallest buildings in Asia. The Shanghai World Financial Center offers stunning views from its three observation decks— the highest being at 474 meters above ground level.

7. **YuYuan Garden**—Occupying an area of approx. 20,000 sq meters, YuYuan Garden is located in Anren Jie. You can marvel over 400 years of Shanghai history and walk on the same paths that were adored by the Ming Dynasty. I recommend you spend half a day if you can spare it.

8. **The Pearl River Promenade**—The waterfront avenue, more formally known as the Bund (Waitan), is Shanghai's symbolic landmark. The Bund offers breath-taking night views for both tourists and residents. Best to avoid it on public holidays as it gets ridiculously busy.

9. **French Concession Tour**—A walk through the old expat enclaves will give you a flavor of how the Europeans lived their luxurious life in pre-war Shanghai. I recommend a gentle stroll in the evening or on a quiet weekend afternoon.

10. **Jade Buddha Temple (Yùfó Sì)**—Founded in 1882 with two jade Buddha statues imported to Shanghai from Burma by sea, the temple was occupied during the 1911 uprising and will provide you with fascinating historical facts about the Qing dynasty (1875–1908), and their relationship with Shanghai.

SHOPPING

The city has observed a see-saw occurrence when it comes to contemporary art and fashion. When mentioning Shanghai Art, usually the first thing that comes to people's mind is 1930s and 1940s. Then there is a pause...a long pause for many years because the Shanghai art scene did not really open to audiences until as late as 2000 when the Chinese government decided that it was OK for Chinese artists to showcase their work to the world.

Although it must be said that independent, foreign-owned galleries were some of the initial "experiments" with the contemporary Chinese art scene, first establishing themselves in Beijing in the early 1990s (Shanghai is relatively new to all of this). In Shanghai, the mother hen of them all was the independent ShangART Gallery, an inspiration by Swiss Lorenz Helbling in 1994; this was quickly followed by galleries such as Biz Art and Art Scene China. Recently relocated to a much larger premises at 50 Moganshan Lu, ShangART represents some of Shanghai and China's hottest contemporary artists, such as painter and visual artist Xu Zhen, visual artist Shi Yong, and Pop artist Zhou Tiehai, the latter known for his painting of former New York mayor Rudy Giuliani framed by elephant dung (anything goes here!). Other famous local artists include photographer Deke Erh and painter Xu Jie, known for her series of China Doll paintings.

Artists and architects from around the world are coming to Shanghai, realizing that it's quicker and cost effective, plus provides more variety to audiences. With this immense growth it is easy to see why Shanghai is the most happening city in China. As an example, the St. Regis Hotel has taken to offering guests "art tours" that are interested in visiting local galleries. But then again, who would require an art tour of Shanghai—a city that itself is a work of art.

Nanjing Road is one of the most famous shopping streets in the world. Giant shopping centers, specialist boutiques, international brands, local upmarket goods—it's all here; it's very busy, and at night it really glitters. It's a fascinating glimpse of modern, commercial China.

Situated next to the Orient Pearl on 168 Lujiazui Rd, the **Super Brand Mall (Chia Tai)** is rated as one of the principal shopping malls in Asia. Chia Tai, with a total of 13 floors and an area of 241 thousand square meters, was designed by the American company Jerde Partnership and at a cost of US$335 million. It is one of the biggest, most exciting, and fashionable commercial community in China. Website: www.superbrandmall.com

With an open-air square of 1600 square meters, the **Shanghai Times Square,** located on 93-99 HuaiHai Road (Middle) is a leisure place. You will see the distinctively huge Bell Tower in the square, and can enjoy roaming around the elegant atrium. It's a shopper's delight with a 200-meters-long frontage of shops. Website: www.shtimessquare.com

It's common to see so many people throng the Bund, especially at the weekends.

Opened in October 1949, the **Shanghai No. 1 Department Store** was the first state large department store that was allowed to operate after the founding of the People's Republic of China. The distinctive green-colored building is located at the corner of 830 Nanjing Road (E). It is difficult not to just take a walk around the 22 floors even if you are not going to purchase anything. The first 11 stories are for shopping and entertainment, while the others are used for offices

The address 1000 Zhaojiabang Road is associated with the **Huijin Baihuo Shopping Mall**, which is situated right at the heart of Shanghai's core area of Xujiahui. With parking space for over 300 cars, it is well known for the "shopping aisle," which conveniently connects to other shopping malls.

Most people know **Xujiahui** as being a commercial center, but are not aware of its history and reason behind its actual existence. Xujiahui literally stands for *the gathering of Xu Family* in Chinese and the *junction of two rivers*. In fact, Xu Guangqi, a famous scientist in the Ming Dynasty (1562–1633) lived here. He is one of the first people to have introduced advanced ideas about astronomy to China. Four roads meet at the junction of Xujiahui: Hongqiao Road, Huashan Road, Zhaojia-bang Road, and North Caoxi Road. This part of Shanghai is also known as a prime location for numerous outsized interconnecting malls and supermarkets such as Grand Gateway, the Pacific Department Store, and the Orient Shopping Center. There is as well an underground shopping mall with uncountable shops at Xujiahui metro station. Overall, Xujiahui can be described as a shopping place for everything from cosmetics to vegetables, from expensive chic global fashion products to your everyday household products.

USEFUL LINKS

* www.shanghaiexpat.com Website for expats in Shanghai
* www.shanghaidaily.com Online edition of the Shanghai English newspaper
* www.shanghai.gov.cn Official Government portal of Shanghai
* www.smtdc.com The official website for the Shanghai Maglev train
* www.shmetro.com The official website for the Shanghai metro (in Chinese)
* www.shanghaiairport.com Both Pudong and Hongqiao airports have one common website

SHENZHEN

Formally established in November 1979, Shenzhen, nicknamed "China's Garden City," is considered to be China's youngest, cleanest, and most modern city. Shenzhen used to be just a fishing village until Deng Xiao Ping declared the city as a Special Economic Zone (SEZ), along with four other Chinese cities on the east coast. Guangdong is known as the most outward-looking of China's provinces and an economic powerhouse. It was here in 1992 that Deng Xiaoping, on a southern tour that included the cities of Shenzhen, Guangzhou and Zhuhai in Guangdong, launched China's economic transformation with the (possibly apocryphal) phrase, "To get rich is glorious." The city is on the list of UNESCO Creative Cities.

It is known as China's garden city because of its abundance of greenery and flowerbeds scattered on almost every roadside and infrastructure. Shenzhen will probably surprise you if this is the first city you come to on your inaugural trip to China. People from the West have usually never heard of it. Hong Kong media tell you that it's the most dangerous place in China and the Taiwanese and Japanese think it's some poor cousin of Shanghai. Shenzhen is actually a city of some 11 mil ion people with the majority of them migrants from other parts of China as well as overseas. It is also the wealthiest city in China, paying the highest average salaries to its inhabitants.

A beautiful view of the skyline of Shenzhen as the sur sets.

To a first-time visitor, Shenzhen would seem a brash and vibrant place. Indeed Shenzhen is China's migrant city where people from other parts of China have come to seek an opportunity, and it provides a sense of freedom for the younger population. With the close proximity to Hong Kong, It also provides an excellent weekend destination for people who live in Hong Kong. The majority of the expatriate community lives approximately 30 km west of the city center in the port area known as Shekou, with most of the expats working in the oil, gas, or electronics industries.

For many Hong Kong citizens, Shenzhen is increasingly becoming a cheaper alternative to live in and commute to Hong Kong on a daily basis. Thus many people are working in Hong Kong, but choose to live in Shenzhen.

GEOGRAPHY

Shenzhen is located in Guangdong province, SE China, on the border of Hong Kong. Shenzhen covers an area of approx. 2020 sq km and is made up of five main districts, Luohu, Longgang, Futian, Nanshan, and Baoan. Luohu and Futian share borders with Hong Kong and there are three main border entry points with Hong Kong, the main one being at Luohu Train Station and the other two being Huanggang and Shekou seaport.

CLIMATE

Shenzhen's climate has the transitional characteristics of subtropical and tropical zones. Overall, the climate can be generalized as long summers often stretching out for the majority of the year, which often makes it difficult to distinguish between other seasons, namely autumn and spring. A high percentage of the year's precipitation falls between November and January, and between April and September. Winter is short and fairly mild (normally experienced for about one or two months in December and January). The average low temperature in January, the coldest month, is about 14.5°C (58°F); the average high temperature in the hottest months, July and August, runs close to 32°C (89°F).

TRANSPORTATION
BUS

Shenzhen has numerous bus connections operating all around the city during the day and a few during night-times as well. Long-distance coaches operate from the main train station at Luohu and also from Futian Bus Station.

AIR

Shenzhen has one major international airport. Bao-an International Airport is located 32 km northwest of the city center, near the Pearl Delta, with connections to major Asian cities as well as many domestic flights. Shenzhen has its own airline, Shenzhen Airlines, with numerous daily flights to destinations within China and several Asian cities.

Although Bao-an Airport is an international airport, most of the flights outside China are destined around the Asia Pacific region. For the majority of international flights outside of this region, connections are made either via Beijing or Shanghai, or the other alternative is to go from Hong Kong or Guangzhou airports.

Bao-an Airport is large enough to accommodate wide-bodied jets such as the latest Boeing 777-200LR, Airbus A340-500, and the Airbus A380 Superjumbo. At the time of writing, there were plans to either expand the current runway or construct another runway. There is a regular daily helicopter service to Macau operated from the airport. In 2009, according to the Civil Aviation Administration of China, the airport handled over 23 million passengers, making it the 5th busiest airport in China. A new 1.6-km-long Terminal 3 building commenced construction in early 2008, and is scheduled to be opened in late 2012 or early 2013.

There is a heliport in the Nanshan District, quite close to the Shekou port; however this is used mainly by the Shenzhen Police Force and the oil & gas companies to transport workers to/from the offshore oil platforms in the South China Sea.

TAXI

Metered taxis are available 24 hours a day. The base rate at the time of writing is 12.50 yuan (approx. $1.50) between 6:00 a.m. and 11:00 p.m. for the first mile. Between 11:00 p.m. and 6:00 a.m. the base rate is 16.50 yuan (just over $2). Inside the city center (Special Economic Zone) the taxis are colored red, while those operating outside the city are colored green. So be aware that if you take a green-colored taxi from outside the city center, that taxi won't be allowed to enter the city center. The red taxis are allowed to go out of the city only to a certain distance, and you will have to pay the toll gate fare if you are traveling between two cities (e.g., from Shenzhen to Guangzhou, and vice versa).

SEA

The main port for traveling by ferry is Shekou. Destinations include Hong Kong (Central and Kowloon), Macau, Hong Kong Airport, Guangzhou, and Zhuhai. At the time of writing the standard fare for going to Hong Kong airport (should take approx. 30 minutes) is 250 HKD (you will get about a 150-HKD refund f you show your flight ticket at check-in), and to go to either Hong Kong (Central or Kowloon and takes approx. 45 minutes) or Macau (takes approx. one hour) will cost 100 HKD one way. Services to these destinations operate every 40 minutes at the time of writing.

You can also check in at the Shekou port for some airlines, including Cathay Pacific and Dragonair.

TRAIN

Shenzhen has many routes connecting to other Chinese cities. The most frequently operated route is the Guangzhou to Shenzhen route. Trains run every 20–25 minutes with some trains stopping in Dongguan, and the trip takes approximately one hour. The one-way fare at the time of writing is 80 yuan.

A word of caution: When you leave Hong Kong and enter Chinese soil, immediately you will notice the remarkable difference—of how much Shenzhen still has to improve (even though it is improving). It feels like entering a different country, or on occasions, even going back in time. At Luohu station you will most likely be met by a large number of beggars, ticket touts shouting "Fa Piao! Fa Piao!" (tickets to sell), and, annoyingly, a number of pimps/prostitutes saying things such as "Hello, you want miss massage?" (This occurs mostly around the Shangri La Hotel, which is situated right next to the station and cannot be missed.) The best response is to ignore this.

Even though it has a crime rate similar to other cities in China, Shenzhen, because of the large influx of visitors each day, has seemingly been the scene of unlawful acts, mostly petty but infrequently serious, aimed at visitors and residents. The border crossings tend to attract the attention of pickpockets and other criminals. There have been reported cases of daytime muggings and individuals being abducted and forced to withdraw cash from ATMs.

METRO

Shenzhen Metro opened in December 2005 and is very clean, fast, and new. Trains are not as crowded as one would experience in other Chinese cities. As of the time of writing Shenzhen Metro has 5 lines, 137 stations, and 178.44 km (110.87 miles) of total trackage in operation.

At the time of writing two further lines were under construction. There is a line that runs direct from the airport to the Luohu border control.

The symbol for the Shenzhen Metro consists of a Green Y logo in a green circle. Fares range from 1 to 5 yuan depending on the length of the journey. The most convenient way to travel is to buy a Shenzhen Tong (深圳通) card at the ticket window. This is a stored value ticket. Touch it on the turnstile reader on entering and leaving the station. It can also be used for purchases in convenience stores.

FOOD

Although Shenzhen may not have as large a variety of restaurants featuring international cuisine as do Guangzhou, Shanghai, and Beijing, there is a sound selection of restaurants available (for a list see the Shenzhen party website link given towards the end of this section). A number of Western-style restaurants (mainly Indian and Italian) are available in the Luohu area, while the MixC center (opposite The Diwang building on Shen Nan Zhong Lu) has an abundance of Chinese, Japanese, and Western style restaurants including "Spaghetti House." It could be considered, however, a waste of precious time in China if you don't try one of the many local eateries in town. For example there are a myriad of Chinese restaurants that offer some scrumptious provincial Chinese cuisine (food from Guizhou, Sichuan, Xinjiang, etc.) for as little as 8 yuan per person. The major setback you are likely to encounter is language problems, as the menu is almost always in Chinese;

therefore knowing a few essential characters or words in Chinese is useful. Some of the words that may be required are listed at the end of this book.

SHOPPING

The following is a list of the main shopping areas:

- **Dongmen** in Luohu district—a bustling and vibrant shopping area in the heart of Shenzhen's most happening place.
- **Hua Qiang Bei** in Futian district—similar to Dongmen but specializes in selling electronic "Made in Shenzhen" goods.
- **King Glory Plaza** in Luohu district—a classy and upmarket shopping area where you can find just about every Western designer shop (including CK, Gucci, etc.); and even a BMW store selling chic leather jackets, baseball caps, and so on.
- **Coastal City** is located in Nanshan (next to Haiwang Da Sha). The area has an abundance of Western shopping outlets, and restaurants.
- **The MixC** is a new shopping center, located opposite the Diwang Building (Shenzhen's tallest building in the heart of the city) on Shennan Road. The MixC is a modern shopping mall with all kinds of restaurants and a supermarket catering to the expat community with imported goods (Olé). The MixC also has many other familiar stores, a huge indoor ice rink, and a cinema.

Another supermarket that is used by both locals and expats is Jusco. It's located in the basement of the CITIC Plaza (Zhong Xin Da Sha) on Shennan Road. Apart from food, Jusco also has housewares, clothing, and sporting goods, but for housewares it's best to go to Walmart (and it tends to be cheaper because it is made under local license rather than imported). There are a few Walmart stores in Shenzhen. The one on Fuxing Road is probably the best. There is also a Sam's Club to the west on Shennan Road that sells Western goods. It's a members-only club but anyone can join and the process is easy.

If you want to buy clothes, CITIC Plaza and the MixC have all the expensive brand names but Dongmen and Luohu offer cheap fakes.

For coffee there are plenty of Starbucks available in Shenzhen. The Starbucks at CITIC Plaza, The MixC, Shekou, and Nanshan are very popular and always packed. Kosmo is a nice alternative offering healthy options. There are also an Illy café (in the MixC building).

KFC, McDonald's, Pizza Hut, and Haagen-Dazs are in abundance. In Shekou there is one Subway sandwiches outlet at the time of writing.

Further information regarding restaurants can be obtained from the Shenzhen party website listed at the end of this chapter.

PLACES OF INTEREST

There are three major must-see places of interest in Shenzhen:

WINDOW OF THE WORLD

Shenzhen's star attraction, it features the world's wonders, historic sites, scenic spots, natural landscapes, folk customs, and world-renowned sculptures. Occupying an area of almost forty-eight hectares, it is composed of 118 attractions set up on different scales from 1:1 to 1:100 including the Eiffel Tower, The Taj Mahal, Niagara Falls, and the Egyptian Pyramids.

HAPPY VALLEY

An amusement park that is especially appealing to the Chinese people because amusement parks are part of the experiment of all things "Western" that China is engaged with. It is Shenzhen's answer to UK's Thorpe Park or Alton Towers. Consisting of a water park and a dry park, it features attractions for both adults and children. The park also has a 4D cinema, the first of its kind in Asia. On a smaller scale than other international attractions, it is a family theme park and quite impressive.

SPLENDID CHINA AND THE CHINA FOLK CULTURAL VILLAGE

Splendid China and the China Folk Cultural Village are located adjacent to the Windows of the World. "Splendid China" features theatrical cultural shows based on China's 5,000-year history and life in the rural areas. The world-famous open-air evening show known as the "Dancing with the Dragon and the Phoenix" made its debut in 2003.

MORE ENTERTAINMENT

There are also other areas such as the **Shekou Sea World**—this is the main restaurant and bar area catering to the expat community; it feels like Hong Kong or Europe with lots of Irish, American, and British expat bars. The magic of this area is that the expats are the ones who make this area feel rather like Europe in China! Inside the bars (including the famous Macawleys Irish pub), you feel as if you are suddenly sitting in Dublin or Manchester; watching a game of footie on Sky TV and drinking the black stuff! Guinness anyone?

LEISURE

Shenzhen has a number of golf courses with many people from Hong Kong coming over for the weekend to play golf here. The most popular and famous venue is the Mission Hills Golf Course, expensive even for China, but it does cater to the affluent market.

BEACH RESORTS

There are two main beach resorts in Shenzhen, both approx. 15 km east of the city center. They are clean, not busy, and safe to swim in:

- Da Mei Sha (free of charge at the time of writing)—a 1.8-km long beach.
- Xiao Mei Sha (20 yuan entrance ticket at the time of writing).

USEFUL LINKS

- www.sznews.com/szdaily *Shenzhen Daily* is the main English daily tabloid
- www.shenzhenparty.com The "What's happening" guide for expats in Shenzhen
- www.szftz.gov.cn Shenzhen Administrative Bureau of Free Trade Zones
- http://english.sz.gov.cn/lis/ Shenzhen Government Online
- www.szwwco.com Window of the World attraction, official website
- www.szmc.net Shenzhen Metro Website
- www.szairport.com The official website of Shenzhen airport

SUZHOU

Originally founded in 514 B.C., the ancient city of Suzhou is situated 120 km west of Shanghai and next to Lake Tai. With over 3,000 years of history and culture waiting to be absorbed, Suzhou is known as the cradle of the "Wu" Culture. Suzhou is nick-named "Venice of the East" because of the many narrow canals, minute bridges, the classical gardens, and the numerous amount of small boats that resemble the Venetian gondola moving through the city. The city is renowned for its conventional gardens, two of which have been recognized as great world heritage sites. Located in between the Yangtze River Drainage Basin and the Yangtze River Delta economic zone, Suzhou has, for a number of decades, been a national tourist center attracting visitors from around the world.

Suzhou is widely acknowledged as a city known for its immense natural beauty, its splendid history, and its rich cultural heritage that brings in many different Chinese people from all over the country to contribute to its booming economy. Suzhou represents more of these qualities than most other Chinese cities of a similar size and status. The city continues to enjoy a considerably high rate of economic and cultural growth. The city's GDP has surpassed any of its other neighboring cities except Shanghai and in the past five years, Suzhou has welcomed more than 85 of the world's top 500 corporations to set up business and industry here. Suzhou is one of the 13 regional cities of Jiangsu province. The cities, including Changshu, Taicang, Kunshan, Wujiang, and Zhangjiagang, are under its jurisdiction. The total population has now topped 13 million, including China's second largest migrant population.

The city of Suzhou is known for its beautiful gardens.

Overall there are over 200 ancient water towns surrounding Suzhou, all of which offer stunning views of canals and the renowned Suzhou architecture. The most popular and "must see" water towns include Luzhi, Tongli, Zhouzhuang, and Qiandeng, all of which are nationally recognized and protected heritage sites.

After Beijing and Xi'an, Suzhou is ranked third in terms of the number of nationally recognized cultural sites. Suzhou's fine reputation nationally and internationally is due to the fact that the city is the proud caretaker of the classical gardens. Chinese gardens are classified into two categories: private garden and royal garden, and Suzhou's gardens represent the latter type. It is the gardens of Suzhou which led Marco Polo to state that Suzhou was China's most gorgeous city. It would most certainly not be an overstatement to state that Suzhou's gardens are like pictures in 3-D space—indeed they are like poetry that has been materialized. Suzhou's gardens are to be cherished and looked after like precious jewelry because they are Suzhou's jewels. There were once over 200 gardens in Suzhou, however over the centuries as the city has become more modern, the majority of these gardens have been either turned into "smaller" backyard gardens that are in villas or hotels or they have been dissolved into the city's modern infrastructure. Sixty of these gardens are still preserved as they were many years ago. Suzhou is highly proud that nine of these gardens have been listed in the World Heritage Sites. When you visit Suzhou, you are sure to appreciate its beauty. The city received over 23 million overseas tourists and just over 52 million domestic visitors in 2010.

The classical gardens in Suzhou were added to the list of the UNESCO World Heritage Sites in 1997 and 2000. Because of the original canals that lurk around the old part of Suzhou, and also the new industrial part of Suzhou, the town is often dubbed the "Venice of the East" or "Venice of China." In 2009, Suzhou's GDP totaled over 774 billion. The population of permanent residents amounted to 10.47 million in 2009, with a per capita GDP of 117,200 yuan! The name Suzhou derives from the "Su" of nearby Gusu Mountain (Gan Su Shan), combined with the common -*zhou* suffix, a term for a Chinese settlement (e.g., Guangzhou, Hangzhou, etc.). Suzhou is a major tourist area of the Lower Yangtze Delta featuring both natural and man-made places of interest.

GEOGRAPHY

Suzhou is located on the Taihu Lake Plain, about 100 km (62 mi) to the west of Shanghai, and just over 200 km east of Nanjing.

CLIMATE

Suzhou has a four-season, monsoon-influenced humid subtropical climate with hot, humid summers, and cool, cloudy, damp winters with occasional snowfall. Northwesterly winds blowing from Siberia during winter can cause temperatures to fall below freezing at night, while southerly or southwesterly winds during the summer can push temperatures above 35°C (95°F). Unless your home has a decent central heating system, it can feel very uncomfortable at night-time in the winter. In the winter it feels somewhat colder than in Shanghai, and sometimes it can snow as well.

TRANSPORTATION
TAXI

In Suzhou (especially in the SIP [Suzhou Industrial Park]area where the expats live), it's very difficult to get a taxi, and most of the public buses stop service after 9 p.m. In order to get a taxi sometimes it's useful to call 67776777, though for that you may require someone to help you translate as the operators only converse in Chinese. In Suzhou it is especially difficult to get a taxi late at night, early in the morning, or during the weekends. For example, I used to go for company meetings in Shanghai, and if my meeting was at 10 a.m. I would usually leave my home in Suzhou at 6:30 a.m. and allow at least 45 minutes to wait for a taxi (normally it takes around 10–15 minutes to get to the train station in Suzhou as it's a small city).

TRAIN

There are two train stations in Suzhou. Suzhou railway station is the major gateway to Shanghai and Nanjing, while Suzhou Technology Park station (known as Suzhou Yuan Qu Zhan), is located in the Suzhou SIP area and is relatively new (and quiet compared to the main station). There are two types of trains that run from both of the Suzhou stations: D-series trains, and the G-series trains. The D-series trains take about 45 minutes to Shanghai, and 1 1/2 hours to Nanjing. The G-series high speed (CRH) train has been in operation since July 2010, and only takes about 20 minutes for the top speed train among all the G-series to travel to Shanghai Hongqiao station and Shanghai station. At the time of writing, the price of a normal ticket on the G-series is about 40 yuan ($6 US) from Suzhou to Shanghai (and around 60 yuan for a first-class ticket). It's best to buy train tickets at least a day in advance from the station because on the actual day of travel tickets may not be available due to the thousands of people traveling every day from the busy station. Suzhou Railway station is among the busiest passenger stations in China, having 139 trains stopping daily. During early morning and late evenings it may be difficult to get taxis from either station (especially from the Suzhou Technology Park station). Public transport in Suzhou is highly limited after 9 p.m. every day.

METRO

At the time of writing, the Suzhou Metro was currently being constructed. Line 1 opened on the 1st May 2012 running from Mudu in the West to Zhongnanjie. There are 3 more lines planned to be in operation by the end of 2016. The opening of the metro has been welcomed by many of Suzhou's citizens that live in the Suzhou SIP area. Most of these people travel early in the morning or in the late hours of the evening, and because it is so difficult to get taxis in Suzhou, it is a relief for them to have the metro in operation. Suzhou SIP can be like a ghost town, with empty roads that can double as airport runways all day and night!!

BUS

Most of the buses running in the city only take exact change so make sure you have some small coins before getting on. The price of regular buses (i.e., those without windows) is 1 yuan per person. Air-conditioned buses, i.e., those with windows, cost 2 yuan per person. Buses running from the city to the suburbs vary in price. Check the sign on the front of the bus to see the fare. Long distance buses stop at the Suzhou North Bus Station, which has the most buses going to the nearby provinces.

A typical road scene in Suzhou with old style homes in the background

Suzhou has five special tourist buses as follows:

- No. 1 goes from Tiger Hill to Suzhou Railway Station (5:15 a.m.–9:00 p.m.); stops at Tiger Hill, Lingering Garden, Suzhou Museum, Humble Administrator's Garden, Lion Grove Garden, Suzhou Silk Museum, and the Beisi Pagoda.
- No. 2 goes from Tiger Hill to The Dock (5:45 a.m.–6:45 p.m.); stops at Tiger Hill, The Suzhou Railway Station, Suzhou Silk Museum, Beisi Pagoda, Suzhou Museum, Humble Administrator's Garden, Lion Grove Garden, and the Garden of the Master of the Nets.
- No. 3 goes from Suzhou Railway Station to Jin Shan Lu (5:30 a.m.–8:45 p.m.); stops at Suzhou Amusement Park, Yushan Park, and the Science and Technology University.
- No. 4 goes from Suzhou Railway Station to the Taiping Mountain (5:00 a.m.–9:00 p.m.); stops at Suzhou Silk Museum, Beisi Pagoda, Ancient Town of Mudu, Lingyan Mountain, and Taiping Mountain.

- No. 5 goes from the Oushang Supermarket to the Lion Grove Garden (6:00 a.m.–10:30 p.m.); stops at the Double Pagoda, Suzhou Museum, Humble Administrator's Garden, and the Lion Grove Garden.

AIRPORT

The nearest international airport is Shanghai Pudong International airport, while the two closest domestic airports are Shanghai Hongqiao airport (located around 100 km away), and Wuxi Airport (located around 22 km northwest of Suzhou). Wuxi Airport used to be a military airport until 2004 when it was also permitted to perform civilian operations. It is located in the town of Shuofang, 12 km (7 mi) southeast of Wuxi and 22 km (14 mi) northwest of Suzhou. The major airlines that operate from Wuxi airport include Shenzhen Airlines, China Southern Airlines, China United Airlines, and China Eastern Airlines. The quickest way to get to both Shanghai Hongqiao Airport and Wuxi Airport is to take the train from Suzhou. For Wuxi Airport, you will need to take a taxi from Wuxi station which will cost you around 60 yuan and will take around 30 minutes; while Shanghai Hongqiao station is located right next to Shanghai Hongqiao airport.

PLACES TO SEE

LINGERING GARDEN

In 1961 the Lingering Garden **was listed as one of the first cultural remnants of national significance.** Occupying an area of 23,410 square meters, the garden is renowned for its creative way of dealing with the various kinds of architectural structures present in its grounds. The vast majority of the space, around 60%, in the garden is dedicated to buildings, including the great hall. Additional space is dedicated to the flowers and statues. The garden is uniquely separated into the middle, eastern, northern, and western parts. The ancestral place of worship and a small home lies to the south of the garden. The entire garden consists of 43 rooms and halls, a 670-meter-long roofed walkway, a network of over 200 windows of various shapes and sizes, 44 parallel couplets, and 17 kinds of precious trees including the gingko and the southern wisteria.

The central part of the garden is situated upon a lake with a man-made mountain in the northwest and a number of attractive buildings situated to the southwest, such as the Hanbi Mountain Villa, the Green Shade Pavilion, the Zigzag Stream Tower, and the Refreshing Breeze Pavilion by the lake. For those who like taking photos in gardens, the Refreshing Breeze Pavilion will provide a very beautiful view.

I would recommend at least half a day to fully explore and enjoy the garden and see the sights in detail. Some buildings that should not be missed include the

Admirable Crane House, The Small Garden of Stone Forest, and the Celestial Hall of Five Peaks. At first the garden may seem like a maze, however, the structures of these buildings are laid out in such a way that you would not get lost. The garden allows visitors to relax, enjoy and smell the flowers, and view the beautiful lake. Entrance for the majority of the year is free at the time of writing.

HUMBLE ADMINISTRATOR'S GARDEN

The largest garden in Suzhou, situated in the northeastern part of the city, occupying an area of over 52,000 square meters, Humble Administrator's Garden (Zhuozhengyuan) has been listed as one of the four most famous national classic gardens in China. The other ones are the Summer Palace in Beijing, Mountain Summer Resort in Chengdu, and the Lingering Garden of Suzhou. This garden, however, is an absolute masterpiece deriving from the Ming Dynasty's classic Chinese design. The best part of the garden is most certainly in the center, which contains small hills peeking over the clear waters of the lake, beautiful buildings, and evergreen trees and flowers.

A treasure house of architectural art, Chinese calligraphy works, carvings, and paintings that depict life in the garden from hundreds of years ago is a key national cultural relic. Among the buildings situated towards the western part of the garden, the Hall of the Thirty-Six Mandarin Ducks and the Hall of Eighteen Camellias are the most magnificent.

SUZHOU SILK MUSEUM

In this region silk has a history of over 6,500 years. The Chinese started exporting the luxury product to Europe and Africa as early as the fifth century B.C. There is a long debate whether Hangzhou beat Suzhou to finding the silk, or vice versa. Nevertheless there is no argument in the fact that the Suzhou Silk Museum located on 661 Renmin Rd was officially China's first silk museum. The attraction combines exhibits with demonstrations of silk weaving, including a live demonstration by literally hundreds of silkworms who are constantly munching away on mulberry leaves while spinning cocoons. It's quite an attention-grabbing affair, although I wouldn't go there just before my meal! Exhibits on display in ts various exhibition halls reflect the origin, evolution, and development of silk production, from prehistoric times to the present.

HANSHAN TEMPLE

Once noted to be one of the top ten temples in China, the Hanshan Temple dates back to the Tang Dynasty when a local monk named Hanshan s said to have stayed in the temple grounds. Located in the town of Fengqiao in the western outskirts of Suzhou, the temple has borne the brunt of being damaged and being rebuilt quite a number of times. Zhang Ji, a celebrated poet in the Tang Dynasty, wrote a poem "A Night Mooring by Maple Bridge," which, as a result, brought even more admirers to the temple. Visitors must see the Main Hall complete with statues of Buddha in many recreations, the Circular Gallery, Sutra Library, and the famous Bell Tower.

NORTH TEMPLE PAGODA

With a history of more than 1,800 years, the North Temple Pagoda was formerly known as the Tongxuan Temple during the reign of Sun Quan, the Emperor of Wu. The North Temple Pagoda is widely known as the best pagoda located in the south of the Yangtze River. It is seen as an important symbol of Suzhou and stands far away from the city facing the Tiger Hill Pagoda. In its beginnings the pagoda was originally an eleven-storied pagoda designed and built by a man called Zhanghui, a monk in the Liang Dynasty. However tragedy struck during the 1920s when the pagoda was destroyed by fire. After this the pagoda, which would be in the shape of an octagon when viewed from above, was reconstructed with brick and wood and has only nine stories. With a height of 76 meters, it is still the highest pagoda in Suzhou. Take a short walk along the stairs to the top floor, and as you stroll along the internal corridor you will be treated to a spectacular view, which is good during the daytime, but even better at night. Suzhou and the lights of the homes on the hills shine like little dots in the distance. Sometimes when it is quiet you can also hear distant noises of singing by the locals in the hilly towns.

THINGS TO DO

Suzhou is certainly not a small city. The place becomes lively at night-time. The obvious destinations are those that make Suzhou popular on the international travel scene, such as the city's many Chinese landscaped gardens which feature traditional Chinese architecture. Due to its close proximity to Shanghai, it also contains a lot of fashionable elements—especially in shopping malls.

Situated in between the Hu Qiu Mountain and the most thriving parts of Suzhou is the 1,200-year-old **Shantang Street**—here you'll find all kinds of ancient ways the local people lived. Not quite like the Hutongs that can be seen in Beijing, but rather as a semi-modern street that does have some remnants of the old Suzhou way of living, such as a butcher "shop" where you can see your much wanted chicken being prepared right in front of you (if you wish to see it!). There are a lot of old works of architecture to be found here.

Suzhou Storytelling House is not exactly hidden from view, but it can be a bit tricky to find. It's located on Wen Hua Square near Guan Qian Street. The place is popular with traditional Chinese storytellers who are masters in the 16th-century art of Suzhou Pingtan, which is a creative form of storytelling. It's spoken in a Suzhou dialect and accompanied by ballad singing. The artists use traditional Chinese stringed instruments. Some of the storytellers are resident in the Storytelling house, while some are wanderers, meaning they travel around the country telling folklore to foreigner travelers as well as local Chinese people. It's well worth a visit even if you do not understand Chinese because just the environment and the style of storytelling are quite compelling. Take a friend who can translate for you if you can.

Suzhou has a lot of water towns to explore, including Zhouzhuang as seen here.

The theatre is not only a strong aspect of the Chinese culture but here in Suzhou it's a lifestyle as well. The **Wuyuegong Restaurant Theatre** provides visitors lively shows, especially in the evening when people have more time. What makes this theatre different is that it's actually located inside the Suzhou Hotel at 115 at Shiquan Street. More specifically it's a restaurant theatre representative of the neighboring culture and customary song and dance art sts.

Suzhou Garden Club on 68 at Shishan Street is a newly built multipurpose leisure and entertainment center. Want to sing karaoke or watch a movie? Or just take a well-deserved rest? Then there is no better place to chill out and relax than at the Suzhou Garden Club. There is even a small Hot Spring (Tangtian) for those who want to enjoy swimming.

SHOPPING

Quite possibly the best location for shopping in Suzhou is the **Guan Qian Street.** It includes many ancient stores, such as the Qian TaiXi'an g Silk Store (more silk shops!); the Cai Zhizhai Candy Store, which is heaven for kids; and the Huang Tianyuan Cake Store. Lying adjacent to Guan Qian Street is Eunuch Lane, which is famous for Suzhou's delicacies. This is the best place to go to for shopping of souvenirs because the coffee shops also act as souvenir shops.

In some big Chinese cities, you come across a lot of "Friendship" stores. These are effectively department stores that have all kinds of shops selling just about anything and everything under one building. The Shi Lu Shopping Center is similar to these "friendship" stores, except that in this department store the majority of the shops sell Chinese goods as opposed to Western designer goods. You can also find some essential shops for everyday goods such as banks, hotels, and post offices. The department store is close to Suzhou Railway Station and Suzhou Bus Station, as well as being conveniently close to famous tourist attractions, such as the Lingering Garden and the Hanshan Temple.

The main specialty of the **Shi Quan Street** is the food and the craftworks. This street is purely a traditional street with a strong emphasis on exhibiting culture. If you like Xinjiang food, the native Xinjiang people will make some fresh delicious kebabs while you wait. Other foreign restaurants feature Indian, Korean, Japanese, and even Thai cuisine. Most are Asian style restaurants. On one side of the street, there are many craftwork shops that sell genuine Suzhou silk, antiques, paintings, and calligraphy.

The **Southern Gate Shopping Center** is a prime example of how much Chinese shopping has changed in years gone by. The center retains some traditional Chinese shops, complete with infrastructure, while at the same it embraces modernity. There are some marine-related product markets, vegetable and fruit markets, and, of course, tea markets. No shopping mall in China would be complete without Chinese tea markets. The port of the famous water flight, "The Heaven Flight," is situated in this area of Suzhou. It is not too difficult to go there and is relatively suitable to get a bus or a small boat to Hangzhou.

You won't find many shopping malls in China that blend modern architecture with original buildings from the Ming and Qing Dynasties. **The Maple Bridge Commercial Street**, named after one of the local bridges in the city, allows the tourist to walk on history while offering the latest range of Western designer goods—a unique mix. There is a section of the street where you will find artists who specialize in Chinese calligraphy. Here you can learn Chinese calligraphy yourself, as well as get souvenirs, such as your name printed in Chinese art.

Located on the shores of Jinji Lake is **Times Square**, a modern shopping area especially made for expats. There are also a myriad of Japanese and Korean stores around the SIP area, especially around the Ling Long area and the Yang'er community. Tianyu near the Crown Plaza, next to Jinji Lake, is also an affluent area where expats live.

TIANJIN

Tianjin is located 137 km to the southeast of Beijing. Officially part of the four largest cities in China (the others being Beijing, Shanghai, and Chongqing), Tianjin is situated at the confluence of five tributaries that derive from the Haihe River, 50 km from the Gulf of Bohai. Tianjin, meaning "the place where the emperor crossed the river," has in recent years started receiving more attention from both tourists at home and abroad due to its numerous travel resources and rich history. Prior to its emergence as a center for tourism, Tianjin was always seen as one of the greatest industrial centers of China. It still has one of the largest shipping ports in China, as well as a long list of foreign multinationals who are seeking to settle their China base in this former colonial metropolis. During the Beijing Olympics in 2008, Tianjin's 65,000-seat Olympic sports stadium served as one of the soccer (football) venues.

Considering its rich and vibrant history, it is no surprise to walk around town and come across many buildings that bear resemblance to architecture deriving from Germany, France, Russia, Great Britain, Austria, Japan, and Belgium. The city was home to many colonial inhabitants from these countries well before the foundation of the People's Republic of China. Of course, this marked an extremely hard period for Tianjin and its inhabitants. The imperialist nations left behind them permanent marks in terms of buildings and other structures such as the thousands of villas in which colonial expatriate population used to reside. Today those villas provide an exotic flavor to Tianjin, enhancing the beauty of the entire city.

Tianjin is one of the most beautiful places in the north of China, not too busy and crowded and just perfect for a weekend getaway if you want to escape to refresh your mind! There are many natural scenes of beauty as well as great historical events. Yes, it may still be a center for industry, but Tianjin has something special to offer to visitors as well.

Various hotels, guesthouses, and hostels can also meet your specific requirements. In addition, there are all types of entertainment available that enable you to relax both your body and mind. Tianjin is a vast city and as such, you would be quite right to expect a variety of restaurants that would cater to all kinds of tastes. These dining venues vary greatly in both price and quality, specializing not only in conventional Chinese cuisine, but also serving dishes of a more international flavor. The world, as they say, is your oyster!

CLIMATE

Average lows in January are at around −8°C (18°F), while average highs in July are about 31°C (88°F). It can feel quite cold in the winter with the wind and chill getting into your bones. The average annual rainfall is around 54 mm.

HOW TO GET TO AND AROUND TIANJIN

The well-planned transportation system of Tianjin allows people to get in and out, and travel around the city with ease. If you prefer to travel by ferry or boat, there are a series of international and domestic sea routes in the port of Tianjin, which is the biggest man-made port in China. Because Beijing has no seaport, Tianjin serves as the nearest port for passenger cruise liners, notably the Princess line and many others. If you plan to arrive by air, Tianjin Binhai International Airport offers excellent non-stop flights to all corners of the country and beyond, as described in detail below.

AIR

Tianjin Binhai International Airport is the city's main gateway to the rest of the world. Appropriately located to the east of the city center, in Dongli District, the aerodrome is also one of the major air cargo centers in the People's Republic of China. It is the hub airport for the newly established Tianjin Airlines, and privately owned Okay Airways. In 2008, the airport handled over 167 thousand tons of cargo freight, and officially became the 11th busiest airport in China. In May 2009, the airport also completed the construction of a second runway, and the number of passengers is expected to exceed 10 million. Frequent flights operate to all the major cities around China. Some international charter flights also operate from here.

RAIL

It can get somewhat confusing when looking for a railway station, because you won't find just one railway station in Tianjin but quite a few. Tianjin Railway Station is the principal one, and the oldest, with trains running on a regular basis to all major cities of China, including, as an example, Guangzhou to the south and Ürümchi to the west. The Tianjin Railway Station is also locally called the East Station, due to its geographical position. Tianjin West Railway Station and Tianjin North Railway Station are also major railway stations in Tianjin. The Tanggu Railway Station is located in the important port area of the Tanggu District, and TEDA (Tianjin Economic Development Area) Railway Station is located to the north of Tanggu. Be careful which railway station you head to as there are several other railway stations in the city that do not handle passenger traffic. In January 2007 a long-term reformation project started involving Tianjin metro lines 2, 3, and 9 as well as the Tianjin-Beijing high-speed rail. Connections are on time and the stations are generally safe.

BULLET TRAIN TO BEIJING

Trains from Tianjin to Beijing start at 6:20 a.m. and end at 11:30 p.m. Trains arrive at Beijing South Railway Station, which is connected to Subway Line 4. Travel time is

30–35 minutes. Ticket prices are 58 yuan for a hard seat and 69 yuan for a soft seat. It's easy enough to buy tickets from an automated machine at the station on the day of travel.

TAXI AND BUS

Extensive bus and taxi services operate. As in most cities in China, taxis operate freely on a 24-hour basis, while buses run from early morning till midnight. Bus fares are 1 yuan for non-air-conditioned buses and 2 yuan for modern air-conditioned buses.

LIGHT RAILWAY AND METRO

Tianjin has an extensive light railway line, the Binhai Mass Transit line, which runs between downtown Tianjin and the TEDA (Tianjin Economic Development Area) located near the seaside region. The eastern part of the line began service on March 28, 2004. The western part of the line was completed in 2006. The Tianjin metro was the second metro system to be built in China and commenced service in the early part of 1984. The total length of track is 7.4 km. This metro has three lines, with Tianjin Metro Line 1, which opened to the public in June 2006, operating through the city center with a total of 22 stations between Liuyuan and Shuanglin. Line 2 and 3 also operate regular services, while the recent Birhai/Line 9 is partially under construction but operational.

PLACES TO SEE

Tianjin Old City is situated at the west of Haihe Shizi Lin (Lion Forest) Bridge. There is no city wall anymore and it is free to go for tourists. A lot of history is associated with this part of Tianjin, and so it is well worth coming here to understand and digest the relevance of Tianjin's past, present, and future. Near to the southern gate of Tianjin's Old City, there is the Guangdong Assembly Hall, which was constructed in the 33rd year of Guangxi Emperor's ruling period in 1907. To add to this splendor, there is also a small mosque in the northwestern corner built in the 42nd year of Kangxi Emperor's ruling period (in 1703) and a "Queen of Heaven Palace" on the northeastern corner of the city, built in Yuantaiding 3rd year (1326), where sacrifices and prayers were offered for safety in navigation. Beside the Lion Forest Bridge the Wanghailou Church was last rebuilt in the 30th year of Guangxu Emperor's ruling period during the Qing Dynasty in 1904. The Laoxi Kai Church at Dushan Road and Binjing Avenue in the Heping District is also open to foreigners.

The popular **Huangyaguan (Yellow Cliff) Pass** takes its name from the somewhat yellow-colored hills and rocks located nearby. Originally constructed in A.D. 557, the Huangyaguan was first restored in the Ming Dynasty, with bricks, and for the second time in 1985. In 1986 the Chinese government listed the place as a key relic and a protector of the history of Tianjin city. The pass is compared to the Great Wall, except that it is the miniature of the Great Wall of China. The entire section is built on a sloped mountain edge. Being gifted with both natural beauty and cultural interest, it has turned out to be famous in its own right as a natural beauty spot and a summer resort for many visitors. The major scenic area is composed of Huangyaguan Pass and Taiping Mountain Stronghold. With a history of over 1400 years, the ancient walls were first constructed in Beiqi, and remained well until today. In the Ming Dynasty brick walls were added. Watch towers, frontier cities, drain holes, emplacements, barracks and other indispensable military facilities are arranged along the wall. The stele forests of the Great Wall, Beiji Temple, the exhibition hall of famous couplets, the Great Wall Museum (the first museum along the Great Wall) and the Phoenix Fortress have been newly built within the area. On Huangyaguan, you will be able to enjoy mountain scenery as well as waterfalls and springs.

Dabei Buddhist Monastery is made up of two parts: the old monastery and the new monastery. The old monastery refers to the three great halls in the west yard. The building of the old monastery commenced at the beginning of the Qing Dynasty era, and was effectively renovated in the eighth ruling year of Kangxi Emperor in the Qing Dynasty. The statue of Sakyamuni located in the Daxiong Palace from the east yard was created in the Ming Dynasty. The Sakyamuni Statue is 7 meters high, weighs 6 tons and has (remarkably) a total of 9,999 small Buddha statues carved on the lotus throne. Someone must have counted them! Inside the Great Compassion hall, a mud statue just under 4 meter high of the thousand-hand "Kwan-yin" is visible. The monastery was once renowned for holding a skull relic of Xuanzang; the relic was presented to India in 1956 when it was taken to Nalanda. The relic is now resting in the Patna museum in India. For that particular reason, the Great Compassion monastery uses the image of the Xuanzang instead of the Buddha. There are memorials for Xuanzang Master and Hongyi Master in the east yard, while the west yard eventually became an office for the Cultural Relic Palace, Abbot Palace, and the Chinese Buddhism Association (Tianjin Branch). Allow around an hour to fully digest the surrounding scenery as well. There are plenty of hawkers who sell water and other cold refreshments such as ice cream.

The **Tianjin Water Park** is the largest urban park and recreation area in Tianjin, China. Even now quite rare for a Chinese city to have such a recreational park, Tianjin was the one of the first cities to have such an attraction, having been opened in 1951. After all these years it is still going strong and covers an area of 127 hectares. The park is one of Tianjin's leading tourist attractions, which was officially acknowledged when it was listed in the National Tourism Administration 4A Level List of Scenic Sites in 2004. The Tianjin Water Park consists of nine sports "islands" and three lakes (East Lake, West Lake, and South Lake). Surrounding the waterways are pathways, pagodas, and gardens. The gardens display both Chinese and foreign architectural styles.

The Memorial to Zhou Enlai and Deng Yingchao is a museum dedicated to the great Chinese Premier Zhou Enlai and his wife, Madame Deng Yangchao in Tianjin. The museum features stunning photos, historical records, and personal accounts of the late premier's life and works, and even documents and dioramas relating to significant events in their lives. The museum is located near the Tianjin Water Park.

THINGS TO DO

The luxurious Notre Dame des Victoires on Shizilin Dajie has a strong feel of France and French culture to it—of course at one time in history Tianjin had a splendid connection with this beautiful country. The Tianjin Notre Dame Cathedral is also recognized for its architectural genius—people appreciate it the moment they set their eyes upon it. The cathedral has been through some turbulent times. The architectural marvel first opened in 1869, only to be sadly damaged one year later in the 1870 Massacre of Tianjin. A massive reconstruction operation was put in place, after which it was rebuilt; it sadly, again, met the wrath of man during the 1900 Boxer Rebellion—when the central government ordered the demolition of most foreign buildings. Revamping immediately followed and this time the cathedral stood until the terrible 1976 Tangshan Earthquake. Major renovations in 1983 restored its architectural glory. In 1988, China declared the church a Major National Relic. Unfortunately, admission for tourists, unless if you are a worshiper, is restricted during Sunday services.

Tianjin Museum is the largest museum in Tianjin and one of the largest in the country. The museum's collection includes an array of cultural and historical relics significant to Tianjin's past and present. An insight into where Tianjin city is heading to is also provided, especially after the completion of the 2008 Beijing Olympics. The museum is situated in the Yinhe Plaza area, which falls under the Hexi District of Tianjin. The premises covers an area of about 50,000 square meters—not small by any means—and will require a fair bit of walking. The unique architectural style of the museum, whose exterior resembles that of a swan spreading its wings, has meant that it is quickly becoming one of the city's iconic buildings. The Tianjin Museum has an extensive collection of over 200,000 ancient Chinese contemporary arts and exhibits on Tianjin's history. There is an admission charge.

The **Hai River**, formerly known as **Bai He**, is a river in Tianjin that also flows through Beijing, and later into the Bohai Gulf of the Yellow Sea. Five rivers known as, the **Southern Canal, Ziya River, Daqing River, Yongding River,** and the **Northern Canal,** have their confluences at the Hai River in Tianjin—this leads out to the sea through Tianjin Port. The southern and northern canals are parts of the Grand Canal. The Southern Canal is joined by the **Wei River** at Linqing. It's quite a spectacular sight, and visitors should take their camera with them at all times because the scenery is just stunning. It will keep you busy behind the lens. The Northern Canal joins with the **Bai He** (or **Chaobai River**) at Tongzhou. The Northern Canal (sharing channel with Bai He) is also the only waterway from the sea to Beijing. At Tianjin, through the Grand Canal, the Hai connects with the Yellow and Yangtze rivers. The construction of the Grand Canal to a great extent transformed the rivers of the Hai He basin. Formerly, the Wei, Ziya Yongding and Bai Rivers flowed independently to the ocean. The Grand Canal cut through the lower reaches of these rivers and fused them into one outlet to the sea, in the form of the current Hai He. There is no admission charge, although if you are going to take a boat trip on the river, then that will, of course, cost. But it's not too much and well worth spending for the experience.

The Tianjin Arts Museum on 77 Jeifang Road has been part of the city's cultural scene since its opening in 1957—not too old by many Chinese museum standards. However it does provide a detailed and much focused outlook on Tianjin's fine art. The museum's collection is modest but interesting all the same time. The two floors of the museum contain some good examples of artwork from both the Yuan and Qing dynasties. The second floor of the facility is devoted to folk art and includes traditional Chinese porcelain objects that have been preserved for many years— these porcelain products have never been sold to anyone because they are rare and treasured by the local government. They consist of many carved figurines and ornately designed giant kites. The third floor is used solely for visiting exhibitions, and is open to anyone if there is an exhibition going on.

Tea houses in Tianjin are not just there for tourists, but are very much part of the culture of the city. Why not join your friends, tourists, and even local people at one of Tianjin's many authentic Chinese tea house attractions and get to observe the ancient rituals of preparing, smelling, and tasting the tea. You will without a doubt enjoy the experience. A waitress (known in Chinese as a "cha si") gives a presentation on the history and formation of tea houses in Tianjin. Following the tea presentation, guests take part in the actual tasting of the tea and learn about the advantages and benefits of drinking different types of tea. Don't think that the tea ceremony in Tianjin will be the same as in Shanghai or Beijing or elsewhere in China, because here in Tianjin (as well as in every different city in China), the tea ceremony is performed differently and the types of tea are different too. After attending the tea sampling, the guests are given the chance to purchase any of many fine Chinese teas. There are quite a few tea houses in Tianjin.

SHOPPING

Guwenhua Jie on Beima Road is widely known as the Ancient Culture Street. It is perfectly nicknamed because that is exactly what is on display for the tourists to purchase. Gold-plated tea pots, jade ornaments, brightly colored red and green painted wooden storefronts capped by elaborate pagoda styled tiled roofs and much more are on offer. The place gives you the feeling that you are in 19th-century Tianjin. Yes, you may come across items that are not real, and you will across items that are very expensive to purchase, even for foreign tourists. But the beauty of even the fake items is that they are well worth purchasing. Are they? Yes, because they work. There are plenty of souvenirs, especially lots of old-style teapots, clay figurines, swords, musical instruments, coins, and books. If you feel that you have seen it all and want to relax and have a bite or two, there are plenty of nice restaurants and cafés scattered in the area.

Locally known as the Jiuhuo Shichang Antiques Market, the Shenyang Dao is Tianjin's most bustling (and quite loud) antiques market. Situated right in the heart of the city center, it runs along Shenyang Jie while spreading narrowly into some of the side streets. This lively market offers a wide assortment of old items of collectible or nostalgic value, including a fascinating collection of Chinese stamps, Chinese and Japanese coins, jewelry, snuff boxes, teapots, and various items related to Chairman Mao's reign—most (such as the stamps and coins) are genuine. If you are lucky enough to be in Tianjin on Sunday morning, visit the market if you really want to see it in full swing. It's a lively place to be—quite nice.

Tianjin Department Store on 172 Heping Road is comparable to Shanghai's Nanjing Xi Lu or Shenzhen's Dongmen area. It's a massive assortment of department and convenience stores all under one roof. Needless to say, you could end up shopping here all day if you wanted to. It offers a serious shopping experience with a highly recommended electronics department, where many modern video games and music-related accessories are for sale at a reasonable price. Amongst the biggest in the whole of China, the Tianjin Department Store also has a special historical significance attached to it—one going back to the colonial times of the city. The store initially opened its doors in the early 1920s and was the main store where foreign residents of Tianjin used to come and do their weekly shopping. The Tianjin Department Store is best reached by using public transport.

Further shopping opportunities in Tianjin present themselves around Xiaobai Lóu, which is close to Qufu Lu and is home to a number of brand-name stores and also the Foreign Goods Market, where second-hand clothing and vintage fashion accessories await. Prices are reasonable and because the store has been in operation for many years, it is popular with the local people and therefore highly recommended.

New World Shopping Center located on Dongma Lu specializes in the selling of electrical and computer related products. If you cannot make it to Hong Kong or Beijing, this store in Tianjin is the place to bargain for that much wanted latest electronic goodie.

WUXI

Located 124 km (77 miles) north of Shanghai is the city of Wuxi (pronounced Wu-She in English) with a population just shy of 5 million. Wuxi, which means "a place without tin," is technically split into two parts by Lake Taihu. The town borders Changzhou to the west and Suzhou to the east. The northern half of the city looks across to Taizhou city over the Yangtze River, while the southern half of the city borders Zhejiang province. Since the beginning of and during the early part of the 19th century, Wuxi gained its nickname "Pearl of Lake Tai" because of its presence next to the lake and the breathtaking surroundings of the city. The city has a history of more than 3,000 years, and it was founded by chance by two princes, Taibo and Zhongyong, both of whom proposed to offer their brother "Jili" the throne. Legend informs us that the two princes settled down in "meili," which is believed to be somewhere close to Suzhou today. When Taibo passed away, because he had no son to whom he could pass on the throne, the emperor of Zhou named a direct descendant of his family king of the "Wu" kingdom The king renamed the kingdom "Gowu."

Located very close to Wuxi and Suzhou is Qionglongshan, a natural beauty spot dotted with beautiful temples.

For a time in history, just prior to the 1990s, Wuxi was dubbed (and still is to some extent) the "miniature Shanghai" not just because of its close proximity to the metropolis but because of its rapid urbanization and roaring economy that is growing at a dizzying pace. Wuxi is without a doubt one of the most delightful municipalities in China, with a population of 4.65 million, and a perfect geographical location that allows its citizens to enjoy day trips to nearby towns in the Shanghai area. Also the city has become a center for investment from foreign business due to its clean air, its beauty, its resources, its excellent infrastructure, and of course its proximity to Shanghai. There are over 9000 foreign invested enterprises present in Wuxi, more than 85 of them standing among the World Fortune 500. That alone explains why Wuxi has become so prosperous in recent times.

CLIMATE

Average low temperatures in January are at around 1°C (34°F), while average high temperatures in July are about 30°C (86°F). The winters in Wuxi make you feel as you are in the old China (or say in the post-war China!) because most Chinese homes don't have proper central heating (except the homes where expats live of course). It gives the city that damp feeling.

HOW TO GET TO AND AROUND WUXI

Wuxi, being a major tourist and industrial city, is well connected to all parts of China by all forms of transport.

AIR

The city is served by Wuxi Shuofang Airport, which is situated 14 km from the city center. There are direct flights to all the major cities in China, including Macau and Hong Kong. The airport is well connected to the city center by all modes of transport. Going in a taxi should not take more than 40 minutes from the center of town to the airport.

TRAIN

Wuxi train station is on the main Shanghai (45 minutes away) to Nanjing (about an hour and half away) main railway line. Other nearby cities are connected by a regular service. Suzhou is only around 20 minutes away.

BUS OR TAXI

Taxis are available at any time of the day or night, and like anywhere else in China, you may need to write down the name and address of your destination in clear

Chinese unless you happen to sit in one where the driver speaks very good English. Buses operate a very good service all around the city, but most stop around midnight. Better ask your Chinese friends or hotel staff to give you detailed advice if you require any.

PLACES TO SEE

LINGSHAN GRAND BUDDHA

The Lingshan Grand Buddha sits on the site of a prehistoric Buddhist Temple— Xiang Temple. This temple derives from the Tang and Song dynasties. Located on the peak of the smaller Lingshan Mountain on the west side of the Qinly peak in Wuxi, this sculpture of Buddha is a staggering 88 meters high. It was positioned on here at the same time when the temple was rebuilt around the early part of the 19th century. The grand Buddha was originally planned to be made of all gold, however because of economic problems that plan was scrapped and instead was built using tin and bronze—which works well in that bronze is resistant to erosion. Bronze objects that derive from the essence of the classical art in the Stone Age are an extremely splendid part of Chinese traditional culture itself.

    It's a place where people can come and take a moment to just relax and ponder over their life's worries or plans. There is a Buddhist canteen that serves complimentary vegetarian food to guests. It's delicious and made by the monks themselves.

MEIYUAN GARDEN

The Meiyuan Garden is situated on the southern slope of Xushan Mountain in the western suburbs of Wuxi. It will take some 15 minutes by taxi to get here as it's approximately 7 km away from the urban areas. The best time to visit this famous garden is when the plum blossom is coming out in early spring. In the garden itself there are just over 45 varieties of plum blossom. In winter or early spring when the flowers are in full bloom, the garden is especially impressive. Most movies are filmed here during this time because of the naturally beautiful background scenery.

    Originally Meiyuan Garden (or Meiyuan Gong Yuan as it is known in Chinese) was a private garden of a prosperous resident in the highest imperial government of the Qing Dynasty. Then in 1912, the garden was owned by the Rong family. They in turn planted thousands of plum trees, roses, as well as a lot of other local types of flowers—some unknown even to this day. Because of the significance of these plum trees, the garden was then renamed as Meiyuan Gong Yuan (meaning plum garden in English).

In the years after the war, a vast collection of new flowers and even more plum trees were introduced in from Japan and Korea; there were also an abundance of oranges, peaches, plums, persimmon, gingko, and pomegranate planted at various periods throughout the garden's history. The garden consists of four sightseeing areas: Junzi (gentleman) Garden, Three Friends in Cold Weather, Sixiu Garden, and Winter Plum. They say that its healthy to walk among flowers and fruit plantations; well that statement is certainly true when one takes a walk along the path lined with these various plants and fruits.

LI GARDEN

The lake located in the Li Garden ripples gently with brightly red colored fish swimming on its banks, eagerly awaiting people to throw food. Rolling smooth green hills lie lazy in the far distance behind the lake. Long corridors, embankments, arbors, and pavilions in the grounds are all exquisitely imprinted with stylish colored drawings. The pavement has black and white chips and marble engraved in the shape of many fish. You will especially enjoy relaxing in the garden in the spring.

Li Garden is uniquely divided into four tourist and sightseeing areas. Each area has a different theme and ambience to it. The following is a direct translation into English. When you get a ticket to the park, the four sections of the park will all make perfect sense. These are (in no particular order): Small hills covered with green vegetation, Spring morning on the south embankment, Long corridor with a collection of sightseeing scenes, and Layers of waves with double images.

In the "Small hills covered with green vegetation," there are boundless views or illusions created by the plants and flowers of springtime, in the Sifang Pavilion. You may prefer to take the path that makes its way beside the lake, and then take the lotus boat for a short tour of the lake itself. The boats come in two forms. One will keep your feet busy as you paddle across the lake, while the other will keep both of your hands busy as you try to keep rowing in a straight line without hitting one of the many edges of the banks of the river (or even other boats).

As you wander around the garden, when you get to the "Layers of waves with double images" section, you will realize that it is the best spot to appreciate the sights and smells of the garden.

You will also come across themes such as Ban Pavilion, Lvyi Pavilion, Chunqiu Pavilion, and Shuimiao Pavilion, which are all centered on water and demonstrate the graceful nature of the lake water in the Li Garden at different levels. Once you get to the area of "spring morning on the south embankment," you will gain a thorough appreciation of the spring scenery. This is where you can really smell the fragrance of the flowers—take your time!

Different seasonal flowers and trees are planted according to the color of flowers and seasons around every pavilion. The spring pavilion of Yihong is planted with plum trees, the summer pavilion of Dicui planted with dogbanes, the autumn pavilion of Zuihuang planted with sweet-scented osmanthus, and the winter pavilion of Yinba planted with calyx canthus. As you stand in any of one of the four pavilions, you can always see the other three without any problems. These four pavilions and their separate gardens can be classified as the "four seasons overlapping with unlimited beauty."

THREE KINGDOM CITY

The Three Kingdom City is an area in Wuxi originally built as background scenery for a Chinese television serial depicting the three kingdoms. It is a re-creation of the chaotic Three Kingdoms period of Chinese history. It is located in the southwest suburbs of Wuxi City and quite easy to get to. The set of the series was so expensive to create that when the filming stopped, the production team, along with the local government, decided to turn the area into a tourist attraction.

Covering just over 40 hectares, the area includes numerous large-scale Han-style buildings in the city, including King Wu's Palace, the Nectar Temple, the water village of Cao Camp, the seven star altar, the fire signal platform, and the wheel-tower gate (outer gate of government official). Plus there are over 20 ancient warships on display that were used as part of the filming. It's worth a visit just to see the enormous props used, and it can provide something new and different for international travelers to China.

TURTLE HEAD ISLAND

The Turtle Head Island (Yuantou Zhu) is actually a small peninsula located in Taihu Lake—the third largest freshwater lake in China. When the lake is covered in light mist at low altitude, then its best to go on top of the Turtle Head Island to get a good view. The entrance is located on Huanhu Road, just behind Mei Garden (see below). The initial object that visitors will come across in the park is a memorial arch. The small park on the island takes advantage of the natural scenery of Taihu Lake and creates a traditional garden with conventional buildings, lavish but well-spaced woods, flowers and unusual rocks along the bank of the lake. After passing through Jianjin gate and the Lishe gate, you will reach the Changchun Bride, where in early spring clusters of cherry trees abundantly bloom in colors of deeply red or Chinese white.

The Wuxi Mei Botanical Garden on 13 BianJiaWan, LiaoXiXi Road, is a fine garden boasting some of the finest flowers in Jiangsu Province. One striking aspect is the immaculate layout of its rose garden, which contains five different types of rose, each a different color, and each section laid out in a different shape.

THINGS TO DO

Wuxi Yanan Theater located on 203 TongHui Road East in Beitang District is the home to the well-acclaimed Wuxi Opera (also called Xiwen Opera). The traditional programs are: Tryst in Nunnery, Turning Mill Stone, Pearl Tower and Couple Pearls Phoenix.

The **Wuxi Grand Theatre**, a brand-new opera house designed by Finnish Architects PES, held its grand opening and inaugural performance on April 30, 2012. The unique complex nestles up against Taihu Lake and provides a stunning venue for not only opera but also ballet and other musical performances.

Wuxi Museum located on 71 Huihe Road is a comprehensive museum that caters to both serious historians and tourists. The Museum introduces visitors to many historical facets of Wuxi city. Constructed in 1957, it was given full authorization by the local government in 1958. The museum building occupies a vast area of 7,000 square meters. Over the past 50 years, it has held over 350 exhibitions and welcomed well over 4.5 million visitors. With more than 30,000 historical artifacts of great historic and economic value on display, the museum is especially well known for its compilation of unusual objects from the Ming and Qing dynasties.

Jiangyin Museum on 159 GongYuan Road in Chengjiang Town is more modern and smaller than the Wuxi museum. There are fewer objects on display than at the Wuxi Museum, but they are of great importance because they reflect the most recent history of the area of Chengjiang and Wuxi. Some rooms display objects only taken since the 1980s. It's a nice place to take a walk and cool off from the hot weather on the streets of Wuxi.

Yixing (a smaller city within the Wuxi metropolitan area) is most renowned for its teapots made using purple sand, known as *zisha*, which is only found in this area of China. The **China Yixing Ceramic Museum** in the Dingshu Town of Wuxi forms part of the collection that focuses on ceramic objects collected from around the early part of the Han Dynasty till the present day. The museum specifically highlights the need to use *zisha* pottery and the teapots; however it also contains celadon items made in the Western and Eastern Jin dynasties and Jun-glaze pieces made in the Song and Ming dynasties (Jun glaze is used primarily in garden pieces).

SHOPPING

One of the things that makes Wuxi different for shopping from Shanghai is that here you can buy genuine pearls at a relatively affordable price. Necklaces made from pearls found in the Taihu Lake are very popular, and locally produced pearl powder, sometimes as a cream, is said to be excellent for the skin and heart. Wuxi is also the home of Yixing teapots, which though not rare, are not easily found in shops either. Sometimes to get something really precious in China, you have to bargain hard.

The Nanchan Temple Market is a very conspicuous building on Jiefang Lu, at the southern end of the main north-south road that goes through the city center, Zhongshan Lu. The area is best seen at night-time when it is more attractive, not just because of the neon lights but because of the whole feeling of being in an area full of activity. Families come out to stroll along the stalls after dinner; there are stalls for fresh flowers, meat and fish, along with souvenirs for tourists. The market is well worth wandering through, even if you don't want to buy souvenirs. You can get just about anything here, from antique marbles to small pet dogs or cats.

Wuxi Red Earthen Art Studio: Center for the Finest Chinese Teapots: Although the southern Chinese city of Guangzhou is known for its year-round fairs, when it comes to specialized products such as clay or red earth clay, places such as Wuxi are your best bet. Wuxi is the host city to China's largest center for red stoneware, especially the one used for making teapots. The center includes eighteen display galleries showing the finest quality Chinese teapots. Collections are original, vast, and unique. Mentors who are based inside the gallery hold demonstration classes in English and Chinese showing visitors techniques for recognizing a good quality teapot.

New World Department Store on 319–339 Zhongshan Road is a conventional modern department store that houses all kinds of goods ranging from designer perfumes to crocodile shoes made locally in China (not to be confused with the Chinese shoe brand "Crocodile"). There is also a fruit and household goods supermarket on the ground floor of the shopping mall. Here you can purchase some products at a fraction of the cost they would be back home, so it can be handy to purchase the products in China while you have the chance.

Wuxi's renowned folk-art "Huis Han" clay figurines, which some regard as highly attractive, are obtainable at the **Huishan Clay Figurine Factory** store at Xihui Lu 26. You can see the figurines being created from just a few balls of clay and then carefully molded into shape and painted before being finished. The business was started around 50 years ago and has grown to be highly popular in Wuxi. Credit cards are accepted.

Wuxi Sanyang Parkson Square Corporation Ltd on 127 Renmin Middle Road is the city's major center for electronic and IT goods. If you want the latest electronic products at a fraction of the cost of what it may be in other parts of the world, then the Sanyang Parkson Square is the ideal place to come to.

BRIEF NOTES ON HONG KONG AND MACAU

HONG KONG

Hong Kong (Xiang Gang is the Chinese name) was a British colony until 1997, and the official name now is Hong Kong Special Administrative Region (HK SAR). It's known as an SAR because it operates on a one government, two systems (the other one being Macau) scheme where the central government is based in Beijing, and a Chief Executive Officer is in charge of affairs in the day-to-day running of life in Hong Kong.

Because Hong Kong is on the border of China, it is convenient to visit for a one- or two-day excursion. Hong Kong's slogan is "Asia's World City" and this statement is most certainly true considering the multicultural environment, which offers a good mix of the East and the West. Immediately as you cross the border from Shenzhen into Hong Kong, the environmental change s so dramatic that it really does feel as if you have stepped 30 years into China's future. Since independence from the British in 1997, Hong Kong has still managed to retain many of the traditions that are forbidden in mainland China. Amazingly it is doing well economically too. Speaking English in Hong Kong is not a problem because of its

Hong Kong, the former British colony, continues to charm tourists from all around the world. Seen here is the famous IFC building and the piers in Central on Hong Kong Island.

history as a British colony. Cantonese (Guangdonghua) is the national language of Hong Kong and not many people understand Mandarin.

In Hong Kong, apart from the multiculturalism, you will notice the free press (there are myriad publications that would be prohibited in the mainland), fashion, the 24-hour hustle and bustle, and food (even the Chinese food tastes different than in the mainland). The general lifestyle of Hong Kong is very appealing, not just to mainland Chinese but also to Asians from other parts of the region. The main drawback is the air pollution, much of which is blown in from the industrialized Pearl River delta area.

Hong Kong is a must for shopping and sightseeing. Don't miss the many beautiful exotic islands scattered around the main Hong Kong Island that you can visit on one- or two-day excursions.

The majority of British expats left after the handover in 1997, but a considerable number have decided to keep Hong Kong their second home. Most British subjects tend to be employed in the financial and insurance sectors (many investment banks have their Asia Pacific headquarters in Hong Kong). A considerable number also work in the airline industry (Cathay Pacific Airways is the national flag carrier of Hong Kong and many of its British staff members, including pilots and cabin crew, are based in Hong Kong).

USEFUL LINKS

- www.discoverhongkong.com Official tourist website for Hong Kong
- www.gov.hk Official government website of the SAR Hong Kong
- www.tdctrade.com Hong Kong Trade Development Council
- www.yp.com.hk Hong Kong Yellow Pages
- www.hongkongairport.com Official website of Hong Kong Airport

MACAU

Macau (Aomen is the Chinese name), a Portuguese colony until 1999, is on the border of Zhuhai to the south of Guangdong province. The Portuguese heritage is evident everywhere as all the signs are in two languages—Mandarin and Portuguese—and the operational currency is "Patacas."

Smaller than Hong Kong (only 26 sq km in size), Macau is now beginning to attract a large number of tourists. However, it is still considered the younger brother to Hong Kong. Macau is famous for gambling and homemade almond butter cookies. The former has been around since licensed gambling was first introduced during the 1850s, and these days Macau is being classed as the Las Vegas of Asia. Macau's casinos are scattered across the region, a peninsula connected to mainland China and two outlying islands by a reclaimed land called Cotai. In August 2007, the world's largest casino, Venetian Casino, managed by the Las Vegas Sands Corporation, officially opened on the island of Cotai. Valued at over $2.4 billion, the Cotai resort contains a hotel with 3,000 rooms, a 15,000-seat sports arena, 1.2 million square feet of convention space, fine dining, and room to accommodate 6,000 slot machines as well as 800 gambling tables.

The Ruins of St Paul's are the most famous landmark of the former Portuguese colony Macau. They were officially enlisted as part of the UNESCO World Heritage Site Historic Centre of Macau in 2005.

Without a doubt that there is a lot of money here and everyday a considerable number of Chinese from the mainland and Hong Kong come to fill its many casinos in search of fortune. Surprisingly you won't find many James Bond type characters with tuxedos in these casinos, as the majority of gamblers seem to be retired pensioners who are just whiling away time and enjoying the company of fellow senior citizens. Nevertheless they do seem to be affluent.

A sizable number of expats from Canada, America, and some European countries are investing in the casino business and have therefore effectively made Macau their second home.

Apart from gambling and almond cookies, Macau is also famous for the Grand Prix (both motorbike and racing car), which is held annually.

USEFUL LINKS

- www.macautourism.gov.mo Official Macau Government website
- www.macau-airport.gov.mo Macau International Airport website
- www.wtc-macau.com Macau World Trade Center
- www.cityguide.gov.mo Macau City Guide
- www.yp.com.mo/en/ Macau Yellow Pages

CHAPTER 3

HOUSING/ACCOMMODATIONS

I T SHOULD NOT POSE MANY PROBLEMS IF YOU WANT TO RENT ACCOMMO-
dations in China. For most expats, employers would arrange some sort of
relocation assistance, such as helping to find accommodation close to the
office. If your employer is unable to assist you with this, an alternative option would
be to ask other expats or any Chinese friend who speaks good English, and go with
them to the estate agent. It should be borne in mind that not many estate agents
can converse in English.

Along with the growing economy, high-rise apartment buildings are being
constructed all the time, offering plenty of choice for price location, and space.
Renting or buying a home in China is not as complex as in Europe or America;
however, for the Chinese, the rocketing pace at which house prices are rising is a
major issue. Most developments will have a management office situated on location. It's usually just a matter of finding a complex that suits your daily needs and
then you can ask to be shown around all the apartments that are up for rent (or
those that are of interest to you). Most apartments have an average living space of
approximately 400 sq ft (approx. 37 square meters) with one or two bedrooms or
a studio apartment.

The Chinese taste in furniture and furnished housing is usually different from
European or Western tastes, so you can specify that you want to have a Western
style kitchen or bathroom and also a Western style toilet, unless you prefer a Chinese style toilet. You should also specify that you want air conditioning in your
apartment as it will get exceedingly uncomfortable in the summer months. Normally most homes only have one air conditioning unit placed in their bedroom,
leaving the rest of the home feeling like a sauna. However, increasingly it is
becoming common in big homes to have at least one air conditioning unit in the
living room, and one in the bedroom.

On the whole, China does have a problem with housing, simply because of
the high population. Homes are generally very simple and seem cramped. The
toilet and the kitchen are usually built side by side. One Chinese friend told me
the reason behind this is that it saves trouble having to go to the other side of the

house if someone needs to go to the toilet or wash their hands while they are in the kitchen. Chinese kitchens and bathrooms tend to be much smaller than those in the West. There are two reasons for this, one being the lack of space and the other being the convenience of having everything within arms' reach in the kitchen, rather than wandering around the kitchen to get your cooking ingredients.

Homes don't have a carpet as they do in the West, even in northern China, where it can get bitterly cold. This does create the problem of having to clean floors filled with dust and small amounts of black soot that piles up due to the polluted atmosphere, especially in industrial cities such as Suzhou, Wuxi, Guangzhou, and Xi'an.

In some homes, people prefer to have a sofa bed in the living room, which can double as extra seating if relatives or visitors arrive and an extra bed for them if they stay overnight. Sometimes it is common for more than two families to live in cramped conditions in one home. In the main cities this is becoming increasingly less common as people are rewarded with higher salaries. Washing machines are smaller in size than in the West and even though they do the job properly, during spinning clothes are vulnerable to being shrunk, torn, or stretched. Clothes dryers are extremely rare.

There may be hidden issues that you won't be exposed to when you initially rent your apartment, such as noise at night-time or early in the morning. Some Chinese people like to play cards or Mah-Jong well into the night while under the influence of alcohol, often with their windows and apartment doors open; this is the case in some hotels as well. And if you are living near a Chinese school, then most likely you will be awakened at about 6:30 in the morning, during schooldays of course, by children arriving in school and singing the national anthem or playing loud instrumental music that is often terribly out of tune!

Most developments consist of high-rise flats. Choosing a high floor is probably the best option to avoid street noise and mosquitoes. It's common that you may get some bad smell through the drainage pipe. The best remedy for this is to use liquid bleach, which can be purchased from any supermarket or convenience store. Most landlords will push you to sign for at least six months, although it is possible to rent a room for three months in some areas—it purely depends on the landlord and the area where the house is up for rent. It's a buyers' market so if you really like a place, even if there are slight flaws such a new paint job being required or a tacky piece of furniture being present, then inform the landlord and he or she may change it for you at no charge. When looking for a home, your top criteria for selection will include such major factors as availability of public transport and the proximity to the center. There are various types of housing available—apartments, courtyards, villas, and compounds.

Landlords in China can require up to 3–4 months' rent when signing a rental contract. Thereafter, you will often pay rent in three-month installments. This is equivalent to an initial, one-time payment between 10,000 and 20,000 yuan (or even more depending on how expensive your accommodation is). You must keep this amount in mind as you plan your budget.

Foreigners who rent apartments with gas appliances should be aware that in some areas, natural gas is not scented to warn occupants of gas leaks or concentrations. In addition, heaters may perhaps not constantly be vented, thus allowing surplus carbon monoxide to build up in living spaces. Due to some fatal accidents relating to foreigners, individuals are advised to make sure that all gas appliances are suitably vented or install gas and carbon monoxide detectors in their residences. These devices are not extensively obtainable in China, and they should be purchased, if possible, prior to arrival.

TYPES OF APARTMENTS

Generally speaking, there are two types of apartments in China.

HIGH-RISE

These homes literally reach for the Chinese sky. They tend to have a wealth of amenities, including security guards, added security, double doors, elevators, modern design, sometimes heated flooring, and sometimes even satellite TV. But the latter few amenities come with a more substantial price tag.

These living quarters often lack much of the charm that makes a house a home. Affordability, size, condition, and location are key considerations when looking for an apartment; rarely are you going to get all four in one high-rise. Great apartments are usually only found in price ranges that demand more than one rent-reimbursement.

CHINESE APARTMENT

Chinese apartments can be found all over China in all cities. These low-slung buildings, which may or may not have an elevator, can come in a wide range of prices, conditions, and sizes. They are often the best deals on the market, but look out for run-down fixtures and amenities, noisy locations, and a lack of security. As elevators are only legal in buildings over eight stories high, you might find that your great deal is just too much of a daily climb (great exercise everyday though can be troublesome in hot weather!). Another downside could be that there may be no central heating, and no proper double-glazed windows. That said, luxurious homes where diplomats and company general managers may reside are also made of a similar design in some cities (Guangzhou, Shenzhen for one). Now the price tags for those luxurious Chinese style homes can go from anything around 40,000 yuan a month to over 150,000 yuan a month complete with butler service. Though I highly doubt that many expat families will reside in these styles of homes unless they are a diplomat or a senior executive.

BATHROOMS AND TOILETS

A Chinese home is most likely to have a shower fitted with access to hot water. Bathtubs are rare, only to be seen in Western-style hotels and maybe the more affluent apartments.

Usually the shower and toilet are in the same room. Modern homes have a Western-style toilet, whereas the majority of homes are fitted with a Chinese-style toilet, which is basically an open drain in the ground where people can squat by putting their feet on each side. Public toilets are much the same except that there is no tissue paper or soap available, so it would be advisable to take some with you when out and about. It can be highly embarrassing and annoying when trying to find a decent public toilet and only to realize that there is no tissue or soap available, and to make matters worse, the flushing system does not even work properly sometimes.

As a foreigner you will find it strange and unhygienic that the Chinese prefer to throw the used toilet paper into the bin rather than flush it down the toilet. This is very much the case in any home, office, or hotel, simply because the quality of the sewage system is poor. This provides a possible explanation as to why perfumed and heavily sanitized/moisturized tissue paper is sold in many convenience stores. From my unfortunate experience I discovered that my toilet got blocked in the five-star hotel in Guangzhou where I was staying –on my first trip to China! The hotel staff politely advised me to put the tissue into the bin in the bathroom, to which at first I thought the guy was joking. That said, in some of the newer homes in China's expat cities, homes have proper sanitation facilities with a proper sewerage system. Some toilets may even have a heated floor and heated toilet seat (sheer luxury in those cold winters!).

MAIDS (BAOMU OR AY YI)

The country's rush to prosperity, and rules that make it easier for rural residents to move to the cities, mixed in with the middle class who are too busy to look after their daily housing needs, has meant an increase in the number of young people from the rural areas (mostly women) taking up employment as maids in affluent households in the big cities. If you are going to lead a busy working life and seldom have time to cook for your family, then perhaps it's more convenient for you to hire a house maid. It's common in China to employ a house maid who would do the cleaning and cooking. The average costs vary between 400 yuan and 1500 yuan per month depending on the area where you live and the amount of hours he or she would work. Back in your own country in the West, having a house cleaner is a real luxury, but it is not as expensive in China to hire an *ay yi* (literally translated "auntie" in Mandarin) to clean the house, do the dishes, and possibly even do the laundry.

The best way to find an *ay yi* is by talking to people who already have one to see if theirs is available. If you can find an *ay yi* who works for people that you know, that is ideal. You can also ask your landlord or realtor for a recommendation. If those don't work, there's always the Internet or contacting a service

The advantage of employing a house maid is that he or she will cook the food just like you want it to be, and also the type of food that you want. With prior notice, the maid will go and buy the required food, cook it, and have it ready for you to eat when you come back from work.

House maids are, of course, Chinese and speak limited amounts of English. In some expat areas in the major cities, in recent times Filipino and Indonesian maids have started being employed. The main advantages of hiring Filipinos are that they can speak English as well as cook Western food if you prefer. The hiring costs may be a little higher than hiring Chinese maids, but it will be worthwhile. For further information on hiring maids, the best source would be to get in touch with your friends or colleagues at work or try any of the local English literature such as the "That's" series of magazines listed in this book. Here are some listings for maids available in some of the cities in China:

BEIJING

Beijing Ayi Housekeeping Service Co., Ltd.
北京家福来劳务服务有限公司
Tel：+86 (0)10-64345647 +86 (0)10-64345648
Address: Room 213A San Xia Zhao Shang Mansion, No.11 Jiu Xi'an Qiao Lu, Chaoyang District, Beijing, China
Email：service@bjayi.com
Website: www.bjayi.com

GUANGZHOU

Guangzhou Bao Mu
Address: Guangzhou City, Guangdong Province, 14 Xi'an Lie Road, Building 601 Huatai Hotel
Telephone: +86(0)20 -88198025
Website: http://www.gzbaomu.com

SHANGHAI

China GNI House Keeping
Address: Room 501,Block 8,Lane 58, Middle Yanggao Road, Shanghai,China

上海市浦东新区杨高中路58弄8号501室
Telephone: (English Speaking) +86 (0)21 6871 2199
Website: www.chinagni.com

SUZHOU

Suzhou Daisy Housekeeping Service
212 Block, 13 Olive Bay
S.I.P., Suzhou
China
Telephone: +86 (0)512 6790 4911
Email: daisyhousekeeping@163.com

TIANJIN

Tianjin Shuimeilian House-Cleaning Service (天津睡美莲家政服务)
Address: No. 904, Block B, Caifu Building, 43 Weijin Lu, He Ping
天津市和平区卫津路43号财富大厦B座904号
Telephone: +86 (0)22 2781 9805

ELECTRICITY AND WATER

China has an efficient power supply throughout the country, with electricity short-
ages and blackouts a rare occurrence. The electric current in China is 220 volts. The
electrical Hertz (Hz) is 50. Appliances in China are relatively cheap and it may be
more convenient if you purchase regular items here after your actual relocation.
Voltage transformers aren't easily found. In case of an emergency it would be wise
to stock up with some candles (Lazhu) and a working flashlight (shoudiantong).

Bills can be paid using a direct debit scheme with your associated bank, or
a monthly deposit can be made from the dedicated bank account. Your landlord
or employer (if the accommodation is provided by your company) would be first
point of contact for any assistance.

It would not be wise to drink straight from the tap (even in five-star hotels or
restaurants). Tap water should be boiled before drinking. Don't be surprised to see
some yellow/slightly muddy water pouring through the taps, even in some five-star
hotels (although the latter is rare). Bottled water is available in most shops. People
seldom use tap water for drinking and only use boiled tap water for cooking. Most
homes get regular deliveries of 19-liter containers of bottled water priced around
8–16 yuan. Water dispensers should be provided by your landlord as a common

kitchen appliance when you first move in. This is operated by the main electricity and has hot and cold water taps.

DRY CLEANERS (GAN XI)

You can get all your laundry washed, dried, and ironed at a small price at most dry cleaners. The service is excellent and professional and at a set price—don't worry about being charged extra because you are a foreigner, because you won't. If you are not provided with a washing machine in your accommodation, then the dry cleaners may be the best option for you.

DIY (ZIJI DONGSHOU)

China's middle class and expats alike have IKEA, B&Q and Dulux Paint shops that cater for those who want to have a go at DIY. Something that started off as an experiment, for foreign investors, has actually proved to be quite successful so far, aiming at the younger generation with high level incomes and who are potentially first-time buyers in China's booming property market. B&Q has over 50 stores on the mainland and has proved popular with the Chinese consumers.

If you are planning on carrying out your own DIY then be assured that you should have no problem buying that much missed BBQ that you wish you had in China—well, now you can!

NOISE

Unlike in other countries, where workmen only work during the weekdays and business hours on construction sites, in China construction goes on 24/7. It's astonishing to observe that when a project is commissioned for construction to start, the workmen first build their own homes, usually with timber and corrugated iron, and then they start building the actual assigned project. It's not just the noise from the construction, but also from the neighbors. In China most homes are constructed using inexpensive materials, so what tends to happen is that the home environment may look nice but the walls or the floorboards may not be as solid as one would imagine them to be, so it's easy to hear the neighbors walk, talk, and even cook food! In extreme cases, you may also tend to hear the neighbors a floor below (or above) you because the materials for construction are so thin. Therefore it's probably better to be careful about which home you choose. Normally, the general consensus is that the more expensive the home is then of course the better the home would be. In some of the expensive homes, you may also have heated flooring.

The Chinese have grown accustomed to such noise in their neighborhoods that many people don't even bother complaining. Therefore, there is not much you can do to stop the noise, say for example, of a drill in the middle of the night or the loud volume of someone's television at midnight, except maybe to complain to the accommodation management office. Even if the staff in the management office take the complaint into account, especially if it's made by a foreigner, it is most likely that the workers won't stop just because one person is complaining. Or they may stop for a while, and then start again by ignoring the plea made by the sleepless residents!

Noise in China doesn't necessarily come from the homes, but from all corners of life such as road traffic, because China is generally a noisy country. A concrete example is people using loud music tones on their mobile phones to show off, and then they also talk very loudly on the mobile phone no matter where they may be (can be on the train, bus, or even in a corporate meeting). One reason for this may be that people want to show off their latest mobile phones, and the interesting musical tones that go with them. The there is a random pointless "tooting the horn" by trucks and cars on the roads—though this horrible practice is banned in the big cities, in second tier cities and rural areas it is common for drivers to toot the horn loudly to tell other drivers to get out of the way.

SECURITY GUARDS

Expats will be relieved to know that every apartment building has security guards on duty 24/7, except the very low end of the housing market where foreigners are highly unlikely to stay. Your landlord should be able to provide you with details of emergency numbers, for which guards can come to assist with any problem, ranging from your water supply not running to any other neighborhood problems. Most homes have a small watch glass in the front door that allows you to see who's outside but doesn't allow them to see you.

Foreigners should not open the door without looking through the watch glass in their door first. The security staff usually doesn't allow a non-resident into the neighborhood; however, sometimes people posing as "mailers" get through, and this can be dangerous if intruders or trespassers find their way in. There have been some cases of foreigners being targeted by prostitutes, thieves, and robbers in expat areas because somehow they know where a foreigner lives. The security guards should be able to assist you with anything and at any time of the day or night. So it could be that your toilet is blocked (hope not!), that your hot water is not on, your electric power is gone and so on.

REGISTERING AS A FOREIGNER IN CHINA

As a foreigner you will need to register your residential address and contact details with your local Public Security Bureau (PSB). It is best that you register as soon as you are aware of your residential address. To avoid potential fines, you should register within 72 hours of moving into your apartment. This is mandatory as infrequently the PSB will carry out random checks, and a fine is most likely to be given if they have no record of you. Also if you want to extend your visa, and you haven't registered, problems are sure to occur.

Property prices in big cities such as Shanghai, as shown here, can be among the most expensive in the world.

Because not many police officers can converse in English, it's best if you can either take one of your Chinese-speaking colleagues or an English-speaking Chinese friend with you. The procedure is simple and takes only a few minutes. All you need is your original passport, visa, and your original rental contract/agreement. The PSB will take copies of all documents and then issue you with two copies of the resident certificate. One copy is kept on file by the PSB while the other you will need to provide when you apply for a work permit. When you are registering your address with the police, make sure that you explain to the realtor or landlord that your visa is currently being converted to a one-year resident permit. After your passport is returned to you, the owner of the apartment or an agent will need to accompany you to the local police station to register your address. If you are residing in a hotel, then the staff will take care of all procedures when you check in, and all you need to provide them with is a copy of your original passport.

In the event you do not register within the required timeframe, the police station may issue a warning that reminds you foreigners are required to register within 72 hours of arrival or moving to a new location. If a warning is issued, you will be required to sign the document and stamp your finger in red ink over your signature. Not registering at all could lead to fines and/or deportation.

COMMUNICATION

Below is a guide to registering with the police containing translated phrases that you can present to them at the station.

If you cannot communicate with the police officer, please show these Chinese messages to him/her:

警察同志, 请帮助我办理临时住宿登记单,谢谢.
(Dear officer, please kindly issue the temporary residence certificate)

若我的材料有缺失或者办理的材料或步骤有问题,请在以下空白处列明,谢谢.

(If there's any problem with my application documents or with the process, please kindly list the problems below. Thanks.)

COMMON QUESTIONS AND ANSWERS REGARDING RESIDENT PERMITS

What are residence and work permits?
These permits need to be obtained for you to be able to live and work legally in China. The Z visa you obtained in your home country is just a single entry visa and is only valid for 30 days once you arrive in China.

How do I obtain these permits?
Your company's Human Resources department will help guide you through the process. You will need to provide the following documents to HR by the deadlines issued to you:

- Temporary Resident Registration Form.
- Original Passport
- 6 Passport Photos
- Employment License

Why are the deadlines so important?

Your company may only have 30 days to transfer your Z visa into a work & residence permit, so the deadlines are extremely tight. However, since your company would likely have successfully helped hundreds of expats obtain these permits, so as long as you submit the required documents by the deadlines provided to you by Human Resources there should be no problems with the process.

Where do I get my temporary residence form?
You can either get this form from the local police station once you have your own apartment or this can be obtained at the hotel. If you are not sure which is best for your individual situation please contact your company's Human Resources department.

What is the Employment License?
The Employment License (EL) is one of the forms you should have been sent by your company before you arrived in China to obtain your Z visa. The original will need to be submitted with your other documents to obtain your work permit.

What is the usual timeframe/sequence?
Conduct Medical Check—You will be provided with the details of the medical check by HR.
• Submit Required Documents to HR by deadline provided
• Attend Visa Interview
• You should receive your permits around 10 days after the interview

SOME IMPORTANT POINTS TO NOTE ABOUT RENTING IN CHINA

In China, most apartments are individually owned, which means you'll find a vast variety in quality and style of interior decoration, electrical appliances, and furniture provided.

Usually the duration of a rental lease agreement is one year, with the option to extend (exceptions can be made for half a year but make sure this is noted on paper when you sign the contract!). However, landlords are quite eager to sign longer contracts. Additionally, you may want to negotiate the inclusion of an "exit clause" in case you need to vacate early. Typically if you have not negotiated an "exit clause" you would forfeit your deposit.

As in any global metropolis, rents vary widely in the big cities in China. In cities such as Beijing, Shanghai, Hangzhou, Shenzhen, and Guangzhou, property can be rented from 1,500 to over 100,000 yuan per month depending on location, size and type of property, lease terms, quality, and so on.

Real estate prices inside the Central Business District of any city are considerably higher than in other parts of the city, with the exception of villas in rural areas. The majority of expats who are relocated to China by their company may be provided with the option to rent a serviced apartment, which comes complete with a housemaid, and all bills are usually included. Serviced apartments sometimes also include swimming pools, heated flooring, and even their own gardener. Most luxury five-star hotels offer the option for guests to stay in a serviced apartment for longer than half a year. The monthly rents for serviced apartments may be anything from around 25,000 yuan onwards. Therefore, unless you live in a serviced apartment, rent does not include utilities (electricity, water, heating, Internet). The cost depends on the size of the property and, of course, usage. For example, a two-bedroom apartment using air-conditioning and a washing machine would typically have electricity costs of approximately 250 yuan per month. Water and gas charges typically cost about 50 yuan per month.

In most northern cities, from November to March, central heating is provided in the vast majority of buildings and is usually included in the cost of your rent, but be sure to read the specifics of your lease agreement. The majority of homes in the South region (namely in Guangdong, Guangxi, and Sichuan) do not have heating installed, which can make the winters an uncomfortable experience because when it is freezing outside then you can't get the interior warmer than, say for example, 12°C (about 53°F). The reason for heating not being installed in buildings in the South region is that usually it only gets very cold for around a month at the most. The prevalence of central heating in the North is one of the main reasons why people there end up warmer and more comfortable in the colder months than those in the South.

Rental pricing can be negotiated. If you are able and willing to pay more upfront you can usually get a small discount on the rent, but don't overdo it. Just remember that once they have your money, some landlords might be less motivated to help resolve any issues that arise. Before signing a contract with your landlord, carefully read each clause with your agent. The contracts are generally written in Chinese and English, but if there are any issues the Chinese version prevails. All verbal agreements made with a landlord should be written down and signed. Any changes you request in the property have to be mutually agreed upon and documented in writing before you can sign.

There are two types of apartments in big cities such as Beijing, Shanghai, Chongqing, Guangzhou, and Shenzhen—more upscale, international apartments and older apartments. One of the differences between the two is the rental agent fee. For the international-type apartments the rental agent fee is paid by the landlord. For older apartments, however, this fee is paid by the tenant. The fee is usually equal to one month's rent. However, be sure to negotiate this fee, as sometimes you can get up to 25% off. This is especially true if you are dealing with an agent with whom a friend or colleague has worked before. However, there are no fixed rules pertaining to who pays the agent commission and it needs to be discussed and negotiated prior to the signing of the lease.

In China, the landlord generally pays the broker's fee, although sometimes the landlord will ask the future tenant to bear the cost, which is an individual decision based upon how badly you want the apartment.

It's a very good idea to insist that you receive either a receipt or a written acknowledgment of all money that is paid to the landlord or realtor. Make a file and save all these documents together.

The only document you should ever sign is the lease (no matter what the broker says). Before signing a lease, always get a photocopy of the landlord's ID card (Chinese people have to carry their ID cards) and a photocopy of the apartment's ownership rights certificate. Make sure that the names match up (if you can't read Chinese, then ask someone who can to accompany you). If the names don't match, then do not sign.

Never hand over a deposit without getting a key in exchange. Never pay more than three months' rent at a time. If something goes wrong, you only have leverage to the extent that you haven't paid. Never give back a key without getting the deposit at the same time, and record this term in the lease agreement before signing.

SOME QUESTIONS AND ANSWERS REGARDING ACCOMMODATION IN CHINA

What do you think about subletting?
It's best to avoid it as foreigners have no rights, protection, or any legal documentation of the stay. Taking a contract to register properly at the police station will be difficult, and a seemingly harmless situation can quickly become unstable if the landlord decides that this is outside of the agreement. If the offer is too good to pass up, make sure that the landlord agrees and has your name added to the original contract or a separate contract drawn up to mirror and be in full accordance with the original contract.

How do monthly utility expenses work?
Every apartment has different ways of paying bills. The methods in which they are paid vary greatly but none are as simple as direct deduction from your bank account. You may have "charge up" cards, you might deposit the cost of utilities into your landlord's bank account directly, or you might have to visit different places to pay the bills for each utility. Be sure to have the landlord explain this to you in *detail*, write it down, and keep it with your contract to find easily. Also, ask what the utilities usually cost on average so that you know if something is costing too much and can find the root of the problem.

Should I buy my own furniture?
Most apartments provide furniture, but some expats prefer to purchase their own. However, be aware that some cities in China have either a dry climate (e.g., Beijing), or a high humidity climate (e.g., Guangzhou, Shenzhen), which can damage wooden furniture with a finish or fine lacquer finishes on dining tables, dressers, coffee tables, etc. Decor and styles vary, and there can be an esthetic cultural gap between some tenants and owners. Keep in mind that most bedding is not

provided and the purchase of linen, towels, blankets, and duvets will be your own responsibility. The latter can be discussed with the landlords themselves.

What penalty will I incur if I break my lease agreement early?
Normally you will lose the deposit, which is usually the penalty stipulated in the contract. Of course this depends on what has been agreed to in your contract. This is sometimes negotiable, especially if you introduce your landlord to a new tenant.

When I encounter a problem, do I contact the agent or the landlord?
Communication with landlords (especially individuals) can often be difficult because of the language barrier and some do not live in the same city as the home. Different agencies employ different approaches to assist with providing solutions for problems such as maintenance repair. It is in your best interest to have a single point of contact throughout your rental contract. In addition it is also important to verify who the official real estate agent is as well. In China some agents act as agents of other agents and thus when a problem occurs in the future it might be difficult determining who is ultimately responsible for resolving a particular issue.

How can I rent an apartment without my passport?
Most landlords will accept a photocopy of your passport and your company's labor contract can serve as proof of employment. Some police stations will accept a copy of your passport in order to issue the Temporary Housing Registration form, but you'll need to go back again after you have your new Resident Permit. If the police station won't issue the Temporary Housing Registration form without your passport, ask them to issue a receipt that you attempted to register in the required timeframe.

ACCOMMODATION IN BEIJING

Rental accommodation in Beijing is generally more costly than other Chinese cities, especially after the 2008 Olympics, as most of the land prices have increased. For example a one-bedroom fully furnished apartment near Beijing University (near Wu Dao Kou area—towards the northwest of the city center) would cost anything between 1500 RMB a month and 5500 RMB a month. Of course if you are an expat who wants to live in luxury then why not experience renting (or even purchasing) an apartment for approximately 50,000 RMB a month in one of the exclusive apartments near the city centre. In winter, most homes are supplied with a heater that can be purchased in advance, usually about 2000 RMB for a six-month lease.

CBD DISTRICT

This area is known for its upscale shopping, restaurants, and pricey accommodations. Between Chaoyang Beilu and Tonghui River, the district features the China World Trade Towers, the Kerry Centre, and New SOHO. Because of the high density in this area, gridlock can be tough during rush hours, but it is easy to catch a subway, as Lines 1 and 2 meet in the center of the district. An apartment can run upward of 80,000 RMB, or be as low as 8,000 RMB per month if you choose to live near Central Park, the Oriental Rose developments, or Blue Castle (a prime location for expats).

HOUHAI DISTRICT

Traditional-style courtyard housing is one of the prime residential characteristics of this area. Starting at around 6,000 RMB per month, apartments can be in serious need of repair, so take a good look. Because this area was a major destination for expats in the past, souvenir shops and less appealing residents have flocked to the area. It still remains, however, a prime location for eating out and shopping for local goods.

LIDO AREA

As one of the furthest points from the central hub of Beijing, Lido is an area that caters to expats with children and families. There is a very strong sense of community, as local outings and events are arranged, regardless of the fact that it is fairly distant from the typical forms of entertainment in Dongcheng or CBD. Apartments with two bed-rooms can be found for 3,000 RMB per month, while the more elaborate complexes, complete with modern amenities and security, can be upward of 20,000 RMB per month. One of the major downsides to living in the district is that the subway doesn't serve the area, so public transportation options are much more limited.

DONGCHENG DISTRICT

Complete with high-rise flats, mid-level apartments, and even courtyard-style homes, the Dongcheng District is one of the most populated areas of Beijing. The area is becoming popular with foreigners, but still manages to maintain the feel of modern China with street lanterns, outdoor markets, cafés, and restaurants. The subway system is also easily accessible, connecting commuters to two lines and the Beijing Railway station, which is only four stops away.

CHAOYANG DISTRICT

The largest district in Beijing, this portion of the city is primarily filled with high-rises and large apartment complexes. Depending on the location, apartments can run from 2,500 RMB for those nearest to the surrounding night clubs to upward of 30,000 RMB per month in an area called Palm Springs. Residents do not have to travel far to find entertainment, by day or by night. Transportation is also readily available—whether you choose to take Line 10 on the subway, grab a taxi, or use the bus. Overall, this is one of the busiest areas of the city, so if you like being in the center of it all, Chaoyang is for you!

FINANCIAL STREET & THE WEST

This particular corner caters to the world of businessmen/women and tourists— complete with high-end hotels, the Central Conservatory of Music, and several concert halls. It happens to be one of the least trafficked areas of Beijing and does not attract many expats, though residential blocks of housing do exist in some areas. Transportation options are also somewhat scarce, as taxis rarely migrate here and significant walking is required to find the train. Slowly but surely, though, the neighborhood is evolving as more and more local businesses move in.

WUDAOKOU & HAIDAN

With a large population of students, Wudaokou & Haidan has the feel of a college town. As it is also the heart of China's music scene, you are sure to encounter a fair share of punk rockers and metal heads as well. The accommodations are fairly inexpensive, with a fully furnished two-bedroom apartment costing approximately 3,000 RMB. Roomier flats can cost up to 6,000 RMB. As with most college towns, inexpensive bars surround the area, as do shopping options such as Wal-Mart and the mall. It can take up to 45 minutes to get to the center of the city, though.

SHUNYI

If you like tree-lined quiet streets and are nostalgic for the feeling of home, you will find Shunyi a very comfortable place. The cheapest rentals you will find would be in the Beijing Euro Village or Capital Paradise, where prices can be as low as 6,000 RMB per month. There are many areas to shop, and Western food is abundant— complete with bagel shops, pizza joints, and many cafés. Most residents have their own cars, since the only option to the center of Beijing is by bus (and that usually takes about one hour).

ACCOMMODATION IN CHENGDU

Most of the expatriates live in the southern part of the city, in particular the neighborhood of Sichuan University and American Consulate General. This is an area with lots of foreign restaurants and clubs are located. The serviced apartment is a good option for the expatriates in Chengdu. Most of the serviced apartments are located in the downtown area, with relatively low service fee.

Recently, the west part of Chengdu has become more and more popular among expatriates who prefer a tranquil and pleasant living environment as there are quite a few nice parks in the area. Zhonghai Faery Villa, Jinxiu Garden, Eldo Garden, Kailai Dijing Garden and Century Garden are some of the nice residential buildings in the area. Prices for rental accommodation range from anything around 2000RMB per month to over 60,000RMB per month.

ACCOMMODATION IN DALIAN

Dalian has not advanced in terms of bringing decent infrastructure for expats to survive in. Though these conditions are set to change in time. There are two major city centers: Qingni Waqiao and Xi'an Road. Apartments in these areas are a bit more expensive than other parts of the city though they are worth paying for because you can have the creature comforts and live a decent life. After all, you need a nice place to crush onto after a long day at work. Like in most parts of the world, one of the major factors influencing house prices is the age of the house.

Accommodation in Dalian is also slightly cheaper than in other Chinese cities. Older houses can be between 600 RMB and 1,600 RMB a month for one to two bedrooms. The lower priced ones are often unfurnished, in poor condition, with a squat toilet, and no air conditioning or internet access. Though for the internet access you can install this, but the air conditioning can be a problem. Even for the ones costing more, the quality can be very low by Western standards. Some common issues include windows that need taping, unreliable heating systems, mold, ubiquitous cockroaches, a shower without a cubicle and foul smelling drainage (expect this to happen even in some of the most expensive homes—it's just the way it is for the time being).

As a result you may prefer a newer house with more western amenities. Newer studio and single bedroom apartments cost between 1,700 RMB and 2,600 RMB, depending on size and location. Larger or two bedroom houses can cost between 2,500 RMB and 5,500 RMB per month. Luxury apartments can cost as much as 15,000 RMB.

ACCOMMODATION IN GUANGZHOU

Areas where expats reside include Tian He, Shamian, Ersha Dao (Ersha Island), Zhujiang New Town, and in luxury residential areas at Jing Hai Wan (next to the Pearl River). The vast majority of the homes in these areas are meant to be for General Managers, Diplomats and senior business people. Prices can range from 5,000 yuan to over 30,000 yuan a month. In Guangzhou house prices are generally cheaper than the big cities, so therefore even if you rent a home for around 6,000 yuan then the quality would be equal to an upscale accommodation that you may find in Shanghai or Beijing.

Guangzhou, the capital city of Guangdong Province, is one of China's big cities after Beijing and Shanghai.

ACCOMMODATION IN SHANGHAI

In Shanghai there is no specific area where only expats reside. So here are some examples of areas where you may consider to move to:

PUXI

The authentic, old, original Shanghai—it's the heart of culture, charm, and history for this city. It also remains the center of most of the nightlife, food, and activities of the city. Quaintness and elegance stroll hand and hand down tree-lined streets, often meeting up with art, culture, music, dance, athletics, and if you're looking for it, a big social scene. Puxi holds just about everything anybody could be looking for in a city, unless of course you're looking for wide-open spaces. Areas to consider include: The French Concession, Xujiahui, Zhongshan Park area.

PUDONG

Pudong is the new commercial, financial, and residential district in Shanghai. A little over a decade ago, nearly all of it was farmland. Now it's the fastest growing district in the city, and one of the fastest in the world. Completely modern, and therefore lacking in Puxi's charm, it does boast some of the nicest new residences in the city. However the community is still being developed and hasn't attracted the nightlife and social scene of Puxi. That can be a big problem if you're looking for a night out, because you'll most likely have to go to the other side of the river. Its time consuming, the subway stops around 10.30 p.m., and also its expensive (around 70 yuan) by taxi to get back to your home, unless if you have your own driver as part of your expat package.

ACCOMMODATION IN SHENZHEN

Rental accommodations in Shenzhen (as well as in other parts of China) include the good, the bad, and the ugly. The majority of foreigners live in either Shekou or Nanshan (Haiwang Da Sha near HaiYa Bai Hu, or near the Overseas Chinese Town in Shi-Jie-Zhi-Chuang).

The first years of the twenty-first century have seen the establishment of a number of new high class International hotels including Sheraton, The Ritz-Carlton, Grand Hyatt, Double Tree by Hilton, and Kemplinski. Located atop the 100 storey Kingkey 100 tower in the heart of Shenzhen's Caiwuwei financial district, designed by famed architect Sir Terry Farrell, The St Regis Shenzhen claims the top 28 floors of the skyscraper. The hotel became the tallest hotel in Shenzhen when it opened at the end of 2011. The vast majority of the expatriate community live in Shekou towards the southwest of Shenzhen where the oil and gas multinationals are based. Shenzhen also has a "Chinese Overseas Town" with a population of around 250,000 "Overseas" Chinese expats. Most of them are Chinese people with Canadian or American passports, while the rest make up Singaporeans, Taiwanese, Hong Kongers, Macanese and others.

ACCOMMODATION IN SUZHOU

Most of the expat community reside in the Suzhou SIP area, namely the areas around the Jin Ji Lake (Ling Long Area, Times Square, and Tianyu are popular with expats with prices for a 2 bedroom home ranging from 4,000RMB to around 50,000RMB a month). The Crown Plaza hotel next to the Jinji Lake has its own luxurious serviced apartments and suites.

REAL ESTATE BOOM

With the rising demand for luxury apartments by the middle class, China's real estate market is one of the fastest growing in the world (i.e., it's a gold mine for investing in property). These properties are being built on farmland that is either no longer in use or where the farmers are being asked to give up the land by Communist Party–friendly "real estate moguls," in return for a small compensation. Communist Party–friendly developers are investing heavily in building an array of real estate across the country as there is a big demand for luxury apartments from China's middle class. Usually the farmers are paid around the equivalent of $40–$50 per month. With nearly 70 million acres of farmland converted to real estate development and approximately 155 million people unemployed in 2009, the disadvantages of real estate development in China are clear. The farmers themselves have no choice.

Taking a look at this real estate does make one wonder where the future of China's middle class is heading. The majority of the estates are beautifully located in the suburbs of major cities, along with their own man-made lakes, sports fields, supermarkets, schools, and even their own small hospitals. The houses themselves are as impressive as their location, with some of the crème de la crème penthouses offering designer furniture, swimming pools, and gold-trimmed bath tiles. It's the kind of stuff that British footballers would love to have. Prices for some of the high-end market homes start from around $250,000. With increasing competition in the region (Japan, Korea, and India are all experiencing such property booms), it may be considered a good investment for the future.

In actual fact purchasing property in China is easier than renting it simply because you don't have to worry about bothering your landlord with monthly payments or any extra costs that may appear out of the ordinary. It's a very simple procedure and there is not much paperwork involved. All you need to do is to register the property with your local PSB (Public Security Bureau) and pay the money in full or as a mortgage to your Estate Agent.

If you are staying in China for a long period of time, or if you like China, then as an expat it may be tempting for you to buy property in one of the major cities such as Shanghai, Beijing, Shenzhen, and Guangzhou. It could make economic sense to invest in China's boom now rather than later. Though there may have been a buying frenzy among keen investors to take an advantage of the over 50% increase in house prices during the three years ending in 2010, business analysts have warned that despite this increase, China's real estate market is starting to weaken. An indication of this has been witnessed in recent years when developers started to offer discounts to unload their unsold inventory. "The dip in home prices will certainly hurt and may lead to the bursting of the Chinese Real Estate bubble, but it's not likely to spark the same kind of crisis it did in the U.S. in 2007," said James A.C. Sinclair, Senior Director at InterChina Consulting, a consulting firm in Shanghai.

For some cities, the law is that foreigners have to reside in that city for at least a year before they can invest in property in that particular city. But China is a gold mine at the moment so it's probably a good investment. The Beijing 2008 Olympics had an immediate impact on increasing land prices, and attracted quite a lot of investors to the capital city as well as other Chinese cities where the Olympics events were held.

The key to being successful in the property investment business is decide carefully which property to invest in and where exactly within the city. Of course the stakes are high if you are investing near the CBD, the lakeside, major highways, the metro stations, or near major ports—but it's more expensive too. Most financial analysts have commented that it's probably a good idea to invest in property in a prime location such as Chengdu, Zhuhai, Chongqing, and even cities such as Tianjin or Dalian.

If you are unfamiliar with China, then buying property here would be awkward as you are not accustomed to the local practices and laws. It would also be helpful to have Chinese friends who can advise on such issues on the mainland. This can sometimes save you a mint because you are not spending much on getting similar advice from relocation consultants.

TEMPORARY ACCOMMODATIONS— HOTELS IN CHINA

Hotel costs in China vary depending on the quality. In China, hotels are generally much cheaper than Western standards and if booked within China, then even internationally renowned five-star hotels can be reserved at a cheaper price. Beijing, for example, has several classes of hotels (these are just ballpark figures; please don't take them as actual prices):

- Five-star hotels—Expensive, comparable with international standards—anything from 600 yuan upwards.
- Middle-range Western-style hotels—400–600 yuan per night
- Middle-range Chinese hotels—200 yuan–yuan per night
- Inexpensive Chinese hotels (may contain just a simple room with a Chinese style toilet and bathroom)—under 200 yuan per night.

Numerous middle-range Western-style hotels have offered discount rates to those who book in advance through travel agencies on the high street or through the online travel companies (such as www.ctrip.com or www.elong.net). The discounts can be as much as 70% off the original price. Some hotels can give discounts if you show your business card or company ID card as some companies in China have partnerships with hotels. Consult the hotel reception upon checking in for this. The above-mentioned prices are just a rough indication. If you are going to be staying at a hotel such as the Ritz-Carlton or the Park Hyatt, then it would cost you anything around the 1,500–4,000 yuan mark per night.

Inexpensive Chinese style hotels may not include amenities that a foreigner from a westernized country might consider essential, such as English black tea, international television stations, or a Western style bathroom. Most hotels in China offer air conditioning and hot water as basic amenities, irrespective of their standards. It goes without saying that in the international five-star quality hotels (for example: the Ritz-Carlton, Hyatt, Kempinski, Banyan Tree, Jumeirah, and the Peninsula hotels), you can expect the finest world-class quality service and food that is perhaps better than elsewhere in the world because they are new.

There are a number of things you may find different as a foreigner in most of the non-international hotels in China, such as that the toilet may get blocked and that the water supply of the shower is either too hot or too cold and you cannot have anything warm in between! The "blocked toilet" problem is partly because the sewage system in China is not as good as that in developed countries, and partly because that particular hotel does not use world class quality materials. Noise may be a problem in some Chinese hotels because if traveling in groups, then Chinese people like to keep their doors open and talk loudly while playing cards or drinking. It creates a nice party atmosphere for them but in the excitement people tend to forget that some people need to get some sleep, especially after a long flight or a long day!

Other minor but important things such as toothpaste, razor blades, and shaving cream are not quite what you would expect in a developed country. Bring your own if you can. Most hotels provide a clean plastic comb, disposable slippers, and clean bathrobes (only in the Western style hotels!). Sometimes there is a fridge provided in the room but it may be empty (of course don't expect this to happen in the international hotels!).

Other inexpensive housing accommodations may likewise be very different from what most foreigners from developed countries may be accustomed to, and therefore you may not find them suitable to your needs, especially with a new baby or toddler. In the major cities, universities are able to offer accommodations at a cheaper price and they are comfortable, clean and offer all the basic amenities that good Western style hotels offer. For example in Beijing, both of the famous universities (Qinghua and Beijing universities) have rooms for rent to foreigners, and in Guangzhou, Jinan University offers very good quality rooms for under 200 yuan per person. It's always best to consult a Chinese friend about university accommodations as staff members seldom speak English and if your friend is a student he or she might be able to get an extra discount for you.

PERSONAL EXPERIENCE

A Tunisian friend I met in a hotel in Foshan once told me that "All hotels in China are more or less the same!"; "it's not like in Europe or Tunisia where we can distinguish the quality of the hotel by the name or the number of stars." Not quite right, I thought to myself, but I think what he actually meant is that all hotels in China have the basic amenities that any human would expect in any part of the world such as a nice clean room with a working toilet and bathroom.

In amusement, I told him that I have had the "pleasure" of seeing the worst! I was on a business trip in Beijing when my Chinese manager decided that we should save the company some money and stay in a Chinese hotel close to the office. I remember arriving at the hotel on a typical hot and dry summer's day. The first impressions of the hotel (which was in the IT area of Beijing, Shangdi) were that it looked like something out of an American western movie with dust everywhere. Inside it was old, dark, and shabby. To my shock there was a pile of live toads and snails lurking in a large green net in the hotel reception, I assumed waiting to go to the kitchen for supper that evening!

The IFC building (left) hosts the Park Hyatt Shanghai, the highest hotel in mainland China. In 2015 this is to be overtaken by the Jin Jiang hotel in the new Shanghai tower.

After checking in at the reception, it took some time for me to first open the room, and then took the same amount of trouble to lock it once I was inside. The air conditioning was working but it sounded rather like an engine of a Spitfire aircraft about to take off, the water supply was a contrast of either being boiling hot or being freezing cold—so having a nice warm shower was out of the question, the bed sheets were smelly but amazingly still white and clean in appearance, and to top it all up there were mosquitoes to keep me company throughout the night (along with that roaring AC!). Oh and I forgot the nuisance calls I got at about two or three in the morning, which went something on the lines of: *"Hello, You like Chinese girl/massage?"* Taking the cable out of the telephone socket solved that problem!

The following morning my manager told me that someone entered his room twice at night thinking that they were booked into his room; clearly both the hotel management's booking system and his door lock didn't work. We decided to have breakfast in the company canteen instead of the hotel.

Without question we checked out in the morning and went to a four-star Western style hotel that was a short taxi ride away in downtown Beijing. To our surprise the cost of the room in the Western hotel was exactly the same as that of the Chinese hotel from hell in which we stayed the previous night. Hence we didn't really save anything by staying there! Plus there was cable television with CNN and the BBC world service, English tea, a daily dose of the *South China Morning Post* (SCMP) newspaper and English breakfast all included in the price! Let me reassure you that not all hotels in China are like this but I was just unlucky to have witnessed one of the worst.

CHAPTER 4

TRANSPORTATION IN CHINA

ONE ARE THE DAYS WHEN CHINA WAS KNOWN AS THE LAND OF BICY-cles. These days it's all about planes, trains, and automobiles, and there are plenty of all three here. Taxis, planes, and the general traffic on the road are susceptible to jams as soon as there is any sign of rain—so expect delays if it is raining—queues at airports (for passengers and for planes waiting to depart) and at train stations can be very long indeed.

THE PEDESTRIAN IS NOT THE KING OF THE ROAD

Shocking as it may seem to any foreigner, in China the driver does not give way to the pedestrian, but the pedestrian has to give way to the driver first. The car driver here is the king of the road, so be careful when crossing the road as it's very easy to get in trouble. If you are crossing the road the driver will not stop to give way, instead they will just keep on driving slowly towards your direction until they either hit you or you move out of the way!

AIR TRAVEL

As in the global aviation industry, flying domestically in China has steadily become cheaper than before and there is plenty of choice in times and destinations. During off-peak seasons flights can usually be bought at the last minute and for a reasonable price. The cabin crews of airlines in China are professional, friendly, and speak good English. Unlike the "dress down code" that some airlines follow these days, Chinese cabin crew and pilots are immaculately dressed in airline uniform throughout the entire flight, complete with pointy hats, which are reminiscent of the 1960s era, the halcyon days for flying. If anything, Western airline companies can learn a few lessons or two from their Chinese counterparts on providing excellent customer service irrespective of the cabin in which they travel.

Flying in China as a Westerner can be a bit of an amusing affair. While even the smallest of the airports is to some extent clean and modern and the aircraft used by the large number of Chinese airline companies are the best in the industry, the manpower behind the operation of the airports and those magnificent flying machines is not so up to scratch with modern times.

China has too many airlines and too many airports, you will be glad to know that there are plans for further airports to be opened in rural and remote areas, as well as more private airlines, thus making it easier for everyone to fly around China at affordable rates. Tickets are available either at travel agents throughout the country, at airline offices (listed in this book), or at the airport. A slight problem that you may encounter is that in most places airline tickets need to be paid for in cash only, although some travel agents are starting to accept credit cards.

One of the key problems experienced by foreigners includes flights being delayed or cancelled without explanation. As air traffic in China is on the increase, and will continue to be so for the next few decades, the logistic problems associated with this industry also continue to increase. Thankfully, however, gone are the days when hair-raising hard landings with aircraft being "kangaroos'" on the runway were the norm. Better airport infrastructure, more experienced maintenance staff, the latest Western manufactured aircraft, and better trained pilots have contributed to the ongoing success and boom in the Chinese aviation industry. Domestic air travel has increased in the aftermath of events such as the Shanghai Expo and the Asian Games in Guangzhou in 2010; and with air ticket prices falling, flying in China is becoming an affordable luxury for many. This trend was even more apparent in the run-up to the Beijing 2008 Olympics.

One particular incident I experienced occurred at Beijing airport in 2004. I had been in China for only about a month and was traveling back to Guangzhou after a holiday in the capital. A considerable number of foreigners, including Canadians and Americans on vacation in China, were on this flight We were due to catch the second from last flight of the day to Guangzhou and while we were waiting at the boarding gate assigned for this flight, suddenly there was confusion all around. It seemed that the gate number was changed at the last minute. Airport staff were clearly panicking and could not offer any direction as to which gate number we had to go to.

Finally, after about an hour of walking up and down the three different gates that were assigned for our flight, we were, to our shock and anger, informed by the airport PA announcement that the flight had by now been cancelled. No explanation was given for this and no financial compensation offered except that the airline did book the passengers into a hotel for the night. Unlike at Hong Kong airport, where the ground staff are exceedingly efficient in getting planes to meet their departure slots, airports in China have quite a way to go before those standards are matched.

Passengers themselves may also contribute to crashes as in China; some passengers ignore the safety warnings and use their mobile phones while the plane is accelerating down the runway for take-off, while it's in the initial climb, or while cruising at 35,000 ft! One time when I was flying on a business trip from Shenzhen to Beijing with a Chinese colleague, we must have been cruising about one hour into the three-hour short-haul flight when the passenger sitting in the front seat started shouting "Wei!, Wei Ni Hao!" ("Hello!"). As I turned to look, I was shocked to see her yelling on the mobile phone rather than talking to her fellow passengers. I did what any other human being would do and advised the cabin crew. Later I found out that this solution seemed to work temporarily; sometime into the flight, as the plane was about to approach Beijing, she seemed to forget the earlier incident (or maybe ignored it!) and started using the phone again.

Airline food on Chinese airlines is another popular topic that crops up when expats are conversing while waiting in airport lounges because the quality of the food varies a lot from one flight to another even if it's with the same airline and on the same route. If you are flying from, say for example, Beijing to Kunming, which is a 3-hour journey, then on some flights you may just get a simple bun for the whole journey, but on other flights with the same airline, you may get a whole meal. Most of the Chinese airlines offer complimentary food, except for China's first privately owned low-cost airline, Spring Airlines.

In-flight catering standards on Chinese airlines are generally seen to be below-par compared to European or Middle Eastern airline companies. Airline catering companies have in recent times recruited expats who specialize in nothing but airline food to try and improve the standards. In the meantime, anyone fancy dry roasted peanuts that taste like rock salt? Or locally branded (copied) Coca-Cola and other fizzy drinks that I have only seen on domestic flights. Vegetarians have to take caution as it is difficult, if not impossible, to get vegetarian options on domestic flights.

There are very few, if any, in-flight magazines that are printed in English. The in-flight magazines for all the airlines in China are published by the state-owned CAAC (Civil Aviation Authority of China), which operates the state-owned flag carrier, Air China.

As for the in-flight entertainment, Kenny G seems to be doing good business with the Chinese airline companies, as every time a domestic flight lands, the cabin crew play one of his tunes on the PA.

You need to pay airport tax when you depart from any city in China. Departure tax on all domestic flights is 50 yuan at the time of writing (approx. US $6.00) and for international flights it is 90 yuan (approx. US $12.00). You need to pay the airport tax at the booth near check-in.

BICYCLES

Cycles are without a doubt still used vastly in rural areas and smaller cities. In the big cities there are separate lanes for cycles, and, as an example, in the run-up to the Olympics in Beijing, steps were taken to create more separate cyclist lanes, which were much safer and much more efficient for moving the traffic along. The same principles applied for other events in China, such as for the Shanghai Expo 2010.

In any city, town, or tourist destination, you can hire a bike for a day. In places such as Yangshou, Guilin, Xi'an, and Beijing, hiring a bike is not a problem for foreigners and it's a highly recommended mode of transport, since you get to see more than you would just by sitting in a taxi. If you are going to be cycling in the cities, it would be wise to wear a mask to cover your nose and mouth to protect yourself from the ever-growing pollution. These masks are available in Watson's drug stores as well as any sports shop.

Pay-As-You-Go bicycles for rent seen in Suzhou.

To own a bike, registration will need to be completed. Registration is normally done at the time of buying. Most embassies and consulates advise people not to buy second-hand bikes unless the owner has proof of receipt or registration, as otherwise these are likely to have been stolen. Cycles can be bought at any sports shop or foreign market such as Walmart, Metro AG, Tesco, and Carrefour. When buying a cycle in China always make sure that the body structure, brakes, lights, and tires are working properly.

Punctures are common in the suburbs due to the dusty uneven tracks and therefore can also damage the brakes. Cycle repair shops, usually managed by young boys, can repair minor faults such as punctures and broken lights for a small charge while you wait.

BICYCLES FOR HIRE

In some Eastern Chinese cities where public transport is not so efficient, it is becoming increasingly common for people to be able to hire a bike. The local government in cities such as Hangzhou, Guangzhou, Shanghai, Suzhou, and Kunshan has installed "pay as you go" bikes. These bikes are securely parked at designated spots around the city. When customers need to hire a bike, all they must do is swipe a pre-paid card into the machine (cards can be purchased from local government offices, and cost an initial 100-yuan deposit), and then the bike is released. There is a tag on the bike, which means that it is tracked automatically by the central computer system. The price per day of the bike depends on the city in which the bike was hired from. The only challenge for expats is that the language used on the "bike hiring machines" is Chinese. So unless you can read and speak Mandarin, it's probably best to get a local bilingual friend to help you. The bikes are colored differently in all the cities. In Suzhou the bikes are green, in Guangzhou they are orange, while in Hangzhou they are red.

E-BIKES

In China electric bikes (e-bikes) currently come under the same classification as bicycles and hence don't require a driver's license to operate. Previously it was required that users registered their bike in order to be recovered if stolen, although this has recently been abolished. Due to a recent rise in electric-bicycle-related accidents, caused mostly by inexperienced riders who ride on the wrong side of the road, run red lights, don't use headlights at night etc., the Chinese government plans to change the legal status of illegal bicycles so that vehicles with an unladen weight of 20 kg or more and a top speed of 30 km/h (19 mph) or more will require a motorcycle license to operate, while vehicles lighter than 20 kg (44 lb) and slower than 30 km/h can be ridden unlicensed. A good e-bike normally costs around 2,500 yuan and should come with two batteries. The batteries take around 8 hours to charge up, and normally provide enough power to ride for about 10 km non-stop. The maximum speed is around 25 kph before the batteries start to drain. Electric bicycles are very common in China, with an estimated fleet of 155 million e-bikes by early 2012. On that note if you thought that the driving on the roads was chaotic, then the driving by e-bikes is worse because people drive carelessly without any concern for their life. Yes, safety helmets are available but (1) Their quality is not good for any kind of safety standards, and (2) Chinese people tend to wear helmets to keep their head warm in the winter rather than for safety purposes. Thus you don't see many people wearing them in the summer months (except for that non-safety standard plastic helmet that looks more like a frying saucepan!).

Most electric bicycles can be locked using keys supplied by the manufacturer. The key is usually inserted into a switch, which is commonly found on the bicycle's handlebars or on one side of the motor compartment. When switched to the "Off" position, the electrical drive system cannot be turned on. In areas of high risk for bicycle theft, these locking mechanisms are used in conjunction with a coil or U-locks. It's probably best to lock your batteries as well because that's what thieves usually go for instead of the bike itself! Also if you have parked your bike in the wrong place overnight, don't be surprised if it disappears in the morning as it has most likely been taken away by the authorities. Normally there is no charge involved to get it back—just don't park it in the wrong place again! As of late 2009 ten cities also banned or imposed restrictions on electric bicycles on the same grounds as motorcycles. Among these cities are Guangzhou, Shenzhen, Changsha, Foshan, Changzhou, and Dongguang.

China is the world's leading manufacturer of electric bicycles, with 25.3 million units produced in 2011. Production is concentrated in five regions: Tianjin, Zhejiang, Jiangsu, Shandong, and Shanghai. China exported 540,000 e-bikes in 2011.

BUSES

The majority of public transport buses in China are air conditioned, clean, and have a non-smoking policy (except the ones with open windows). However, they normally tend to be overcrowded, hence pickpocketing and groping are common in the big cities. On the whole, petty crime against foreigners on public transport is rare and China is safer than London or New York. Nevertheless like anywhere in the world, just be careful not to put your mobile phone or wallet in your breast pocket or somewhere thieves may find it an easy target. Pickpockets normally operate in groups of three or four people; usually one person steals as the bus comes to a stop, then the rest of the group scatter in different directions to deceive the victim.

COACH TRAVEL

Coaches are clean and air conditioned with televisions that show Chinese movies or songs. Bottled water is provided free of charge on majority of the routes and coaches are equipped with toilets, although ironically, on long journeys these may be out of service. Apart from the normal coach, there is also the sleeper coach, which is slightly pricier than the former. The sleeper coach contains beds aligned in a dormitory style configuration with no privacy and with very little space to move around, making them less than comfortable to say the least. They are used for journeys involving more than seven hours and are normally meant to be operated during the night; however, they can be used for daytime travel if it's a long journey.

There is also the possibility that "unexpected" maintenance stops may be made, hence delaying the journey. For those who detest the smell of cigarettes, it may be delightful to know that smoking is not permitted on any sleeper coach. You will have to bear with passengers snoring loudly, which is common on packed trains, buses, and planes throughout China!

Pedal power is still at large, though these rickshaws are for tourists rather than for normal public transport.

Foreign travelers may find it strange that before every long-distance journey the driver or the coach staff normally takes photos of every passenger; rest assured this is for your own good in case there is a crash, so that they have a record of all passengers aboard. This may, however, give you the uncomfortable feeling that coach operators are well aware that road crashes are common in China! The service on the coach is similar to flying as the coach hostesses are always dressed like 1960s-style air hostesses with pointy hats.

DRIVING YOURSELF

It goes without saying that driving in China is an erratic and nerve-racking experience. It also may seem dangerous to the newcomer. Even though car ownership has soared in recent years, the private car is still very new in China and therefore driving is also a very new concept in China. Despite there being set rules in place it's fair to say that people tend not to think much when driving because they just drive without observing or considering the consequences of an accident. One Chinese friend told me that in China people like to drive the way they want to drive. People always have the thought at the back of their minds that "it will never happen to me."

Therefore don't be surprised to see a person driving a Ferrari at 30 mph in the fast lane on the highway or a car suddenly changing lanes without putting on the indicator. The driving and therefore the traffic in Shenzhen are somewhat better than most other cities in China; however, it is still considered very poor compared to international standards. On average, six people get killed on the roads of Shenzhen every day, as compared to over 200 in the rest of China. In the many years that I have lived in China, almost every day to and from work, I witnessed at least one accident (normally it's a car versus a large vehicle or a small bus).

OBTAINING A DRIVER'S LICENSE IN CHINA

The following is the information obtained from the Shanghai Vehicle Management Bureau. With their kind permission, this has been translated into English. This information gives you an idea of what is involved in the process of obtaining a driver's license in China. On the whole, it's strongly recommended that in case you do decide to embark on getting a driving license in China, the best channel to go through would be the local Shanghai Vehicle Management Bureau in your city.

Foreigners should provide their passport along with the script and copy of their Resident Permit or work visa (Z Type). Individuals are authorized to submit an application for a driver's license if their resident permit is for over one year. You are allowed to apply only for a temporary driver's license if your resident permit or work visa is for over three months but less than one year. As a holder of an international driver's license, you have to go to an authorized "Foreign Language Translation Company" to translate the driver's license into Chinese. This is important because your Chinese driver's license cannot be issued if it is not printed in both Chinese and English.

The following is the procedure in all cases, even if you have an international driving license, then you still need to apply for a Chinese license (International Driver Permits and Overseas Driver's Licenses are not recognized in China). The steps required to obtain a Chinese driver's license:

1.   Normally require two to five color passport-sized photographs with white background.

2.   A completed driver's license application form, available from the local Vehicle Management bureau.

3. Take the driving practical test and supply the medical check certificate issued by the hospital (normally this can also be a copy of the medical certificate that you obtained before applying for a work permit).

4. Need to show your original foreign driver's license and a photocopy. Driver's license in non-Chinese language must have a Chinese translation attached.

5. Finally you need to take the test that checks your communication regulation knowledge—this is a short theory test that is sometimes conducted verbally if the learner cannot read Chinese. Therefore expats would be asked questions verbally by the examiner instead of a proper test.

6. After the submission of all the above-required documents to the driving bureau, a payment of 20 yuan needs to be paid as the commission fee.

7. The test itself!

After the Motor Vehicle Administration accepts the application, the applicant may reserve a time to complete the "Course 1" test. If you are applying to drive a large-sized passenger vehicle, tractor, mid-sized passenger vehicle, a mid- or large-sized freight vehicle, you must also reserve a time to take the 'Course 3" test.

Both Course 1 and Course 3 can be taken on the same day, and in case you fail, you can re-take it once more. If however the applicant fails the exams twice, the test is considered over, and the application procedure can be re-initiated again after a gap of 20 days.

Upon successful completion of the test, normally it takes approximately one week to get your Chinese driver's license.

DRIVING RULES IN CHINA

While it may seem as if people drive blindly all around the country, China does have strict driving rules in place. On February 25, 2011, the Standing Committee of the National People's Congress approved an amendment to the Road Traffic Safety Law aimed at making the country's roads safer. In accordance with the new law, drivers are considered to be intoxicated if they have 80 milligrams of alcohol or more for each 100 milliliters of blood. Those drivers that are caught over this limit will have their licenses revoked for five years. That's a serious wake-up call for anyone thinking that they can get away with drinking and driving while driving their brand new Ferrari down the dusty lanes of Guangzhou and so on! Furthermore anybody who causes a fatality to occur by drinking and driving will be liable to face serious punishment from the Chinese government (as well as a lifetime ban on their license).

SPEED LIMITS AND PENALTIES IN CHINA

- 30 km/h (19 mph) on city roads where there is only one lane per direction, 40 km/h (25 mph) on Chinese National Highways.
- Up to 70 km/h (43 mph) on city roads where there is a major road with central reservation or two yellow lanes or 80 km/h (50 mph) on Chinese National Highways.
- 100 km/h (62 mph) on city expressway roads
- 120 km/h (75 mph) on expressways

There is a tolerance generally around 10 km/h (6 mph), however some expressways may have a tolerance set all the way up to 20 km/h (12 mph); however, anything around 15 km/h (9 mph) to 20 km/h (12 mph) over the stated speed limit is relatively high risk.

A penalty of up to 200 yuan for excess speeds of over 10 km/h (6 mph) but under 50% above the speed limit.

A penalty of up to 2,000 yuan and a possible loss of license for excess speeds over 50% above the speed limit.

FERRY TRAVEL

Taking a boat ride on the river at night-time in a city such as Shanghai or Guangzhou can be a very pleasant and romantic experience. Various types of tickets are available depending on if you want to sit on the upper deck to marvel at the scenery or enjoy a meal, which normally is a Chinese buffet accompanied with free-flowing Chinese tea and drinks.

For long-distance trips such as Guangzhou to Hainan Island or pleasure boat journeys along the Yangtze River, for example, the experience can be quite memorable and nice. Boats are clean, offer plenty of sightseeing opportunities, and usually have an on-board restaurant. As with other modes of transport during the holiday season in China, ferries are usually overbooked and crowded.

METRO AND TRAINS

Unlike the older, nosier, dirtier, and often non–air-conditioned metro system in most developed countries (London Underground and the New York subway are prime examples), China's metro system (called Subway in Beijing) in comparison seems much more advanced in terms of technology, very safe, much cleaner (graffiti-free and free of bad odors), and very comfortable. The metro does have slight drawbacks; with China being the world's most populous country, it is no surprise that trains are likely to be extremely crowded in rush hours. Be on guard against thieves, both on the train and on the platform, especially when it is particularly crowded. Thankfully all metro trains in China are air conditioned—which is a relief, especially in the summer. On-board announcements in both trains and metros are made in Chinese and English.

There are stations where several metro lines meet. Be careful not to confuse the words **interchange** and **transfer**. An **interchange** station is a station where you can change for other lines without having to go through a ticket barrier, and a **transfer** station is one where you have to leave the first line through a ticket barrier and then be charged for another line.

Trains in China are still the preferred mode of travel over long distance for the vast majority of the population, and more so during the national holidays when seats need to be booked well in advance. Bear in mind that trains are subject to delays and/or cancellations due to the severe winter weather, as was the case during the 2008 Chinese New Year season when thousands of people were left stranded at train stations across the country. Most trains in China have glass windows, are air conditioned, and have an on-board restaurant or trolley service for snacks and refreshments. As opposed to air travel, trains in China are exceedingly efficient in getting off the station platform on time. Trains for long-distance journeys are not overcrowded as they used to be (exceptions can still be made for the hard seat compartments!), as only passengers with seat bookings are accommodated on board. There are four types of ticket available for all long-distance journeys in China:

1. Hard Seat

This is the cheapest ticket on offer; however the seat is not comfortable because it's similar to a hard wooden bench with no cushion or headrest, except maybe the window seal. Bear in mind that for many people this is more than enough as people look for the cheaper option and seats are booked well in advance during the holiday season or on weekends. There is also no privacy and compared with Western standards it is dirty and smelly.

2. Hard Bed

This is similar to a hard bench seat except you have room to stretch your legs. There is no bedding provided, although on some routes you can rent bed sheets and pillows for a small charge. There is no privacy as the berths are arranged in a bunk bed configuration with no separate cabins. For long journeys it can cause a headache for those of us who are not used to the Chinese way of living. It can also be very noisy as people start playing cards, conversing loudly, and perhaps even enjoying a drink or two; mix all of that with babies crying, the stench of body odor or people smoking like chimneys and I'll leave the rest to your imagination.

3. Soft Seat
Depending on the train used and the length of the journey, seats may be leather padded or just soft cushions; nevertheless it is considerably much more comfortable than the hard seats, and less noisy.

4. Soft Bed
The soft beds are very comfortable and in quiet cabins, with each cabin having its own separate lockable door and four berths arranged in a bunk bed configuration. Each berth has its own reading light, a comfortable and clean pillow, bed sheet and quilt provided, along with a coat hanger. On some routes a toothbrush, disposable pair of slippers and washing-up soap are also provided. If you have time on your side, then for an overnight trip this may seem a comfortable alternative to air travel. As opposed to air travel there is no need to check in for domestic train journeys, end to end journey time is reduced because the train stations are in the heart of the city, unlike airports, which are located in the suburbs. There is more room to sleep or stretch your legs, it's roughly the same price as a flight on that route, and a nice hot complimentary dinner is provided, which actually tastes better than airline meals!

For business travel it may not be convenient to take a day journey from Guangzhou to Shanghai, for example; however, some people do take sleeper trains for journeys involving less than twelve hours of travel, so they can reach their office in the morning the following day. I once met a German businessman on a sleeper train from Beijing to Shanghai. He told me he found it much more comfortable and convenient to take the sleeper train than to take a two-hour flight between the two cities. His reasons for choosing the sleeper train were understandable too: From Beijing the train leaves at seven in the evening and arrives twelve hours later straight in the heart of Shanghai, with enough time at the destination to get him refreshed before going to his office. There is also the high-speed train between Guangzhou and Shanghai, which takes only four hours, and costs around 550 yuan for an economy class soft seat. The prices are somewhat similar to that of a one-way economy class flight ticket, and you could end up being pleased taking the comfortable train rather than the plane because trains in China are normally on time as opposed to the unpredictability of air travel. Tickets may be purchased on the day of travel; however depending on the time of the year (holiday season etc.), they may not be available at the last minute, so it's best to book a few days in advance.

Passengers on long-distance journeys can purchase a Western breakfast or a Chinese one. From experience, I would recommend eating your breakfast once you arrive at your destination or try the Chinese option, unless your train journey takes you past breakfast time. The Western breakfast is expensive and would most likely contain just two pieces of white bread with a spoonful of fruit jam placed in the middle or a fried egg liberally soaked in cooking oil—not appetizing at all.

With the opening of the 714-mile Qinghai to Lhasa (Tibet) rail link, Chinese train travel has become among the most modern in the world and offers some unique features that have been introduced for the first time in China. These include having cabins that are fitted with oxygen masks (because of the high altitude that the railway line goes through), air conditioning to keep the temperature warm in sub-zero freezing conditions (outside temperature can go as low as −35°C with crosswinds of over 50 mph), signs and announcements in three languages (English, Mandarin, and Tibetan), the train's crew include both Tibetan and Chinese nationals, for the on-board meals there is a choice of Western, Chinese, and selected Tibetan dishes on offer, and the stunning views of the Tibetan plateau provide the perfect icing on the cake for the passengers. The plateau covers approximately 2.3 million square km and is situated on average 4,000 meters above sea level.

PRIVATE JETS—THE FUTURE OF FLYING IN CHINA?

With an increase in the number of China's super-rich businessmen, and as their average age becomes younger, affluent Chinese travelers are becoming more choosy because they want their own private jets to be able to save them the hassle of waiting at airport queues. Of course the beauty of private jet travel is that travelers can go anywhere, any time of the day, and without the hassle of aircraft delays.

Many aviation analysts believe that China is set to become a booming market for private jets in the coming years, especially with the aftermath of the Beijing Olympics, the Guangzhou 2012 Asia Games, and the Shanghai Expo 2010, as well as other important events happening in the context of China's rising economy. China's private jet industry is destined to offer a more efficient, affordable means of traveling in a world that is becoming ever more congested. DeerJet has been one of the companies that has excelled in providing a personalized flying service for customers. The passengers can choose to fly where they want to fly and when they want to fly.

The line between business and luxury travel is not clear because workaholic Chinese travelers, who have grown accustomed to being constantly in contact wherever they are, continue to conduct business even while they are on vacation. I remember one of my former Chinese directors had his phone on "standby mode" 24 hours a day so that colleagues in China could contact him anytime for work-related issues, even when he was on holiday with his family in Europe. Put this into perspective—with the fact that by around 2020, it has been predicted that China will have a staggering five million "super millionaires" with assets of more than $2 million. Given that the private jet business is booming in Europe and the USA, it will undoubtedly boom further in China.

TAXIS IN CHINA

Taxis are metered and available 24/7 throughout the country. There is no need to book in advance or go to a designated taxi stand as all can be hailed on the street. Available taxis have a bright red light displayed on their front panel behind the windscreen.

Most taxi drivers cannot speak English, so it is best to get a friend to write down your destination in Chinese so you can show it to the taxi driver. Most hotel staff would be pleased to assist you on this matter and you can always show the business card of the hotel or your destination address.

Travelers should have small bills (10-, 20- and 50-yuan notes) for travel by taxi. Reports of taxi drivers using counterfeit 50- and 100-yuan notes to make change for large bills are increasingly common. Be sure to get a receipt from the taxi driver. Taxi drivers can refuse to take you if you are drunk and behave disorderly. Generally speaking taxi drivers will not cheat you deliberately. Unlike in some Western countries where you can pay your taxi fare using a credit card, in China you can only pay using cash.

Taking a taxi in China is, on the whole, safer than in most parts of Europe and the USA. Nevertheless there have been some reports in local Chinese media outlets of illegal taxi drivers who either spray passengers with a gas or turn on the air conditioning system that contains a gas to make the passengers fall asleep. This is in order to take the passengers to secluded locations where their partners in crime are waiting for the purpose of mugging. You can rest assured that these are highly rare cases, and it can be said from experience that the vast majority of taxis in China are perhaps the safest in the world. You can be sure that no one will take you in the wrong direction because in the big cities taxis are fitted with a GPS system which can be tracked by the authorities.

If possible inform your friends or hotel staff about where you are going. In any case it is wise to use only licensed taxis, avoid carrying large amounts of cash or walking alone, and exercise due caution in public areas.

CHAPTER 5

EMPLOYMENT AND BUSINESS

JOB HUNTING

If you are sent to China as an expatriate on a contract through your employer in your own country, then you don't need to worry about the material in this chapter as it won't apply to you.

On the other hand if you have just arrived in China and are looking for work then there are a few options you can consider. If you are not looking for a job as a language teacher, then as a foreigner you will find it somewhat difficult to look for corporate employment, but it's not impossible. You have to keep trying hard to find the job or career you are looking for. The following information offers a few tips that may assist you in your job hunting:

LOOKING FOR A JOB AS A TEACHER

There is a great demand for teachers who can provide tuition in English, Russian, Italian, Spanish, Japanese, Portuguese, French, or German. Most educational establishments would be willing to reward you handsomely if you can also teach a scientific or humanities subject in these languages. Teachers are respected in China and there is even a Teachers Day when students present gifts for their teachers and sing songs or read poems. Please note that this chapter does not apply to those who will be teaching in International schools because International schools have different standards that are compatible with "International educational law." This section is only for those foreigners who are thinking of teaching in a Chinese school.

English, being the international language, is in more demand than the other languages mentioned above. There are number of channels you can use to find the job that you want. You can apply directly to local schools, either by paying an ad-hoc visit to meet members of the staff, or by telephoning the school beforehand and asking them for vacancies. Don't be afraid of gate crashing into a school and asking the staff politely if they have any vacancies. Staff members at Chinese schools are generally more than happy to see a foreigner enter their school offering to teach a language. It would of course benefit you to wear a suit or look smart and take any proof of your credentials (certificates and similar documents) with you.

There are various websites on which you can register your resume, and some of these websites (listed below) provide direct links to the colleges and universities in most cities in China. You can also try applying to the list of schools and colleges that are provided in this book. Due to the increasing number of language teachers applying for openings, the minimum requirements to be a qualified language teacher in any school/college or organization include having a TEFL certificate (or a TEFL-C for teaching children), and at least a Bachelor's degree, and being a native speaker of the language. The reason why organizations have become strict about requirements is that in recent years there have been quite a number of individuals, native speakers or not, who don't hold the relevant qualifications to teach language. This has been a nuisance for schools/universities especially when the language involved is English. Because most foreigners can speak English, Chinese schools used to be fooled into thinking that any foreigner who can speak English would be a good teacher. In actual fact this is not true at all and, thankfully, organizations that need teachers are realizing this.

Salaries can range anything from 5,000 yuan per month up to approx. 15,000 yuan a month for those with extensive experience. There may be better offers than these; it just depends on the organization. An Australian expat teacher whom I met in Beijing said that he was offered an all expenses and accommodation paid English teaching job for 9,000 yuan a month. Then there was an American teacher who was offered a similar all expenses paid job, but for only 3,000 yuan per month.

When you are offered a job as a language teacher here are few things you should be on the lookout for:

Read your contract carefully before accepting the offer and don't sign anything until you are fully satisfied with the package. Except for the basic salary, the benefits vary for different schools, with some offering any or all of the following:

1. Furnished accommodation with paid bills

2. Paid telephone for local calls

3. Free Internet

4. Drinking water supplied weekly or monthly

5. Three free meals a day provided

6. Five-day or six-day working week

7. One return flight back home (normally this is given after you have completed your contract).

• Be sure to know how many hours of teaching you would be required to do per week. There have been cases in China where the number of teaching hours is changed without notice after the contract is signed. This has resulted in teachers being asked to do overtime without being paid.

- There was one case where a foreign teacher gave his one-month notice to his employers; however, the university did not pay for his flight (as stipulated in the contract) and did not pay his one-month salary.

- If you are going to be working outside the major cities, be well prepared for additional culture shocks such as possible power cuts, foreign food, dusty air, blocked sewage system, the weather, and of course language problems.

- If you are going to provide private tuition then be sure you confirm the hourly rate for tuition with the establishment or your student before you start teaching. As a rough guide, hourly tuition rates range from 120 yuan to 250 yuan in the mainland (this depends on the teacher's qualification as well as to whom you are providing tuition—whether it's on an individual basis or to corporations). This may change according to the individual agreement between schools or students and their teachers.

- Foreigners teaching in China, particularly at newly established private secondary schools and private English training centers, have often found their employers unable or unwilling to honor contract terms or to assist in obtaining Chinese employment-based visas and other permits required for foreigners to teach lawfully in China.

- Potential teachers should always ask for references from other foreign teachers who have completed a contract teaching term and have returned to their home country.

- Potential teachers should certainly not arrive in China without receipt of the proper "Z" or work visa from the Chinese Embassy in their country. In some cases, it may be that you will arrive in China with a one-month tourist visa and then your school will provide a "Z-Type" work visa for you.

- Potential teachers must not accept any pledge by a school or institute to acquire the proper visa after their arrival. Health insurance that is provided by Chinese employers ought to be supplemented as described above.

- Prospective teachers should always insist that they be given a contract from their employer rather than from an agent or any third party member. These agents or middle men often get a large part of the monthly pay promised to the teacher. This leaves the teachers without significant financial income. These "fees" are at times not disclosed until after the prospective teacher arrives in China. To date, courts and police in many authorities have declined to interfere in these cases on behalf of foreign teachers.

The most popular English tuition organization is English First. They have a myriad of opportunities around many cities in greater China and they are very professional in their approach to signing on English teachers.

ENGLISH CORNERS

When employed as an English teacher you will most probably be asked to attend an English corner. Basically it's an informal open session outside of teaching hours where Chinese students can discuss and ask you, as their English teacher, anything and about any subject. This is designed to improve the students' practical spoken English because they have no other chance to do so. It does test the teacher's patience and professionalism, especially when different sets of students will ask the same questions over and over again. And not surprisingly, most of the time, you are the one who is doing the talking because you have to explain lots of meanings, whereas it should be the other way around.

LOOKING FOR A CORPORATE JOB

The saying goes that if you have a degree, can use the computer, and can speak English, then you can get a job anywhere in the world. In China that is also possible, but it can be a little bit tricky because the corporate language is Mandarin. Even in multinationals the staff members discuss all problems in Mandarin. Most of the documents are also in Chinese and meetings are conducted in Chinese. These days there is a dire need for highly qualified professionals, both local and foreign expats, in multinationals that are setting up base in China. Highly qualified bilingual Chinese-English speaking manpower is difficult to find in China. Most middle managers can command a handsome 30,000-40,000 yuan a month in most multinationals in China. The PowerPoint slides might be in English but the discussion is in Chinese. So therefore it can be a bit of a lonely feeling if you are asked to attend the weekly meeting and you are ignored. It can also cause a few problems if you are an engineer and need to look at technical documents for reference.

While the average salary in China is still around 2,800 yuan per month, the corporate sector has started to see an increase in salaries during the past few years, especially in the major cities.

Depending on experience and qualifications, foreigners in general can demand more than the natives. Taxable income from corporate employment includes salaries, wages, and bonuses. A universal stipend of 900 yuan per month is deductible by the Chinese employers from taxable employment salaries. In areas such as Shanghai, Shenzhen, and maybe even Beijing, the amount is greater because of their monetary presence.

Foreign nationals are entitled to an additional allowance of approximately 3,000 yuan per month, which would bring their total allowable deduction per month to approx. 3900 yuan. Here are a couple of salary examples I know from personal experience, but salary is a negotiable matter between the recruiter and the employee.

Case 1: A foreigner with five years of experience and a master's degree was employed by a foreign investment bank in Guangzhou for approx. 30,000 yuan per month before tax.

Case 2: A foreign graduate engineer with a bachelor's degree was employed by a multinational in Beijing for approx. 7,000 yuan per month before tax.

Apart from the national holidays, especially the Chinese New Year (February), May Day (May 1), and the Mid-Autumn Festival (October ˙), employees of foreign multinationals can enjoy anything up to twelve paid holidays a year, while those working for Chinese companies may get a few days fewer. In the old days of Chairman Mao, people seldom used to take holiday; hence most senior executives have an ethos based on working hard and saving lots of money.

China is increasingly being seen as an attractive market for job seekers.

A few companies, such as Philips, Boeing, and Siemens, for example, encourage their staff to discuss problems in English and organize team exercises in English. However, language is not the only problem reported by most of the foreign staff members with whom I have worked. Some of the challenges and problems experienced by foreign employees working in China:

Normally in China you cannot just go and see your manager or senior member of staff and most certainly you cannot argue over any point with your seniors—irrespective of how professional you are in your approach. The corporate environment is built around a hierarchical structure where seniority comes first. Employees have to do what they are told, without their bosses giving them a chance to ask questions, is shocking for most foreigners. Even in corporate meetings, ideas may be shared among colleagues; however, the final decision has to be made by the Manager or Director. It gives the image that the juniors treat their seniors like father/mother figures, and this is very much true because the Chinese are extremely status conscious in all business matters.

If an employee wants to make a point to his or her manager, then the usual channel of communication is through email. It fits in better with the Chinese style of business negotiating and ethics because if their English is not good enough then it saves them from being embarrassed in front of clients, for example, and it allows them to reflect more on their answer. If you are doing a good job, your managers will not mind you contacting them on their mobile phone, whereas on the other side of the coin, it would be better to go through the secretary or email. Also, Chinese managers usually don't reply to emails. This is again a sign of seniority and it may be the case that you first have to send an email and then follow up that email with verbal communication.

In China the corporate culture is such that the Manager or Director does what he/she thinks is best for their employees. In some companies if the employees don't agree with their senior's advice then they risk being fired on the spot. This is common in Chinese companies, especially state-owned ones. This poses a challenge for foreign employees because if you are manager, your employees will expect you to give them tasks to carry out and they won't use much initiative.

On the other hand your manager will not expect you to ask him or her questions directly about your work; this can also pose problems because you are expected to know how to do your job or else your manager will probably think that you are not qualified enough for the job.

There tends to be certain amount of jealousy amongst the Chinese staff members about a foreign staff member's salary. Staff members will openly say to you "I think you get a higher salary then me!", "What's your salary?"—don't be shocked to hear such questions as in China it is considered normal to build trust between your colleagues. The best way is to use diplomacy and try to change the subject.

There is a certain lack of trust and underestimation of the ability of foreign employees to carry out their duties. Your duties may be changed because your manager may not know what task to give you. You must be aware of the constant reserve (or ridiculous laughter) Chinese display in front of foreigners due to bewilderment at what we might do next. This can be very upsetting, especially when you know what you are doing and how to do it and then someone tends to openly criticize your work to give the image that they are more intelligent than you. Despite any misunderstandings, it is best to present a positive, friendly, and professional image to your peers and your manager and most important not to openly criticize anything or anyone. It is better to keep your integrity and professionalism rather than to let the boat sink.

If Chinese staff members do something wrong, they shouldn't be openly criticized for their mistakes because losing face for the Chinese is a very important thing. Criticizing them won't do any favors for your career. It is best to just go with the flow and focus on your task that is given to you.

If you are working for a Chinese company then you may run the risk that on paper you are employed as an engineer, for example, but in reality they may just use you as a English tutor to assist the department with its advertising or other English documents. This means that you won't be given much exposure or advancement contributing to your career. Definitely you will gain some excellent international experience by working in a Chinese company; however, don't expect to be promoted or given a salary increase every six months to a year, as you would in a multinational corporation.

Flattery is common in all parts of corporate culture in China. Praising your peers in front of other colleagues is a way of keeping trust and negotiation going. It is also common to express reverence to the senior management in front of them.

If you can communicate in Chinese then this is a huge advantage in your favor because then you will most likely be given real work and responsibilities, rather than just be a PR stunt for the company to show that they are international.

In some corporations, especially state-owned traditional Chinese companies, the meetings will start off in a formal manner; however, take care not to be shocked to see people spitting (though this habit is phasing away slowly), or interrupting the speaker by talking loudly on their mobile phones. The worst I have observed is women cutting their fingernails in the middle of corporate meetings!

Business hours are from 8 a.m. till midday and from 2 p.m. until 6 p.m. Some companies, including multinationals, operate a five-day work week; most factories, Chinese corporations, and state-owned companies are open six days a week.

When negotiating in a corporate meeting, a Chinese person may feel that he or she will risk embarrassing both parties by directly offering a negative response. Normally the response from the Chinese side is to remain silent or offer a vague smile.

In the West, it is usual to ask questions of the speaker if someone is unclear about something. In China, however, audience members rarely ask questions of the speaker, even if they don't understand a point. This is because not being able to understand something is a possible loss of face. On the other hand, if the speaker is saying something wrong in his or her presentation, the audience will also remain silent and not criticize or correct in front of others to save the speaker from losing face. In one meeting when this happened (speaker making mistakes), the audience did not question or correct the speaker, but instead just started leaving the meeting.

During meetings, the Chinese can be very argumentative and competitive in their approach to make a point. As a foreigner you may not notice this at once; however, if you are around in the company for a while then you will become familiar with this whenever you attend meetings.

You may find that meetings or a simple talk with your colleague in China may seem to drag on for ages. People actually like this because since childhood, the Chinese are used to listening and observing the other party's views very carefully. Trying to rush the meeting would give the impression that you are not taking your job seriously and it will also seem rude if the speaker talks quickly. In the West people like to wrap things up quickly and not sound boring. For these reasons, in China meetings take some time.

AFTERNOON SIESTA AND EXERCISE

In most Chinese workplaces, including some multinationals, employees (including senior managers and directors) usually take a lunchtime siesta (Xiuxi) either on their chair or under their tables. In some of the traditional Chinese companies, employees are encouraged to buy a mobile mattress and pillow when they join the company. If you are working for a traditional Chinese company, you may even end up having to do group exercise in the morning or after sleeping in the afternoon. This is to boost staff health and morale. The secretary will put on the cassette player and with the vocals "Yi, Er, San, Si… etc. (One, Two, Three, and Four…etc.), and the employees take part in an army style exercise!

NETWORKING (GUANGXI)

Although networking takes place all around the world, in Asia, especially in China, it has a special meaning to it altogether. Networking, or Guangxi, in China is used for everything from finding a job for your friends or relatives to acting as a matchmaker. If you are looking for a job then Guangxi can work greatly in your favor because it is very common for friends to consult each other if they have an open vacancy or if they know someone who is offering a job. It can be much better than sending your resume through a company corporate website where it may not even get more than just a quick glance by HR.

In China, when a foreigner meets another foreigner on the street, or on public transport, it's a great opportunity to network and you never know who you are going to bump into. You may end up meeting people who you would normally not come across in your home country because in your home country you are in a majority, whereas as an expat you are in a minority that have things in common. These people may be company directors, CEOs, or key HR decision makers within corporations. All of this, of course, provided you are a good networker and comfortable with meeting new people. But on the whole, in China, gaining the skill to "guangxi" with new people would come naturally even if you are not a good networker.

BUSINESS FORMALITIES

The Chinese can be exceptionally formal when it comes to corporate events, especially if it involves the participation of foreign clients. Most professionals (including lawyers, corporate executives, investment bankers, and civil servants) wear formal dress to the office. In southern China, where it's hot (and other parts of China where it's hot in the summer), people generally dress down. In some companies, men usually roll up their shirt sleeves and trousers in the summer (especially engineers!).

Whenever two business persons meet for the first time, the formalities are instigated by first shaking hands and then exchanging business cards. Although shaking hands is common with everyone, irrespective of their age or gender, in business terms it is very important to bear in mind that when you are introduced to a colleague or client, you should stand up and shake hands. Even if you are familiar with your Chinese colleagues and even if it is common in your culture to do so, avoid kissing your Chinese colleagues (male or female) anytime during the beginning or conclusion of a meeting or dinner.

Friends or colleagues who know each other quite well will often shake hands firmly and for a little bit longer than in Europe or America. When you give someone your business card, it should be held at the top with two hands, and the person receiving the card also takes it with two hands. It is customary to read the card once someone gives it to you, and maybe even try to repeat their name in Chinese and their position. This will give them a feeling of importance in front of their colleagues and will show that you are giving them your absolute attention. If there are a group of people in the meeting then it is polite to go around the table and meet everyone one by one and not just a few people.

During the meeting people keep the business cards in front of them on the table to remind themselves of who's who, rather than store them away—which again can be seen as impolite. Almost all meetings are held in Chinese, even in multinationals. English may be spoken with foreign clients, although most companies have professional translators present, in case the client's first language is also not English. If you are giving a presentation in English, it would be polite for you to talk slowly, patiently, and clearly, so that those who understand English can follow what you are talking about. It would be an error to shout or talk loudly, and most certainly never show any signs of frustration when talking or explaining to your audience. Even a little sigh may seem rude and will make the Chinese feel embarrassed or uncomfortable.

Maintaining long eye contact with your counterparts is a good sign of business. Constantly looking away from the person you are talking to will give the impression that you are being rude, impolite, and not interested in the business meeting. It can also make your interlocutor lose trust with you. In the West it is different, where too much eye contact can be uncomfortable.

Business cards in China are printed double-sided, one side in English and the other in Chinese. If your colleagues might find it hard to pronounce your name, then you will most likely be given a Chinese name. Normally this is chosen by your colleagues and sometimes you are given a number of Chinese names to choose from, as in my case. It's a good thing because if you are a sales guy constantly in contact with Chinese clients, it saves them the hassle of pronouncing your English name! In return your friends and colleagues may ask you to give them a good English name (see the section on Chinese Names in Chapter 11).

Most professionals keep an album for their business cards, and in time you may end up with quite a number of albums, as I noticed from personal experience! Having a business card collection is very useful for the purposes of guangxi; when you may want to look for a business opportunity or a new job, you can always flick through your album to find any useful contacts that may be of assistance to you.

BUSINESS MEALS

A business lunch is normally taken within the timeframe that is allocated by the company for a lunch break. Business dinners however, tend to take a much longer time because there is no need for anyone to go back to the office. Employees usually sit with their colleagues rather than according to which department they belong to. I do remember, however, a time when one of my colleagues kindly whispered to me that "the Engineers are not so sociable as the Sales & Marketing guys, so they tended to sit separately during formal dinners."

During formal dinners and events senior management start by giving a short speech and then go around carrying out the toasts with every employee. Normally non-managerial employees don't make a speech; however exceptions may be made to welcome new foreign employees to the company. So if you are asked to make a speech then it's best to make it short, offer gratitude to your senior managers, and make a few comments as to how you will contribute to the company's success.

In the West people normally only offer a loud "Cheers!" maybe once during a meal. In China, during a formal meal, the first "Cheers!" is offered by the senior management, and thereafter during the meal follow several toasts, usually starting by everyone banging the table with spoons or holding their glasses together high in the air over the table and loudly shouting "Gambei!" (the Chinese equivalent of saying "Cheers!").

TAXATION OF PERSONAL INCOME IN CHINA

Economic reforms since 1979 have brought China step by step into line with other economies. In December 2001 China finally joined the WTO.

China imposes individual tax on the basis of a person's residence and domicile. In China a person is considered domiciled if they are resident in the country due to personal commitments such as family relationships or because they hold a registered householder with a personal residence record.

Any person who resides abroad for reasons such as education, employment, work assignment, visiting relatives, or touring, and who thereafter must return to China is regarded as being domiciled in China. Expats must be aware that Western style (UK, USA, and European) pension schemes are not available to foreigners working in China.

The extent to which persons who are not domiciled in China are liable to income tax depends on their period of residence in China. After five consecutive years of residence in China, foreign individuals will be subject to individual income tax (IIT) on their global income (income paid from their native country), just as a Chinese domiciliary is liable. Subject to the approval of the tax authorities, however, foreign nationals who have been resident in the PRC for between one and five years are liable to be taxed on their Chinese sourced salary and the non-Chinese income paid by a PRC establishment. (This applies if you want your company to pay your salary in a foreign currency.) Usually this is in USD or euros.

Foreign nationals who have been resident in China for under a year are liable to pay the IIT on their Chinese-source income only. Foreign nationals who are employed in China for less than ninety days during a calendar year are exempt from the IIT if their income is paid by a foreign establishment and not paid by a Chinese company.

The following shows categories of income that are subject to the Chinese IIT; they include:

1. Wages and Salaries—5% to 45%;

2. Income from personal services—20% to 40%;

3. Business income from sole proprietorships, contracting and leasing—5% to 35%;

4. Interest, dividends, royalties, and other income (including capital gains)—20%.

Income is computed separately for each category of income and IIT is levied at the appropriate rate on taxable income of each category after deducting allowable expenses. The tax year is the calendar year, but tax returns must be filed and tax paid monthly.

In China, interest and dividends for investments are taxable with no allowable deductions. The tax rate is 20%. Income from investments in real estate property is taxable, and after deduction of a standard 20% of the gross income, in respect of expenses.

In terms of double tax treaties, China has over 70 solid treaties in force with other countries for the elimination of double taxation on the income, including treaties with the UK and the United States. In terms of keeping your money safe, Hong Kong would be the nearest best place for this. Most expats in China have a monthly stipend (more commonly known as a local allowance), paid for them to use on a daily basis while they are on the mainland (this "stipend allowance" is taxed according to Chinese laws as stated above) and a tax-free salary (paid in £UK, $US or Euros) in an off-shore bank account in Hong Kong or one of the offshore islands (such as Jersey, Isle of Man, Bermuda, Barbados, or the Cayman Islands).

As an expat in China will I be subject to tax on the salary that my company pays to me?
Yes, you will be subject to tax in China on the salary that you receive from your company, regardless of how long you are physically present in China in during the tax year. This is because your salary is considered China "source" income as you have earned it in China.

What are the tax rates in China?
At the time of writing, foreign nationals are able to exempt the first 4,800 yuan per month of their taxable income. The remainder of employment income is taxed at progressive rates ranging from 3% to 45%. Tax is calculated on a monthly basis. The tax rates are below:

Taxable Income (yuan), after exemption of 4,800 yuan	Applicable Tax Rate	Quick Deduction
0—1,500.00	3%	0
1,500.01—4,500.00	10%	105.00
4,500.01—9,000.00	20%	555.00
9,000.01—35,000.00	25%	1,005.00
35,000.01—55,000.00	30%	2,755.00
55,000.01—80,000.00	35%	5,505.00
Above 80,000.00	45%	13,505.00

The formula for calculating monthly tax payable is:
(Monthly income—deductions) x applicable tax rate—quick deduction

As an example, the tax on a monthly salary of 15,000 yuan is 1,665 yuan, calculated as follows: (15,000 yuan—4,800 yuan) x 20%—375 = 1,665 yuan

What is my filing status in China?
Individuals pay tax on a separate basis in China—i.e., there is no "married filing joint" status.

Do I need to file a tax return in China?
All companies (multinationals and Chinese companies) are required to file withholding tax returns monthly, reporting amounts that the Company pays to you, and the amounts of individual income tax (or "IIT") that has been deducted from

those payments. In general for most individuals, this withholding tax is the final tax for that month and there is no need to file an annual tax return in China. However, individuals who earn an annual total (gross) income of over 120,000 yuan are required to file an annual tax return that is due by March 31 after the close of the tax year, with no extensions.

Rules change frequently with respect to the annual tax return; therefore you should confirm each year with your tax advisor whether or not you are required to file a Chinese tax return. If you are required to file a tax return in China, this is your own responsibility to manage and meet.

What if I receive a bonus—how is it taxed in China?
Most likely bonuses that are paid once a year, in recognition of your and your company's performance, are subject to a separate tax calculation from your monthly salary. The tax rate that applies to your bonus might be different from the tax rate that applies to your monthly salary. The tax calculation on the once-a-year bonus is a two-step calculation as follows:

1. Divide the bonus by a maximum of 12 (or the number of months you worked for your company, if less than 12 months) and look up the *applicable tax rate* and *quick deduction* from the table on the previous page

2. Calculate the tax as follows:
Tax = (Annual bonus x *applicable tax rate*)—*quick deduction*

As an example, the tax on an annual bonus of 15,000 yuan is 1,475 yuan, calculated as follows:
15,000 yuan / 12 = 1,250 yuan
Applicable tax rate on 1,250 yuan is: 3% and the quick deduction is: 0 yuan
Tax payable = 15,000 yuan x 3%—0 yuan = 450 yuan

What deductions can I claim in China?
For most individuals, the monthly exemption amount of 4,800 yuan is the only amount that is "deductible." Cash charitable contributions can also be deducted from calculating your monthly taxable income if the donation is made to a qualified PRC charity, and a valid Chinese receipt ("*fa piao*") is submitted within the month the contribution is made.

Unlike some other countries, in China, deductions must be made on a monthly basis. It is not possible to file a year-end tax return to claim a refund of tax due to a higher amount of deductions claimed.

Do I have to pay social insurance taxes in China?
The China Ministry of Human Resources and Social Security (MOHRSS) has recently made the announcement (referred as "Interim Measures" approved by the State Council on 6 September 2011) requiring all foreign individuals working in China to participate in the PRC social security scheme effective from October 15, 2011; the

practical implementation timetable may vary city by city based on the readiness of local social authority, but for those cities officially launching later than October retroactive contributions to the plan may also be required.

Will I be subject to Chinese tax on any income that I earn in China outside of my corporate job?
You will always be subject to PRC tax on other income if that income is considered to be derived from "sources within China." Below are some common types of China source income that may be earned by foreign nationals in China:

- Salary income earned in China
- Interest from a Chinese bank account
- Rental income received from a rental property purchased in China

It is strongly suggested that you contact your own tax advisor if you have questions.

Will I be subject to Chinese tax on other income that I earn outside China?
You will not be subject to tax on income that is derived from sources outside China until *after* you have resided in China for more than five consecutive "full tax years," and if the current year is also a full tax year spent in China. A "full tax year" in China is any year where you do not spend more than 30 consecutive or 90 cumulative days outside China. Days of departure from and arrival into China are counted as separate China days.

For instance, let's assume you arrived in China at the end of 2008. You then lived and worked in China, making only occasional trips outside China that did not exceed 30 consecutive or 90 cumulative days per year. Under this scenario, the first year you would be subject to Chinese tax on your worldwide income is 2014. Before 2014, you are subject to tax on your Chinese-source income only.

If at any point *before* meeting this five-year "clock," there is a year where you are physically outside China for more than 30 consecutive or 90 cumulative days, the "clock" is re-set and a new five-year period starts again the next year.

Who should I contact if I have more questions about Chinese taxes?
You should make arrangements to engage a qualified tax advisor if you have additional questions about your personal taxation in China.

BUSINESS INTERESTS WITH CHINA

With the economy booming, most Western economic pundits believe there is no better time than now to either set up a business in China or directly do business with China while being based in their home country with the assistance of affiliates on location in cities like Shanghai and Beijing.

Setting up in China is by all means not as easy as setting up in Europe, India, or anywhere else where there is a sense of "internationality" in people's thinking and operability on business and cultural terms. Also setting up a new business in China requires a lot of homework and preparation. It's not a simple case of one or two trips and you are in; it has more to do with commitment by your company's senior management to have strategically set inroads into China where an expat or a number of expats from the European or American office need to relocate and live in China on a long-term basis and manage the resources on location rather than remotely from the HQ, which simply won't work. So companies must be able to work out whether they are actually up to this market place. Knowing your company's limitations, strengths, and weaknesses would be of great advantage.

Another good approach is to find local partners because it is inevitable that you will have to work with local partners when the business is up and running, and in China networking, as mentioned before, is, in most cases, more important than a brand image of the company. Chinese society is about building and sustaining trust between people. It is quite different from Western history, which alternatively raises a caste division to control society or relies instantaneously on punishment to enforce conformity.

Global economists have come up with a general prediction that China's future is bound to accommodate an augmented shift of technology and proficiency, a larger inflow of foreign capital, and huge amounts of productivity, both in the manufacturing and financial business sectors. In a nutshell, to do business in China, one needs to have a plan of staying in the country for a long period. Building trust, relationships, and "Guangxi" with local partners are all equally important; as well as finding a location where you can have competition and repeat business (i.e., one of the major cities).

Here is just a guide to what you can expect to be the advantages or disadvantages. This list is by no means intended to make it look as if China is a very difficult place to do business for foreigners, because it's not. The advantages actually outweigh the disadvantages, and it's always the challenges that make the fruits of the labor taste sweet afterwards.

ADVANTAGES OF DOING BUSINESS WITH CHINA

- Reach—world's largest population (1.3 billion people) makes it one of the largest consumer markets in the world. Doing business in China can be quite lucrative.

- Exposure—The majority of Chinese people, especially the younger generation, like to try Western consumer goods such as food, clothes, and so on.

- Opportunity for investment and sales at a large scale.

- New market—There is enormous opportunity for business growth for both Chinese and Western companies.

- Cheap labor costs—at a fraction of what it costs to manufacture the products in the West (total cost of ownership is improved vastly).

- The sheer size of China and its capability to "compete right across the price chain" makes it a much more of a strategic threat than any other competitor in the world, past or present.

- China is no longer a massive cheap sweatshop; instead foreign companies are flocking to China and setting up manufacturing plants and research centers in major cities without the need of having large "sweatshops"—Chinese high tech is on its way.

- WTO membership allows China to stop the granting of zone and industrial based allowances to foreign business ventures. Foreign businesses can make their judgments around cost strategy (such as tax, labor, corporate and employee insurance).

- The Chinese pay close attention to detail, especially when dealing with foreign companies. Presentations and corporate meetings are well prepared in advance and are much well-ordered than in the West.

DISADVANTAGES OF DOING BUSINESS WITH CHINA

- Great time differences with Europe, North and South America, and Australasia.

- Language problems—A major obstacle for many Western companies when they want to open an office in China. Even the newly styled "Chinglish" is difficult to for Westerners to understand!

- Cultural differences—Losing face, giving an impression that everything is ok when it is not. This can lead to challenges such as lack of trust among Chinese colleagues and their counterparts in the business world.

- Laws regarding import/export of goods are strict, and the costs are one of the highest in the world.

- In case of any company legal issues, the legal process can take a long time; even for the smallest of cases it can take months, if not years.

- Western businesses remain worried about having their intellectual property (IP) stolen. The Chinese government is working hard at stamping down on Chinese companies/individuals who are involved in the abuse of IP; however there are always holes left unfound.

- If you are an exporter you may find it difficult to find the right business partner.

- Many Western economies are strong in professions such as financial services in consumer and investment banking, accountancy and engineering; currently very few if any of these markets are open in China. This provides a tough challenge for Western companies.

- Strict guidelines in regards to advertising and marketing of foreign goods on the mainland. Because Chinese companies are not used to dealing with Western markets and vice versa, there can be many misunderstandings in terms of what products are sold and how they are sold. For example one Western company that specializes in offering travel incentives carried out a marketing campaign in China, with offerings such as "When customers purchase a one-year contract deal with [a particular telecom company], they can take advantage of a "two return flights for the price of one with an airline company on any of their destinations." The Chinese telecom company management were very confused as to why the Western company was offering a free flight to its customers because they had never heard of such a thing before. What they did not realize is that the customers are not being offered anything free, but they have to actually buy.

- The increased competition within the mainland can lead to the shut down or closure of smaller enterprises because they simply lose out in the market.

- Be careful when entering into the China market because all the excitement of China being the "world's fastest growing economy" may lead one to think that one could get left behind; however, the truth may be far from that. There are a lot of hidden dangers such as the high cost of setting up the business, the high amount of import/export tax in China, plus all the other problems that are highlighted in this chapter. It's a challenging market but it can be equally rewarding provided you hit the right notes and meet the right people at the right place.

- Contract terms may be changed by the Chinese side even after both parties have signed and agreed on the terms and conditions. It would be in the best interest of both parties to have documents in both Chinese and English.

- Christmas and Easter are treated as normal working days in China, whereas in the other countries (except in SE Asia), the long Chinese national holidays are not accounted for.

- There are no trade unions present in China, thus leading to moderately nonchalant rules and regulations regarding health and safety. Many companies do not have Health and Safety as part of their induction for new employees. It may not be easy to get the business license for foreign firms because of all the bureaucracy and the hideous amounts of paperwork involved (and networking).

With so many books, websites and guides on how individuals can manage themselves when conducting business activities in China, it can be a daunting process for a person interested in doing business with China who is not familiar with the country and its business ethics. It goes without saying that doing business in China is not easy for any foreign company or person irrespective of how long they have lived, worked or had some sort of connection with China. It may be just that little bit smoother if you have a Chinese business partner (person or company); however if you are going to go and try to set up a base for your company all by yourself, then you are, I am sorry to say, going to drown yourself into deep waters. Having been there, and done that myself, here are some tips I would like to share. These, of course, take into account that I have had experience of working for a Chinese company in China, as well as working for a foreign company in China. Two very different corporate cultures operating within an embedded common Chinese environment—it sounds like an experiment at a large scale but in actual fact the beauty of it all is that it does work (IF good corporate advice is followed):

DO BACKGROUND CHECKS: If you are going to employ foreign individuals in your company in China, especially if they are senior executives who would be responsible for making day-to-day decisions, then I would strongly recommend carrying out detailed background checks. This would, of course, apply also to Chinese nationals being employed. There are many companies specializing in these services. You can contact your local Chamber of Commerce or search on the internet.

KNOW THE CORPORATE LAW IN CHINA: Be very careful when treading into issues such as Import and Export Tax Laws. Select a reliable and known law firm that can guide you in the correct way. Corporate laws are different in China. With common sense any company will investigate this first before making their moves. I have come across some expats who believe that because they are foreigners, so they will get some special VIP treatment and can "get away" with some laws (such as import/export tax). Well, this is not true at all; in fact the corporate laws in China are stricter than in most other countries.

PROTECT YOUR IP: In China, you would be amazed at the number of fake and copied goods that are openly available on the consumer and corporate market. Ranging from your "Iron Bru drink" to even manufactured Chicken Eggs, ANYTHING can be produced by those who wrongly believe they can outwit the Chinese law. Unsurprisingly, Intellectual Property is the most sought after advice topic by foreigners thinking of investing in China's booming economy. Sincere advice would be to use the same due diligence you would outside of China.

AVOID ARGUING: It would not be a nice idea if you decide to argue or force your Chinese counterparts to come to agreements with you. Negotiation is not a smooth process in China. If the two sides do not agree, then it's common for Chinese business officials to just go quiet and maybe not even respond to questions at all. Your best approach is to go in the meeting not aiming to make a deal—otherwise you will become frustrated easily. Explain your position in clear, concise words. Be respectful and state your points by the book. Then be prepared to walk off if your conditions are not met.

AVOID REJECTING THE CULTURE: Many foreign business people ask me what are the wrongs and right of business etiquette in China. The most important thing I would say is to respect face. Never quarrel or voice a difference of opinion with anyone—even a member of your own team. Never make the other person wrong. It is common for people to answer the phone or talk among themselves loudly in a meeting. Never say "no" directly, as that is considered impolite and superior. It makes sense to educate individuals on the cross-cultural factors that have a direct impact on your Return on Investment (ROI).

BE ACCURATE: Avoid making assumptions or hoping that YOUR personal judgments will make you stand out among others in meetings or presentations. Logistics and facts are the core ingredients of any successful business in China. Not taking this into account can be very dangerous because if your facts are not validated then you will end up losing your credibility, and your audience will lose trust in you. In the West mistakes are somewhat accepted to a certain extent, but in China a single mistake is enough to kill trust. Once trust is lost, it's very difficult to get it back in China.

AVOID SARCASM: When you are having a business meal or in a break between meetings, then sharing a light joke is perfectly acceptable, provided you don't start talking about anything political or anything which may involve sarcasm. People will not understand Western humor (especially British humor!), and your intended sarcastic joke may be taken as offensive or completely misunderstood. In some circumstances, the consequence of this may lead to the difference between winning and losing a negotiation.

NETWORKING: We all know that globally in the business culture maintaining rapport with like-minded individuals can make the difference between a win-win and a loss situation. In China this networking goes just that extra mile. Networking is a lifestyle in China that extends beyond the boardroom. Making your client feel special and treating them to dinner or any other entertainment, such as, say for example, a day at the Golf Club, even before setting up a formal meeting, would be a very good idea. Concentrate on building the relationship before talking business. Most certainly never undervalue the significance of existing connections.

SENSE & SIMPLICITY: When making presentations to Chinese clients or colleagues, speak slowly, clearly, and concisely. Make your presentations simple and easy to follow, almost like an "Idiot's guide to so and so" but without making the audience feel as if they are idiots. Avoid telling jokes and avoid making the Chinese audience look as if they do not know anything. People may be quiet or may not pay much attention to a presentation, but they do understand and are willing to take part if given the chance.

RESEARCH: Before heading to your new market, do as much detailed research as possible. There is a whole range of advice provided by Chamber of Commerces, Embassies, your country's Trade & Industry organization (UK, USA, etc.), expatriate website blogs as well as sound advice from other corporate professionals who have lived and worked in China.

A crude example may be taken into account, such as, if a person who has lived in, say, Canada, for 25 years and managed his business the Canadian way. Then one day as he comes to open a new branch in China—apart from the normal culture shock in all aspects of life, you can imagine the immediate corporate culture shock he will also experience. Above all else, common sense should prevail and more importantly the above ten tips may be applied anywhere in the world, however, in China they have a special significance because the culture (both outside and inside the corporate world), language, and laws are different.

BUSINESS CONSULTANCIES IN CHINA

Foreign companies that are planning on entering the Chinese market would be strongly recommended to carry out their research thoroughly even before entering China, including getting plenty of advice from their respective Chambers of Commerce (a list of Chambers of Commerce of most countries is provided in Chapter 22), from their embassy, from their country's trade and industry department, and from international management consultancies.

One of the most central concerns faced by Western businesses making strategic decisions in China is of obtaining accurate market information. James A. C. Sinclair, Senior Consultant at Interchina Consulting in Shanghai, comments in his report "Market Information Paradox":

China is an enormous, complex and dynamic market. In the West, the market information structure is such that businesses have often been operating in their markets long enough to have developed a strong understanding of their markets. In contrast, the market information structure in China is relatively weak. Many Western businesses are new to their markets in China, and for almost all the first impression is one of opaqueness rather than transparency. Western businesses can't just turn to their investment bank analysts, as the view from the ivory towers in Shanghai looks quite different from the reality on the ground in say, Sichuan for example.

Western governments are taking China very seriously (the other country being India of course), and so if you have a strong proposal to trade with or invest in China, you will need to know who does what and how to go by the more strategic routes. A deep support mechanism will be provided by your Chamber of

Commerce as well as governments. There are various organizations that specialize in providing professional assistance to individuals or companies who want to move into the China market.

A list of some consultancies that provide assistance to foreign businesses in China is included in this book.

QUALITY OF GOODS

These days almost everything from designer clothes to the latest electronic gadgets that are sold in the USA and Europe is imported from China, and the labels proudly declare "Made in China." The standard of quality of those goods is equally high. However, ironically, goods of the same brand names that are sold domestically in China do not conform to the same international standards of quality as do the goods that are sold internationally. This is because manufacturers can get away selling bad quality products in the domestic market. Nevertheless with increasing competition from foreign companies that are choosing to manufacture goods on the mainland, as well as running a rat race with local "copy cats," Chinese manufacturers are taking steps to polish up the image of bad quality goods on the mainland.

Some Chinese companies are taking further steps to form international corporate partnerships with Western companies in order to give the "good-looking" image to the consumer. Their efforts are duly paying off as this does bring the quality of goods in China up to scratch with global standards.

While you are on the mainland, if you are going to buy your children toys or electronic devices such as an MP4 player, it would be advisable to check if the products conform to ISO9001 quality standards and especially if they have full money back international guarantee, in case you want to return them. It's important to check this because if you buy most electronic goods on the mainland such as laptops or mobile phones, then they are only covered for guarantee in mainland China, not even Hong Kong or Macau. Some goods are covered under international guarantee; it's just a matter of finding the right shop that sells them. In Hong Kong, most electronic goods are cheaper than on the mainland and are covered under a world-wide guarantee.

Some fakes are so good that it is hard to detect if they are real or not. Even though the price of the goods may be reasonably low compared to your home country, there is a fine line between quality and pricing of the products. Poor quality can be a particularly important issue for items such as children's toys and shoes because toys can break easily and are harmful to young children if they swallow small parts or are exposed to lead paint, especially because infants and toddlers are apt to put anything into their mouths.

CHAPTER 6

FINANCE—BANKS AND INSURANCE

THE NATIONAL CURRENCY IS THE RENMINBI (PEOPLE'S MONEY; ABBREVIA-tion is RMB) and is also known as the yuan. It comes in denominations of 5-, 10-, 20-, 50-, and 100-yuan notes, and there are coins in the denominations of 1 yuan and 5 jiao. The Renminbi is broken into 100 fen and 10 fen make up a jiao or mao. When buying goods you can refer to the money as "kwai." So 5 yuan is referred to as "Wu Kwai" ("Wu" stands for five in Mandarin). A full translation of essential Chinese is given towards the end of this book.

In banks, foreigners are given respect and special attention by the staff. If, for example, there is a large queue in a bank, the chances are that a staff member will take you to the VIP counter and deal with your problem promptly. Service is gen-erally fast and efficient. All banks in China have at least one security guard at the entrance and CCTV is in operation 24 hours a day. Even cash machines that have 24-hour access are manned by security personnel 24 hours a day. At the time of this writing, the maximum amount that can be withdrawn from cash machines is 20,000 yuan in one day. If in doubt, please check with your bank.

Every province and major city has a bank named after it (i.e., Bank of Suzhou, Bank of Zhuhai, and so on). Because there are too many Chinese banks in China to list here (that would require another book about banks alone!), I have listed some of the top ones:

CHINESE BANKS

Agricultural Bank of China (state owned)

Global HQ
Jia 23, Fuxing Road
Beijing, China 100036

Telephone: +86 (0)10 6821 6807/ 6842 4439

Fax: 86 (0)10 6829 7160/ 6842 4437

Website: www.abchina.com

Bank of China (the main state-owned bank)

Bank of China Global HQ

1 Fuxingmen Nei Dajie

Beijing 100818, China

Swift: BKCH CN BJ

Tlx: +86 (0)10 22254

Telephone: +86 (0)10 66596688

Fax: +86 (0)10 66593777

Website: www.bank-of-china.com

China Merchants Bank

Global HQ

News Palaza

2 Mid Shen Nan Road

Fu Tian District

Shenzhen, China

Website: http://english.cmbchina.com/

China Merchants Bank is a private bank and is widely cor sidered a bank with a high level of professional service that conforms to international standards.

Construction Bank of China (state owned)

24-hour hotline: 95533

Website: www.ccb.cn

ICBC (State Owned)

Global HQ
55 FuXingMenNei Street
Xicheng District
Beijing, 100032, P.R.C
Nationwide 24-hour Service Hotline： 95588
Email: webmaster@icbc.com.cn
Website: www.icbc.com.cn

Then there are various other banks:

Bank of Beijing (Government)
Headquarters
17 Finance Street
West City District
Beijing, 100032, China
Website: www.bankofbeijing.com.cn

Bank of Communications (Government)

188 Yinchengzhong Road
Shanghai, 200120
Telephone: +86 (0)21 95559
Email: 95559@bankcomm.com
Website: www.bankcomm.com

China Citic Industrial Bank

Block C, FuhuaMass
8 Chaoyangmen Bei Dajie
Dongcheng District
Beijing 100027
Telephone: +86 (0)10 6554 2388
Website: www.ecitic.com

China Minsheng Bank

2 Fu Xin Men Nei Road
West City District
Beijing 100031
Email: service@cmbc.com.cn
Website: www.cmbc.com.cn

Shanghai Pudong Development Bank

Global HQ
12 Zhongshan Dong Yi Road
Shanghai
Telephone: +86 (0)21 6329 6188
Fax: +86 (0)21 632 32036
Website: www.spdb.com.cn

Shenzhen Development Bank

5047 Shenzhen Development Bank Plaza
East Shen Nan Road
Shenzhen, Guangdong
China 518001
Email: netbank@sdb.com.cn
Website: www.sdb.com.cn
Fax: +86 (0)755 8208101

In smaller banks, the service may not be as efficient and the number of offered services may be less than at one of the larger banks. Smaller banks may not be as well represented in the major cities. ICBC is the largest lender on the mainland, and has branches in the USA, Hong Kong, U.K., and Russia.. While foreign banks have been making significant inroads into the booming Chinese economy in recent years and pushing hard for access, Chinese banks on the other hand are excluded from foreign markets. This is simply because of a history of poor risk management and corporate governance.

China's banks are cash-rich and ready to take on the world, just as the Japanese banks were doing half a generation ago. In actual fact the Bank of China is the only one of the nation's state-owned lenders that has any significant offshore presence—and the vast majority of the operations are in neighboring Hong Kong and Macau.

Peoples Bank of China
32 Chengfang Street
Xi Cheng district
Beijing
China 100800
Telephone: +86 (0)10 6619 4114
Email: webbox@pbc.gov.cn
Website: http://www.pbc.gov.cn/english/

FOREIGNERS OPENING BANK ACCOUNTS IN CHINA—REQUIREMENTS

If you are coming to China through your employer in your country, then your employer should be able to assist you in setting up a bank account for your salary and personal income.

If you want to open a normal savings account, then as a general requirement, all that is needed is your passport with a valid residence permit or work permit if you have one.

You can open a credit card account in China only if you are a Chinese national and have property in China. Foreign nationals are not allowed to open a credit card in China but can only open a debit card with one of the major Chinese banks. Further details may be obtained from the www.bankofchina.com. In some respects, banking is extremely convenient in China compared with most other countries. In China you will walk out of the bank with your debit ATM card as soon as you open the account. On the other hand, problems, such as losing your ATM card, can create a hassle.

Most of the banks in China are open seven days a week and are busy with long queues. Sometimes the queues start to form outside the bank even before the bank has opened. Cash machines are available everywhere just like in the West. In China all business matters related to your account must be done at the original branch where you opened the bank account. So it is very important you remember where you opened the bank account in case you need additional services. If you are moving from one city to another in China, then you will have to open a new bank account in that new city, and also transfer all the cash into that new bank account. The transfer costs at the time of writing are around 50 yuan (around US$9). These days, in the big cities, most banks have someone that can communicate in English.

With the rising Chinese economy, a large number of poor migrants are pouring into the major cities (especially Shenzhen) in search of fortune and fame.

If you are without money in China, the best option would be to get in touch with your consulate or embassy. They can advise you on how to transfer money from your country or elsewhere, and they maybe even able to contact friends and relatives if you wish.

What do I do if I lose my bank card or change my account?

a) Inform your bank and start the process to get a new card. Different banks will have different processes. At some, you have to wait 7–15 working days before they will reissue a bank card. That means that you may have to be very frugal for a week or ask for extensions on payments due in order to get by! If you lose your credit or debit card, the bank will FREEZE your account for a minimum of 15 days. As a result of this, your company won't be able to deposit your salary into your account because of this. Additionally, you won't be able to able to withdraw any funds you have in your account or even pay for anything. If you lose your credit or debit card, then you must report it to the bank branch along with your passport (it has to be reported to the branch that issued the card). Which means that if you lose your card in another city or when you are on business or holiday then you are in serious trouble! In a nutshell, please do whatever you can not to lose your card! The bank branch will ask you to return to the bank within 7–15 days and choose a new password. On one side it is good because it prevents fraud, however it does cause a hassle for you for those 15 days.

b) As soon as possible let your company's payroll supervisor and accounting department know so that they can be aware for any payments in process.

c) Once you have your new card, make sure that you provide the account information to your company's payroll supervisor and to accounting to ensure that both your salary and expense payment records are updated accordingly.

d) When you provide your new bank card information, make sure you give your payroll supervisor a copy of both the card itself as well as the account confirmation slip.

Chinese banks only have one field to record your name and foreign names are inconsistently entered:

- Sometimes they are recorded with spaces and sometimes without
- Sometimes Family names are entered first and sometimes last
- When you get a new bank card, sometimes the name on your account will change (when it happened to me they added a space between my first and last name)

Name-Account mis-matches are the most common reason for payment rejections so make sure that you communicate any changes to your company's HR department.

INTERNATIONAL BANKING

While Beijing has many branches of international banks, there has been an increase in the number of Western banks in the other three major cities in China within the past few years. HSBC, DBS, Bank of East Asia, Woori Bank, IBK (Korea), Citibank, and Standard Chartered Bank have branches in all the major cities (Guangzhou, Shenzhen, Suzhou, Beijing, and Shanghai). There are plans to open branches of these banks in some other cities in the next few years as well as having some other Western banks in the major cities. Banks in China operate differently from how banks operate in Western countries. Because banking policies vary, you may receive your salary and reimbursement from your company on different days (irrespective if it's a Chinese or multinational company). If your e-deposits seem slower or encounter difficulties on a regular basis, it would be wise to check with your human resources department or even switch to another bank.

All the above listed banks have cash machines in selected areas in all the major cities mentioned. These cash machines accept international bank cards and there is a charge for their service.

American Express has branches in Beijing, Guangzhou, and Shanghai.

MONEY TRANSFER

SENDING MONEY OVERSEAS

Financial obligations back home often necessitate transferring money from China to your home bank account. Transferring money to a bank account, as opposed to sending money to a receiver through a service like Western Union, can be somewhat time-consuming because the bank staff may not have experience with the process. Here are some useful tips on how I have managed to do this:

You may be required to bring the following documents to the bank: Although banks can help you convert currency and wire it back to your country, the process is somewhat slow and bureaucratic. Under Chinese law, the bank may require a copy of your pay stub to prove payment of taxes and/or your employment contract. It is recommended that you bring the following with you to the bank:

- Employment Contract
- Paystubs
- Personal Salary Tax statements
- Work Permit (Red Booklet)
- Passport (with valid residence permit)

Many expats use services such as Western Union or MoneyGram to send money overseas. You will need to bring your passport to send or receive money. It is unlikely that anyone will speak English at the service counter, so bring a Mandarin speaker with you to ensure a smooth process.

After arriving at the service counter, inform the bank teller that you wish to remit money. The words for this in Chinese are "huì kuǎn"; however there should be someone that speaks some communicative English. Banks in China are normally open 7 days a week, so you can go anytime.

Complete the remittance form with your name, contact information, the amount you wish to transfer in the desired currency, and your signature. The form will also require you to place the name of the recipient and their bank information, which should include bank name, address, and SWIFT code. You may also require the BACS code of the bank account you want to transfer to in your country.

If transferring non-yuan currency, the teller will exchange the funds at the current day's exchange rate. Additional fees from the bank include service and wire fees. Service fees are calculated by either a flat fee (usually 200+ yuan), a percentage of transfer amount (larger amounts have smaller percentages), or are sometimes complimentary if the transaction is within the same city for the same bank. Wire fees are incurred for using the bank's telephone line. Some banks may add a cost of service fee, while others may charge 50 yuan or more. The bank employee will tell you how much to pay, including fees, in order to remit the amount designated on the form.

Once processed, the teller will give you a copy of the remittance form, your passport, and currency exchange receipts. It is essential that you save all these documents for tracking purposes.

It can take up to one week for the funds to reach the bank account. If the transfer is unsuccessful, the bank should notify you via your contact information requesting more information.

Other alternatives are as follows:

WESTERN UNION

The fastest and most efficient method to send money internationally, including to China, is via Western Union. Western Union operates in China in partnership with China Post. The money transfer information is sent through the company's international computer network. The recipient can collect the funds a few minutes after the transaction is complete. Funds can be picked up in person, or delivered by courier to the recipient at the address provided by the sender. At present, only US dollars or Chinese Renminbi can be transferred through this service. At the time of writing, Western Union charges a 0.5% service fee.

Contact Information:

Western Union

1-800-325-6000
www.westernunion.com
www.westernunion.cn/en/

MONEYGRAM

Similar to Western Union, MoneyGram transfers funds electronically through its network of over 50,000 international agents. However, unlike Western Union, which charges a flat fee, MoneyGram's fee is based on the origination and destination cities, amount of money sent, and the desired speed of transaction. MoneyGram has many locations throughout China. Most CITIC Industrial Banks are MoneyGram agents.

Contact Information:
MoneyGram
1-800-MONEYGRAM
(1-800-666-3947)
1-800-926-9400
www.moneygram.com

CURRENCY EXCHANGE

The Bank of China, ICBC, and the China Merchants Bank all have foreign exchange counters. You should not have any difficulty exchanging American Express travelers cheques in the majority of the Western banks or in your hotel. You can use international credit cards throughout China to withdraw money (as long as the Union Pay and Visa sign is visible) from your accounts at home, although foreign transaction fees will usually be added. So plan ahead!

It is best to keep the receipts with you of all your money-changing transactions to make sure you have no problems when you change the currency back to your own country's when you leave China. At the time of writing the maximum amount of hard currency you can take out of China is 20,000 yuan (equivalent to approx. $2500).

Foreigners are believed to be rich so be careful not to be deceived by conmen approaching you with a laptop or the latest mobile phone in the shopping malls! Be careful of being handed counterfeit money (especially 100-yuan and 50-yuan notes), and there seem to be a lot of "on the street" money changers in the black market—this can get you in deep trouble with the Chinese police as it is illegal to exchange dollars for yuan except at banks, hotels, and official exchange offices.

You will generally receive a higher exchange rate if you convert currency in China than in other countries. You need to convert currency as soon as you arrive in China at the airport because you may need money as soon as you arrive at the hotel (most likely you would either be moving into a hotel first and then into your accommodation or if your company has a house for you, then you still may require money for the everyday essentials of life). Most expats will have a driver come to pick them up at the airport to take them to their new home or hotel. If you are checking into a hotel, you may be required to submit a deposit of anything between 500 and 3000 yuan in cash (or credit card in international hotels). These deposits and their recovery upon check-out from the hotel are your sole responsibility. Also it is important to remember that, shortly after your arrival in China, your company will collect your passport to begin processing the work permit.

This process can last anything up to 5 weeks, during which time you will not be able to convert currency without your passport. So take enough cash out because you will also need enough cash to pay your housing deposit. During your first month in China as an expat, you will incur significant out-of-pocket costs. This includes your medical examination (which can cost around 300 yuan), taxi fare, and also as mentioned, your housing rental fee. Other ordinary personal expenses that you can expect in the first 24 hours include the purchase of a cell phone, a telephone number, and food.

Due to the large volume of counterfeit currency in China, unofficial exchanges usually result in travelers losing their money and possibly facing charges of breaking foreign exchange laws. If detained by police under suspicion of committing an economic crime involving currency, an individual may be delayed for weeks or months while police investigate the allegations.

INSURANCE IN CHINA

Many insurance companies in your own countries can provide short-term insurance if you are going for a month or so. However for longer periods as an expat, the following two Chinese companies provide insurance:

Ping An Insurance Company (www.pa18.com) is the famous, largest, and most reliable insurance company in China. The staff at Ping An Insurance are very professional and there is always someone who can speak good English.

China Life Insurance Company Ltd is China's second largest insurance company after Ping An.

Your employer should have insurance provided by your employer automatically; however, if you need insurance for your personal belongs or life insurance for yourself, Ping An Insurance is the best option for you. In China it is no longer compulsory to buy insurance with your mortgage.

The AIA insurance company is internationally renowned and has branches in all of the main cities throughout China.

CHAPTER 7

INTERNATIONAL EDUCATION—
EXPAT CHILDREN IN CHINA

A CHILD'S EDUCATION IS OF MAIN CONCERN TO PARENTS WHEN THEY relocate to China. Unlike in most European countries where parents have a choice of state-run (free education) or private schools, in China you will have to pay for your child's education. With the growing number of expats flocking to China, there has also been an increase in the number of international schools. Some expats have children's education included in their job package, as this can be very expensive. Prices can range anywhere from approximately $10,000 up to $25,000 per annum depending on the school and the age of your child. Scholarships and bursaries are available in some schools, and realistically these are not easy to secure as the competition for places can be demanding.

INTERNATIONAL SCHOOLS

When choosing a school for your child's education, you should be aware of the curriculum available in the various institutions. It may go against your child's interests and future career if, for example, they are introduced to a totally different curriculum from the one they have been used to studying back in their country. The majority of international schools teach the American or British curriculum and the age ranges are from Kindergarten up to International Baccalaureate (or A-Level if a British curriculum–based establishment). Some schools are specialized only for children of a certain nationality, such as French, German, Japanese, and Korean schools. The teaching and the curriculum in these schools is provided in their native language rather than English. The teachers in international schools are highly educated professionals, normally with extensive international teaching experience, and are usually hired from their native countries.

Presently government laws don't allow Chinese nationals to attend international schools in the mainland. The majority of the foreign schools are located in the major cities of Shanghai, Beijing, Guangzhou, and Shenzhen. A comprehensive list of international schools in the major cities is included under the listings in this book. It may be better to send expat children to an international school that really is international, rather than send them to schools that call themselves international but may have a higher proportion of students from one particular background.

Remember that children are just as vulnerable when joining a new environment as you would be when you join your new office environment in China. Children need to feel comfortable and happy in their new school, so that they can start making friends with other children who are in the same situation. Otherwise, if they feel lonely and "left out of the crowd," they may start feeling homesick, which can of course have a devastating effect on their education.

International schools should not be seen as just examination factories that intend to churn out the brightest of expat kids; rather, they are grooming grounds for providing expat children with the same education that they would get back home, which should better prepare them for entrance to British and American universities.

Dulwich College Management (DCM) is one of the leading organizations providing consultation on the establishment of international education in China. Based in Shanghai, DCM has in recent years assisted in the establishment of some of the most famous international schools in China, such as Dulwich College International (for which DCM is the franchise holder). DCM used to be formally known as the GEICC. Richard Barnard, senior consultant at DCM in Shanghai, comments:

By Chinese law the schools can only enroll foreign national children, thus the strength of the schools' enrolment is a reflection of the high number of foreign families who settle in China for work. DCM is therefore in the process of developing education projects that will target Chinese nationals. These include United High Schools (joint ventures between Dulwich and local High Schools) enabling Chinese students to graduate with an internationally recognized high school diploma, and bilingual kindergartens.

Dulwich College Management
901 Aviation Center
1600 Nanjing Xi Lu
Jing'an District
Shanghai 200040 China
Telephone: +86 (0)21 6248 7878
Fax: +86 (0)21 6248 6899
Email: info@dulwich-management.com
德威士教育管理信息咨询（上海）有限公司
中国上海市静安区南京西路1600号上海机场城市航站楼901室，邮编
200040

KINDERGARTENS

Most of the cities where there are expat communities (especially in the cities mentioned in this book) you are bound to come across one or two kindergartens that cater to the kids of international expats. The trainers at these kindergartens are normally a mixture of local and foreign staff. The majority of the international kindergartens are mostly managed by foreigners. Your company or the relocation company should be best able to advise you on which kindergarten to go to for your children. Some international schools, such as Dulwich College, have kindergartens established as well.

EFFECT ON THE CHILDREN

When moving to a new country, the environment can be stressful for you as the parents, and equally stressful for the children. Some children find it exciting to travel abroad and experience a new environment, and will look forward to making friends with other foreign children, while others can be trapped by homesickness and missing their life back in their country. Of course, if you are offered a job in China through your company, then before accepting the contract, it is best to talk it through with your family and research the many options of what may and may not be right.

For the children, it would be exciting for them to know that they will be flying halfway across the world to China and experiencing a new culture and a new environment. They will of course feel proud that they will be gaining a little bit extra advantage over their classmates by going overseas, and that not every child has the chance to study and live overseas. However, once they get to China, they may enjoy being there or they may not. This can depend on many factors such as whether they like the new environment (food and language can be the most important things for children when making these decisions), whether they are following up with their studies or are falling behind their peers from back home, whether they have made many friends in China—local or expatriate—and how long they can manage to live happily in China.

It is worth pointing out that children should be told that once they are in China, they will most probably remain in China for the majority of the year rather than coming back and forth frequently—unless the parents have a large wallet! It all depends on your personal budget or what expat package your company has provided you with. While most packages include just one or two return flights a year, some corporations can provide up to three or four return flights a year back to your country.

I knew one Canadian couple in Shenzhen who had left their jobs in Toronto, sold their house, and moved with their four children to China. For the parents it was a long break that they always had wanted to take from their careers and do something special, while for the children it was more homesickness than anything. I asked them how the children were coping and the father responded hazily:

They [the children] don't seem to be enjoying it. They have not made many friends in the expat community and they find life here very boring because there is not much for them to socialise except the odd day away to a touristy place with the family. The kids didn't like the local food, the weather was too hot for them, and they found it difficult to make friends because of language and cultural problems, and majority of the time they just stayed at home playing computer games. We could not bear to see them suffer like this so we looked at all the various options again.

The children were signed up for daily remote "online" education tutorials from their school in Canada. This made sure that they didn't miss out on the curriculum and it's a much more economical solution than sending them to a local international school. However it proved challenging, and it was obvious that sadly the China trip did not work out for them as they had intended before they left Canada.

LIBRARIES AND BOOK CITIES!

There is no charge to become a member of a public library in China or to borrow books. The majority of the books are in Chinese. There are a handful of English books as well; however, most of these are for learning the language rather than being a novel or any other particular genre. Most libraries have a separate section for international books; however, these books may be considered boring or out of date. The majority of them are about scientific subjects such as Mathematics and Physics.

Most libraries also have an Internet room and the rates at the time of writing are ranging from approximately 3 to 5 yuan per hour. The only problem may be that computers are installed with a Chinese windows operating system.

China is heaven for budding bookworms as people will read just about anything and especially if it is concerned about foreign countries or written by Western authors, all translated into Chinese of course. Another new phenomenon in China is the abundance of "book cities"—buildings which double as bookstores and libraries (as well as English learning centers). There is a "book city" in almost every major city. Most of these books are in Chinese except English tutorials and some movies. These "book cities" are busy, overcrowded, and noisy (not your ideal "quiet" place to read a book).

CHAPTER 8

HEALTH CARE

DOCTORS AND HOSPITALS

The old saying "Health is wealth" is very much true when it comes to looking after yourself anywhere in the world, but even more so in a difficult environment such as China where basic essentials of life such as proper sanitation and clean water may be limited in availability (though things are getting better on the whole). No matter how healthy you think you are, it would still be a good idea to go and see your doctor about two to three weeks before you arrive in China so that if there are any vaccinations or medication (such as for malaria, in case you are visiting the southern state of Hainan Island) that you need to start taking in advance, you can have enough advance notice.

As an expat you should have the contact details of your doctor given to you by your employer. If you happen to fall ill in a hotel, then consult the hotel staff, who would be happy to arrange a doctor to visit you. In China normally patients have to go to the hospital's Accident & Emergency unit. There is normally a small charge for registration upon your arrival at the hospital, and depending on the illness, you may have to pay for the medicine too. Above all else, it is best to make sure that you are covered by adequate medical insurance either before you enter China or get medical insurance as soon as you arrive. Most expats are covered by medical insurance automatically as part of their employment contract before they arrive in China (such as the BUPA Gold scheme). If not, then it's best to ask your employer for advice on this. It's important to have insurance because medical care is not free in China as I realized on one occasion:

In the first few months of my stay in China, I sprained my ankle by falling down a set of stairs on an overhead walkway bridge in Shenzhen. In deep pain and panic, I had no choice but to go to the nearest clinic (it was a small hospital doubling as a doctor's surgery in the Liantang area of Shenzhen). It wasn't clean and not too crowded either. I got to see the doctor, who was able to speak a limited amount of English. I immediately phoned one of my English-speaking Chinese friends, who were very helpful in exchanging translations between the doctor and me. To my amazement, after looking at the injury, the doctor just told me that I'd need an x-ray and left it at that. Then my friend on the phone advised me that the doctor will only carry on further if I paid first. I was lucky to have company medical insurance to claim back the expenses, even though they weren't that much. But this example goes to show the bureaucracy that patients have to deal with in order to get what they require.

Friends and/or neighbors would be more than happy to assist in any way possible in case you fall ill in your home, and it may also be helpful to have a friend who is a doctor. The Chinese doctors are very helpful and professional, and they treat foreigners with great respect. This is especially true if a foreigner falls ill in their country—they feel it's their duty as a host to look after you properly and they will do whatever is possible so that a full recovery is made quickly. Most doctors can speak "technical" conversational English.

If in the unlikely event that you are involved in an accident, get a taxi and inform friends. Ambulances are just used as a fast mode of transport from the scene of the accident to the hospital; they do not carry sophisticated medical equipment, and ambulance personnel generally have little or no medical training. Therefore, it is recommended that injured or seriously ill foreigners take taxis or other immediately available vehicles to the nearest major hospital rather than waiting for ambulances to arrive.

In rural areas, only rudimentary medical facilities are generally available. Medical personnel in rural areas are often poorly trained and have little medical equipment or availability of medications. Rural clinics are frequently reluctant to accept responsibility for treating foreigners, even in emergency situations.

If the injury or illness is serious try to get in touch with your consulate at the first instance so that they can get hold of your next of kin back home or friends in China. Your consulate or embassy should visit you in the hospital, if friends and family are not available.

If you need to be medically repatriated, it can be very expensive, particularly if a medical escort or special equipment is required for the journey.

Hospitals in China are clean and spacious with separate wards for inpatients and outpatients. The queues are not as long as they used to be in the past. The one thing you may find a bit annoying is that there is a certain lack of privacy when you visit the doctor. While you are in a private consultation with a doctor, other patients will come into the room and openly listen to your conversation. This is something that you just have to get used to in China, especially if you are a foreigner—as people are always curious.

I went to a military hospital in Guangzhou once with a Chinese-speaking friend of mine. While the doctor was physically examining me and advising me what to do, there were three other patients who came into the room at the same time and while they were waiting for their turn to be seen, one of them started giving me advice too! This seemed a bit strange to me as there was no privacy and the doctor just told me to relax. It can be an unbelievable situation for first-time visitors.

If you are not accustomed to traditional Chinese medicine, you should be aware that Chinese doctors will tend to give you lots of tablets to take even for the most minor of ailments. For example, I had a slight fever in Guangzhou once, and the doctor prescribed me to take eight tablets a day for one week. Once a friend of mine was prescribed to take six tablets a day for four days for a normal cold. In both cases, the medicine seemed to work; however in my case, I did find it hard to stay awake for almost a couple of days!

As a foreigner wishing to work in China you will be required to have a full-body medical check-up before a visa is issued, including tests for HIV, hepatitis B, and syphilis, and an ECG/ultrasound. You will be issued with a Certificate of Health Examination in paper form and as a booklet. The paper certificate needs to be handed to the PSB when applying for the work permit, while the booklet form should be kept with your passport at all times in case of inspection.

China has one of the world's highest incidences of hepatitis B and HIV, especially in migrant cities such as Shenzhen. Indeed, it was reported by the Shenzhen daily newspaper on World AIDS day in 2009 that there had been a 35% rise in HIV infections within one year. More recently there have been worries about bird flu and SARS.

If you are admitted into a hospital, you will be given a uniform to wear in the ward. Normally these clothes consist of white pajamas with a blue or black striped design. Pharmacies in China are different from those in Europe and the USA. They sell medicines only. Do not expect suntan lotion or deodorant or any toiletries from them. The largest difference may be that you can buy prescription drugs at any dosage on the street.

Beijing United Family Hospital and Clinics ("BJU") is the first and remains the only foreign-invested full service international standard 50-bed hospital operating in Beijing, China. BJU was opened in 1997 by Chindex International, an American company, which in 2002 was awarded the US Secretary of State's Award for Corporate Excellence. BJU offers the full range of specialties including Family Practice, Internal Medicine, Surgery, Obstetrics/Gynaecology, Pediatrics, Dentistry, Psychiatry, and Physiotherapy, in addition to a 24-hour Emergency Room staffed solely by expatriate staff specialists. These physicians are all board qualified (or equivalent) in their respective fields and include specialties such as Anaesthesiology and Intensive Care Medicine. Additionally, staff are fluent not only in English but also in a wide range of languages including French, German, Japanese, Spanish, Swedish, and Finnish. At the time of writing, in Beijing they have six clinics/hospitals, one hospital in Shanghai, one in Tianjin, and one in Guangzhou.

Beijing United Family Hospital (北 京 和 睦 家 医 院)
2 Jiang Tai Lu
Chao Yang District
Beijing 100016

Telephone: +86(10) 5927 7000 (24-hour number)
Fax: +86 (0)10 64333963
Emergency Hotline: **+86(10) 5927-7120**
Website: www.unitedfamilyhospitals.com

Guangzhou United Family Hospital
1F, Annex Building
PICC Building
301 Guangzhou Ave Middle
Guangzhou PRC 510600
Telephone: +86-(0)20 8710 6000
Fax: +86 (0)20 8710 6059
Email: gzptservice@ufh.com.cn
Website: www.unitedfamilyhospitals.com

Shanghai United Family Hospital
1139 Xianxia Lu
Changning District
Shanghai
China 200336
Emergencies: +86 (0)21 2216 3999
Telephone: +86 (0)21 2216 3900
Email: shuptservice@ufh.com.cn
Website: www.unitedfamilyhospitals.com

Tianjin United Family Hospital
No. 22 Tianxiaoyuan
Tanjiang Road
Hexi District
Tianjin, China 300221
Emergencies: +86 (0)22 5856 8555
Telephone: +86(0)22 5856 8500
Email: patient_services_TJU@ufh.com.cn
Website: www.unitedfamilyhospitals.com

Amenities include two operating theaters, international standard five-star LDRP birthing suites, neonatal ICU, a four-bed adult ICU, general inpatient facilities, and standard support services such as digital radiology, ambulance services, pharmacy, laboratory, and a 24-hour on-site blood bank with emergency blood prescreened to the International Blood Bank standard.

Global Doctor, Ltd. has opened clinics staffed by English-speaking doctors within the VIP wards of government-run hospitals in Chengdu, Nanjing, and Beijing. Global Doctor can be reached by telephone from China at +86 (0)10 8456-9191

Also you can check these international clinics in Beijing:
* Bayley & Jackson Medical Center +86(0)10 8562 9998
* Beijing International Medical Center +86(0)10 6465 1561
* Beijing International SOS Clinic +86(0)10 6462 9112
* Beijing Union Hospital +86(0)10 6529 6114

BIRTH

Giving birth in China can be a trouble-free experience for the expat expectant mother, provided the quality of the medical care is excellent. It is absolutely essential that a good hospital is chosen, one where the doctors and midwives can communicate in English and where the quality of the doctors is also on a par with international medical standards. A list of hospitals that cater to foreigners is provided in this book. You can also find more information from your consulate or embassy.

It goes without saying that locally trained Chinese doctors can be as good as doctors in the West, and remember that giving birth in a country where doctors are used to delivering on average fifteen million babies every year should not pose too many problems! China boasts some top-quality hospitals with world-class facilities catering to the middle class, and they charge good money too.

The first few weeks after the birth of a baby can be quite stressful and without a doubt can keep the new parents busy. In China, English-speaking midwives and nannies are available in the big cities; however there are costs associated with this assistance. It may also be quite useful for the new mother to have friends around to assist with minor but important chores such as cooking or cleaning the home. If you are living close to other expats or Chinese who can speak English, then this should be no problem at all as people are nice here and would take the first opportunity to help. Having close relatives, such as the newborn's grandparents, for example, fly over to China may be another option; however, bear in mind that costs will be high especially if they are flying from Europe or the USA.

In China, childbirth can be a surprisingly expensive experience for foreigners, as all medical facilities and post birth care charge fees. Birth registration for foreigners is not compulsory in China. The baby may be eligible for Chinese nationality if one of the parents is a Chinese passport holder. Otherwise the baby will have the same passport as that nationality to which the parents belong. That said, it purely depends on the rules and regulations of different countries because for some countries, the baby is disqualified from acquiring the same passport as their parents (such as the UK, where a child born outside the UK to holders of a UK passport, who were also born outside the UK, might not be eligible for a UK passport, unless one of the parents was born in the UK). Sounds complicated and for further information, the best source is your consulate or embassy.

Your consular birth registration may be able to provide your newborn child with a birth certificate in the same style that is given in your country. Essentially this means that your child can obtain any future duplicate copies of the birth certificate from the General Registrar's office in your country. Again it is best that you speak to your consulate or embassy regarding this.

If your wife is Chinese, then both before and after birth, she may prefer to spend time with her parents in her hometown or village, unless of course, the grandparents are already in the same place as the newborn. This will provide a sense of care and comfort for the new mother and baby while the baby's father may be busy with all the other important household chores that are associated with childbirth. In Chinese culture, a child is considered to already be one year old at the time of birth as age is supposed to be judged from the moment of conception.

DEATH

In the unfortunate event of a death in China, the hospital or the police must contact your consulate or embassy at the first instance, so that your friends and family are informed. The death of a relative or friend is very distressing, particularly if it happens abroad.

Below are local procedures involved:

DEATH IN A HOSPITAL

1. A death certificate should be issued by the hospital stating the cause of death.

2. The Public Registry Office would then need to notarize the death certificate. There would be a charge for this service.

DEATH ELSEWHERE

1. The Public Security Bureau (PSB) needs to be informed of the death and details.

2. Once the PSB staff members have seen the deceased, a death certificate is issued.

3. The Public Registry Office needs to then notarize the death certificate. There would be a charge for this service.

Your embassy or consulate can provide you with a variety of services such as advising on burial costs, local cremation, and transport of the remains and personal property back to your country. A comprehensive list of some major companies that specialize in international relocation is provided in this book (please see Chapter 22).

Should you have to attend a Chinese funeral, white is the color to be worn. Chinese people believe that the body should depart into the next life intact; therefore cremation is not a popular choice—although in recent years with the lack of space in major cities, people are starting to opt for cremation. People also believe that the older the person is at the time of death, especially if they are over the age of 70, then they are considered to have lived a good life, and so not many people would grieve seriously.

TRADITIONAL CHINESE MEDICINE

One Chinese friend courteously advised me that "Chinese medicine works slower and only on a temporary basis as compared to Western medicine, but it still works!" Traditional Chinese medicine is widely accepted in Western countries as well as in every province within China and is recognized by the World Health Organization (WHO). It is based around the concept that in a healthy individual, the significant "internal energies" that flow along the body (known as Qi) try to balance the temperature of your system between the hot and the cold.

Normally the Chinese doctor will first look at your tongue and your pulse rate and then determine whether your body belongs to the "hot" or "cold" set of energies according to the color of your tongue and the speed of your pulse rate. This is similar to the ancient Chinese philosophy of "Yin" (Passive energy) and "Yang" (Active energy), where Yin applies to such things as cold and female and Yang applies to hot and male.

Whereas in the West you would normally take one or two tablets at one time, for the same medical condition, in China you would most likely end up taking maybe five or six tablets perhaps three times a day. Therefore don't be put off by Chinese doctors giving you lots of small packets of herbal medicine to mix with warm water and drink with your meals or to mix with your hot meal. Herbal medicine contains lots of vital ingredients, some of which may be derived from exotic plants, organs of animals, or standard household ingredients found in Western countries such as nutmeg, black salt, black pepper, and other spices. The filling of a traditional Chinese prescription ordered by a Chinese doctor is a fascinating process to observe. The pharmacist selects a few particular ingredients from the hundreds on his shelf. It may sound like a tedious task having to prepare the medicine every time you take it, but it can have a good effect. Most taste like bitter tea.

Be sure to ask the doctor if the herbal medicine has any side effects, as Chinese bodies handle herbal medicine differently than Western bodies. Normally Chinese doctors will shrug off any problems and give it to you anyway. For example I once tried using herbal medicine as an alternative to paracetamol (acetaminophen) for a headache I had. It took the headache away within a few hours; however I also had to get by with a lot of unwanted deep sleep for a couple of days!

A traditional Chinese pharmacy has a unique smell made up of thousands of scents emanating from jars and cabinets stocked full of dried plants, seeds, animal parts, and minerals. Among them are the well-known ginseng roots, dried or immersed in alcohol and often looking like a human figure.

Tongrentang Pharmacy (同仁堂), in an old part of Beijing south of Tiananmen Square, has been in business for over 300 years. Founded in 1669, this pharmacy was once a royal dispensary during the Qing Dynasty and still produces all the capsules and secret mixtures once used by royalty. The enormous size of this pharmacy is overwhelming, as is the selection of remedies that contain among others: small and large eggs, snakes coiled in spirals, dried monkeys, toads, tortoises, centipedes, grasshoppers, small fish, stag antlers, rhinoceros horns, and testicles of various animals. And then there are the thousand kinds of dried and preserved herbs, blossoms, roots, berries, and fruits.

While in China, although you may be cautious about using Chinese medicine, it does boil down to personal choice. You can have peace of mind that there is no harm in trying it as Chinese medicine will not make your illness worse; however, it is highly likely that either it will take longer to have any significant effect or it will make no change to your current situation.

In drug stores and pharmacies you can purchase a range of traditional Chinese medicines that are readily prepared for various needs, such as if you have a muscular pain then "hot patches" are available. These "hot patches" are made up of a sticky plaster smeared with traditional Chinese medicine that you can apply to the affected area.

ACUPUNCTURE

Having needles stuck into your body may not be your cup of tea; however, it does work effectively for some conditions such as back or muscular pain. Using the principles of Qi along with the body's energy channels of Yin and Yang, needles are inserted into the body's acupuncture points that lie on these energy channels. It is a proven method of treatment and has been for the past 2500 years in China. The risks of getting any disease such as HIV are negligible as the majority of medical centers use disposable and sterile needles. Costs vary depending on the clinic you go to.

Some Chinese people prefer to be treated using the traditional method of **Moxibustion** for treating minor ailments such as a fever or back pain. Normally this procedure requires the dropping of burning Moxa (made from wormwood) onto the required points of the body.

There are various other methods including using **Suction Cups.** These are glass cups that are heated using a burning piece of alcohol-soaked cotton and then placed over the required point on the body. As unpleasant as it may seem to the observer, these suction cups cause the skin to be "sucked out" and leave a temporary mark on the body. Usually if you happen to see someone with circular marks the size of a small glass cup on their forehead, then most likely they have had the treatment for a fever or headache.

"MIRACLE CURES" FOR ILLNESSES

Some foreigners come to China to get affordable surgical treatment or even a "cure" for illnesses that would otherwise be untreatable, let alone curable, in the West. Some hospitals and private practitioners in China advertise internationally to promote experimental medical procedures to treat diseases such as Alzheimer's, epilepsy, Down syndrome, AIDS, and others. Other practitioners advertise that "new procedures" are available to extend life expectancy or to make people taller using traditional Chinese medicine, and to provide other cosmetic procedures.

These advertisements state that these procedures are safe, cheap, and effective. Formal complaints have been reported to the British and American embassies from foreigners with regard to many of these experimental practices. The embassies and consulates are aware of fatalities and permanent disfigurements that have sadly followed some of these treatments. Foreigners are advised not to enter China for treatment of advanced diseases without first consulting their physician in their own country. Others are prepared to take the chance, because to them, this could be the only hope that their illness may be treatable if not curable.

"MOBILE DOCTORS" AND PHARMACIES

In both rural and urban areas, doctors sometimes set up mobile surgeries to carry out diagnostic procedures—all free of charge. Diagnostics may include blood tests, eye tests, investigation of hair loss problems, and other minor, treatable problems that can be detected without the need for the patient to go to a major hospital. These mobile doctors (or "street doctor" as they are commonly known) are highly unlikely to be real doctors but could be medical students or nurses who are taking an opportunity to practice their trade. If you have a minor ailment such as a cold or fever then it's no harm to go to your nearest pharmacy and get the required treatment but if it's something more serious, your best bet is to pop into the nearest hospital.

There is an ongoing problem with fake medicines and out-of-date medicines being sold in some pharmacies, something that the government is trying to clamp down on, but without much luck. You will also find in China that just about any medicine is available over the counter without prescription from the doctor (except some rare traditional Chinese medicines).

OPTICIANS

Prescription glasses are available widely in major opticians. On-the-spot free eye tests can be performed by the optician; normally it's best to take a Chinese-speaking friend with you as only a limited number of opticians can speak English. Again it may be a case of trial and error to see which ones are the best. Providing a list of opticians would prove difficult as there are too many around, although you should be careful which opticians you choose. Usually the ones where the staff members are wearing uniforms are recommended by the locals because they are more professional and have better qualified staff available to help you.

If you are a contact lens wearer then you need not worry about poor quality materials. Both Bausch & Lomb– and Johnson & Johnson–manufactured contact lenses are widely available throughout the big cities. Nevertheless you should be cautious, as with everything else in China, about fakes in the smaller stores on the high street.

BEAUTY SALONS

With rising salaries and a much more stressful work life, there has been a huge demand for beauty salons that cater to young professiona Chinese women. Chinese women go to beauty salons to relieve the stress of the day or just to relax and chat with their friends and colleagues while being pampered. Normally staffed by young women dressed in 1930s-style pink nurses' uniforms, offering facial beauty treatment as well as body, foot, and head massage for women only, these salons are becoming ever more popular with the middle-aged Chinese women too. Some salons offer a hair wash, perm, cut and style as well.

As a foreign woman, you would be most welcome to try out the beauty treatments on offer—just take a Chinese lady friend with you as the staff is unlikely to speak English. The costs are much cheaper than in Europe and the States, and the hospitality is excellent.

Genetically the vast majority of Chinese men are not known for going bald; nevertheless due to work-related stress or other causes, there has been a huge demand in the mainland for hair salons. These salons (known as ZhangGuang 101 Hair Salon, www.101.com) specialize in herbal treatment of hair loss for both men and women and offer a variety of treatments to suit your health needs. Again if you want to try, it's best to take a Chinese-speaking friend with you. There is a 101 Hair Salon in almost every major city in China.

Companies that specialize in beauty and healthcare products, such as Amway and Pharmanex, have started business in China with promising results that have attracted the country's middle class, who appreciate these luxuries.

SMOKING AND DRINKING

China is the world's leading consumer and producer of tobacco products. The tobacco market is dominated by the China National Tobacco Corporation (CNTC), which is a government monopoly.

According to a report by the World Health Organization (WHO), about 60% of men and 3% of women smoke. The Chinese government has reported there are about 350 million Chinese smokers. In restaurants and at formal meals, it is common for people to be offered a cigarette along with traditional Chinese tea— and smoking is considered a kind of status symbol amongst the wealthiest in China. When I took a domestic flight from Beijing to Guangzhou, I was surprised to see that both of the pilots started smoking in the cockpit when the plane landed at Guangzhou (with the window open)!

If you happen to be in a smoke-filled restaurant, then you cannot do much except perhaps change your seat as far away as you can or change your restaurant as it is very hard to escape from other people's cigarettes in public places.

The majority of Chinese people don't seem to be worried about the health risks associated with smoking. Tobacco kills 1.2 million Chinese each year. In the mid-1990s, tobacco use cost the Government US$6.5 billion annually in health-care costs alone. Approximately 130,000 deaths from passive smoking occur annually according to a recent survey from the Ministry of Health in China.

Alcohol is an important part of formal meals, and wine is always offered to guests. In larger restaurants, normally there will be two or three glasses on the table, one for the beer (Tsingtao Beer, named after a town in northern China, is the most common brand in China), one for wine (Great Wall wine is one of the most popular red wines available, but be careful as some Chinese wines are strong, especially the one that looks like water but is almost 70% proof!), and another glass for a toasting liqueur such as Mao-tai, again this is approx. 70% proof. Mao-tai is normally provided in a small glass.

According to Euromonitordata, China has become the world's largest beer market by volume, overtaking the USA in 2002. With a desire for Western style beers, Chinese consumers are gradually shifting from drinking spirits to beer.

Carlsberg, Heineken, and Guinness "Stout" beer cans are wicely available at local prices in convenience stores and supermarkets around the country. Plus there is increased domestic competition from Chinese brewers such as Tsingtao, Kingway beer of Shenzhen, and Snow beer of Beijing.

CHAPTER 9

FOOD

W HILE I WAS SHOPPING WITH AN EXPAT FRIEND IN GUANGZHOU ONE day, he told me, "There is more variety in China and the food is fresh, rather than being frozen as is in Europe or the States." Judging from what is available in supermarkets, his statement is correct. It is only in recent years that some ready-made meals have become available in the supermarkets (such as ready-to-steam dumplings) because, as a culture, the Chinese like to have their food freshly cooked rather than frozen. Although in most Asian countries the perception is that Westerners prefer to have their food frozen rather than freshly cooked, it shouldn't really be seen as a preference, as it may well just be that the British/American people are more accustomed to "convenience" food. With the ever increasing number of Western supermarkets such as Walmart (American), Olé (French), Tesco (British), Mykel (German), Metro (German), Park n Shop (Hong Kong/ USA), Carrefour (French), and Jusco (Japanese) as well as the numerous Western food restaurants, there is certainly much more choice available for the expat than in the past. The British supermarket Tesco, which has about 110 stores in China, opened its first outlet on the mainland in 2007 but it's very much localized, and nothing like the Tesco in the UK.

Don't be surprised to see live chickens, game, fish, crabs, and tortoise in super-markets or in your local outdoor market, as they are killed only a short time before being cooked. In the supermarkets you will find a wide variety of meat available such as pig's feet, ears, face, and hands; chicken feet; duck's head and eggs. The Chinese love pork and chicken eggs and it's no surprise to find one of these two products in most dishes. Outside the major cities, the menus in most restaurants are printed in Chinese only, so if you are trekking on an adventure and become hungry, it would be advisable to keep a small dictionary with you at all times.

Red bean (Hong Dou) and green bean (Lu Dou) are widely used in desserts such as ice creams and fruit drinks because they are healthy. Fresh mixed fruit juice is also widely available, either sold by roadside hawkers or in shopping malls. Rice is the staple food, usually plain boiled.

Exotic food galore! Deep fried hairy crabs decorated in lemon sauce.

If you are not too adventurous with your meats, then the best way to stay healthy is to stick to eating plenty of fresh fruit, vegetables, and fish. In China, freshly cooked and uncooked seafood is available in abundance and there are restaurants that are dedicated to just serving seafood.

There are numerous amounts of dried fruits and pickles, usually packed in tight plastic bags. Unfortunately there are also a lot of fake-branded goods available openly in supermarkets and convenience stores; these include everything from copied "Red Bull" energy drinks to copied "Great Wall" wine—these goods are copied so well that it is very easy to confuse them with the genuine products as everything about the products, including the packaging and the taste, is the exact copy of the genuine article.

In 2006, there were a number of reported cases on state TV of shoddy and unsafe goods such as toothpaste mixed with industrial chemicals and eggs tainted with dangerous dyes. There was one case where a man in Guangzhou was "manufacturing" eggs in his home that looked and tasted like real chicken eggs.

The government is taking stiff measures to improve nutritional safety and China's dismal food safety record. The Health Ministry openly reported in 2005 that there were more than 34,000 food-related illnesses and in 2006 a state-owned journal reported that a survey by the quality inspection administration found almost one-third of China's 450,000 food production companies had no licenses. However on the whole, it is very safe to eat restaurant food in China. Just like anywhere else in the world, common sense should prevail when eating from places that you do not know about; and of course if you stick to the old rule of "Do as the locals do," then you should be just fine.

BREAKFAST—CHINESE AND WESTERN

A bowl of warm congee (Zhou, a rice porridge) is a favorite among the masses. It's great because you can mix it with anything. Some people like to mix congee with instant noodles and pickles, while some like to mix it with powdered milk and cereal packets to make it into a sweet porridge. Soy milk with simple bread or a steamed bun is another favorite. Then there are other treats such as a steamed bun with a sweetened egg yolk inside (Lai Huang Bao) or fried bread sticks (You Tiao).

If you are feeling homesick there are a variety of cakes (Dan Gao), bread (Mian Bao), and preserved milk available in supermarkets and convenience stores. Nestle 250ml carton milk and powdered milk (550ml packets) are widely available.

Green tea comes in all different tastes and brands. Outside the major cities, black tea and coffee are still quite a rare luxury. Lipton "yellow label" black tea is available, both ready made with milk and sugar (just add hot water) or in tea bags. Recently, imported cereal packets, oats, Earl Grey tea, and McVities Digestives, HobNobs and Rich Tea have started to become available in Western supermarkets such as Carrefour, Walmart and Olé.

Dim sum (Dian Xin in Mandarin) is eaten all over China; however, it is still the favorite in Guangdong (Cantonese) province, where Chinese tea is served with hot and steamed dumplings (Jiao Zi) filled with either vegetables or pork meat.

CHINESE CUISINES

Westerners will be shocked to find that the Chinese food in China tastes nothing like what is available in Europe or the States, and that's because the Chinese food outside China is catered for the tastes of the Western mouth. Obviously, chicken chow mein and prawn crackers are not staples in China! If you have not already got used to it, then the art of eating with your chopsticks will be a new experience for you—don't be embarrassed to make a fool of yourself in a restaurant. Even for Chinese people it is tricky enough when they start using the chopsticks for the first time in their childhood. When I used chopsticks for the first time, I had a competition with my friend to see who could eat the greatest number of peanuts quickly—it was a good way to practice and master the skills!

An essential part of any Chinese diet is ginger and garlic because they are cheap, available in abundance, and act as a natural cure for minor ailments such as headaches. Some Chinese believe that if you are experiencing nausea, the best treatment is to mix Coca Cola with a little bit of ginger or salt.

Unlike in the West, the experience of going to a restaurant in China can be a bit of a noisy affair and very busy indeed—with waitresses dressed in brightly red colored Qipao standing at the entrance to greet guests. Foreigners will notice that despite most of Chinese food being healthy, some regional dishes can also be very salty, oily, or sugary (sugar-coated tomatoes are a prime example). So considering this statement, amazingly, the vast majority of Chinese people are slim and appear healthy compared to Westerners. One of the many reasons for this may be that Chinese people naturally have a better metabolism than non-Chinese (although there is no scientific proof of this and don't take my word for it!), and the other reason may be that the people tend to eat small amounts of everything that's on the table, rather than eating large bowls of one dish.

CANTONESE FOOD

Considering the content available on most of the menus in restaurants in Guangdong province, Cantonese food may be classed as the most varied in the whole of China. There is a saying that the Cantonese "will eat anything with wings, except a plane, and anything with four legs, except a table." If you venture around restaurants in the major cities such as Guangzhou, Shenzhen, Zhuhai, or Zhongshan, you will observe that this statement is very much true. In outdoor markets, buying fresh meat is defined in an entirely different way, as you will find all kinds of game, snakes, rats, snails, insects, and seafood, all waiting to be sold while still alive. In one market in Guangzhou, I was shocked to observe a woman sitting on the pavement on a busy crowded street, killing and then scooping the insides of frogs right in front of impatient customers.

In a restaurant, the most shocking sight I have come across is people eating a very expensive dish called "Buffalo's Penis" accompanied by drinking snake wine, which is served in some of the high-class restaurants. The chef brings in a glass of wine (usually Great Wall wine) in one hand and a live snake in the other hand. Then within seconds the chef severs the snake's head to pour the blood from the body into the wine glass. Utterly distressing for the faint-hearted observer and not recommended if you want to sleep peacefully without having nightmares.

Some other famous Cantonese dishes include cactus cat meat, chilled monkey brain, casserole mountain turtle, and hot pot dog. Unlike in Europe and the USA, where hot dog usually refers to pork meat, in China, a hot dog is actual cooked dog meat and is usually served in the winter months, as dog meat is known to provide a warm feeling. Then there is also pig's blood, which looks like thick brown jelly and is eaten as a delicacy in Guangdong province. Many foods are believed to have medicinal properties, such as black chicken soup with coconut being good for heartburn.

STREET FOOD

The various kinds of street foods include kebabs of lamb, chicken and beef meat (usually provided by Xinjiang Muslim people), "stinky" black bean curd, and a variety of other barbecued meats. In some parts of Jiangsu, Xinjiang, and Hebei provinces I have come across unusual types of meats including donkey meat, shredded snake, and even goats' eye balls. Many people have commented that the street food in Xian is perhaps the best they have come across in China, although it has to be said that the smell and the smoke generated from some of this food can make one feel uncomfortable.

SICHUAN FOOD

Sichuan province is famous for a number of things, including the giant panda and some of the most beautiful scenery throughout China. But all of them are incomparable to the exquisite cuisine of this province because Sichuan is known throughout China for producing spicy food. Sichuan cooking relies on the heavy usage of chilies and spices in dishes, so those of you who are not used to hot food should take precautions.

There are also other regional cuisines such as Shangdong food (a high concentration of seafood), Shanghai cuisine (sweet and sour), and flavors from northern China, including Inner Mongolia.

Street food is very popular in all parts of China.

MUSLIM FOOD

Throughout the country you will find Muslim restaurants that are owned and operated by the Chinese Muslims, namely the Hui and Uighur people, from the Xinjiang province. They are famous for making delicious halal food such as lamb koftas, lamb and vegetable kebabs, thick noodles (known as "La Mian"—that means pulled noodles), Peshwari naan breads and Ma-Dang, which is a very sweet sticky toffee-like dessert that is sold by peddlers. It contains a mixture of exotic fruits and nuts. Naturally, you won't find any pork dishes in a Muslim restaurant.

VEGETARIAN FOOD

Vegetables are available in abundance everywhere and have been popular for over 2,500 years in Chinese cuisine; however, because China is a nation that loves eating meat products, if you are strict vegetarian, you will find it a bit of a challenge as most dishes contain meat, usually pork, in some form or other (except of course if you go to a Muslim restaurant).

Normally during formal meals, it is considered a status symbol to offer the guest meat dishes rather than "simple and cheaper" vegetable ones. Vegans would be disappointed to know that even McDonald's in China does not offer a veggie burger. Nevertheless there are many other options available such as "Subway sandwiches." "Mian Dian Wang" is another Chinese fast food outlet that offers vegetarian options including various noodles and dumplings.

You can politely mention "Wo bu yao rou" or "Wo bu che rou" (both mean "I don't eat meat") to the waitress in the restaurant, and she would be more than glad to show you the myriad vegetable options including lotus root, boiled cabbage leaves, and shredded carrots ("Bai/Hong lobo"—white/red carrot). Bean curd (Tofu) is made from soy beans and is widely served in restaurants. It's delicious eaten either with rice and pickles, or just plain with any other dish.

INTERNATIONAL CUISINE

In the major cities, there is plenty of choice for international cuisine that includes Japanese, Korean, Indian, Italian, French, Mexican, and Middle Eastern food. There are a few American steak houses in the cities of Beijing, Shanghai, and Guangzhou. Most of these restaurants are managed by natives from those respective countries with well-trained Chinese cooks. Don't expect to see an expat bar in every city and it may be that you will have to stick to Chinese beers such as Tsingtao or Kingway beer, which are comparable to most foreign beers. Foreign beers are available (such as Carlsberg, Heineken, and Guinness made under license) but not in every city.

FAST FOOD OUTLETS AND COFFEE HOUSES

Western fast food outlets first started operating in China during the late 1980s as an experiment in a market that had no previous experience of this kind of food. It was either make or break for companies like McDonald's, KFC (KFC celebrated 20 years' operation in China during 2007 with a nationwide marketing campaign), and Papa John's, Costa Coffee, Starbucks, Jamaica Blue Coffee, and Pizza Hut. These days you will have little problem finding your nearest KFC, McDonald's, or Pizza Hut in any major city and this trend is on the increase. In 2005 McDonald's opened its first ever "drive thru" in Dongguan city (halfway between Guangzhou and Shenzhen), and since 2006 Pizza Express and Papa John's home delivery have become available in some of the larger cities. With the increasing number of fast food chains and sugary brands such as Coca-Cola, Nestle (chocolates and ice creams), there is also the rising risk of young Chinese children becoming obese. Evidence of this is clear in the larger cities, where young overweight kids take their parents and grandparents into the local KFC/McDonald's.

Subway Sandwiches and Croissant de France can be found in the major cities as well. You may prefer to try Chinese fast food, from outlets such as "Real Kungfu"— whose corporate logo consists of Bruce Lee doing a karate kick. Chinese fast food consists of healthy steamed vegetables and meats usually cooked without using oil.

Coffee is still a relative luxury in China for many people as green tea is the preferred option. Starbucks has managed to break this culture barrier by opening quite a number of outlets in the major cities, much more rare in the rural areas, for now. There are a number of other coffee houses such as Mingtian Coffee, Kosmo, and SPR Coffee among other local outlets.

DRINKING TEA AND WATER

Chinese people drink large quantities of water (usually boiled) as it is believed that water helps to wash away the pollutants in the body as well as keeping the digestive system flowing. When you enter as a guest in anyone's home or an office, usually the first thing that is offered is hot water in a plastic or paper cup from the water tank. Every household and office in urban China has a mobile water tank. The water tank can be ordered from the supplier once the container is finished. If your company has provided an accommodation for you, then most likely your apartment will contain a free supply of drinking water. Bottled water is also available ubiquitously throughout the country; the most popular brands are Cestbon, Watson Water, Nanfeng Spring Water, and Ginten Water. Western brands such as Evian or Vittel mineral water are available, but, as expected, cost more.

It goes without saying that the Chinese drink large quantities of "green tea," without adding sugar or milk. Tea shops are widely located everywhere and sell beautifully decorated boxes and hand-painted tins full of various types of traditional Chinese tea. The Chinese drink tea frequently in offices, homes, restaurants, and formal gatherings. Tea bags are a relatively new thing and only available in the major cities. Small amounts of fresh tea leaves are mixed with boiled water and require about five minutes to infuse before you start drinking. Trying to drink Chinese tea without swallowing the tea leaves is a skill in itself and for this reason Chinese tea should be drunk in a mug with a lid in the shape of a Chinese pagoda roof. Every time a tea leaf gets to the top of the mug, you should push it away with the lid before you end up swallowing it.

Tea houses (Cha-dian) are places where Chinese people can go, usually in groups with friends or colleagues, and relax after a long day in the office. Tea houses are located in quiet and beautiful surroundings, usually with the presence of traditional Chinese music being played with a Zheng instrument in the background, either a recording or live. Chengdu, the capital of Sichuan province, is famous for tea houses, which can be found in most parks, theatres, and narrow lanes in cities. The most popular tea house in Beijing is the "Xi Bei Cha," located in the northwestern area of Shangdi—which is also known as the Silicon Valley area of Beijing. The unique aspect of this tea house is that you can get your feet massaged while you are sipping your tea and chatting with your friends.

CHAPTER 10:

RELATIONSHIPS

PERSONAL RELATIONSHIPS— BOYFRIEND AND GIRLFRIEND

Unlike in the past, when it used to be rare for couples to be together before marriage, times have changed and China has become a bit more liberal and open minded with regard to relationships. While holding hands is common, kissing in public is still very rare. This has nothing to do with being a taboo; it's just not in the culture. Asians generally (including Indians, Thais, etc.) are shy when it comes to romance in public because you would get "onlookers," and it may seem offensive to the elders and traditional people. That said, modern China is presenting a few surprises, as a recent trend has been for couples to head for parks or get romantically attached in quiet neighborhoods.

Nevertheless, living together before marriage is rare and arranged marriages are still widely practiced in China. However with the emergence of the internet and modernization, couples in urban areas are more and more often choosing their own partners.

Foreigners ought to be aware that if they are in a relationship with a Chinese national, normally this may be assumed to be a strong indication for marriage, both by their Chinese partner and his or her parents. For example, if a couple are seen romantically tied together in a neighborhood, people start gossiping and asking the parents whether they will be getting married, and so for parents to marry off their children is a matter of respect and honor. So what may seem to be a "casual friendship" to a Westerner may be considered something a bit more serious by her or her Chinese partner.

MARRIAGE IN CHINA

Weddings in China are normally held in a local registry office followed by a lavish reception for friends and family at a restaurant or hotel. It's providing a booming business opportunity to international five-star hotels these days with lavish banquets being laid out.

Most marriages in China are still arranged by the parents, relatives, or friends of the family who may act as matchmakers; this is very much the case in the rural areas. In some remote villages often the bride and groom only meet each other on the day of their marriage, although this practice is slowly fading away as increasingly couples have the freedom to choose their own partners, and usually start dating before marriage. Women are not allowed to marry in China until they are 20 years old (22 for men). And while the Asian fear is prevalent (i.e., if you are not married by 30, then no man will have you); many Chinese women are putting off marriage in favor of gaining an education and enhancing their careers. Due to a desire to have boys in the past, there is now a shortage of women (over 505 million Chinese men aged 18–64 years old compared to just 478 million women aged 18–64).

Unlike in the West, engagement ceremonies before marriage are not practiced on the mainland. Even though things are getting a bit more liberal, nevertheless both the bride and bridegroom have to get consent for the marriage from their respective parents. In some parts, especially the rural areas, the bride and bridegroom wear traditional costumes according to the part of China where they are from, such as Mongolia or Shaanxi for example.

In the major cities the bride and bridegroom usually wear Western style wedding clothes, with the bride wearing a beautiful white dress and the bridegroom wearing a tuxedo. Irrespective of the weather conditions, newlywed couples flock to parks and lakes to take photos, posing in front of beautiful flowers and sculptures. All in all, getting married in China can be a rewardingly romantic experience.

One thing that you may find confusing is that Chinese women don't change their surname when they get married, and the children adopt the father's surname. A Chinese woman married to a foreigner may or may not change her surname depending on the couple's personal decision.

MARRYING A CHINESE NATIONAL

An increasing number of Chinese nationals, more women than men, are marrying foreigners. Indeed some expats whom I have met have come to China for no purpose other than marrying a Chinese girl, and then they don't leave China. Either they have met their Chinese partner in their home country and followed them to China or they just come to China, usually leaving their life behind in their own country, in search of true love; of course that's not to say that they could not find true love in their own country. I have managed to gather information on what steps are required in order to get married in China, either to another foreigner or to a Chinese national.

BASIC INFORMATION ABOUT GETTING MARRIED IN CHINA

Foreign nationals planning on getting married in China, either to a Chinese national or to another foreigner, should review the following general information provided by the Chinese Government for the proper procedures. All marriages, by foreigners and natives, in China are registered according to the laws of China, regardless of the nationality of those being married. Contrary to popular belief, the diplomatic and consular officers from your embassy or consulate do not have the authority to perform marriages and are not required to witness the marriages of foreign nationals.

The current Marriage Law of the People's Republic of China was approved in September 1980 and came into practice in January 1981. Under this law, marriage registration procedures are administered by the local civil affairs office (minzhengju), in each authority. Individuals planning to marry ought to visit one of these offices for explicit information. There will be a charge for this visit. If one of the spouses is a Chinese national, the appropriate civil affairs office will be the one in the authority in which the Chinese national was born (i.e., their national ID card, which is known as *Hukou*). So for example, if a lady who was born in Beijing is marrying a man from Singapore, then the lady's Hukou belongs to Beijing even if she marries in Shanghai. The marriage registration process may take anywhere from several days to several months to complete, depending upon how quickly the required documents are obtained. For example, some Chinese citizens have difficulty getting a "release" from their danwei to obtain the "certificate of birth" or the "certificate of marriageability."

The **danwei (work unit)** is the basic-level organization through which party and government officials control the social, political, and economic activities of inhabitants. The danwei typically controls the share of accommodation, grain, edible oil, and cotton rations; the issuance of permits to travel, to marry, and to bear or adopt children; and permission to enter the army, Communist Party, and university as well as if an individual wants to change his or her job.

It is recommended that the couple dress up (coat and tie for the male). From past experience, it appears that whenever a couple appeared in jeans and sneakers the registration process took over a month whereas couples who dressed formally and displayed a "correct attitude" were usually registered within a few days.

If both are foreigners, they go to the civil affairs office in the city in which they live. In general, at least one of the partners must reside in China. Two foreigners visiting China temporarily on tourist visas are unlikely to be able to register a marriage.

Certain categories of Chinese nationals, such as diplomats, security officials, and others whose work is considered to be crucial to the state, are not legally free to marry foreigners. Chinese students generally are permitted to marry if all the requirements are met, but they can expect to be expelled from school as soon as they do. Foreign nationals wishing to marry Chinese students should bear this in mind. It also should be noted that the school may require Chinese students to reimburse the school for hitherto uncharged tuition and other expenses upon withdrawal from school to marry foreigners. The school will not release documents the student needs to register the marriage until the fees are paid. Some work units may also demand compensation for "lost services."

Upon the receipt of an application to register a marriage, the civil affairs office will ascertain that both parties are of minimum marriageability age (generally this is 22 for men and 20 for women, although a higher minimum may be established by the local civil affairs office) and that both parties are single and free to marry. Persons who are divorced will be asked to submit original or certified copies of final divorce or of death certificates if widowed.

Foreign nationals who want to marry in China will generally be asked to submit the following:

- A current passport
- A Chinese residence permit
- A health certificate from the local hospital designated by the civil affairs office
- A "certification of marriageability," which can be prepared at your consulate on the basis of an affidavit in which the foreign national swears or affirms before a consul that he or she is currently legally eligible to marry.

Individuals who have previously been married need to show a certified divorce decree, annulment decree, or death certificate both to their consulate when preparing this certificate and to the local authorities. Since proof of termination of all previous marriages will again be required when you file an immigrant visa petition on your spouse's behalf, it is highly recommended that you do not surrender the certified copies of death certificates or divorce or annulment decrees to the civil affairs office. You should take a good photocopy with you when you go to register the marriage. Generally, if you present the certified copy with the copy for their review, the Chinese authorities will accept the copy. This is also true for your spouse if he or she has previously been married.

- Three photos of the marrying couple, taken together
- A registration fee

The Chinese partner to the marriage will be asked to submit the following:

- A certificate of marriageability (obtainable from the office that has physical control of his or her file)
- A certificate of birth
- Household registration book
- Health certificate (obtainable from a regional level local hospital)

A letter from the parents of the local partner giving permission for their child to marry a foreigner (this letter should include the index fingerprint of both parents below their signature and date).

All English-language documents must be translated into Chinese. Translation of documents usually takes about a month, but can be completed within 10 days at double the original cost. Translations should be obtained from and certified by a Public Notary office or a lawyer (list provided in this book) in your city.

It takes the marriage registration office about an hour or so to review the submitted documents and approve the application. Once the marriage registration office approves of the application and registers the marriage, it will issue a marriage certificate to be picked up by the couple.

For some nationalities, the rules to get married to a Chinese national vary slightly. For example British citizens have a requirement to obtain a Certificate of No Impediment in order to get married in China. It's a British legal requirement to confirm that a British national has been resident in China for 21 consecutive days before swearing an Affidavit and completing a Notice of Intent to Marry. The notice of intent to marry will be displayed at the British consulate for a period of 21 days, after which a Certificate of No Impediment will be issued in both English and Chinese languages. This certificate is valid for three months from the date of issue.

DIVORCE IN CHINA

Divorce is still quite rare and seen rather as a taboo, although in the big cities, just as Chinese couples have the freedom to choose their partners, they also have the freedom to leave them—so much so that in the big cities divorce is providing quite good business for lawyers. Because of the culture in China (as well as most parts of Asia), what tends to happen is that couples get married because their parents and relatives pressure them to, and then they have kids because again it's a cultural thing (grandparents want to play with their grandchildren as soon as possible after their kids get married!). But then as those new parents become more mature, they realize that they may not be right for each other (this is more prevalent in middle-class familes), and the end result sadly is a divorce.

ADOPTING CHILDREN IN CHINA

Whenever I used to go to the Shamian Island of Guangzhou, I would come across quite a number of expat families with Chinese children, and I would think to myself that those children looked nothing like either of the parents. Then someone told me that it is common to adopt Chinese children in this part of Guangzhou.

Interested foreigners should be aware that the process of adopting a child in China and bringing the child to their country may be expensive, time-consuming, and difficult. Although the number of Chinese children adopted by foreigners has steadily gone up, in recent years the number of available children has been reduced and the timelines have been considerably increased. Most of the information listed in this chapter is obtained with kind permission from the American and British Embassies in Beijing. All the information is correct at the time of writing this book and neither the author nor the Embassy authorities are responsible for any m sapprehensions that may arise after consulting with or relating to any adoption organizations.

CHINESE ORGANIZATIONS/AGENCIES INVOLVED IN THE ADOPTION PROCESS

There are many child adoption centers in Western countries. Anyone wishing to adopt children in China should first start doing research by consulting their local adoption center in their country. Responsibility for the various procedures necessary to adopt a child in China in accordance with Chinese law is divided among the following Chinese government authorities:

THE CHINA CENTER FOR ADOPTION AFFAIRS (CCAA)

The China Center for Adoption Affairs, a branch of the Ministry of Civil Affairs, is the central authority for adoptions in China. Since its establishment in 1996, the CCAA has taken measures to regulate adoption procedures and make them clearer.

CCAA
103 Beiheyan Street
Dongcheng District
Beijing 100006
Telephone: +86 (0)10 6522 3102 or 6513 0607
Fax: +86 (0)10 6522 3102.

DEPARTMENT OF CIVIL AFFAIRS

China's provincial and county Civil Affairs Bureaus are officially in charge for orphaned and abandoned children. The Ministry of Civil Affairs administers the Civil Affairs Bureaus.

Department of Civil Affairs
147 Beijeyan Street
Beijing 100032

CHILDREN'S WELFARE INSTITUTE (SHEHUI FELI JIGOU)

The Ministry of Civil Affairs, through provincial Civil Affairs Bureaus, administers the Children's Welfare Institutes. These are government-operated homes for orphaned and abandoned children. Children can only be placed in welfare institutes if their parents have died or abandoned them. For abandoned children, the authorities do make efforts to trace the parents before allowing adoption from the institutes.

NOTARIES OFFICES

The provincial Notaries Offices, which are managed by the Ministry of Justice in Beijing, issue the concluding adoption certificate. That process terminates the parental rights of the birth parent(s). Each adoption certificate comes with a notary's birth certificate for the child and either a statement explaining the reasons for desertion or notary's death certificates for the orphaned child's parents.

PUBLIC SECURITY BUREAU (PSB)

The local police station in China or Public Security Bureau (PSB), as known in China, in the locality where the adoption takes place, is responsible for issuing Chinese passports and exit permits to children adopted by foreigners.

HOSPITALS

Chinese law states that it is not permitted for a hospital to release a child directly to prospective parent(s) for adoption. Prospective adoptive parents have to go through the correct channels for adoption.

CHILDREN ELIGIBLE FOR ADOPTION

Only children processed by the CCAA are available for international adoption. The CCAA matches individual children with prospective adoptive parent(s) whose completed applications have been submitted to the CCAA by a licensed adoption agency in your country. Only applications submitted by agencies whose credentials are on file at the CCAA will be considered. A list of these adoption agencies is available from any one of the websites listed at the end of this chapter. An important issue that is made is that prospective parents *may not* choose the child they wish to adopt because the CCAA does not consider requests to adopt specific children.

ADOPTION CATEGORIES

The Adoption Law of the People's Republic of China, adopted by the twenty-third meeting of the seventh National People's Congress Standing Committee in December 1991, presented that, with a few exceptions, children under the age of 14 in the following categories may be adopted by foreigners:

- Orphans—Any child whose parents are deceased or who have been declared deceased by a Chinese court.
- Abandoned children—these are children who have been abandoned by their parents or guardians.
- Hardship cases—these are children whose birth parents are incapable of looking after them because of unusual hardship such as financial or other valid reason(s).

DEFINITION OF A SPECIAL NEEDS CHILD

As of the time of writing this document, no legal definition of a special needs child (or "disability") was developed by the CCAA. In the absence of a specific definition of special needs for the purposes of foreign adoptions, the CCAA relies on the criteria for disabled people approved by the State Council in October 1983. There are five kinds of handicaps as defined here:

- defects in vision
- defects in hearing and language
- mental deficiency (such as low I.Q. and development)
- handicap/impairment of arms and legs
- mental illness

The determination is made on the basis of "obscurity or loss of social function." Financial hardship is not classed as a disability.

Some illnesses that may be considered to cause an individual to become disabled in Western countries may not necessarily be considered to be so in China. Potential adoptive parents should be very clear in their applications as to whether they are interested in adopting a disabled child. The medical report provided by the CCAA gives specific details about any disability or medical abnormality that does not comprise a disability under Chinese law. If and when in doubt about any specificity of information received, prospective adoptive parent(s) should feel free to request clarification from Chinese authorities directly or through the adoption agency in their country. If, prior to signing the final contract, adopting parent(s) believe that a disability or medical condition that has not been considered a disability under Chinese law may be more serious than otherwise presented, an independent medical examination may be considered and can be requested.

Foreigners traveling to China to complete adoptions will ultimately have to stay a period of time in China during the immigrant visa process. Foreign citizens interested in adoption in China have often inquired about inexpensive housing in the city where the child is located in China. Your adoption agency or travel agent may be in the best position to assist you in this regard.

OUTLINE OF REQUIREMENTS
FOR ADOPTIVE PARENTS

(table provided courtesy of the American Embassy in Beijing)

Section of China Law	Adoptive Parent(s) requirements	Adoptable Children's requirements
Article six	• Age 35 or over • Childless • May adopt only one child	• Abandoned child (Parents cannot be found or have relinquished parental rights to control)
Article eight, Paragraph two	• Age 35 or older • Not childless • May adopt more than one child¹	• Orphaned child (Requires proof that both parents are deceased) • Handicapped child
Article seven	• Age 34 or under • Not childless • May adopt more than one child	• Orphaned child (Requires proof that both parents are deceased) • Handicapped child
Article ten	• Unmarried	• All above age restrictions, limitations *re* number of children and category of children apply (implied)
Article nine	• Unmarried Male	• If adopting a female child, the adoptive parent must be at least forty years older than the adoptee

CHINESE DOCUMENTARY
REQUIREMENTS AND
AUTHENTICATION PROCEDURES

As stated in article twenty of the PRC adoption law, a foreigner interested in adopting a Chinese child must present proof of age, marital status, occupation, financial status, health condition, and police check record. It is advisable to bring several copies of the authenticated documentation with you to China in addition to the package of documents forwarded by your adoption agency to the CCAA for approval. Authentication means that the documents must bear the seal of the Embassy or Consulate of China in your country in order to be acceptable in China.

REQUIRED DOCUMENTS FOR ADOPTION

Birth Certificate(s): Certified and authenticated copies of the adoptive parent(s)' birth certificate(s). The birth certificates should include the applicant(s)' name, sex, date of birth, place of birth, and parents' names. Please note that only original certificates would be accepted.

Marital Status Certificate: A certified and authenticated copy of the adoptive parent(s)' marriage certificate (if applicable) and/or proof of termination of any previous marriage (certified copy of spouse's death certificate or divorce decree). Single adopters must submit a document attesting to single status—this is obtainable from a public notary in your country.

Health Examination Certificate(s): A medical certificate(s) for adoptive parent(s) executed by physician before a notary public and authenticated. Each applicant should submit a completed "General Physical Examination for Adoption Applicant" form. This form may be available from any adoption agency in your country. Please note that medical reports will only be considered valid if sent to the CCAA within six months of the date of issuance.

Statement of Childlessness: A notarized and authenticated statement is needed that clearly states that adoptive parent(s) is/are childless and has/have not adopted other children.

Certificate of Infertility: If this condition is present, a medical certificate (executed by a physician before a notary public and authenticated) is required. Note that infertility is <u>not</u> a requirement for adoption in China any longer.

Certificate of Criminal or No-Criminal Record: A certificate of good conduct for the adoptive parent(s) from a local police department in the country of the adoptive parent(s), notarized or bearing the police department seal and authenticated, is required. For example an FBI report (USA) or a Criminal Check Bureau (UK) is acceptable in lieu of a local police record; however, this is separate from the criminal records checks that are conducted by INS as part of the petition process.

If the adoption claimant has lived overseas, away from his or her country of regular residence for one year or more during the last five years, the claimant must put forward a corresponding certificate to indicate whether the applicant has any criminal record in the overseas locality.

It must be noted that certificates of criminal or no-criminal record will be considered valid only if sent to the CCAA within six months of the date of issuance. A criminal record does not automatically mean a rejection from the adoption process for the adoptive parent(s) as it depends on the seriousness of the crime committed. Needless to say, any individual who has been convicted of sexual offenses, irrespective of whether the case involved children or not, would be automatically rejected from consideration for adoption. For more details you can consult your embassy or consulate in confidence about this issue.

Certificates of Profession, Income and Property: Every applicant must submit a certificate of profession issued by his or her employer. This would include the applicant's position, the length of employment, and annual salary denominated in local currency. If the applicant is self-employed, the certificate must be submitted by a certified public accountant; if the applicant is an accountant, another certified accountant must submit the certificate.

Letters of Reference: Two letters of reference, notarized and authenticated, are required.

Certificate(s) of Property: If applicable, copies of any property trust deeds are required.

Home Study Report: A home study prepared by an authorized and licensed social agency must in all cases be submitted. The report must describe in detail:

- the applicant's motivations and reasons for adopting; whether the applicant has children, including any from previous marriages or any other adopted children; any conditions the applicant places on the adoption, including whether special needs children are acceptable (and indicating what kind of special needs); and whether older children are acceptable.

- the applicant's family background, including education, experience, and relationships with parents and siblings.

- Whether the applicant has a history of alcoholism, substance abuse, pilferage, domestic violence, child abuse or other harmful behavior, or whether the applicant has a criminal record or any penalty meted out against him or her.

- The health status of the applicant, including whether the applicant suffers from any mental or psychological illness or any unfavorable elements that would affect the bringing up of the child. Licensed physicians in connection with the conditions mentioned above should supply the health certificate.

- The marital status of the applicant should include a description of the relationship between husband and wife, any previous marriages, the number of divorces and their causes.

- Who shall act as guardian for the child in the event of an accident or health problem, or premature death of the applicant(s)? What will be the commitment on the part of the guardian?

- The reason for any cohabitation between family members or others living with single applicants, in order to ensure that the single adopter is not a homosexual. Homosexuals are prohibited from adopting children in China.

- The community environment in which the applicant lives, and in particular the attitude toward accepting children from other cultures and ethnic groups.

The Home Study should be investigated and completed by a certified, licensed social worker. The social worker should provide an assessment as to whether the applicant is qualified to adopt, as well as suggestions for the adoption.

Bank Statements: This is to prove that the applicant has enough funds to take financial responsibility for the adopted child.

Power of Attorney: This is required if only one spouse will travel to China. In the case of married couples, if only one adopting parent comes to China, the spouse traveling to China must bring a power of attorney from his or her spouse, notarized and properly authenticated by the Chinese Embassy or one of the Chinese Consulate Generals in your country.

Letter of Intent to Adopt: describing the child the adoptive parent(s) is/are willing to adopt, notarized and authenticated. Please be mindful of Chinese law regarding those children that are eligible for adoption by given applicants.

Certificate of China Adoption Approval: All applicants must submit a Certificate of China Adoption Approval, or its equivalent, by the competent department of the applicant's country of constant residence. The applicant must also submit a certificate of effective approval of travel to China for adoption.

WHAT TO BRING FOR YOUR NEW BABY

It is difficult to predict how long it may be obligatory for you to remain in China with your adopted child. Many stores, including foreign supermarkets such as Walmart and Carrefour, sell products for babies. Most hospitals and Western style hotels have personal stores and shops that sell some products for babies. It may also be useful for you to bring your own things from your own country in advance. This would save you time and the effort of looking for the right products that may be difficult to buy.

These items may include:

- Plastic or cloth baby carrier
- Bottle nipples
- Disposable paper diapers
- Baby wipes
- Baby blankets

- Infant wear
- Thermos bottle—for hot water to prepare dry formula
- Milk bottles (plastic, glass, and disposable)
- Disposable plastic bags for milk bottles

CHAPTER 11

WOMEN IN SOCIETY AND IDENTITY

ATTITUDES TOWARDS WOMEN

Women in 21st-century China, irrespective of whether they are white collar professionals or not, are treated the same as males. In the major cities, there has been a significant increase in the number of women opting to focus on their career rather than marrying in their early twenties and starting a family, as was the case in the past and still is in the rural areas. Even though China does not have official laws in place that define equal opportunities, as they do in the West, the people still have the common ethos built into them, through years of communism, that everyone should be treated with unity and equality irrespective if they are rich, poor, male, or female.

Women participate in all kinds of professions, such as police officers, judges, lawyers, doctors, engineers, senior corporate executives, and even politicians. Nevertheless, some male-dominated professions still exist, such as fire-fighters, construction workers, or taxi drivers, where the absence of women is due to personal choice or other reasons rather than on discriminatory grounds—which is not the case.

Women in China are increasingly doing jobs that otherwise may have been done by men years ago.

As a foreign woman in China, you will be treated with respect and no different from how a male foreigner would be treated. Sexual harassment towards foreign women (even locals) is rare, and you don't need to feel unsafe walking on your own, for example, late at night. When it comes to interacting with foreign women, the majority of Chinese men are shy, although they would be most willing to jump at the first opportunity to become friendly. In saying this, caution should always be practiced, as you would anywhere else in the world.

Wearing a bikini on the beach should not pose problems, although it would be common sense to avoid wearing revealing clothes (i.e., short skirt for example) in busy shopping malls or late at night as you will be likely to attract unwanted attention. The worst you may encounter is giggling men saying such things like "Hello, English/American women!" from a distance (with a hint of shyness).

CHINESE NAMES

Around the world we have perceptions of various surnames such as that most Muslims and Arabs are known as Mohammed or Ali, Smith is a popular Western name, and most Indians can be distinguished by the surname Singh, Patel or Shah. However, no country can quite match up to China's record for the contest of most used surnames in the world. If you happen to be in a bank or a hospital or anywhere where there is a genuine need for customers to book business appointments, then it's not surprising to hear the names of two people with the exact surname and forename being called up.

With 1.3 billion people sharing about 430 surnames, it can get pretty confusing. In contrast to the growing economy, China is also going through a name crisis, which means there are too few names for too many people. The number of Chinese people named Wang is 94 million, a number that exceeds the population of most European countries including France, Germany, or the UK. There are a staggering 90 million people surnamed Zhang, much more than any surname in the whole nation or country of Australia. The most popular Chinese names are Li, Wu, Xiao, Zhang, Wang, Hu, Jiang, Zhou, and Guang.

In my Shenzhen office, there were twelve colleagues named Wu and three of them had the same exact full name only to be set apart by having them called Wu junior (Xiao Wu, where Xiao means Small or Junior), Wu senior (Lao Wu where Lao means Old or Senior) and Wu number two (Er Wu)! The idea of addressing your seniors by putting "Lao" in front of their surname and your juniors by putting "Xiao" in front of their surname, is a more respectful but informal way of greeting people. It's best to only start using this once you know someone well enough. Sometimes the Chinese find it easier to solve the "too many people with the same name" problem by putting their job titles before their names, so for example Professor Jiangzhi, Captain Xiaopang (for Pilots etc.), Dr. Deng, or Nurse Yixia.

The government has started making efforts to propose a few changes to the law in order to allow parents to create double-barreled surnames for their children, combining the father's and the mother's surnames, thus greatly increasing the number of unique surnames.

The Chinese put their surname first followed by the forename. So for example the name "Deng Xiao Ping" would be known as Mr. Deng and not Mr. Xiao Ping, and "Mao Zedong" where Mao is the surname and Zedong is the first name would be called Mr. Mao and not Mr. Zedong.

Most Chinese students, people who work in multinationals, or those who live in the major cities, tend to have an English nickname that replaces their Chinese first name. When using an English nickname, a Chinese name can be written in a Western style, for example if someone is called James Wu then they would be, of course, known as Mr. Wu.

A Chinese may not be offended if you pronounce their name wrongly; however they will appreciate your effort to try to say it correctly. The most frequent mistakes that Westerners make is reading "Ang" as "Aen" as in Bang, instead of "Ah-n."

In the corporate office, unless you know your colleagues quite well, it is best to be formal when addressing someone (as in Mr./Ms./Mrs.) regardless of whether they are senior or junior to you. It all depends on how you are introduced to your colleagues when you first join.

When I joined my first corporate position in Shenzhen, all the colleagues (including the senior management) were known by their first name. Even I was given a Chinese name (Lei-Xinge) and some colleagues asked me to christen them with an English name. Chinese people can be quite adventurous when choosing English nicknames—I have met people who have decided to call themselves "Top Gun," "Milky," "Magic," "Stone," "Scorpio Legend Mei," and "Hoofball" just to name a few.

MISTAKEN IDENTITY?

Even though there are officially 56 ethnic minority groups in China, the country is not considered a multicultural society as such because those minorities are still Chinese by blood rather than being from other parts of the world, as is the case in Western Europe, Australia, and North America.

Foreigners are known as a "Wai Guo Ren" (外国人) and anyone who looks mature or is generally over the age of 30 is known as a "Lao Wai," meaning old foreigner. In Hong Kong and Guangdong province, a rather blatantly curse word, "Gweilo," is used, literally meaning "white ghost." Africans or people with a dark complexion are known as "Hei Ren" (黑人, black person) and white people as "Bai Gwe" (white person). In years gone by it used to be that irrespective of your race, you were the star attraction just because you were a foreigner in China, with your differences in facial features, body shape, and hairiness.

In the rural parts of China, if you are a non–white-skinned foreigner or even a "foreign born Chinese" in China, then this is something that you may end up explaining to people if they ask. Because of many years of poverty and low incomes, the vast majority of the people have not been abroad (although this is changing nowadays); therefore it is most likely that people will judge your origin from what you look like rather than your nationality.

Foreign-born Chinese, more commonly known as "Overseas Chinese" or "Non-Resident Chinese" (NRCs), are treated with great respect when they return to China, just as any other foreigner is.

However if NRCs have relatives who live in China, usually they are expected to bring back gifts or money when they return to their motherland. It is usually the case of emigrant Chinese going to the USA, Australia, or European countries and working hard to save as much as they could, so that when they returned back to China, they could build a new home or set up a business in China. Although this is the same with most emigrants including Indians and Pakistanis in Europe and the USA, the NRCs actually contribute to the growing success of their country and work hard.

Therefore it is best to politely mention your nationality as well as your ethnic origin, whether you are a British Indian, British-Chinese, and so on, otherwise people get confused. Don't take it personally if someone consistently refers to you as an Indian or a Chinese, even if you are a British-born Chinese or an American-born Indian for example. Most Chinese people still have an image in their minds that London is foggy and industrialized, that British people are gentlemen wearing a bowler hat and carrying an umbrella, and that the ladies are elegant and wear posh hats and dresses. However, in recent years, with the huge surge of foreign expats flocking to China, being a foreigner in China is not seen as a rare thing, and the Chinese people have become more aware of the customs and culture of Western people (i.e., foreigners are no longer treated like royalty like they used to be!). So unlike in the past when people would even get together to take a photo next to a foreigner, that does not happen anymore except in rural areas or if you are in an area filled with rural tourists. These days you would be lucky if anyone bats an eyelash when a foreigner walks past!

CHINESE LAW

ESPITE THE COUNTRY EXPERIENCING AN ECONOMIC BOOM, WHERE there is a feel of rapid improvement in living standards, the Chinese legal system is one where communism thrives and this is where China is still lagging behind the rest of the world. The Chinese police force (known as Jing Cha) is one of the largest and the best in the world. The police in China have more power than the courts and lawyers. There are numerous plain-clothed C.I.D. officers patrolling the streets, shopping malls, and even state-owned companies/offices. China has one of the toughest criminal laws in the world. The death penalty by lethal injection or the firing squad is used for serious crimes such as murder, rape, engaging in sexual activities with a minor, bribe of a large amount, fraud of a large amount, and drug-related cases. For other crimes, the penalty can range anything from a simple warning to imprisonment.

ENTRY AND EXIT

It is highly prohibited to carry out any of the following while passing through any ports of entry/exit within the People's Republic of China:

1. To forge, alter, misuse, lend, buy, or sell visas.

China has one of the best police forces in the world.

2. To be in possession of illegal, pirated disks (CD/VCD/DVD/Cassette/Computer hard disk/video tape, etc.), or pornographic disks.

3. To smuggle out of the country protected cultural relics, gold, silver, diamond, ivory and other precious metals; rare animals and rare plants and their derivatives; contraband goods.

4. To be in possession of or consume illicit drugs—this is a very serious crime and punishable by death.

WHILE IN CHINA

All of these are highly prohibited within the country:

1. To assault someone or to instigate a quarrel; to infringe on someone's rights and freedom.

2. To steal, rob, gain by deceit, vandalize public or private property, or purchase stolen goods (be very careful what you buy because in China the buyer also gets punished if the goods don't belong to the real owner).

3. Prostitution and having a massage by women are illegal activities in the PRC. Sexual harassment and rape are also very serious crimes, as is having sexual intercourse with a minor. If you are found guilty, these crimes can all lead to serious trouble.

4. To log onto pornographic websites, or to distribute or trade in pornographic or obscene materials, is strictly illegal.

5. Don't disturb the peace and order in public places; especially train stations, airports, shops, cinemas, or market places. Please take note that being intoxicated doesn't constitute a proper defense and doesn't reduce responsibility and liability.

Note: The above examples are only a partial list of prohibited activities in China. You need to pay attention to all the laws, although, like anywhere else, just be careful and sensible in life. Your behavior in China should be no different from how you behave back home. A good rule of thumb from an old Chinese idiom is: "Ruxiang Suisu"—When in Rome, do as the Romans do.

The crime rate in China is relatively low in comparison to other countries, but it's always best to take safety precautions as you would in any other country. In case of any problem, dial 110 at once and ask to speak to the police, ambulance or fire. If you don't speak Chinese, most likely there will be somebody on the phone that does communicate with a little bit of English! With the large number of foreigners coming to China, and with the large emergence of English language learning schools in China, the Chinese police forces are training their staff to communicate in English.

ARREST AND DETENTION

If you are suspected of any criminal activity in China, the legal procedures can take a very long time irrespective of how serious a crime is committed. This can be a very distressful and stressful time for a foreign suspect and his or her family members back home. While you are questioned and detained in China, you are subject to Chinese law.

It is absolutely imperative that when you are taken in for questioning, you get in touch with your consulate or embassy at the first instance. Then at least you can have the peace of mind that the authorities will follow proper legal procedures in accordance with the Chinese law and that you will be treated fairly. Your consulate or embassy can also get in touch with your friends or family, provide you with information about a lawyer, and get you money if you are detained. Foreigners detained for questioning may not be allowed to contact their national authorities until the questioning is concluded. Foreigners suspected of committing a crime are rarely granted bail, although your embassy or consulate may apply with reasons. There was a rare case of a foreign woman given bail because she had a newborn child who needed breast feeding.

Foreign lawyers cannot represent a criminal case in China, and so a foreign suspect must hire a Chinese national as his or her lawyer. Normally, criminal suspects are not allowed access to a lawyer until they are formally charged, although sometimes for small cases and foreigners, it may be possible to get a lawyer to visit the suspect before being charged.

Initially a suspect can be kept for a maximum of 12 hours for questioning at a local police station (known as PSB), after which the authorities have to either release the suspect or formally press charges. If however, there is still no progress after the 12 hours of questioning, the PSB may pass the case onto the C.I.D. (Criminal Investigation Department), who can keep the suspect for questioning for a further 12 hours. After a maximum of 24 hours of interrogation, the police must either release the suspect or formally issue a warrant for detention. Then the suspect can be detained for up to 30 days without formal charge, after which authorities have 7 days in which to release the suspect or formally charge and issue a written arrest warrant.

Your consulate or embassy can visit you in the detention house within 7 days of your detention, and can assist in passing messages to your next of kin or friends in your native country. Your consulate can also take up medical problems or any justified complaints with the police authorities. The British, Canadian, and American embassies visit their nationals once every month while in detention. Other countries have similar procedures. Police authorities are always present during visits by the consulate or embassy and everything is censored.

If you are formally arrested after the 37 days in detention, you can be kept for a further 60 days so that the C.I.D. can continue their investigations. Normally even if the case is minute, the police take their time and unless there is some special backing from the senior police or the government, they will take the full specified time to complete investigations, or even longer if the case is important. For example, the senior police or government can argue that a case involves state secrets and is important.

Unfortunately nobody, including any embassy or government of any country, can push the Chinese police authorities into releasing a suspect—because it's not in the Chinese government's nature to do that. They can take as much time as possible in order to prove that a crime has been committed.

Once the police feel they have enough evidence to prosecute the suspect, the case is passed to the provincial government for approval to formally prosecute the suspect. The government will send three members of the prosecution to interrogate the suspect in order to be sure that what the suspect says is in line with what the police have in their files. If what the suspect tells the prosecution is different from what the police have filed, then the case will be passed back to the police for further investigation. The prosecution will only pass the case to the court once the facts stated by the suspect are in line with the police authorities. Therefore, if the suspect says he is not guilty, it will take a very long time before the case is passed to the courts.

If a suspect has admitted to a crime, then even if the police cannot prove the charges or formal arrest, they can still try a suspect for charges and give the suspect the maximum punishment. This is China and the courts can do this. Sadly, no international government or human rights organization can intervene.

Chinese defense lawyers do not work the same as they do in Europe or America. This means that Chinese defense lawyers basically go through the motions and are too afraid to push or raise impropriety or questions. The minimum time it takes for a defendant to go to a court hearing for the first session is normally anything between 5 and 7 months from the initial day you are taken into detention. Anything less than that is considered rare. In some cases foreigners detained pending trial have waited over a year for their trial to begin.

Chinese courts consist of three judges at the high table in the center, a maximum of three members of the prosecution, a defense lawyer, a translator if needed, and a court clerk. The defendant is brought in and sits in a small bench in the center of the courtroom, facing the judges, defense, and prosecution. The majority of the questions are asked by the judges and the prosecution. Evidence is produced. Witnesses may also be produced, but in most cases they don't bother coming to the court because in China, the prosecution already has collected all the evidence before passing the case to the court.

From the first session of the trial to the second session, a maximum of 6 weeks is permitted. Courts can apply for an extension of up to one month. For foreign nationals it takes anything between one to two and a half months to get the verdict, and for most cases only one court session is required.

The defendant has the right to appeal within 10 days of the end of the trial. On paper, from the appeal being lodged to being heard by the High Court, a maximum of 6 weeks is permitted. However in reality this can take a minimum of 5 to 6 months for any case. Therefore there is no point appealing a decision if it contains a small sentence. Otherwise the case will just drag on for another few months.

Visits by family members are not allowed until the detainee has been formally sentenced. An application has to be made through the relevant Public Security Bureau. Family members or friends can visit the prisoner once every month and for a maximum of 30 minutes only. While in prison there is very little communication with the outside world as no phone or email is allowed. Foreigners can write letters, in both Chinese and English; however they are censored and read by the police authorities. In short—avoid going to jail in China!

CHAPTER 13

FESTIVALS AND RELIGION

C HINESE FESTIVALS ARE SPLIT ACCORDING TO EITHER THE SOLAR CAL-
endar or the lunar calendar. There are nine holidays according to the
former while there are five official holidays according to the lunar calendar.
Christmas day in China is no different from any other day as it is not officially celebrated here. Foreign hotels and multinational corporations have a Christmas tree
in the foyer along with a Santa Claus. Christmas celebrations are not quite like what
they are in the West as in one particular example I saw in Shenzhen: The foyer of the
Hilton Hotel was decorated in silver and blue instead of the usual red and green that
is associated with Christmas in the West, plus the dragon was used instead of the
reindeer and the legendary Chinese monkey king replaced Santa Claus.

During the official Chinese holidays, streets are decorated with the national
flags, and special entertainment shows are provided in cities, where famous
singers and actors mingle with the crowds and promote a sense of nationalism.
Crowds are encouraged to participate in the singing of patriotic songs, as well as
traditional songs that tell stories about village life and the struggles during the
Cultural Revolution.

CHINESE NEW YEAR (CHUN JIE)

Chinese New Year (known as the Spring Festival) usually falls towards the beginning of February and is the highlight of the year for everyone. During the official
three-day holiday, China is effectively closed for business in banks, law courts, and
other government offices. Companies normally offer 7 days, so employees have to
compensate by working the following weekend.

Many people take extended leave from the office for about 3 weeks. It's the
time of the year when people get the chance to return to their villages and hometowns and have large family reunions. People clean their home the day before the
start of the New Year and this may include relocating the furniture in the home

to give the home a new look for the New Year. Old clothes and furniture may be thrown away and replaced with new ones. If you are planning on traveling within the country, it would be a good idea to book your holiday in advance as it is very difficult to get a seat on any form of transport at the last minute.

Weeks before the start of the Chinese New Year, streets shops, homes, and offices are decorated with red lights in the shape of Chinese lanterns, the legendary monkey king, or other things associated with Chinese culture. People put up red and yellow colored decorations on their front doors and inside the house to bring good luck for the coming year. Loud firecrackers are set off, in a belief that they will scare away evil spirits and bad luck.

In the major cities, especially Shanghai and Shenzhen where there are a considerably high number of migrants, be wary of thieves and gang robbers who try to look for anything expensive like laptops and mobile phones so that they can take them back to their villages or hometowns and give them as gifts to their families.

QING MING FESTIVAL

This is in the third month of the Chinese calendar. It's a day when people visit the cemeteries and burial sites to pay respects to their ancestors. There is a public holiday but no major celebration. The day is actually seen in most parts of the country as a welcoming for the spring and summer months. In most Chinese cities people may be seen flying kites in the parks and lakes.

OCTOBER MID-AUTUMN FESTIVAL (ZHONG QIU JIE)

Also known as the golden week holiday or the moon festival, the mid-autumn festival is a time when people eat lots of delicious moon cakes. These are round cakes made with the standard ingredients of wheat, sugar, and one or two dried egg yolks. Other moon cakes come with a variety of stuffings, according to the area of China in which they are sold, including dried fruit, nuts, and meat (usually ham, duck, or chicken). The legend goes that you should climb your nearest hill or mountain late in the evening to admire the full moon and eat moon cakes with friends, family, or your loved one.

Rather expensive in some places, these cakes can be an ideal gift for anyone. Foreigners often find them very heavy and they are considered quite fattening.

The story behind this holiday reverts to a legend called Hou Yih, who was an officer in the Imperial Guards in the year 2000 B.C. It goes that one day there appeared a sighting of ten suns in the sky. The Emperor, greatly concerned and afraid that this sighting foreshadowed some great evil to his people from the almighty, ordered Hou Yih, who was an expert archer, to shoot nine of the suns. Hou Yih did not let the emperor or the Goddess of the Western heaven down, for he did exactly as requested and accomplished the feat with impressive results.

Knowing that Hou Yih was also a renowned architect, the Goddess asked him

In China, festivals are a time when families get together after a long time being apart in different cities.

to build her a remarkable palace made of multicolored jade, as jade is a very important stone in the Chinese culture. He did not fail and with that the Goddess rewarded him with a capsule that would give him a chance of having everlasting life. The legend states that he was not to take this pill until he had undergone a year of prayer and fasting.

Hou's wife was not aware of the capsule that Hou had hidden away safely. Or so he thought, because his wife, a very beautiful and charming young lady named Chang Oh, found it and swallowed it. By the time Hou found out, it was too late. His wife was already airborne and was sent to the moon. Ever since, the legend has it that Chang Oh's face gleams in the moon on the 15th day of the 8th month of the Chinese lunar year— hence the moon festival!

MAY DAY HOLIDAY

The May Day naturally falls on the 1st of May. It's not much of a celebration of any sort; however the relief for many people to get a three-day official break from the office is welcome.

DRAGON BOAT FESTIVAL

Apart from Chinese New Year, the dragon boat festival, known as the "Duan Wu Jie," is perhaps the best known symbol of a traditional Chinese festival. It falls on the fifth day of the fifth lunar month. The highlight of the festival is contestant teams racing on their local river in slim wooden boats in the shape of a dragon (usually with the front part representing the dragon's face and the back part in the shape of a tail). Each team may have up to eight contestants, all dressed in colorful traditional costumes and chanting patriotic songs to the beat of drums in the background.

On the ground, shops sell boiled rice (known as "Zhongzhi") mixed with vegetables or meat and wrapped in a banana leaf, made to the shape of a pyramid (known as "Ketupat" in some parts of SE Asia such as Malays a and Brunei).

The festival is said to commemorate the death of a minister and great poet of the State of Chu (Qu Yuan) during the Warring States (475–221 B.C.), who according to legend, drowned himself in protest in the river after learning that his king did not accept his advice. To avoid sea life consuming his body, the people of Chu launched their boats and threw rice dumplings wrapped in bamboo leaves into the rover where he drowned to feed the fish.

It's a very colorful event in cities such as Shanghai, Guangzhou, and Hong Kong, where people line up on the banks of the rivers and cheer on the contestants. At the end of the race, in a gesture of good humor, the captain of the winning team is jubilantly thrown into the river by his teammates before collecting the trophy from the mayor of the city.

RELIGION

In China, people are allowed to practice their religious beliefs in places of worship; however, it would go against the government's wishes if those beliefs were spread around or if others were encouraged. Several cases have been reported of foreigners who have been detained and deported from China for passing out unauthorized religious literature. Sentences for distributing this material may range from 3 to 5 years' imprisonment, if convicted.

For these reasons, many Chinese keep their religious beliefs a private matter. There are of course many beautiful Buddhist temples around, as well as Christian churches and Muslim mosques. The main religions are Buddhism, Taoism, and Confucianism. While the majority of Chinese

Religion in China is practiced but people are not encouraged to promote it. Here is a devout priest in Suzhou.

people don't believe in God or any particular religion, China is home to approximately 102 million Buddhists, approximately 9 million Muslims, and around 14 million Christians.

CHAPTER 14

HOBBIES/INTERESTS

THERE ARE PLENTY OF OPEN AIR AND INDOOR SWIMMING POOLS. MOST real estate developments have their own in-house gym and swimming facilities that can be used by the residents for a minute cost compared with public facilities.

Every major city and town in China has numerous beautiful parks and lakes. These parks are kept clean and have a small entrance fee. The country has approximately 2,800 natural lakes with a total area of more than 80,000 square km. Some of the more popular parks and lakes have traditional Chinese instrumental music being played, normally with the recorded sound of a "Zheng," an 8- or 25-string plucked instrument. The speakers are camouflaged in shrubs and flowers, creating a romantic atmosphere. Public parks are extremely congested during the holiday season with families, tour groups, and couples.

Chinese people have in the past been known to save money for future investments and not spend on holidays or unnecessary purchases because it was thought of as a waste of money. Nevertheless, with increasing salaries and more free time on their hands, Chinese families are starting to enjoy all the kinds of entertainment and lifestyle choices that would normally be seen in other more advanced developing nations in Asia. Everything from artificial skiing slopes to traveling abroad is on the activities list for the modern Chinese person.

Irrespective of the city you are living in, there are things to see and do everywhere in a country that is host to at least 33 official UN World heritage sites, including the Beijing Great Wall, the Giant Panda reserve in Sichuan, and the Xi'an terracotta warriors.

During the winter months, hot springs, some natural and some man-made, are popular tourist attractions for families and couples alike. Hot springs are normally located in beautiful rural surroundings next to mountains, parks, or lakes. Most hot springs offer special packages that provide hotel accommodation, breakfast, and unlimited access to the pools. As with other parks, tea houses, and lakes in China, hot springs also have beautiful Chinese instrumental music being played in the background, usually the stringed "Zheng." An ideal way to take away your stress in the winter.

Excursions can be easily booked through travel agents, some of whom can speak very good English. There is the risk that some expats can make themselves fall into the trap of just staying around their expat neighborhood because they are afraid to wander around the country due to lack of language or cultural knowledge.

CATS AND DOGS

Chinese people, especially women, love to keep small dogs as pets. Chihuahuas seem to be a favorite choice and in many neighborhoods people normally go for an evening stroll with their dogs. For unexplained reasons, Chinese girls get very excited when they see dogs, not so much with cats. Even if a girl is walking hand in hand with her boyfriend, and she sees a cute dog, she will almost forget her boyfriend and focus on the dog! On the other hand if you are a young single man walking with a cute dog, then girls will take note of you too, not just the dog!

MAH-JONG

There is a general belief among the Chinese elders that by playing Mah-Jong, they can help eliminate any irregularities that are usually associated with the brain's functionality as a person gets older (such as Alzheimer's or Parkinson's disease for example). So because of this physiological effect, blended with the fact that some elders have nothing else to do all day, they often play Mah-Jong all day. The phrase "all day" implies exactly that—most people start playing the game early in the morning and carry on until sunset with the occasional break for essentials or to have a quick snack at lunch time. These pensioners play for fun of course.

The Chinese as a culture like to gamble and some serious players like to indulge in this rather addictive game for financial purposes. There is plenty of this going on in the Las Vegas of Asia, Macau.

TAI CHI

With its origins in China, Tai Chi (known more commonly as "Tai Chee Chuan") is a popular Chinese martial art practiced ubiquitously throughout the country in schools, parks, and residential communities. The theory behind Tai Chi agrees with many of the philosophical principles of Taoism, and Confucianism.

If you venture out in the early morning around 6 a.m. or so, it is common to come across a group of old-aged pensioners practicing Tai Chi in motion complete with fake swords in their hands. The martial art is actually more challenging than it looks, and the art of a perfect Tai Chi session involves the testing of all of the body's and mind's senses so that the person's health, meditation and martial arts are all blended into one. Many scholars have pointed out the strong benefits of Tai Chi for a person's health and longevity, including that the slow gentle movements of the martial art can burn more calories than surfing or hiking. Apart from renowned Chinese actors who openly practice Tai Chi in real life, such Jackie Chan, Bruce Lee, and Jet Li, recently the most famous person to adorn this martial art is China's Premier Wen Jibao, who has been regularly seen practicing Tai Chi with local elders in parks around the country.

Tai Chi is a popular choice of exercise for early mornings and evenings throughout the country.

There are plenty of schools that teach Tai Chi in almost every Chinese city. The prices vary from around 100 yuan for an hour to around 300 yuan an hour depending on the experience of the teacher and the reputation of the school. It's best to ask your neighbors or colleagues to give the best suggestion for a good Tai Chi school.

LITTLE EMPERORS/EMPRESSES!

China's one-child policy may seem to be working well in the government's roadmap to having a smaller population; however it has also tended to create a large population of spoiled and discourteous kids. This is much more apparent within China's middle class where each young kid has the close attention of their parents, both sets of grandparents, and all other relatives who are willing to buy anything for their loved ones. Hence these middle-class Chinese kids have been given the nickname "little Emperors" or "Empresses." On the whole children are treasured in China. The subject of children is probably the best starting point of your talk with your host. Therefore when you do ask about children, always start with your own kids, or your friends' kids. It a nice way to get into the inner circle with your host and mix in well with your Chinese friends.

CHAPTER 15

ENTERTAINMENT

CHINESE OPERA

Chinese opera comes in various styles, such as Beijing opera (more formally known as Peking opera and "Jiangxi" in Mandarin), Cantonese opera, from Guangzhou, and Sichuan opera. Of all the Chinese operas, the most famous is Beijing opera, which is thought to have been established around 1790.

Chinese opera requires the actors to go through hours of preparation in skilled face painting, which itself is like a work of art. Chinese opera is performed by actors who express their singing and moods with prolonged high-pitched notes lending a very strong emotional connection to the story they are performing. Even some Chinese people cannot understand what the actors are saying when performing the opera. If you come to China and you don't get a chance to watch a genuine opera show, then it may be said that you have not experienced the real China.

Tickets can be expensive during the holiday season. In touristy places such as Beijing, almost all shows are fully booked. If you love watching Chinese opera then you can either head off to your nearest theatre or find out more or watch it on Channel CCTV 11, which is dedicated to nothing else but Chinese opera.

KTV BARS

The Chinese usually like to relax in the evening either at home with their families, or go out with their colleagues and friends to a KTV (Karaoke Bar). KTV venues have rooms to hire of all different sizes depending on how many people want to rent the room for singing. The prices for hiring a room per hour depend on the type of service you want, such as food and the number of songs. Each room consists of a couple of televisions with microphones to sing with and a PC from which you can choose the songs that you want to sing. Convenience food, such as snacks, fruit, and drinks, can be ordered. For those who cannot understand Chinese, or who are not budding singers, then KTV may prove to be a boring affair. Some KTV machines do have a limited selection of English songs.

Unlike in Japan and Korea, where KTV bars also double as "hostess bars" for exhausted businessmen in search of some of the unmentionable pleasures of life, in China the KTV culture has not reached such adventurous altitudes. Nevertheless in some big and modern cities such as Shanghai, Shenzhen, or Harbin, such KTV bars do exist in minute numbers with the majority of "hostesses" being migrant girls from the villages, attracted to the neon lights.

In the northern cities they are usually young women from Russia or Mongolia. Normally the trend is for businessmen to go to a KTV bar after work and perhaps act as host to their counterparts from the overseas offices, staying there until the wee hours of the following day, not doing much except singing songs, drinking, and watching TV. Quite monotonous actually but it's effective if you just want to while away the time after a stressful day.

THEATRE & CINEMA

Theatre plays are a way by which folk Chinese stories are told in many public parks around the country.

There are a number of good cinemas in the major towns and cities. In smaller towns and villages sometimes there is a common television set up in the middle of the street where everyone can come to watch the latest movie. Hollywood movies are normally shown a bit later than in the rest of the world because of license reasons. While Chinese cinema has not quite hit global popularity as Hollywood and Bollywood (Indian cinema) have, there is a general interest in Chinese movies throughout Southeast Asia. With the rise of modern Chinese stars such as Jackie Chan, Jet Li, Gong Li, Zhang Ziyi, and Chun Fat Yuan making their mark in Hollywood movies, Chinese movies are no longer stereotyped for being full of just simple kung fu action. Increasingly foreign filmmakers are looking towards China to choose their locations because of its beautiful and magical landscapes.

Most of the theatres and cinemas are large, clean, modern, and have a roof, although some have open sides, which makes it difficult in the winter because there is no heating system—this more applies to southern China because of the hot weather for most of the year. The other thing that you may find annoying when in a theatre or a cinema is that people will talk with each other and on their mobile phones all the way through the entire show only to stop if there is an important scene or something special happens in the show. All of this seems discourteous to the foreigner. But rest assured that the Chinese see it as simply a way to enjoy a good day out with the family.

CHAPTER 16

COMMUNICATION

EMAIL AND INTERNET ACCESS

China has plenty of Internet Service Providers (ISPs) who will be happy to help connect you.

There are surpluses of private and joint-venture ISPs, many of which have their own World Wide Web sites, some of them bilingual, others Chinese only. Data published by eTForecasts suggested that the American share of the world's online population declined from around 20% in 2004 to about 13.4% in 2009, while China's share increased from about 10.7% to just over 17%. Nearly 90% of China's internet users are surfing the Web with a broadband connection, which is an increase of 190 million from 2008. Mobile phone internet users totaled 245 million by the beginning of 2011. According to the latest figures from CNNIC, the number of internet users in China rose to 420 million at the end of June, 2010, an increase of almost 36 million users in the first 6 months of year 2010 and including 115.1 million users in the rural areas. The current internet penetration rate in China is 31.6% according to Internet World Stats statistics.

Broadband is widely available through China Mobile or China Unicom, the two main state-owned service providers on the mainland. It's best to take a Chinese-speaking friend with you to a local China Mobile store. For a relatively small price, between approx. 100 yuan and 200 yuan a month at the time of writing, you can have unlimited internet connected through broadband access plus your China Mobile landline. They even install the equipment for no extra charge. In a nutshell, internet access in 21st-century China is much faster and cheaper than in the West.

Another success story is that China is now Skype's biggest market. In September 2009, Skype had just over 75 million registered Skype users in China, approximately 17% of the total, and more than in any other country. Western social networking websites such as Facebook, Twitter, YouTube, and other similar websites were blocked at the time of writing by the central government server. When these sites would be accessible to the general public is anyone's guess as the government does not wish to have these websites being accessed by the general public. Some people have tried to use VPN to access these blocked websites; however sometimes even that is blocked. While Western websites may be banned in China, the influence on the public comes from the 30% of the Chinese population who are using domestic social networking websites such as Sina, QQ, Tencent Weibo, Weixin, and RenRen. If one looks at the bigger picture, it's not the Western influence or dominance in China of big brands such as KFC, Starbucks, Pizza Hut, etc., but it's the national Chinese rivals that are going head-to-head with their Western competitors. All of that influence is actually being fueled by the Chinese social networking websites.

When you apply for your internet access account, it's best to take your passport and a copy of your passport with you. Although you're technically required to register with the Public Security Bureau (PSB) before you can open an account, many ISPs will do this for you.

INTERNET CAFÉS (WANGBA)

Internet cafés are located in all the main cities. Most coffee shops such as Starbucks, Jamaica Blue Coffee, Costa Coffee, and Illy provide a complimentary wi-fi service to their customers. However if you end up using a local Chinese internet café, then take good care as the vast majority are in dark and smelly rooms accompanied by a cloud of cigarette smoke—unhygienic and to be avoided if possible. It gives a whole new meaning to surfing online, as in any internet café, you can find an army of at least 50 people, usually teenagers, all playing Counter-Strike with each other! Be careful as some of these internet cafés are operated without a proper license and are prone to random checks by plain-clothed police. Costs at the time of writing are about 5 yuan per hour. As there aren't many smoke-free cafés in China, a nice and clean internet café can cost between 7 and 10 yuan per hour.

INTERNATIONAL CALLS

You can request access to making international calls from your home phone when you set up with China Mobile. Calling internationally from China is not cheap, because there is only one provider, so therefore no competition for prices. International calling cards provided by either China Satcom (known as 17970 or "Yao-Qi-Jiu-Qi-Ling") or by China Unicom (known as 17910 or "Yao-qi-jiu-yao- ing") are available at street kiosks in values of 50 yuan or 100 yuan. Most people at the kiosks don't understand English, so you can ask for them in Chinese as follows:

English: I would like to buy the "17910 International Calling card" for 50 yuan/100 yuan please, thank you.

Mandarin Pinyin: "Wǒ yào yì zhāng yāo-qī-jǐu-yāo-líng guó jì diàn huà kǎ—Wǔ Shí Kuài dē/Yī Bǎi Kuài de，xiè xiè"

Mandarin: 请我要一个17910购机点卡 50快的/100块的

English: I would like the "17970 International Calling card" for 50 yuan/100 yuan please, thank you.

Mandarin Pinyin: "Wǒ yào yì zhāng yāo-qī-jǐu—qī-líng guó jì diàn huà kǎ—Wǔ Shí Kuài dē/Yī Bǎi Kuài de, xiè xiè"

Mandarin: 请我要一个17970购机点卡 50快的/100块的

Skype is easily accessible in China, and customers that wish to use the Skype phone service can also do so by paying using their international Visa card (or a local Chinese credit card).

PHONE LINES/MODEMS

As is the case in other developing countries, phone lines in China can be awkward, so your ability to dial in to a server may depend on how your office (or hotel, home, university, or work unit) is connected. If you're in a Western-style business office, you should be able to dial in easily. If you're at a university or some other state-run organization where the telecom equipment is old, you may have problems since phone lines are frequently overloaded. Keep trying, however, and you can usually connect.

On the whole, China has a very high bandwidth compared to most European and Asian countries. Internet connection is fast, reliable, and much more efficient.

NOT A CENTRALIZED SYSTEM

China's internet and mobile telephone system can be highly tricky, and at times, troublesome. Every city in China has its own mobile phone system, even if those cities are in the same province. So for example, if you live in Shenzhen then you will find it cheaper and more convenient to have a Shenzhen mobile number, and if you then relocate to Guangzhou (which is in the same province as Shenzhen), then you will find it cheaper and more convenient to have a Guangzhou mobile phone number. In addition, if you want to deactivate your Shenzhen mobile number then you have to go back to your service provider in Shenzhen to deactivate your number, even if your service provider has a branch in Guangzhou. Of course, you can keep your original phone number; nevertheless, if you have any issues then you have to speak to your service provider in the city where you bought the sim card (and the costs are higher too). It's the same issue that people have to face with banks too. It's best to open a bank account for every new city you have to live in even if it is with the same bank; otherwise you will end up paying a commission every time you take money out of the ATM machine outside of your home city. It's a highly bureaucratic system, which does not benefit anyone.

PERSONAL EXAMPLE

I relocated from Shanghai to Guangzhou, which is a journey of two hours by plane. When I left my apartment in Shanghai, I forgot to deactivate my internet account, and I forgot to deactivate my mobile phone account for Shanghai too. Once I got to Guangzhou, I called the service provider (China Mobile), and asked them to deactivate my Shanghai internet account. To my frustration, they told me that I have to physically go back to the branch outlet where I originally signed up for the internet account to be able to permanently deactivate the account. That meant that I would have had to take at least a day (make that two days just in case of flight delays, etc.) to go back to Shanghai just to close an internet and mobile phone accounts.

Now, to make matters worse, the person who moved into my home in Shanghai started using the internet for free under my account because it was still open. The only solution for this dilemma was for me to change my password for both my internet account and also my mobile phone number, and until I returned to Shanghai I could not close both accounts down.

PHOTO PROCESSING SHOPS

Getting your photos processed should not be a problem, as there are photo processing studios everywhere in most towns and cities. These photo processing studios also double as "luxury photo" studios, where you can go and have your photos taken in various poses, with super Kodak type quality and much cheaper than what you would pay for the same quality in the West. It's also a kind of fashion among the unmarried couples or Chinese girls to have their photos taken complete with a wedding dress or a tuxedo—just so they can see what they will look like when they get married!

Newly wedded couples as well as toddlers can often be found in parks and lake areas during the weekend having their photos taken, rain or shine.

NEWSPAPERS AND MEDIA

Chinese media, including the internet, is censored by the central government. Sometimes the news pages of the BBC, CNN, and some other selected news websites are blocked. The timing of these blockages is random and unannounced, so for example, one minute you may find that you can access any of the BBC website pages, but the next minute they be blocked.

The state owned CCTV (China Central Television Channel) has twelve official channels, with CCTV 9 (www.cctv-9.com) being the only English-speaking channel in the whole of China. CCTV1 and CCTV5 are the main flagship channels, and both show major sporting events live such as the World Cup and the Olympics. There are two other English-speaking channels that are available on cable TV, TVB Pearl broadcast from Shanghai and ATV broadcast from Hong Kong. BBC and CNN are available on cable TV or in four-star and five-star hotels. If you don't have STB (Cable TV), then the other 70 state-owned channels are all in Chinese. Apart from CCTV, every province, or cities in a provinces has its own state-owned television channels with local news and shows. Occasionally Western movies are shown with subtitles.

China Daily is the major English-speaking newspaper and is available in hotels and reception halls of multinationals, but it's difficult to find it in a street stall. Then there are various state-owned newspapers that are available only in those particular cities or provinces; for example the *Shenzhen Economic Zone* daily is only available in Shenzhen, and the *Guangzhou Nanfeng Daily* is only available in Guangzhou, and so on. All these newspapers are of course printed in Mandarin.

South China Morning Post (www.scmp.com) is a Hong Kong–based English daily that is only available in all major hotels and multinational offices on the mainland.

Glossy fashion magazines from the West have only started being sold in recent years, and not many are available on the market. *GQ, Marie Claire, and Good Housekeeping* are just a few that are available on street stalls, and are printed in Chinese. If you are coming to China with foreign magazines or newspapers, they may be confiscated at the entry/exit port if the customs staff members feel that the material is not appropriate to bring into China, which includes publications that contain pornography, that are political in nature, or that are intended for religious proselytism.

Foreigners seeking to enter the mainland with religious materials in a quantity larger than that required for personal use may be detained and fined. Chinese customs authorities may confiscate books, films, records, tapes, and compact disks to check whether they infringe Chinese prohibitions.

CHAPTER 17

LEARNING CHINESE

THE OFFICIAL CHINESE LANGUAGE, KNOWN AS MANDARIN OR PUTON-ghua (common language), is one of the world's most complex languages. Unlike the ease with which foreigners can pick up languages such as French and Spanish with considerable fluency, this is not always the case with Chinese because no matter how expert you are at mastering this marvelous language, you will never be as good as a native Chinese, as one of my friends quite rightly pointed out:

No matter how fluent foreigners are at speaking Mandarin, they always sound funny to us because to us it looks strange that a foreigner is talking in Mandarin, but we are most willing to assist of course. It's all part of the fun of learning any new language.

Mandarin is spoken by approximately 95% of the population of mainland China and Taiwan. It is also known as *Hanyu* (the language of the Han people) and *Zhongwen* (language of the middle kingdom). The majority of the population keeps Mandarin as their first or second language along with their local dialect.

There are more than 150,000 foreign students in China, with the vast majority learning Mandarin. China's only English-speaking television channel, CCTV-9, quoted that in 2006 there were more foreign students in China than the number of mainland Chinese students (125,000) studying overseas.

Considering that one in five people in the world are from China, along with the fact that Chinese is one of the most difficult languages to learn, it would be a good idea to learn to speak some useful phrases before coming to the country. By learning Chinese you can begin to understand the cultural differences, and often it will help explain to you why those differences make you particularly uncomfortable.

Some schools in European countries, such as the UK and France, have already taken notice of the need to introduce Mandarin as an optional subject into their school curriculum. Clearly, European governments are realizing that they need to help equip the youth of today to handle the future challenges of working along-side their counterparts from emerging economies such as China.

Because of China's large geographical presence, many dialects are spoken in the different provinces. Apart from Mandarin, which is based on a northern dialect, with a few exceptions, with Beijing pronunciations as the standard, there are seven other dialects spoken widely throughout China, including Shanghainese, Hakka, Guangdonghua (Cantonese is spoken in Hong Kong, Macau, and Guangdong Province), Amoy, Fuzhou, and Wenzhou. In some of the villages and remote areas there are many minor local dialects spoken only within the tribes.

The Chinese phonetic alphabet is called the Pinyin and uses letters from the pronunciations of the Chinese characters. As the characters themselves don't correspond to the sounds, the phonetic alphabet is a well-established tool that helps overcome any problems in reading, writing, and remembering the characters.

Many of the letters have the same sound values as in English, but a few are different. Other Asian languages such as Vietnamese, Burmese, and Thai, for example, work in a similar way to Mandarin because they belong to the Sino-Tibetan family of languages as opposed to the Indo-Aryan family, to which English, Arabic, and Hindi, for example, belong.

The tone of the Chinese word is just as significant as its pronunciation. This feature of verbal communication of Chinese is the challenging part for foreigners to learn. In English, the tone of a word varies with the mood of the sentence; in Chinese, the tone stays the same whether the sentence is a question, exclamation, or a simple statement. The mood is signified by stress on some words. To use a wrong tone in a Chinese word would transform its meaning entirely.

There are four tones in Putonghua, expressed as 1st, 2nd, 3rd and 4th. The first tone is a relatively high level pitch (-); the second tone is a rising pitch (/); the third tone is a fall-rise pitch (\/) and the 4th tone is a falling pitch (\). Now considering Mandarin has four tones, other dialects may have more, such as Shanghainese has eight in some words and Cantonese has up to nine. Therefore Mandarin may seem quite straightforward in that respect.

Many Chinese words are made up of one or two syllables, and each syllable is represented by one character. Even if two syllables have the same initial and final letters, the tone may give them totally different meanings. For example: Yi said in the first tone means the "number one" and Yi said in the third tone means a chair.

Besides the four basic tones, there is one special tone known as the neutral tone. The neutral tone is not a syllable that stands by itself; it occurs only in relation to the tone that precedes it. There is no tone mark written above syllables of the neutral tone. The neutral tone is considered short and weak, but don't think that neutral is far less important than the four main tones, since not many English speakers can master the language accurately and with a natural flow if unaware of how and where to use a neutral tone in communication.

Normally the tone mark is written on top of the vowel. If there are several vowels in a word, the tone mark is written on top of the major vowel that is pronounced clearly and the loudest (or the vowel that is visibly the most important). The structure of a Chinese sentence is relatively simple to understand and can be put as: Subject, Verb, and Object.

In some circumstances there are bound to be changes in the tones. Quite a number of words, such as Wo (Me, 我) are not necessarily at all times marked with a similar tone when they emerge in various phrases. The simple explanation behind this is that the tone of some words depends entirely on the tone of the word that follows it. So for example Wo ought to be only spoken in the first tone when it's used by itself; if the next word consists of either a 1st, 2nd or 3rd tonal word, then Wo can be spoken in the fourth tone, Wo; if then the fourth tone is present in the next word, Wo should be read in the second tone Wo.

Effectively, if the 1st tone is followed by a neutral tone, then it may be possible to stress the 1st tone, if however, there are two similar tones, then the tone on the first syllable should be short and then the tone on the second syllable can in actual fact be stressed.

Let's say if a syllable of a second tone is followed by a syllable of the 3rd, 4th, 1st, or the neutral tone, then the second tone is pronounced with only the falling part of the tone without its final rise. However, in case the second tone is followed by another second tone, then the first second tone is read as a first tone. Sounds confusing—and it is for anyone who is alien to the language. Also note that all questions are normally followed with a "Ma" at the end.

With China's advancement, some linguists have predicted that Chinese may be one of the world's dominant languages after English. Birds flying next to the China Shanghai Expo 2010.

Unlike Beijing and Shanghai, a person living in a second tier city such as Suzhou, Nanjing, Hangzhou, Tianjin, Dalian, Chengdu, and others may experience some difficulties if they do not have knowledge of the local language or have assistance from a local Chinese person in such cases as banking matters, public transportation, shopping for items at a local store, etc., but overall the Chinese people are very patient and accommodating to foreigners with the most basic Chinese vocabulary. Most Chinese people in second tier cities do speak and understand Mandarin Chinese as that is the national language. Learning a few key Mandarin phrases definitely helps.

CHINESE CHARACTERS AND WRITTEN CHINESE

As pointed out earlier, the Chinese language is one of the oldest and most complex of languages to learn. Every Chinese character depicts a picture and it is upon this principle that the written form is based. Chinese characters are believed to have been created more than 3800 years ago out of simple pictures of things they represented. For example a person (Ren) looks like a little human with two legs as if he is running (人), and mouth (Kou) looks like a square (口). The written form is the same throughout most of the Southeast Asian region where the majority of Chinese people reside. The complexity comes in the spoken form, where there are a myriad of regional dialects and forms of the Chinese language. Cantonese for example is only spoken in Guangdong Province and Hong Kong, while Hokkien is spoken in some parts of Singapore, Malaysia, and some parts of Fujian and Anhui provinces. The vast majority of the words are compounds that are created by joining two or more characters together. For example, the characters for the "sun" and "moon" put together make the word "bright," while the words "electric" (Dian, 电) and "shadow" (Ying, 影) make the word "cinema" (Dian Ying, 电影). Modern Chinese characters consist of two parts: the radical and the phonetic. The radical shows the class to which a word belongs, while the phonetic illustrates how a word is pronounced. Most of the characters without a phonetic component are believed to have been developed from simple pictures.

For example, the radical word "mouth" (Kou, 口) may be found in a whole host of words such as "to eat" (Chi, 吃) and "drink" (he,|喝). There are approximately 250 radicals; some of them are common while others are rarely required for everyday usage. It's a very useful skill to be able to learn and practice using the radicals with phonetics.

The phonetic part of a character is often itself a character. Mastering the pronunciation of the core character from which some words are derived can often assist in the pronunciation of most of those words. Westerners frequently find it very difficult to distinguish between the various sounds of words when they are pronounced in Pinyin, even though they may look different when written. Just practice having a go and you'll be able to impress the locals sooner than you think!

For Westerners, learning all these concepts can take a long time; indeed the spoken version of standard Mandarin is easier to pick up then the written version, where the latter may take years and even then it is difficult to master some words. Various sources indicate that there are around 60,000 characters, bearing in mind that for everyday use (perhaps to read a magazine, newspaper, or road signs); you will only require on average between 5,000 and 7,000 characters. Even this is a lot to swallow considering that in the English alphabet there are only twenty-six!

Road Signage	Meaning
Jie (e.g., Sichuan Jie)	Avenue/Street
Lu (e.g., Beijing Lu)	Road
Zhong (e.g., Nanjing Zhong Lu)	Middle
Nan (e.g., Nanjing Nan Lu)	South
Bei (e.g., Nanjing Bei Lu)	North
Xi (e.g., Nanjing Xi Lu)	West
Dong (e.g., Nanjing Dong Lu)	East
Da Dao (e.g., Shennan Da Dao)	Expressway (or Highway)
Yi, Er, etc. (e.g., Zhongshan Yi Lu)	One, two etc.

My personal Chinese class tutor in Guangzhou advised me that for any beginner to the Chinese language, the best way to study is to learn to write and pronounce one or two characters a day and keep on memorizing those characters on a regular basis, so by the end of a year you will have mastered at least 365 characters!

Hello	你好 (NiHao)
Me	我 (Wo)
How are you?	您好吗? (Ni Hao Ma?)
You (Singular)	你 (Ni)
You (Plural)	你们 (Nimen)
We	我们 (Women)
I have a question	我好一个问题 (Wo you yi ge wen ti)
I am fine.	我很好 (wo hen hao!)
My name is …	我的名字是 (wo jiao…)
What is your name?	您叫什么名字? (Ni Jiao Shen me ming zi?)
Do you speak English?	你说英语吗? (ni shuo ying yu ma?)
Good morning	早上好 (zao shang hao)

Good afternoon	下午好(xia wu hao)
Good evening/night	晚上好/夜(wan shang hao)
It is nice to meet you.	真的很高兴见到你 (hen gao xing ren shi ni)
Do you understand me?	你明白我的意思吗? (ni ming bai wo de yi si ma)
I don't understand	我不明白 (Wo bu ming bai)
Could you speak more slowly?	你能说慢一点吗? (ni neng shuo man yi dian ma?)
Are you from here?	你是本地的吗? (ni shi ben di de ma?)
Bye	再见(zai jian)
Thank you	谢谢您 (Xie Xie Ni)
You are welcome.	不客气 (bu ke qi)
Please	请 (qing)
Excuse me.	劳驾 (Lao Jia)
I am sorry.	对不起 (Dui Bu Qi)
Pardon me.	请愿 凉 (Qing yuan liang)
You are very nice.	你真好 (ni zhen hao)
I don't know	我不知道 (Wo bu zhi dao)
Thank you for your help.	感谢您的帮助(xie xie ni de bang zhu)
Can you help me, please?	你能不能帮忙? (Ni neng bu neng bang mang?)
Help!	救命! (jiu ming)
Please call a doctor!	请叫医生! (qing jiao yi wei yi sheng lai)
Where is the police station?	警察局在哪里? (jing cha ju zai na li)
I am lost.	我迷路了 (wo mi lu le)
Yes	是，对 (Shi, Dui)
No	不是 (Bu Shi)
Where is the embassy?	大使馆在哪里? (da shi guan zai na li)
I need a doctor!	我要看医生! (wo yao kan yi sheng)
Where is the pharmacy?	药店在哪里? (yao dian zai na li)

Someone stole my belongings.	有人偷走了我的东西 (you ren tou le wo de dong xi)
I lost my passport!	我丢了我的护照 (wo diu le wo de hu zhao)
Stop	停 (ting)
Go straight	直行 (yi zhi wang qian)
Turn left	左转 (xiang zuo zhuan)
Turn right	右转 (xiang you zhuan)
Where is…?	…在哪里？ (…zai na li)
Where is the exit?	出口在哪里？ (chu kou zai na li)
Where is the entrance?	入口在哪里？ (ru kou zai na li)
Keep going.	一直走 (yi zhi zou)
I am looking for a hotel.	我要找酒店 (wo zai zhao jiu dian)
Where is the bathroom?	洗手间在哪里？ (xi shou jian zai na li)
Is it far from here?	离这里远吗？ (li zhe li ma)

CHAPTER 18

CHINA: HOST TO GLOBAL EVENTS— IMPACT ON EXPATS

OWARDS THE CONCLUSION OF THE FIRST DECADE OF THE 21ST CENTURY, China was at the center of the world's attention at a huge scale when the greatest sporting event on earth came to Beijing on the 8th day of August in 2008, in the form of the world Olympic Games.

The Chinese put forward an ambitious bid to host the Olympics on the eighth day of the eighth month of the year 2008, because in China the number eight is considered to bring good luck and fortune. And luck was indeed on the side of the Chinese, when in 1991, the IOC formally awarded the 2008 Olympics to the city of Beijing. For many the Olympic Games were hailed a success far beyond what Chinese authorities had even imagined to be.

Expats can enjoy the endless beauty that the country has to offer.
Seen here are the dreamy mountains of Yangshuo.

270

In the run-up to the Olympics many events and exhibitions had created tremendous economic and social opportunities for Chinese citizens as well as foreigners. To China, the Olympics meant more than just a showcase for the largest sporting event in the world. The Olympics opened many corridors for massive economic trade at the highest level between China and the rest of the world. These opportunities are expected to continue for many years, even in the decades that follow in the aftermath of the 2008 Beijing Olympic Games.

The Beijing Olympic Games brought in many sponsorship and trade opportunities for foreign investment into Chinese cities. It wasn't just Beijing that benefited but also Shanghai, Tianjin, Dalian, Qingdao, Hong Kong, and Macau—although the latter two did not have much of an impact on foreign inward investment as the northern cities. Nevertheless, these inward investment opportunities have paved the way for foreign corporations to set up their offices, sometimes even their China or Asia Pacific Headquarters (again moving away from setting up HQs in places such as Singapore and Hong Kong) in these major Chinese cities that hosted the events of the Beijing 2008 Olympics. These business contracts have allowed the opportunity for foreign corporations to bring in foreign leadership and workforce to settle in China. So the number of expats will of course greatly increase in China, especially in these main cities. Henceforth this brings a need for all these expats to learn a new culture, a new language, and get acquainted with their new home in China. It goes without saying that an increasing number of Chinese people are learning English, however to counter-balance this trend, an equally increasing number of foreign expats in China are willing to learn Mandarin. The knowledge of the local language goes way beyond any relationship building exercise that foreigners may involve themselves in because if you can speak and understand the language then at least there is some indication that your efforts will be recognized by your hosts—whether in the business or personal environment.

Nobody should be blamed for the lack of correct English in China; it's a natural occurrence because the Chinese language and the English language are totally different. It must be borne in mind that China has not been exposed to the international arena for a long time, and so English is still very much a new language. It's difficult for the Chinese people to learn English, just as it is for foreigners to learn Chinese.

Just as an example, prior to the Beijing Olympics, one of the trends to have hit the capital was taxi drivers practicing their English while driving around foreign passengers. Simple sentences such as "Where would you like to go?" or "It will cost you X amount of yuan" were played on the car cassette player and occasionally the taxi driver might like to practice talking with the passengers. It was all good fun and a great way for the drivers to enjoy their work because it's something new and exciting for them.

China has gained a lot of global attention in the recent years because of its ability to host world class events. The Beijing Olympics in 2008 were just the beginning. Then arrived the 60th Anniversary of the founding of the People's Republic of China on October 1, 2009. Some other events that have put China in the global limelight are the Shanghai 2010 World Expo, Guangzhou Asian Games in 2010, and the 2011 Shenzhen Universiade. All of these events were a showcase for China to present the best of its infrastructure, its economy, and how well the country can plan and host major international events of significance. The key trend from these events is that the event advertisers/sponsors brought in foreign investment, and this in turn brought in the large number of expatriates that we see today in China.

The rice fields of Guilin.

CHAPTER 19

MOVING TO CHINA—DECIDING
WHAT TO PACK

O NCE YOU KNOW FOR SURE THAT YOU ARE OFF TO CHINA, YOU NEED TO decide what to pack up depending on the following factors:

• What time of the year you are going and which part of China you are going to—this is very important because if you are going to south China during the winter then you don't need to pack too many warm clothes. Winter in southern China lasts no more than two months at the worst and the majority of the year is warm and humid. On the other hand, winter time can present some exceedingly freezing conditions in the northern cities such as Beijing, Shanghai, and Xi'an for example.

• How long are you going to China for? Obviously if you are going for a contract that is lasting for at least a year then it would be wise to take quite a considerable amount of clothing with you.

• Take sensible amounts of clothes with you, maybe seven sets of clothes, one for each day of the week, with an extra set for other occasions. Don't fall into the trap that buying clothes on the mainland is necessarily cheaper than in the West because it's not surprising to see Western-labeled designer clothes or other high-quality material available at more or less a similar price to what you would pay back in the West. Of course on the other side of the coin, there are various outlets that offer high-quality "fake" designer labels at a fraction of the cost you would get in the West. Remember that you will have to bring the whole lot back again, so avoid over-packing at all costs!

• Some corporations offer a "relocation allowance" for those who are going to be moving abroad for a long period (anything from six months and beyond is considered as "long period"), while others might cover the cost of extra luggage on top of the basic amount that airlines offer (typically this extra luggage can be anything from 80 kg up to 180 kg, depending on your company's policy). It

273

would be advisable to move as many personal belongings as you like and make the most of the allowance that is given to you.

• Even if you do qualify for a "relocation allowance," do bear in mind the small size of Chinese homes. Unless you are lucky enough to be put in a luxurious and spacious expat villa in Shanghai or Shekou, do try to keep your luggage on a small scale because storing it would be a problem. Most Chinese homes don't have the storage space that Western homes do, and especially if you are moving from Canada or the USA, where many homes have a basement level that can store extra luggage, you will be in for a shock as there is no such thing in a Chinese home (even in the expat areas). You may need to pay extra to a relocation company to have your extra luggage stored in their warehouse. The costs associated with this are available from your China relocation company, and a list of these is provided in this book.

• There is no need to bring your furniture to China, unless you want to of course. There is IKEA and B&Q in some cities in China.

• Be careful of bringing electrical items into China. Although in Hong Kong and Macau you should have no problem with using Western style three-pin plugs, in China the plugs are configured with either two pins, or narrow-type three-pin plugs. If you have to take an electric shaver, a portable games console, mobile phone/laptop charger, and so on, then it is advisable to buy an international plug adaptor. Electrical adapters compatible with international standards are widely available in China. It would be advisable to purchase one from your home country or at an international airport.

• Bear in mind that import/export laws in China restrict certain items from being brought into the country, such as some publications. For example, a British friend of mine who relocated to China had copies of the *Sun* newspaper and men's magazine *Nuts* confiscated by customs officials upon arrival at Shanghai Pudong Airport—much to his embarrassment in front of on-looking locals, who, of course, had never seen such publications in their life.

• You might want to bring your favorite snack foods to China, such as Walkers crisps or chocolate—these are not widely available. Although they may not last long once you are there! Dove Chocolate (Mars group), Snickers, Cadbury, and M&M's are available on the mainland.

• For children, think about items such as toys, computer game consoles, books, and anything else they cannot live without. Involving children will help reassure them that they will find it comfortable living in China just as they did back in their home country. Important things such as favorite hobbies (stamp collecting materials, skateboarding shoes, favorite books, music, and DVDs) should also need to be taken into account.

- There is no need for you to bring your bicycle to China. After all, China used to be known as a "bicycle country"! You can purchase good quality cycles in many stores in every city at a reasonable price.

- Unlike in past times there is no need to bring your own cutlery and utensils to China because Western-style kitchenware is easy to find (e.g., in Walmart, Jusco, Carrefour, and Tesco supermarkets). Increasingly Western style cutlery is available in China. Though if you are going to a rural area, then Chinese-style spoons, and chopsticks would be in abundance! The Chinese spoons are not the same as Western-style spoons, and even if you are in a Western-style restaurant (except in five-star hotels and foreign-owned restaurants), then eight times out of ten you will probably get a fork and a sharp kitchen knife instead of a dinner knife matched to the fork! It's just like in the West, where supermarkets don't stock as many chopsticks as Western cutlery, so the same in Chinese supermarkets, where they don't stock as much good quality Western-style cutlery as they do Chinese ones.

- Don't worry about taking the bedding, because there are plenty of good quality pillows, quilts, and bed sheets available in China, and there is more variety too. You can easily purchase genuine silk bedding for a fraction of the cost you would pay in the West, plus it's a rare luxury to have silk material bedding in the West.

- In terms of your dress code, pretty much anything goes in China and you can dress however you feel comfortable. Because of history, there is no particular fashion style in China and it's especially the women who tend to wear an odd and interesting mix of clothes that might make you wonder for example, why someone in the office wants to dress in tight leather pants as if they were going to ride a motorbike! Of course as a woman, if you go out in a tiny top and shorts, don't complain if you get stared at more than you normally would as a foreigner, especially from construction workers who have not seen their wives/girlfriends for years!

- If you are on medication, it is advisable to take it with you, especially if you know that it may be difficult to purchase in China. Some medication (for epilepsy and diabetes for example) may not be available in China, so talk this over with your doctor at home before bringing a reasonable quantity to China. If the medicine is prescribed in limited quantities, you may need to arrange the delivery of further prescriptions.

- Antiperspirants and shaving cream are available in stores such as Watson's and Mannings, but not common, so it would be wise to take a sensible amount of stock with you. (These products are not available in abundance and are expensive because they are imported.) The same goes for designer fragrances (Gucci, Armani, CK, etc.). They are available in China but because of duty tax, they tend to be double the price of what you may find back in the USA, or Europe.

- Pets can be brought into China as long as they are not endangered or protected wild animals. You should check with the Chinese Embassy in your country and you should also check with the local Agricultural and Fisheries department in your country. Furthermore the Chinese Embassy in your country may be able to provide detailed information on any customs laws regarding the importing of pets into China.

- You may want to take along your favorite music tracks (either as a MP3/4 or CD format) and your favorite DVDs as foreign music and films are still not widely available in China. Be aware of the customs restrictions on what to bring and how much.

Minor but important things that you must take care of and need to take with you are listed here:

1. Mandarin phrase book and English-Chinese dictionary

2. Passport

3. Work Visa & Resident Permit

4. Your contract in English and Chinese (if you have one)

5. Birth Certificate, Marriage Certificate, etc. (although you can get copies in case you lose these)

6. Local Driver's License and International Driver's License (but neither allows you to drive in China)

7. It would be useful to have contact addresses and phone numbers of people you know in China (friends, colleagues and so on).

8. Medicine and any medical certificates

9. Copies of credit card numbers, mobile phone Sim cards and local currency need to kept safe with at all times (never leave valuable belongings open in your home in China—thieves know where foreigners live and can target them in any case).

10. Take care of your mobile phone, laptop, and all other valuable belongings.

11. Important numbers of the local police station and emergency numbers of your local consulate and embassy in China.

12. International calling cards

CHAPTER 20

CULTURE SHOCK IN CHINA

N O MATTER HOW WELL YOU PREPARE YOURSELF MENTALLY, YOU WILL nevertheless experience culture shock. It's something that will stick with you irrespective of how long or how many times you travel between China and other countries because for you China will never be the same as your native country. In some way or another it will, without a doubt, affect you emotionally and perhaps even physically. The good thing is that the longer you stay in China, the more you get used to the surroundings and then you start treating it as your second home. This is when at least some of the emotional signs of the initial culture shock start to dissipate. Getting to identify what is acceptable and what isn't can at times prove to be tricky.

Settling in any foreign country for the first time can be challenging yet exciting. It's fair to say that for the first few months you are no more than an excited tourist taking photos everywhere, digesting the sights, smells, and sounds of China.

Before you go you need to think carefully about questions such as "How long do you really want to stay in China" and "For what reasons will you stay in China?" or "Is it beneficial for your future life or career?" You may be in a situation where you are going to China for the first time to experience what it's like before you embark on a longer stay there afterwards. The answers to all of these questions are vitally important because those answers will inevitably determine how you feel and react after returning from China. If you can, try to take a short break to go and experience what it's like in the country that you may be living in for a long time. It will be better than going there with no preparation and then not liking the place—you will just end up wasting your money and time. The other side of the argument may be that you don't have the time and/or money to go to China for a holiday.

There are a number of ways to overcome the initial homesickness. One way is to treat it like a lucky break or a working holiday because every day you know that you are experiencing something new and different, something that your friends and relatives back in your native country never got the chance to do. Treat it as no different from migrating to a different city, that you never been to, in your native country. Even though China is moving towards becoming a country that is exposed to "internationalism," it still has time to go before it becomes as international as, say for example, Hong Kong, where it is normal for everyone to speak English or to see a foreigner. It would be fair to say that these days in China you can get almost everything that you would be able to get back home (food wise especially), though it may still be expensive because it may be imported. The main difference is that when you are abroad you experience a different "culture" in terms of language and not just the environment.

The symptoms of culture shock occur naturally and start even before the journey begins in your home country, as you prepare to leave the comforts of your accustomed surroundings. It sounds like a sad love story but that's exactly how it may be viewed, because you are leaving something that you love and going to a destination that you are not familiar with, and in the process you will most likely end up making new friends and starting a new life. It's as much a physical experience as an emotional one and it is something that any individual will experience every time he or she moves to an unfamiliar location anywhere in the world.

Try to look at it the other way around. Take a moment and just imagine how Chinese people feel when they come to your native country to work, for holiday, or to study. Of course it is not easy for Chinese people to settle into a foreign environment, especially a Western culture such as Europe or the USA. Everything for the Chinese seems a challenge, from holding a fork and knife in a restaurant to not being able to mix in with the locals for entertainment. Thinking about this may put your mind at ease because you as a non-Chinese suffer the same culture shock when you are in China.

Language can be a barrier for most expats and locals.

I remember when I was at university in the UK, I used to see lots of Chinese students going to the local supermarket and buying nothing but eggs, rice, and ready-made noodles. It seemed funny at the time but when I was in Shenzhen, I realized that I was in their shoes and the locals must have been wondering why this weird foreigner was buying lots of hamburgers and cereal bars!

Suffering from culture shock may include confusion, loneliness, disorientation, homesickness, anxiety, disliking the local food, missing loved ones or friends back home, and stress. This all takes its toll with the time difference (+8 hours GMT and +12 hours from New York) and the cost of international calls For example, making that extra effort to telephone home can be a headache especially if you have had a long day and you need to call back to your parents or loved ones. For long-distance relationships, couples can find it stressful to say the least.

Quite amazingly you will be surprised that in China, you w ll end up making more friends than you ever did back in your home country. These friends may consist of fellow expats and locals alike. There are two reasons for this. The first reason is that you will be surrounded by a group of people from different countries and cultures but who have something in common; you are all expats in a foreign land. So there will be plenty of friends to make, to share stories about each other's experiences.

The other reason is that you will find it much easier to make friends with the locals because to them you are different, and being different has its advantages. Both you and your host friends can share stories about each other's culture and countries. Chinese people will often consider it a privilege to invite a foreigner into their home for a meal. Even on the street or in the office, it is very easy to make friends with the locals because you are different.

This "over-friendliness" by the Chinese and the VIP treatment given to foreigners can actually make foreigners become too spoiled in a way. For example, I realized that I got used to being treated like a VIP for everything and it got to the point where sometimes I expected it all the time, whereas this was not always the case. For example if I went to a bank and there was a large queue, then the bank staff would give me the privilege of jumping the queue simply because I was a foreigner; or if I went to a restaurant and there were no tables available, then on a few occasions I saw that the waitress took the trouble to ask some Chinese people to either move to another table or hurry up so that a foreigner could take a seat.

One side of me was always thinking that this is a good thing, while on the other hand I was always feeling a bit guilty of taking "liberties" to some extent in China. One day on a crowded train from Guangzhou to Shenzhen, a Chinese man offered me his seat; I politely kept on refusing but finally I sat down after he declined my refusals. At the moment that I sat down, another young Chinese man came up to me and spoke in an American accent: "I have lived in New York for over twenty years and no one has done this for me in America, why should we give up our seat to foreigners in China? Why? Can you tell me?" Meanwhile a lady, presumably his other half, calmed him down. I thought to myself that he did make a point and he was brave enough to say it. So I politely told him to take it easy, in Chinese, and then got up and changed carriages. He seemed surprised and I assume he wasn't expecting me to answer back in Chinese.

But my point is that the American-Chinese man made me think that most foreigners (including me) get sucked into the habit of being treated like a VIP everywhere we go in China (this is while under the influence of suffering from culture shock), but we don't realize that when foreigners come to our country we ignore the culture shock that they are going through. It's an interesting concept, one which I am sure many foreigners would wonder over!

One of the most important things that I would advise to new expats is to stop thinking in terms of your home country's currency, and start to think in terms of your local Chinese currency. While it is natural to think of your Chinese salary in terms of its equivalence in your home currency, you will be in a much better position if you plan your budget around your new salary in Chinese currency.

Most people are able to lead comfortable lives in China on their expat salary and benefits. In fact, you can earn a much higher salary than the vast majority of the country and at least five or even ten times as much as some of the local staff in your office. Having said that, your finances will largely depend upon your lifestyle. Trying to re-create a Western lifestyle in China can be costly. Western products are increasingly available in mainland China, but import fees mean that those same products will cost more.

REPATRIATION—THE EFFECTS OF REVERSE CULTURE SHOCK

Even though this book is aimed at expats who have not yet set foot in China, the issues involved when you do return from China to your home country need to be addressed. It's best to know what you may expect beforehand rather than later.

After spending a long time in China, coming back to your home country may seem strange, especially if it's in Europe or North America. For some people it may be a relief to come back while for others it can actually be more stressful to return than it was to move to China in the first place. No matter how long you have lived in China, you will without a doubt see things differently, think and behave differently, than you did before you left your home. Some people experience more of the reverse culture shock after returning from China to their homelands, while others experience more culture shock when they go to China. It purely depends on the individual.

A Dutch friend of mine who returned to Holland after spending nearly two years in Guangzhou told me that he didn't find much of a reverse culture shock when he returned to Holland, but he had suffered from culture shock when he first arrived in China because he wasn't prepared for the shock, mentally or physically—whereas he knew what it was like in Holland and nothing much had changed upon his arrival.

From my personal experience, every time I come back to the UK, it seems so boring and dull compared to the excitement and busy atmosphere of Hong Kong and China. Strange as it may seem, when you have been in a country like China for a long time, every time you come back to the UK it makes you think how life is more laid back and relaxed in the West. I suppose, apart from my parents, the second best thing I missed must be the food. It's always good to tuck into a bag of nice cod & chips or cheese & onion pasties!

The beauty of it all is that most expats complain when they are in China, but when they are away they start missing their expat life so much that it hits them emotionally. This is because they don't get the same star "VIP" treatment in their home country that they became accustomed to as expats in China.

If you are living in the West (especially the UK, America, or some parts of Europe), you will definitely notice that it's much easier to make friends in China, simply because you are different. In the West people are more conservative and have an attitude of minding their own business, whereas in China or anywhere else in Asia, people may be nosy and curious, but out of that you will end up making more friends than enemies.

For example, in the UK, it is rare for someone to go up to a total stranger on a bus or train and start introducing themselves and becoming friendly; people will start having doubts about your character. But in China you will have to get used to Chinese people coming up to you and asking questions and trying to become friends with you. As an expat you may find out that it's easier to make friends with other foreigners in China, because as foreigners you are a minority in someone else's country; and through this networking opportunity you never know who you may bump into.

As an expatriate away from home for a long time, you will realize that you will have changed more than your family or friends who have stayed behind. Even though they have carried on with life without you, they generally would have maintained the same routine of life for the period that you have been away whereas you will have met many people from diverse cultures and backgrounds, experienced different environments, and faced different challenges and benefits of life, which actually can make someone more mature about life, especially if they are young.

PERSONAL STORY

I first went to China for a one-week holiday during the spring festival of 2004. I was lucky that I knew a very close friend there who welcomed me and showed me around because I knew nothing about China. I was not prepared for the culture shock. I could not speak the language, could not even hold chopsticks properly, and was just like a kid in a candy shop—very excited and running around Guangzhou with my camera taking photos of anything that seemed new and strange to me.

When I came back to the UK I felt like as if I had woken up from a dream because it was such a short trip and even though I had been away for only seven days, I was in actual fact experiencing the effects of "reverse culture shock." One of the many reasons for this could have been that I enjoyed my holiday so much and I did not want to come back to the UK.

I liked the place so much that I could not wait to go back. It was almost as if I had fallen in love with China and Hong Kong, because they are so far away from the UK and it's something exotic, something new, and it's something special to have when you are moving around between Europe and Asia.

I kept my faith and I did manage to go back later in the same year after completing my degree, but this time it was for a longer period. This time around I did not know how long I was going to stay in China and where my future would take me with my job. Nevertheless after the first few months, when the "honeymoon period" was effectively over, the reality of living and working in China started to hit me.

The two major shocks that foreigners are likely to encounter in China are that of language problems and the lack of good-quality Western cuisine. It's usually after the first couple of weeks that you start to realize that you have to live without eating cereal with milk in the morning or have a Sunday roast. The only places near the mainland where you are guaranteed to get some genuine Western food are in Hong Kong or Macau. Thankfully living in Shenzhen meant that I could always nip across the border to Hong Kong for a day or two during the weekend and spoil myself with as much Marks & Spencer food as I liked!

Living so far away can, without a doubt, be exciting and life rewarding; however, there are other minor but important things that you have to worry about. For me the pressures of life such as worrying about my parents' health were always lurking at the back of my mind. It was the thought of "What if things went wrong." Of course I kept in touch through email, internet, and the phone.

Nevertheless, being so far away meant that naturally my parents would not disclose any bad news to me, such as if my mother was ill for example (which she was on one occasion and I only found out when I returned to the UK after a few months!). Of course I was livid with them for not telling me and they obviously didn't want to worry me so they kept saying everything was fine.

I was lucky to have a job that enabled me to effectively "commute" between China and the UK on a fairly regular basis and hence I got used to the 13-hour non-stop flights so much that after a few times it really felt no different than catching a long-distance coach with the exception that I had to deal with the effects of the time difference both mentally and physically!

I found out that having lived in China for a long time also made me effectively "become Chinese," and I only realized this when I came back to the UK. My parents and family were astonished that I could speak Mandarin, and it didn't end there. In the first week I came back, while assisting my parents with the weekly shopping in a local supermarket, after getting my change back from the cashier, without realizing it, I accidentally said thank you to her in Chinese, and she looked at me in surprise!

It is fair to say that I wasn't fully prepared for the shock that I got when I arrived in Guangzhou; however, I am glad that I wasn't because it has made me better prepared to tackle the culture shock no matter where I go in the future. I always maintain the principle that if you can survive in China then you can survive in any other country (except war zones, natural disasters, and so on of course!).

From my experience, I would certainly advise expats to go on a short crash course on Chinese culture before they come to China, if possible. It would definitely help to have friends or colleagues who are from the mainland and get to know as much as possible about the culture from them. Even speak with expats who have been resident in China for a long period of time and try to get useful advice from them. It will boost your confidence and morale tremendously.

CHAPTER 21

HOW TO STOP CULTURE SHOCK FROM RUINING YOUR LIFE IN CHINA!

A VOID REJECTING OR OFFENDING THE CULTURE. YOU MUST REMEMBER that you are in someone else's country, so it's only fair to respect their way of living—no matter how strange you may find it. In England, there is a saying that an "Englishman's home is his Castle"; there goes a similar saying in China: "A Chinaman's home is his Imperial Palace." Trying to change local methods to make life easier for you will not work. Instead it will do you more harm than good and build up your stress and frustrations. The best way is to just go with the flow and accept the local practices and ways of living. It would be advisable to steer clear of talking about certain political issues involving China. If you find yourself in a conflict situation, a better way to get what you want is not to raise your voice but to calmly persist. Local residents tend to react to another's anger equally or more strongly. Loud voices are used quite frequently and often what sounds like an argument is just a lively discussion—for example, when bargaining for goods at a local market.

Do as much background reading about China and in particular the part of China that you are going to. A good start would be to read the *The Rough Guide to China, The Lonely Planet* guides to China, and other useful travel guides. Go to Google or yahoo and just type in the name of the Chinese city you will be traveling to. Look at the photos, maps and so on to get a virtual feel of the place. It will mentally prepare you for the place. The physical preparation can come later when you are physically there and that should not be a problem as you will get used to it after a few days or couple of weeks at the most.

Avoid whining and complaining about everything that makes you feel uncomfortable, such as people staring at you or asking you too many personal questions. The Chinese people are very nice and friendly towards foreigners and those that have seldom come across foreigners will want to be as hospitable towards you as possible. For these reasons people in the suburbs and rural areas (and even in some major cities where there's a large migrant community) will stare at you and will be curious to find out more about you. Most Chinese people are shy in front of foreigners—by all means you can meet the other end of the spectrum too. It will do you no good to take things personally, say for example if nobody sits next to you on a bus or train, despite that seat being the only empty one. Don't be upset by people staring at you or being nosy. Instead try to start a conversation if you can; in the process you may learn something new about their culture and life. If you smile, then 90% of the time you'll get a smile back.

FOOD

Most foreigners I have met in China are very careful about eating the meat, especially street meat. There is no harm in trying any new food for the first time, and then you don't have to eat it again if it doesn't tickle your taste buds. As long as you buy what the natives are eating or if there is a large queue of people including foreigners buying the food, then it should be no problem. As mentioned earlier, the Chinese are very careful of what they eat and where they eat—if a restaurant is empty then normally it means that the restaurant is under-rated by the natives.

LANGUAGE

Learn the language—inability to speak Mandarin is a problem for most foreigners in China. To put your mind at ease, try to learn the essentials of the language before you go to China and then try to keep learning on a regular basis while you are there. Normally the best way is to learn one or two words a day and then memorize them after a few days. The Chinese language is very different from all the Indo-Aryan languages so therefore it is difficult to learn for Westerners. Practice and repetition help.

BEHAVIOR

Even though China is changing and people are becoming a bit more liberal, nevertheless, do try to avoid kissing, hugging, or engaging in any other "touchy" behavior with your partner in public—as it will not go down well with the locals. For example, I once saw a foreign gentleman giving a piggyback ride to his girlfriend in Beijing's Tiananmen Square. This resulted in him being politely told by a guard to put her down as it caused offense to the locals.

Try not to be put off by people spitting, clearing their throat with a loud noise, or sneezing loudly without a tissue in public places (including offices, public transport, etc.). This kind of behavior is normal among the deprived and those who have not been in contact with Westerners. Unfortunately it is ubiquitous in China. caused either by excessive smoking, bad air pollution, or just an unpleasant habit. There is nothing you can do about this, because if you look at someone with disgust, they will get confused and think that something is wrong with you. Try to ignore the negatives and think of the positives and you will see the world in a different way.

When putting down chopsticks on the table during dinners, avoid putting them facing downwards into a bowl of rice, as this indicates a symbol of death or bad luck. Normally a chopstick stand is provided for each person, where you can place the chopsticks on the side of your dishes.

Avoid giving a clock to anyone as a gift, as this indicates death. I made this mistake when I gave a Millennium clock in 2000 to a Chinese friend of mine. Of course if a foreigner gives such gifts (unknowingly), then it can be taken with a laugh.

MIDDAY SUN

Just as in other countries in Asia where the midday sun is dangerously hot—especially from noon to 3 p.m. (India, Malaysia, Vietnam, etc.), Chinese women use an umbrella to protect their skin from the blazing hot sun. I have seldom seen men use an umbrella to protect against the sun because the Chinese believe that "the man should be strong and face the sun!" If you are a foreign woman, it would be advisable that you use an umbrella to protect yourself. You will be the odd one out if you don't!

INVITATIONS

If Chinese friends invite you to their home or to attend a dinner with them or their family, it's best to accept the offer if you have the time. The Chinese consider it an honor to invite a guest, especially a foreigner, to their home. Even if you politely refuse the offer, it may seem rude, so you should try to make an effort to attend because, as mentioned before, losing face in China is very important.

GETTING UPSET

Avoid getting upset and certainly don't verbally lash out at anyone if they push you and then they don't apologize for it. Since China is the world's most populous country, undoubtedly people are going to push and shove each other unintentionally in crowded places such as airports and train stations. People, especially those from the rural areas, are not used to saying sorry, as it is seen similar to "losing face." In saying this, elderly people are given more respect than any other group of people.

It is very easy for a foreigner to get upset in China, and for the smallest of things—all because of culture shock. What makes it worse is that the locals will usually start laughing and this would of course give you the impression that no one is taking you seriously. This is because in China facial expression goes a long way to show your emotions. When Chinese people are upset they normally open their eyes wide, their eyebrows are then pointing upwards and they stare with disgust. However when Westerners get upset, they frown, have their eyebrows pointing inwards towards the eyes and start moving their arms and hands in all different directions to show anger and then the Chinese people start laughing because they think you seem confused and not upset.

When conversing with your Chinese friends or colleagues, don't have any perceptions of rudeness or "no-manners," especially when words such as "Thank you," "Sorry," "Please," or "Excuse me" are not used as often in Chinese as in other languages.

SENSE OF HUMOR

Avoid jokes or using sarcasm in the office, with friends, or at formal dinner gatherings/parties. Given that the vast majority of Chinese people have not been exposed to sarcasm, and mix that with language problems—you will not be doing anyone any favors—and if the joke is rude then you best be careful as people may take t seriously enough to feel insulted. In the process, you will end up feeling embarrassed and effectively "talking to yourself"—because not many people will understand what you are trying to imply. The sense of humor of Westerners is just totally different from a Chinese sense of humor. In saying this, the best advice would be to "to keep your sense of humor," and in China it's a must to beat culture shock!

CLOTHING

The general sense of dressing is very informal throughout the country, partially because of the hot weather (in southern China) and partially because of cultural differences. People generally don't judge you on the way you are dressed although saying that, there is the chance that in their own circles and within their own class, people will tend to show off. Even in many multinationals, unless you are a senior Manager or Director, not many people wear a formal suit. Sales and Marketing professionals normally keep a suit in the office, in case a client visit is required at short notice. It does make you think how affluent people in Europe and the States are when it comes to dressing up. In the evening you may come across people going to the supermarket to do shopping wearing their night pajamas and slippers and in hot weather the men usually roll their shirts up to their chest and rub their belly.

Don't be shocked to see someone cleaning the road while wearing a blazer jacket, or someone dressed in tight leather pants in a corporate meeting in a multinational. It goes without saying that because of historical reasons, such as that people only started wearing Western clothes around the early 1980s; many Chinese don't conform to Western concepts of how to dress up properly and for what occasion. This applies very much more for women than men and the proof is everywhere.

PROSTITUTION

All over China, women outside hotels in tourist districts frequently use the prospect of companionship or sex to lure foreign men to isolated locations where their accomplices are waiting with the intention of robbing you. You should not allow yourself to be driven to bars or an individual's home unless you know the person who's making the offer.

If you need a haircut, then be careful which hair salon you venture into. Don't be fooled by the numerous amount of so called "hair salons" that are actually illegal massage parlors or brothels, and the shocking thing is that they are everywhere in China. The government is taking great efforts to tackle this problem; however, like most things in China, it's easier said than done. It's sadly a vital ingredient for a waiting pandemic of diseases such as AIDS. Thankfully these "haircutting brothels" are being phased out by the Chinese government but nevertheless in most parts of the country they do give a somewhat negative image of a country that is nevertheless a beautiful and prosperous one.

You should take care and be wary of the fact that in the big cities, it is common for prostitutes to place nuisance calls to your hotel room number (somehow they know where foreigners stay!) in the middle of the night—the best defense is to disengage the phone from the socket. Some cases of theft of personal belongings have in the past been reported by foreigners, who have been either intoxicated or drugged in their hotel rooms. Hotel guests should refuse to open their room doors to anyone they do not know personally.

LEARNING

On the whole learn as much as you can about China. Try to catch up on current affairs by watching the news, reading the internet and newspapers, and doing research on your embassy's website. Also try to read travel books to learn more. On the internet go to any search engine and type in keywords such as: "Expat + China" or "living in China" or anything about the particular city that you are going to travel to. This could range from any subject such as the availability of foreign foods to school options. Being able to speak in the language of the province or city you are in is absolutely key to understanding and perceiving from the Chinese point of view. On the language level it is one thing, but on the cultural level it is a problem to be accepted within Chinese society.

PROFESSIONAL RELOCATION CONSULTANT

If you want, you might like to hire a professional relocation consultant who can advise you on any worries that you may have regarding settling in China. Your company may have resources and information for getting hold of a relocation consultant on your behalf, as the prices may be high if hired on an individual basis. If there are a group of expats in your company who have come to China for the first time, then perhaps a cost- and time-effective solution may be for your company to hire a relocation consultant for you. A good consultant will not only save your money and time but also provide encouragement to you to mentally take control of yourself and provide you vital information as to how you can achieve that in a way that's comfortable to you.

ATTITUDE

Having a positive attitude can go a long way to diminishing the stress that is connected with culture shock. Having a good attitude toward most things can eliminate the bad and sad feelings that you may develop once you have settled into your Chinese environment.

This one comes down to personal choice; however I would put myself in the situation of avoiding wearing too much perfume or aftershave. Chinese people are not used to wearing too much of these products. Although with the change of the times, the younger generation from China's middle class would jump at the first opportunity to try the latest CK1 or Christian Dior.

As an expat in a foreign country you need to prepare yourself for challenges and benefits. However, no matter how bad you feel or how bad your experience has been, don't be taken too much by stories and experiences that other expats or repatriates (people who have returned back from China) tell you. They may not have been able to beat the culture shock in the same way that you may do or they may not be experienced travelers and so on. It's good to get different opinions and listen to other people's stories, and then you can judge for yourself of what the place looks like and feels like. Every country has good people and bad people and every country has good areas and bad areas.

You will not be doing yourself a favor by just hanging around in expat bars and areas where the majority of foreigners (Laoweis) stay as this will not give you exposure to the real China. As a foreigner in China you have to go out and experience the country as the locals do—otherwise it's a waste of time and money. I remember venturing into a few expat bars in Shekou (Shenzhen) and Shanghai, where I happened to meet quite a number of foreign expats who proudly told me that they had been living in China for many years. I was, however, a bit shocked to find out that when I asked them if they could speak the language or knew anything about general Chinese life, they shrugged their shoulders and said, "Nah, buddy, there is no real need, I have my free home, my expat bar, and my corporation looks after me well here; I don't need to speak Chinese or eat Chinese food!"

Don't be put off by friends or family members who try to scare you with any ancient stereotypes that they may hold about China. On one of my trips back to the UK, I once met up with some of my university alumni friends, and they were stunned to hear that I had been living in China for such a long time. They were telling me things like: "You'd better take care," "Do you know anyone there?" "Oh god, China? That's where they have public beheadings right?" It was the funniest thing I ever heard. I politely reassured the gentleman that he was probably thinking about Saudi Arabia and in my time in China I have never heard or seen such things. He was shocked to hear that I feel much safer walking on the streets of Guangzhou in the middle of the night than I do walking in broad daylight in some parts of London or New York.

There is a saying that "Give a Chinese an Apple and he will in return offer you an Orange. If he does not have an Orange readily available, then he will remember it and returning you the Apple will become one of his life's goals."

The best way is to make as many Chinese friends as possible—which shouldn't be a problem because Chinese people will jump at the first opportunity to make friends with a foreigner. One American friend of mine put it into perspective:

I have been to so many places around China with my Chinese wife that I would not have been able to see had I been lurking around with other foreigners or by myself. Having a Chinese partner certainly helps in many ways such as language problems, food, companionship, a sharing of cultures and you get to experience China in an exciting way that can greatly eliminate any physiological effects that you get with the normal culture shock because you feel safe in the company of your Chinese partner.

CHAPTER 22

LISTINGS FOR CHINA

WHILE THE INFORMATION PROVIDED IN THE FOLLOWING LISTINGS was correct at the time of going to press, neither the author nor the publisher is liable for responsibility for any changes that may occur in any contact information for any of these listings. Since China is experiencing a rapid change, any of the listed companies may change their address at short notice, and that would be without the knowledge of the author or the publisher.

MANAGEMENT CONSULTANCIES

Accenture China
21/F West Tower, World Financial Center
No. 1, East 3rd Ring Middle Road
Chaoyang District
Beijing, 100020
Telephone: +86 (0)10 5870 5870
Fax: +86 (0)10 6561 2077
Website: www.accenture.com

APCO China
16th Floor, NCI Tower
12A Jianguomenwai Avenue
Chaoyang District
Beijing 100022
People's Republic of China
Telephone: +86 (0)10 6505 5128/7
Fax: +86 (0)10 6505 5258
Website: www.apcoworldwide.com

A.T. Kearney (Shanghai) Management Consulting Co., Ltd.
22/FL, Hang Seng Bank Tower
1000 Lujiazui Ring Road, Pudong New Area
Shanghai 200120
Telephone: +86 (0)21 5182 2000
Website: www.atkearney.com

Bain & Company Consulting Group—China
Unit 2407-09, Office Tower 2
China Central Place
79 Jianguo Road
Chaoyang District
Beijing 100025
People's Republic of China
Telephone: +86 (0)10 6533 1199
Fax: +86 (0)10 6598 9090
Website: www.bain.com

Boston Consulting Group China
21/F, Central Plaza
227 Huangpi Bei Lu
Shanghai 200003

People's Republic of China
Telephone: +86 (0)21 2306 4000
Fax: +86 (0)21 6375 8628
www.bcg.com.cn

CapGemini China
CapGemini Center
Shanghai, PRC
Post Code: 200021
Telephone: +86 (0)21 6182 2688
Website: www.cn.capgemini.com

CEC—China Expert Consulting (China) Limited
1718 Forture Times Building
1438 North Shanxi Road
Shanghai 200060
Telephone: +86 (0)2162271673
Fax: +86 (0)2162271024
E—mail: Shanghai@chinaexpert-consulting.com.cn
Website: www.chinaexpert-consulting.com

Deloitte China
Deloitte Touche Tohmatsu CPA Ltd.
8/F Office Tower W2
The Towers, Oriental Plaza
1 East Chang An Avenue
Beijing 100738
People's Republic of China
Telephone: + 86 (0)10 8520 7788
Fax: + 86 (0)10 8518 1218
Website: www.deloitte.com

Droege Management Consultants China
Rm. 811 Green Land Commercial Center
1258 Yu Yuan Road
Shanghai 200050
People's Republic of China
Tel.: +86 (0)21 6240 9090
Fax: +86 (0)21 6240 9881
Website: www.droege-international.com

EAC—Euro Asia Consulting Rep. Office
Sunyoung Center, Rm. 1702
398 Jiangsu Road
200050 Shanghai

China
Telephone: +86 (0)21 6350 8150
Fax: +86 (0)21 3250 5960
Email: eac-sha@eac-consulting.de
Website: www.eac-consulting.de

Ernst & Young
Level 16, Ernst & Young Tower
Oriental Plaza
1 East Changan Ave. Dongcheng District
Beijing, 100738
China
Telephone: +86 10 5815 3000
Website: www.ey.com

Fiducia Management Consultants
Unit 1907-1910, Central Plaza
No. 227 Huangpi North Road
Shanghai, 200003, China
Telephone: +86 (0)21 6327 9118
Fax: +86 (0)10 6327 9228
Email: info@fiducia-china.com
Website: www.fiducia-china.com

Far Eastern Limited China
Room B1805, Top Land (DiSanZhiYe),
Jia 1 of ShuGuangXiLi,
Chaoyang District
100028 Beijing, China
Telephone: +86 (0)10 5822 1042
Fax: +86 (0)10 5822 1049
E-Mail: beijing@far-eastern.cn
Website: www.far-eastern.de

InterChina Consulting
Suite 3110
Haitong Securities Tower
No. 689 Guangdong Road
Shanghai 200001, P.R. China
Telephone: +86 (0)21 6341 0699
Fax: +86 (0)21 6341 0799
Email: Shanghai@InterChinaConsulting.com
Website: www.interchinaconsulting.com

JLJ Management Consultants China
Unit 603-605
Shanghai Oriental Center
699 Nanjing West Road / 31 Wujiang Road
Shanghai 200041
People's Republic of China
Tel +86 (0)21 5211 0068
Fax +86 (0)21 5211 0069
Email: info@jljgroup.com
Website: www.jljgroup.com

KPMG China
8th Floor
Office Tower E2, Oriental Plaza
1 East Chang An Avenue
Beijing 100738, China
Tel +86 (0)10 8508 5000
Fax +86 (0)10 8518 5111
Website: www.kpmg.com

LEK Management Consultants
Floor 34, CITIC Square
1168 Nanjing Road West
Shanghai 200041
People's Republic of China
Telephone: +86 (0)21 6122 3900
Fax: +86 (0)21 6122 3988
Email: info@lek.com
Website: www.lek.com

McKinsey China
17/F Platinum Building
233 Tai Cang Road
Shanghai 200020
People's Republic of China
Telephone: +86 (0)21 6385 8888
Fax: +86 (0)21 6386 2000
Website: www.mckinsey.com

Mercer Investment Consulting/HR Consulting China
Room 3601
Hong Kong New World Tower
300 Huaihai Zhong Road
Shanghai 200021
People's Republic of China
Telephone: +86 (0)21 6335 3358
Fax: +86 (0)21 6361 6533
Website: www.merceric.com
Website: www.mercerhr.com

Monitor Consulting China
Unit 3905-3906, K. Wah Center
1010 Middle Huaihai Road
Xuhui District
Shanghai 200031
People's Republic of China
Tel +86 (0)21 6145 8900
Fax +86 (0)21 6145 8901
Website: www.monitorgroup.com.cn

PWC China
26/F Office Tower A, Beijing Fortune Plaza
7 Dongsanhuan Zhong Road
Chaoyang District
Beijing 100020
Telephone: +86 (0)21 6123 8888
Fax: +86 (0)21 6123 8800
Website: www.pwc.com

Roland Berger Strategy Consultants (Shanghai) Ltd
23rd Floor Shanghai Kerry Center
1515 Nanjing West Road
Shanghai 200040
People's Republic of China
Telephone: +86 (0)21 5298 6677
Fax: +86 (0)21 5298 6660
Website: www.rolandberger.com.cn

HOSPITALS

ANHUI PROVINCE

Anhui Provincial People's Hospital
1 Lu Jiang Road
He Fei City
Telephone: +86 (0)551 2652 797

Affiliated Hospital of Anhui Provincial Medical Institute
218 Ji Xi Rd, He Fei City
Telephone: +86 (0)551 3633 411

BEIJING

Alcoholics Anonymous
Telephone: +86 139 1138 9075, +86 (0)10 6940 3935
Beijing AA Fellowship: www.aabeijing.com
Email: Beijingfellows@yahoo.com

Centers for Disease Control and Prevention
Travelers Website: www.cdc.gov
Telephone: 877 394 8747

American-Sino OB/GYN Service
218 Anwai Xiaoguan Beili
Beijing
Telephone: +86 (0)10 6496 8888 (24 hours)
Email: info@asog-beijing.com
Email: billing@asog-beijing.com
Website: www.asog-beijing.com

Arrail Dental (瑞 尔 齿 科)
19 Jian Guo Men Wai Da Jie
Chao Yang District
Beijing 100004
北 京 建 国 门 外 大 街19 号
Telephone: +86 (0)10 65006472/3, 85263235/6
Website: www.arrail-dental.com

Asia Emergency Assistance Ltd. (AEA)
14 Liangmahe South Road, 1/F
Beijing 100600
Telephone: +86 (0)10 6462-9112, 6462 9100
Fax: +86 (0)10 6462-9111

Bayley & Jackson Medical Center
7 Ritan Dong Lu
Chaoyang District
Beijing 100020
北 京 朝 阳 区 日 坛 东 路7 号
Telephone: +86 (0)10 8562 9998
Fax: +86 (0)10 8561 4866
Website: www.bjhealthcare.com

Beijing Anding Hospital (Psychiatric Hospital)
5 Ankang Hutong, Deshengmenwai
Xicheng District, Beijing
北京安定医院
北京市西城区德胜门外安康胡同5号
Telephone: +86 (0)10 58303000 (operator)
Telephone: +86 (0)10 58303225 (Foreign Department)

Beijing First Aid Center
103 Qian Men Xi Da Jie
Xuan Wu District
Beijing
北 京 前 门 西 大 街103 号
Telephone: +86 (0)10 120 (24-hour), +86 (0)10 65255678, 66014336

Beijing Airport First Aid Center
首 都 国 际 机 场 急 救 中 心
Telephone: +86 (0)10 64591919
Inside the Beijing Capital Airport Terminal 2
地址： 北 京 首 都 国 际 机 场 2号航 站楼内
Telephone: +86 (0)10 64530120
Inside the Beijing Capital Airport Terminal 3
地址： 北 京 首 都 国 际 机 场 3号航 站楼内

Beijing Hengsheng Hospital
12 Dongzhimenwai Dajie, Chaoyang District, Beijing

北京恒生医院
北京市朝阳区东直门外大街12号
Telephone: +86 (0)10 64178040

Beijing Hospital Affiliated to Ministry of Public Health
卫生部北京医院
北京市东城区东单大华路1号
#1 Dahua Lu, Dongdan, Dongcheng District, Beijing
Telephone: +86 (0)10 65132266

Beijing Huilongguan Hospital (Psychiatric Hospital)
北京回龙观医院
Telephone: +86 (0)10 62716286 psychological
hotline (Mon.—Fri: 6:00 to 11:00 p.m.)
Telephone: 800-810-1117 24-hrs hotline for suicide
prevention
Telephone: +86 (0)10 82951332
Website: www.crisis.org.cn

Huilongguan Town, Changping District, Beijing
Telephone: +86 (0)10 62715511 ext. 6383 or 6387
北京市昌平区回龙观镇
Clinic in Andingmen:
安定门诊所
#A-35 Cheniandian Hutong, Andingmennei Dajie,
Dongcheng District, Beijing
Telephone: +86 (0)1 -64077669
北京市东城区安定门内大街车碾店胡
同甲35号
Clinic in Yuetan:
月坛诊所
No. 1 Yuetan Nanjie, Xicheng District, Beijing
北京市西城区月坛南街1号
Telephone: +86 (0)10 68049865

Beijing Red Cross Chaoyang Hospital Affiliated to Capital Medical University
首都医科大学附属北京红
十字朝阳医院
8 Bai Jia Zhuang Lu
Chao Yang District
Beijing 100020

北京朝阳区白家庄路8号
Telephone: +86 (0)10 6500 7755 Ext. 2380, 6502
4704

Beijing United Family Hospital
2 Jiang Tai Lu
Chao Yang District
Beijing 100016
北京朝阳区蒋台路2号
Telephone: +86 (0)10 59277000 (24-hour number)
Fax: +86 (0)10 59277200
Emergency Hotline: +86 (0)10 5927 7120
Website: www.unitedfamilyhospitals.com

Beijing United Family Clinic—Shunyi
Pinnacle Plaza, Unit 818
Tian Zhu Real Estate Development Zone
Shunyi District
Beijing 101312
北京顺义区天竺房地产开
发区日祥社区818号
Telephone: +86 (0)10 80461102
Fax: +86 (0)10 80464383
Website: www.unitedfamilyhospitals.com

Beijing United Family Health & Wellness Center—Jianguomen
St. Regis Hotel
21 Jianguomen Waidajie
Beijing, CHINA
地址：建国门外大街21号国际俱乐部
饭店
Telephone: +86 (0)10 85321678; 85321221

Capital Institute of Pediatrics
#2 Yabao Lu, Chaoyang District, Beijing
Telephone: + (0)10 85695555
首都儿科研究所附属儿童医院
地址：北京市朝阳区雅宝路2号

China Academy of Medical Science-Beijing Hospital (Peking Union Hospital)
协和医院
1 Shui Fu Yuan
Dong Cheng District

Beijing 100730
北 京 东 城 区 帅 府 园1 号
Telephone: +86 (0)10 65296114; +86 (0)10
65295284
Fax: +86 (0)10 6529-5283
Website: www.pumch.ac.cn

Chaoyang Hospital Affiliated to Capital Medical University
首都医科大学附属北京朝阳医院
北京市朝阳区白家庄路8号
#8 Baijiazhuang Lu, Chaoyang District, Beijing
Telephone: +86 (0)10 85231000, +86 (0)10
85231653

Confidant Medical Services
北京纽曼德美容整形外科诊所
701 Changan Club
10 Dongchan'anjie
Beijing, CHINA
地址：东长安街10号长安俱乐部701室
Telephone: +86 (0)10 65596769
Website: www.cmsclinic.com

Ever Care Clinic
伊美尔整形美容医院
1/F Building A Lucky Tower
3 Dongsanhuan Beilu
Beijing, CHINA
Telephone: +86 (0)10 64627575
Website: www.evercare.com.cn

Friendship Hospital—GlobalDoctor Clinic
95 Yong An Lu
Xuan Wu District
Beijing 100050
北 京 宣 武 区 永 安 路95 号
Telephone: +86 (0)10 8456 9191 or +86 (0)10
83151915
Email: gdbjing@163bj.com

Global Doctor Medical Center—Beijing
环 球 医 生
9/F Mingri Building
No. 69 N. Dongdan Ave.

Chaoyang District
Telephone: +86 (0)10 83151915
Website: www.globaldoctor.com.au

Hong Kong International Medical Clinic—Beijing
9/F Swissotel Office Building, Chaoyangmen Beidajie
Dongcheng District
Beijing 100027
北 京 东 四 十 条 立 交 桥 港 澳
中 心9 层
Telephone: +86 (0)10 65012288 Ext. 2345/6

Intech Eye Hospital (Dr. Hu) (英 智 眼 科 医 院)
12 Pan Jia Yuan Nan Li
Chao Yang District
Beijing
北 京 朝 阳 区 潘 家 园 南 里12号
Telephone: +86 (0) 10 6773 2909
Website: www.intecheye.com

International Medical Center (IMC)—Beijing
Lufthansa Center, Office Building
Suite 106
50 Liang Ma Qiao Rd
Chao Yang District
Beijing 100016
Website: www.imcclinic.com
北 京 朝 阳 区 亮 马 桥 路50 号
燕 莎 中 心 办 公 楼106 室
Telephone: +86 (0) 10 64651561/2/3 (24-hour number)
Fax: +86 (0) 10 64651984

International SOS (Medical Emergency and Evacuation Service)
北 京 亚 洲 国 际 紧 急 救 援 医 疗 服 务 中 心
Suite #105
Tower I, Kunsha Center
16 Xinyuanli
Chaoyang District, Beijing
Telephone: +86(0)10 64629112
Fax: +86 (0)10 64629188，64629111

Emergency: +86 (0)10 64629100

Website: www.internationalsos.com

地址：朝阳区新源里16号琨莎中心1
座105室

King's Dental

经典口腔

Rm 118 1/F

Beijing Towerrest Plaza

3 Maizidian Xijie

Beijing

CHINA

Telephone: +86 (0)10 8458 03888

Website: www.kingsdental.com

MEDEX Assistance Corporation (Medical Evacuation Service)

871 Poly Plaza

14 South Dongzhimen

Beijing 100027

Telephone: +86 (0)10 65958510

Fax: +86 (0)10 65958509

Email: Operations@medexassist.com

Website: www.medexassist.com

Ministry of Public Health-Beijing Hospital

1 Da Hua Lu, Dong Dan

Beijing 100730

北 京 东 单 大 华 路1 号

Telephone: +86 (0)10 65132266

New Century International Children's Hospital

北京新世纪国际儿童医院

56 Nan Li Shi Rd.

Xicheng District (west side of the 2nd ring road)

Telephone: +86 (0)10 6802 5588 (general number)

+86 (0)10 8804 6000 (24 hour emergency)

Fax: +86 (0)10 8804 6166

Website: www.ncich.com.cn

No. 3 Hospital of Beijing Medical University

49 Hua Yuan Bei Lu

Hai Dian District

Beijing 100083

北 京 海 淀 区 花 园 北 路49 号

Telephone: +86 10 82256699, 82265537

Peking Union Medical Hospital

1 Shui Fu Yuan

Dong Cheng District

Beijing 100730

Telephone: +86 (0)10 6529 6114 (registration)

Telephone: +86 (0)10 6529 7292 (information)

Telephone: +86 (0)10 6529 5284 (24 hours)

Modern Facilities with English speaking staff.

Separate ward for foreign patients.

Ping Xin Tang Clinic

218-2 Wanfujing

Beijing

China

Telephone: +86 (0)10 65235566 (Chinese),

13501003692 (English)

Fax: +86 (0)10 65236611

Email: yjzx@cuiyueli.com

Website: www.pingxintang.com

Sino-Japanese Friendship Hospital

Ying Hua Dong Lu

He Ping Li

Beijing 100029

北 京 和 平 里 樱 花 东 路

Telephone: +86 (0) 10 6422-2965; 84205566

Fax: +86 (0) 10 6422-2965

SK Hospital

11 Shuiduizi Beili (Opposite Chaoyang Gym)

Telephone: +86 (0)10 35961677 (Chinese/Korean),

+86 (0)10 85961678 (Chinese/Korean)

北京伊美尔爱康美容整形医院

地址：北京市朝阳区水碓子北里11号

（朝阳体育馆对面）

Website: www.skhospital.com.cn

SOS International (Medical Emergency and Evacuation Service)

北 京 亚 洲 国 际 紧 急 救 援 医
疗 服 务 中 心

Building C, BITIC Leasing Center

1 North Road
Xing Fu San Cun
Chao Yang District
Beijing 100027
北 京 朝 阳 区 幸 福 三 村 北 接
1 号 北 信 租 赁 中 心C 座100027
Telephone: +86 (0)10 64629100 (24-hour), +86
(0)10 64629112
Fax: +86 (0)10 6462-91111

TCM Traditional Chinese Medicine OHS Clinic—
Oriental Health Solution
Rm D 25/F Building B Oriental Kenzo Building
Dongzhimenwai Dajie
Dongcheng District, Beijing
北京仲和中医研究信息咨询
北京市东城区东直门外大街东方银座
B座25层
Telephone: +86 (0)10 84476886
Email: ohsclinic@hotmail.com
Website: www.ohsclinic.ucoz.ru

Vista Clinic （维 世 达 诊 所）
Kerry Center Shopping Mall B29/B30
1 Guanghua Road
Chao Yang District
Beijing 100020
北 京 朝 阳 区 光 华 路1 号 嘉
里 购 物 中 心 B29B/B30
Telephone: +86 (0) 10 8529 6618
Fax: +86 (0) 10 8529 6615
Website: www.vista-china.net

DONGBEI
PROVINCE
(INCLUDING LIAONING
PROVINCE)

SHENYANG

Shenyang District includes China's three northeast
provinces: Liaoning, Jilin and Heilongjiang. There
are several hospitals which can provide services

for foreigners in each province. Not all hospitals,
however, have a designated English-speaking doctor
for foreigners. This list is provided for reference only
and does not constitute a recommendation.

American Medical Center—Global Doctor
Medical Staff
54 Pangjiang Rd.
Dadong District
Shenyang
Telephone: +86 (0)24 2433 0678; +86 (0)24 2432
6409
Fax: +86 (0)24 2433 1008
Emergency No: +86 (0)24 2432 6409

First Hospital of China Medical University
155 Nanjing North Street
Heping District
Shenyang 110001
Telephone: +86 (0)24 2326 8760
Fax: +86 (0)24 2326 4417
Telephone: +86 (0)24 2325 6666

He's Eye Hospital
128, Huanghe Bei St
Huanggu District
Telephone: +86 (0)24 8653 1325 (president's
office); +86 (0)24 8652 0800

The No. 2 Hospital of China Medical University
26 Wenhua Rd
Heping District
Shenyang 110003
Telephone: +86(0)24 2389 3501
Emergency: +86 (0)24 2389 2620 (day)/2389-2430
(night)

The People's Hospital of Liaoning Province
This hospital is designated for use by foreigners
English-speaking doctors available.
33 Wenyi Rd
Shenhe Dist.
Shenyang, 110015

Telephone: +86 (0)242414 7900 Director's Office: +86 (0)24 2481 0438
Emergency: +86 (0)24 2481 0136/2414-7900

DALIAN

Dalian Friendship Hospital
8 Sanba Square
Zhongshan District
Shenyang 116001
Telephone: +86 (0) 411 271 8822
Admin office: +86 (0) 411 271 3281

Dalian Railway Hospital
6 Jiefang St.
Zhong Shan District
Telephone: +86 (0)411 282 1120
Foreign Line Ward: +86 (0)411 2636293/2834447

The No. 1 Hospital of Dalian Medical University
222 Zhongshan Rd
116011
Telephone: +86 (0)411 363 5963
Special Need Medical Department which can meet medical needs of foreigners, Ext.2126/2127/2128/2129 (night) or +86 (0)411 4394743.

FUJIAN PROVINCE

Fujian Provincial Hospital
134 Dongjie
Fuzhou
Fujian 350001
Telephone: +86 (0)591 755 7768

Union Hospital Affiliated to Fujian University of Medical Science
11 Xin Quan Road
Fuzhou
Fujian 350001

Telephone: +86 (0)591 335 7896 Ext. 8291, 8292 (Emergency)
Xiamen

Lifeline Medical System
123 Xidi Villa Hubin Bei Road
Xiamen City
Fujian 361012
Telephone: +86 (0)592) 532 3168 (24 hours)
Fax: +86 (0)592) 532 6168
Email: lifelinexiamen@yahoo.com
Working Hours: Monday–Friday 8:00 a.m.–8:00 p.m., Saturday 8:00 a.m.–noon

GANSU PROVINCE

The People's Hospital of Gansu Province
160 Dong Gang Xi Lu
Cheng Guan District
Lan Zhou 730000
兰 州 市 城 关 区 东 岗 西 路 160 号
Telephone: +86 (0)931 8281973 emergency; 8281763 operator

Lanzhou Military General Hospital
#333 Binhe Nanlu, Qilihe District, Lanzhou, Gansu
Telephone: +86 (0)931 3975497 (emergency), +86 (0)931 8975491, +86 (0)931 8975003
兰州军区总医院
甘肃省兰州市七旦河区滨河南路333号

GUANGDONG PROVINCE

GUANGZHOU

Affiliated Hospital of Zhongshan University of Medical Science
58 Zhongshan 2nd Road

Guangzhou 510080
Telephone: +86 (0)20 8775 5766 Ext. 8511; +86
(0)20 8733 0808 (Emergency)

Global Doctor Medical Center
Guangzhou City No. 1 People's Hospital
Outpatient Department, 7-floor, 1 Panfu Lu
Guangzhou, Guangdong, 510180
Telephone: +86 (0)20 8104 5173
Fax: +86 (0)20 8104 5170
Email: guangzhou@eglobaldoctor.com

Guangdong Concord Medical Center
9/F of the Guangdong Provincial Hospital
96 Dong Chuan Road
Guangzhou
This hospital is clean and modern and has a private
inpatient floor. It has an inpatient and an outpatient
unit located in a large government hospital.
Outpatient visits are handled by staff physicians by
appointment. Specialists are called in as needed
or the patient is escorted to see the specialist.
There is a membership fee. Be sure to make an
appointment before going in for a check-up since
this facility gives priority to its members and does
not guarantee service to non-members.
Telephone: +86 (0)20 8387 4283, +86 (0)20 8387
4293
+86 (0)20 8387 4313
+86 (0)20 8387 4283 (Emergency)

**Guangdong Hospital of Traditional Chinese
Medicine (Ersha Island Hospital)**
Da Tong Lu
Ersha Island
Guangzhou 510100
Telephone: +86 (0)20 8190 4609; +86 (0)20 8188
9683

Guangdong Provincial People's Hospital
96 Dongchuan Road
Guangzhou 510080

Telephone: +86 (0)20 8382 7812 Ext. 2603; +86
(0)20 8384 8627 (Emergency)
Telephone: +86 (0)20 8188 5119; +86 (0)20 8387
4283

Guangzhou Can Am International Medical Center
5/F Garden Hotel
368 Huanshi Dong Lu
Guangzhou
The Guangzhou Can Am Medical Clinic offers a
second choice for Guangzhou expatriates who wish
to visit a Western standard health care setting.
No membership is required, though those who
are members ($120 fee) received a 20% discount
on services. On-site laboratory, radiology, and
pharmaceutical services are part of the operations.
Four medical doctors, one dentist, and one
professional counselor are on staff.
Visitors are welcome if you'd like to have a tour of
their facilities. The clinic has also arranged direct
billing with 10 insurance companies and is looking
to increase this list.
Clinic hours: Monday through Friday 9:00 a.m. to
12:30 p.m. and 2:00 p.m. to 6:00 p.m.
Saturday 9:00 a.m. to 12:30 p.m.
Telephone: +86 (0)20 8386 6988 (24-Hour hotline)

Guangzhou Children's Hospital
318 Renmin Central Road
Guangzhou 510120
Telephone: +86 (0)20 8188-6332 Ext. 5103
(Emergency)

Guangzhou Emergency Center
Telephone: +86 (0)20 120
Anyone who needs emergency medical service
can call the city Emergency Center (Guangzhou:
020-120), which will inform the hospital nearest
the patient to arrange an ambulance and a medical
team to the patient's location as soon as possible.

Guangzhou No. 1 People's Hospital
602 Renmin Road North

Guangzhou 510180
Telephone: +86 (0)20 8108 2090; Telephone: +86 (0)20 8108 0509

Guangzhou No. 2 People's Hospital
Telephone: +86 (0)20 8181 4711

Guangzhou Red Cross Hospital
396 Tongfu Road Central
Guangzhou 510220
Telephone: +86 (0)20 8441 2233x1108; +86 (0)20 8444 6411 (Emergency)

Guangzhou Overseas Chinese Hospital
Shipai, Guangzhou 510630
Telephone: +86 (0)20 3868 8102 (Emergency)

Nanfang Hospital
Shahe, Guangzhou
Telephone: +86 (0)20 8514 1888 Ext. 87287; +86 (0)20 8770 5656 (for foreigner service) +86 (0)20 8770 6163 (Emergency)

No. 1 Affiliated Hospital of Guangzhou Medical College
1 Yanjiang Road
Guangzhou 510120
Telephone: +86 (0)20 8333 7750 Ext. 3046; +86 (0)20 8333 6797 (Emergency)

No. 2 Affiliated Hospital of Guangzhou Medical College
Telephone: +86 (0)20 8444 9613

No. 1 Affiliated Hospital of Guangzhou University of Traditional Chinese Medicine
Telephone: +86 (0)20 3659 0957, +86 (0)20 3659 1316

No. 1 Subsidiary Hospital of Zhongshan Medical Sciences University
Telephone: +86 (0)20 8777 8314

Overseas Chinese Hospital affiliated to Jinan University
Telephone: +86 (0)20 8551 6025

SOS Alarm Center in Hong Kong
Telephone: +852 2528 9900 (Provides medical services in Hong Kong only)

SOS Guangzhou Clinic
1/F North Tower
Ocean Pearl Building
No.19 Hua Li Rd.
Zhujiang New City, Guangzhou
Phone Number: +86 (0)20 8735-1051
Fax: +86 (0)20 8735 -2045
Office Hours: Monday to Friday 9:00 a.m. to noon and 2:00 p.m. to 6:00 p.m.; Saturday (by appointment and emergencies only) 9:00 a.m. to noon
This clinic is run by foreign doctors who have overseas training and experience. They have a program called "one week program" in which you can become a member for a week. Consultation fee and commonly prescribed medicines such as antibiotics, cough syrup, and antihistamines are covered under the membership fee once you sign up for the one-week program. Multiple visits to the doctor during that week period are also covered.

Sun Yat Sen Memorial Hospital
107 Yanjiang Road West, Guangzhou 510120
Telephone: +86 (0)20 8133-2199; +86 (0)20 8133-2469, +86 (0)20 8133-2648 (Emergency)
The urgency and the location of the patient would have to be the primary factor in making the decision to use this facility. Assurance has been given that they use disposable needles and syringes, and sterilization is in evidence for those requiring such but there is no way to confirm the validity of this information. They also have an outpatient department in this hospital.

Dentists in Guangzhou

Guangdong Provincial Dental Hospital
366 Jiang Nan Da Dao
Guangzhou 510260

Telephone: +86 (0)20 8444-6867 (Director Office);
+86 (0)20 8442-7024 (Medical Dept.)
+86 (0)20 8442-7034, +86 (0)20 8443-8740
(Medical Office)

Sun Shine (Kai Yi) Dental Clinic
2 Tianhe North Road
Telephone: +86 (0)20 3886 2888 Ext. 3111

SHENZHEN

Shenzhen Affiliated Hospital to Beijing University
Telephone: +86 (0)755 8392 3333

Shenzhen People's Hospital
Dongmen Road North
Shenzhen
Telephone: +86 (0)755 2553 3018 Ext. 2553-1387
(Outpatient Dept.)

Shenzhen Red-Cross Hospital
Telephone: +86 (0)755 8336 6388

GUANGXI PROVINCE

GUILIN

Guilin People's Hospital
70 Wenming Lu
Guilin
Guangxi 541002
Telephone: +86 (0)773 282 9065, +86 (0)773 282 3767
Telephone: +86 (0)773 282 5116 (Emergency)

GUIZHOU PROVINCE

ANSHUN

People's Hospital of Anshun Prefecture
22 East Hongshan Road
Anshun City
Telephone: +86 (0)853 3222403

GUIYANG

Attached Hospital of Guiyang Medical College
28 Guiyijie Street
Guiyang
Guizhou
Telephone: +86 (0)851 6821113

KAILI

Hospital of Kaili City
418 West Beijing Road
Kaili City
Guizhou
Telephone: +86 (0)855 8220700 (operator)

ZUNYI

Attached Hospital of Zunyi Medical College
113 Dalian Road
Zunyi City
Telephone: +86 (0)852 8622042

HAINAN PROVINCE

Haikou People's Hospital
68 Desheng Sha Road
Haikou City

Hainan Province 570001
Telephone: +86 (0)898 6622 3897 (Outpatient Dept. Office)
Telephone: +86 (0)898 6618 9675
Telephone: +86 (0)898 6622 2412 (Outpatient Dept.)

Hainan People's Hospital
Xianlie Lu, Xiuying Qu
Haikou City
Hainan Province 570011
Outpatient Dept. 8 Longhua Rd
Haikou City
Hainan Province 570001
Telephone: +86 (0)898 6864 2660
Telephone: +86 (0)898 6622 3287 (Outpatient Dept.)
Telephone: +86 (0)898 6622 5866; +86 (0)898 6622 6666
Emergency: +86 (0)898 6222 2423

HEBEI PROVINCE

People's Hospital of Hebei Province
河北省人民医院
348 He Ping Xi Lu
Xin Hua District
Shi Jia Zhuang 050011
Telephone: +86 (0)311 85989696
地址：石家庄市新华区和平西路348号

Bethune International Peace Hospital
白求恩国际和平医院
河北省石家庄市中山西路398号
#398 Zhongshan Xilu, Shijiazhuang, Hebei
Telephone: +86 (0)311 87998114

The First Hospital of Hebei Medical University
#89 Dong'gang Rd. Shijiazhuang, Hebei
Telephone: +86 (0)311 85917000

河北医科大学附属第一医院
河北省石家庄市东岗路89号

The Second Hospital cf Hebei Medical University
#215 Heping West Rd. Shijiazhuang, Hebei
Telephone: +86 (0)311 87046901
河北医科大学附属第二医院
河北省石家庄市和平西路215号

The Third Hospital of Hebei Medical University
#398 Zhongshan East Rd. Shijiazhuang, Hebei
Telephone: +86 (0)311 85990114
河北医科大学附属第三医院
河北省石家庄市中山东路398号

HEILONGJIANG PROVINCE

HARBIN

Provincial Hospital
82 Zhongshan Rd.
Xiangfang District
150036
Telephone: +86 (0)451 566 2971

The No. 1 Hospital of Harbin
151, Diduan St
Daoli District 150010
Telephone: +86 (0)451 468 3684 (Admin office)
Telephone: +86 (0)451 461 4606; 461 4636

The No. 1 Hospital of Harbin Medical University
5 Youzheng St
Nangang District 150001
Telephone: +86 (0)451 364 1918/360 7924/364 1563

The No. 2 Hospital of Harbin Medical University
247, Xue Fu Rd
Nangang District 150086
Telephone: +86 (0)451 666 2962

QIQIHAER

The No. 1 Hospital of Qiqihaer
20 Gongyuan Lu
Longsha Dist, 161005
Telephone: +86 (0)452 2425 981

HENAN
PROVINCE

The People's Hospital of Henan Province
7 Wei Wu Lu
Jin Shui District
Zhengzhou 450003
郑 州 市 金 水 区 纬 五 路7 号
Telephone: +86 (0)371 65580014 daytime,
65951056 night
Fax: +86 (0)371 5964376

Zhengzhou People's Hospital
郑州人民医院
河南省郑州市黄河路33号
#33 Huanghe Lu, Zhengzhou, Henan
Telephone: +86 (0)371 67078012
Fax: +86 (0)371 67078012

HUBEI
PROVINCE

**No. 1 Hospital Affiliated to Hubei Medical
University**
湖北医科大学附属第一医院
湖北省武汉市武昌区解放路238号
#238 Jiefang Lu, Wuchang District, Wuhan, Hubei
Telephone: +86 (0)27 88041919, +86 (0)27
88066234

**Zhongnan Hospital Affiliated to Wuhan
University**
(Formerly known as : No. 2 Hospital Affiliated to
Hubei Medical University)

武汉大学中南医院（原名：湖北医
科大学附属第二医院）
湖北省武汉武昌区东湖路169号
#169 Donghu Lu, Wuchang District, Wuhan, Hubei
Telephone: +86 (0)27 87824212

**Union Hospital Affiliated to Tongji Medical
University**
同济医科大学附属协和医院
湖北省武汉汉口解放大道1277号
#1095 Jiefang Dadao, Wuhan, Hubei
Telephone: +86 (0)27 85726114

Yichang Central People's Hospital
宜昌中心人民医院
湖北省宜昌市夷陵大道183号
#183 Yiling Dadao, Yichang, Hubei
Telephone: +86 (0)717 6481969, +86 (0)717
6483495

HUNAN
PROVINCE

The People's Hospital of Hunan Province
61 Jie Fang Xi Lu
Changsha 410002
长 沙 市 解 放 西 路61 号
Telephone: +86 (0)731 2278120 emergency,
2278048 duty phone, 2278120 ambulance

**No. 1 Hospital Affiliated to Zhongnan University
(Xiangya Hospital)**
中南大学附属第一医院（湘雅医院）
湖南省长沙市湘雅路87号
#87 Xiangya Lu, Changsha, Hunan
Telephone: +86 (0)731 84328888, +86 (0)731
84327196

**No. 2 Xiangya Hospital Affiliated to Zhongnan
University**
中南大学湘雅二医院
湖南省长沙市人民中路139号
#139 Renmin Zhonglu, Changsha, Hunan

Telephone: +86 (0)731 85295888
Fax: +86 (0)731 85533525

INNER MONGOLIA

Inner Mongolia People's Hospital
#20 Zhaowuda Rd. Hohhot, Inner Mongolia
Telephone: +86 (0)471 6620000, 6620225
内蒙古自治区人民医院
内蒙古呼和浩特市昭乌达路20号
English service available

Inner Mongolia Medical University Hospital
内蒙古医学院附属医院
内蒙古呼和浩特市回民区通道北街1号
#1 Tongdao Beijie, Huimin District, Hohhot, Inner
Mongolia
Telephone: +86 (0)471 6636643, 0471 6636126

The Affiliated Hospital to Inner Mongolia Medical College
1 Tong Dao Bei Jie
Hui Min District
Inner Mongolia 010050
内蒙古呼和浩特市回民区
通道北街1号
Telephone: +86 (0)471 6636643, 6636126

JIANGSU PROVINCE

NANJING

Jiangsu Provincial People's Hospital
300 Guangzhou Rd
Nanjing City
Telephone: +86 (0)25-371-4511

General Hospital of Nanjing Military Base
305 Zhong Shan Dong Rd

Nanjing City
Telephone: +86 (0)25 4826 808

SUZHOU

Affiliated Children Hospital of Suzhou
Jingde Road
Suzhou
Telephone: +86 (0)512 6522 3820

Kowloon Hospital Suzhou
No. 118 Wansheng Street
Suzhou SIP
Telephone: +86 (0)512 6262 9999

Suzhou Eye Hospital
No. 18 Shuyuan Lane
Suzhou
Telephone: +86 (0)512 6960 7660

Suzhou Sheng'ai Hospital International Treatment
2F, No. 36 Jinshen Road
SND, Suzhou
Telephone: +86 (0)512 6807 8039/6227 7755

Tokushinkai Dental Suzhou Clinic
1F, Suxin Building, No. 88 Jinjihu Road
SIP, Suzhou
Telephone: +86 (0)512 5763 5720/5721

WUXI

Tokushinkai Dental Wuxi Clinic
B-1F, No. 8, 6-7 Euro-Plaza
Xinchuang 6 Road (near Guolang Donglu)
SIP, Wuxi New District
Telephone: +86 (0)510 8528 1121

Wuxi Women's Children's Hospital
48 Huashu Lane
Suzhou
Telephone: +86 (0)510 8272 5161

Wuxi 4th People's Hospital
200 Hui He Road
Telephone: +86 (0)510 8868 2999/3114

JIANGXI PROVINCE

The People's Hospital of Jiangxi Province
152 Ai Guo Lu
Nanchang 330006
南昌市爱国路152号
Telephone: +86 (0)791 6895533 emergency

No.1 Hospital Affiliated to Jiangxi Medical Institute
江西医学院附属第一医院
江西省南昌市东湖区永外正街11号
#11 Yongwai Zhengjie, Donghu District, Nanchang, Jiangxi
Telephone: +86 (0)791 8692715, +86 (0)791 8692748

JILIN PROVINCE

CHANGCHUN

The No. 2 Hospital of Norman Bethune Medical University
18 Zhiqiang Street
Nanguan District
Changchun, 130041
Telephone: +86 (0)431 8974612
Emergency same as above, Ext: 621

The Hospital of Changchun Chinese Medical University
20 Gongnong Road
Changchun, 130021
Telephone: +86 (0)431 5955911

YANBIAN

Yanbian Hospital
119 Juzi street
Yanji, 133000
Telephone: +86 (0)433 2532435

NINGXIA PROVINCE

The People's Hospital of Ningxia Hui Autonomous Region
2 Li Qun Xi Jie
Yinchuan 750001
Telephone: +86 (0)951 120 ambulance; 6192221 emergency
宁夏回族自治区第一人民医院
银川市利群西街2号

Ningxia Medical University Hospital
#804 Shengli Nanjie, Xingqing District, Yinchuan, Ningxia
Telephone: +86 (0)951 4091488, +86 (0)951 6744200
宁夏医学院附属医院
宁夏银川市兴庆区胜利南街804号

QINGHAI PROVINCE

The People's Hospital of Qinghai Province
(The First Aid Center of Qinghai Province)
2 Gong He Lu
Xining 810007
Telephone: +86 (0) 971 120, 8177911 Ext. 215
青海省西宁市共和路2号

Qinghai Medical University Hospital
#13 Tongren Lu, Xi'ning, Qinghai
Telephone: +86 (0)971 6143103

青海医学院附属医院
青海省西宁市同仁路13号

SHANDONG PROVINCE

Qingdao Municipal Hospital
#1 Jiaozhou Lu, Shibei District, Qingdao, Shandong
Telephone: +86 (0)532 82827191
青岛市市立医院
山东省青岛市市北区胶州路1号

International Clinic
5 Donghai Zhonglu, Qingdao, Shandong
Telephone: +86 (0)532-85937600; 85937690
English
国际诊所
山东省青岛市东海中路5号
Website: http://qdslyy.cn/

Qingdao Medical University Hospital
青岛医学院附属医院
Telephone: 0532-82911219, 0532-82911847,
0532-82911546
Add: #16 Jiangsu Lu, Shinan District, Qingdao,
Shandong
地址：山东省青岛市市南区江苏路
16号

Qianfoshan Hospital of Shandong Province
66 Jing Shi Lu
Jinan 250014
济 南 市 经 十 路66 号
Telephone: +86 (0)531 82968900, 0531-82967113

SHANGHAI

GENERAL

Lifeline Shanghai is a community-based,
confidential hotline providing emotional support

and information to Shanghai's expatriate
community.
Hotline: +86 (0)21 6279 8990

World Link Clinic (Expatriate doctors and imported vaccines)
Portman Clinic: Shanghai Center
203 W, 1376 Nanjing Xi Lu
200040
Telephone: +86 (0)21 6279 7688
Appointments: +86 (0)21 6279 8678
Fax: +86 (0)21 6279 7698

Hong Qiao Clinic: Mandarine City
Unit 30, 788 Hong Xu Lu, 201103
Telephone: +86 (0)21 6405-5788
Fax: +86 (0)21 6405-3587

Shanghai United Family Hospital and Clinics
1111 Xi'an Xia Xi Lu
Chang Ning District
Shanghai 200336 PRC
Website: www.shanghaiunited.com

MEDICAL/SURGICAL EMERGENCIES

Hua Dong Hospital
2nd Floor, Foreigner's Clinic
221 Yanan Xi Road
Telephone: +86 (0)21 6248 4867
Telephone: +86 (0)21 6248 3180 Ext. 3106

Hua Shan Hospital
15th Floor, Foreigner's Clinic
Zong He Lou
12 Wulumuqi Zhong Lu
Telephone: +86 (0)21 6248-3986
Telephone: +86 (0)21 6248-9999 Ext. 2531

Rui Jin Hospital
197 Rui Jin Er Lu
Telephone: +86 (0)21 6437 0045 Ext. 668101
Telephone: +86 (0)21 6437 0045 Ext. 668202

The First People's Hospital
International Medical Care Center
585 Jiu Long Lu (near the Bund)
Telephone: +86 (0)21 6324-3852 (24 hours)

DENTAL PRACTICES

DDS Dental Care in Shanghai
2F/1, Tao Jiang Rd. (Dong Ping Rd.)
Telephone: +86 (0)21 6466 0928
Fax: +86 (0)21 5456 2311
Email: cabuduo@hotmail.com

Dr Harriet Jin's Dental Surgery
Rm 17C Sun Tong Infoport Plaza
55 Huai Hai West Rd, 200030
Telephone: +86 (0)21 5298 9799
Fax: +86 (0)21 5298 9799
Email: harrietjin@online.sh.cn

The No. 9 People's Hospital
7th Floor
Shanghai Dental Medical Center Cooperative Co.
(Sino-Canadian Joint venture)
Outpatient Service Building
639 Zhi-Zao-Ju Lu
Telephone: +86 (0)21 6313 3174

MATERNITY AND GYNECOLOGY

International Peace Maternity Hospital
910 HengShan Road
Telephone: +86 (0)21 6407 0434 Ext. 1105

The First Maternity and Child Hospital
536 Changle Road
Telephone: +86 (0)21 5403 5335

Pediatric Hospital
Shanghai Medical University

183 Fenglin Road, 2nd Floor
Telephone: +86 (0)21 6403 7371; +86 (0)21 6404
7129 Ext. 5009

SHANXI PROVINCE (INCLUDING XI'AN)

No. 1 Hospital of Shanxi Medical University
85 Jie Fang Nan Lu, Taiyuan 030001
地址:太原市解放南路85号
Telephone: +86 (0)351 4044111 Ext.25463/26706

No. 2 College Affiliated to Xi'an Medical University
157 Xi Wu Lu, Xi'an 710004
地址:西安市西五路157号
Telephone: +86 (0)29-87679323, 87678421

Shaanxi International Travel Healthcare Center
陕西国际旅行卫生保健中心
陕西省西安市含光北路10号
No. 10 Hanguang Beilu, Xi'an, Shaanxi
Telephone: +86 (0)29 85407057 or 85407061;
Fax: +86 (0)29 85407059

Xijing Hospital Affiliated to Shaanxi No.4 Military Medical University
#15 Changle Xilu, Xi'an, Shaanxi
Telephone: +86 (0)29 84774114 (operator), +86
(0)29 84775541 (Emergency)
陕西第四军医大学西京医院
陕西省西安市长乐西路15号

People's Hospital of Shaanxi Province
256 You Yi Xi Lu, Xi'an 710068
地址：西安市友谊西路256号
Telephone: +86 (0)29-85251331

SICHUAN PROVINCE

CHENGDU

Chengdu Children's Hospital
Taishengnai Road 137
Emergency: +86 (0)28 662479

Chengdu Children's Special Hospital
The east part of Jiangjun Street
Telephone: +86 (0)28 6691296

Chengdu Military Bayi Orthopaedics Hospital
Beijiaochang Houjie, Chengdu
Telephone: +86 (0)28 6637492

Chengdu No. 1 People's Hospital
The east part of Chunxi Road 2
Telephone: +86 (0)28 6667223
Emergency: +86 (0)28 6659298

Chengdu No. 2 People's Hospital
10, Qingyun Nanjie
Telephone: +86 (0)28 6621522
Emergency: +86 (0)28 6740843

Chengdu No. 3 People's Hospital
82, Qinglong Jie
Emergency: +86 (0)28 6638387

Hospital Attached to Chengdu Traditional Chinese Medical University
39, 12 Qiao Road
Telephone: +86 (0)28 7769902

No. 1 Hospital Attached to West China Medical University
37, Guoxuexiang
Emergency and Emergency +86 (0)28 5553329, 5422286
Appointment: +86 13808005795 (English, Japanese)
Medical Service: +86 (0)28 5551331(Chinese)
Office of OPD: +86 (0)28 5422290

No. 2 Hospital Attached to West China Medical University
20, Section 3, Renmin Nanlu
Emergency: +86 (0)28 5501340

Sichuan International Medical Center and Foreigners' Clinic
Telephone: +86 (0)28 5422408 (English and Chinese, Monday to Friday 8:30 to 5:30)
Telephone: +86 (0)28 5422777(English and Chinese)

Sichuan Province People's Hospital
1st ring road, west section 2, No. 32
Telephone: +86 (0)28 7769981;
Emergency: +86 (0)28 7769262

Stomatological Hospital Attached to West China Medical University
14, Section 3, Renmin Nanlu
Telephone: +86 (0)28 5553331; +86 (0)28 5501437; Emergency: +86 (0)28 5501452

Ya Fei Dental Clinic
25 Xifuhuajie (not far behind the Mao Statue), Chengdu
Telephone: +86 (0)28 5276100, +86 (0)28 6697436, +86 (0)28 6274034.
Email: yfdental@mail.sc.cninfo.net

DAZHU

People's Hospital of Dazhu County
West Zhongshan Street
Telephone: +86 (0)23 43722184
Telephone: +86 (0)23 43722184

FENGDU

People's Hospital of Fengdu County
251, Zhonghua Road
Mingshan Town

Fengdu County
Telephone: +86 (0)23 70623569

Telephone: +86 (0)833 2119310, +86 (0)833
2119311
Emergency: +86 (0)833 2119328

FENGJIE

People's Hospital of Fengjie County
61, Xinqiao Road
Fengjie County
Telephone: +86 (0)23 56522704

FULING

People's Hospital of Fuling District
2 Gaosuntang Road
Fuling District
Telephone: +86 (0)23 72224460
Te: +86 (0)23 72223629 (Outpatient department)

GUANGYUAN

People's Hospital of Guangyuan City
28, Jinjia-xiangzi (Jinjia Lane)
Telephone: +86 (0)839 3222256
Telephone: +86 (0)839 3223672 Ext. 3266

KANGDING

People's Hospital of Kangding County
63, Xiangyang Street
Telephone: +86 (0)836 2811445
Telephone: +86 (0)836 2832445

LESHAN

People's Hospital of Leshan City
76, Baita Street
Central District
Leshan

LIANGSHAN

First People's Hospital of Liangshan Prefecture
82 Shunjie
Xichang City
Telephone: +86 (0)834 3222761, +86 (0)834
3226779
Telephone: +86 (0)834 3222138

PANZHIHUA

(also known as JinJiang, near the border of Yunnan
Province)

Central Hospital of Panzhihua City
North Dahe Road.
Telephone: +86 (0)812 2223255, 2222512
Telephone: +86 (0)812 2222941 Ext. 3346

SONGPAN

People's Hospital of Songpan County
1 Shoubei Lane South
Shuncheng Road
Jin-An Town
Telephone: +86 (0)837 7232497

URBAN AREA

Chongqing Emergency Medical Center
1 Jiankang Road
Yuzhong District
Telephone: +86 (0)23 63862747

First Attached Hospital of Chongqing Medical
University
1 Youyi Road

Yuanjiagang
Telephone: +86 (0) 23-68816534
Emergency: +86 (0)23 69012330

Third People's Hospital of Chongqing City
104 Pibashan Zhengjie
Telephone: +86 (0) 23 63515394

WANZHOU
DISTRICT
(WANXIAN)

Three Gorges Central Hospital of Chongqing City
165, Xincheng Road
Wanzhou District
Telephone: +86 (0)23 58122821
Telephone: +86 (0)23 58122622 (office)

TIANJIN

General Hospital of Tianjin Medical University
154 An Shan Da
He Ping District
Tianjin 300450
天 津 和 平 区 鞍 山 道154 号
Telephone: +86 (0)22 60362255; 60362538

The First Center Hospital of Tianjin
24 Fu Kang Lu
Tianjin 300450
天 津 复 康 路24 号
Telephone: +86 (0)22 23626600

The Third Hospital of Tianjin
83 Jin Tang Lu
He Dong District
Tianjin 300250
天 津 河 东 区 津 塘 路83 号
Telephone: +86 (0)22 24315150 or 24315670

Tianjin Hospital
#406 Jiefang South Rd.

Hexi District, Tianjin
Telephone: +86 (0)22 28332917; 28302006
天津医院
天津河西区解放南路406号

Tianjin Central Maternity Hospital
#146 Yingkou Rd.
Heping District, Tianjin
Telephone: +86 (0)22 58287742
天津市中心妇产医院
天津和平区营口道146号

Tianjin Tianhe Hospital
#122 Munan Rd.
Heping District, Tianjin
Telephone: +86 (0)22 23317703
天津市天和医院
天津和平区睦南道122号

Tianjin United Family Hospital
天津市和睦家医院
Telephone: +86 (0)10 59277345 (inquiry)

Tianjin Huanhu Hospital for Head Trauma
#122 Qixiangtai Lu, Hexi District, Tianjin
Telephone: +86 (0)22 60367500
天津市脑系科中心医院（环湖医院）
天津市河西区气象台路122号

TIBET
AUTONOMOUS
REGION

LHASA

People's Hospital of Tibet Autonomous Region
7 North Linkuo Road
Lhasa
Telephone: +86 (0)891 5332462

Tibet Autonomous Region No. 1 People's Hospital Emergency Medical Facility
This is a 24-hour facility (unlike the rest of the hospital)
18, North Lin Kuo Road, Lhasa, Tibet 850000
Emergency number: +86 (0)891 120
24 hour emergency number with an English language speaker: +86(0)891 632 2200.

Tibetan Medical Hospital of Tibet Autonomous Region
Sickward Department:
14 Buliangre Road (Liangre road in Chinese)
Out-patient Department: No.10, Yutuo Road
Telephone: +86 (0)891 6322351

WUHAN

No. 1 Affiliated Hospital to Hubei Medical University
湖北医科大学附属第一医院
238 Jie Fang Lu
Wu Chang District
Wuhan 430060
Telephone: +86 (0)27 88041919, 88066234
地址：武汉市武昌区解放路238号

Zhongnan Hospital affiliated to Wuhan University
Former known as: No. 2 Affiliated Hospital to Hubei Medical University
湖北医科大学附属第二医院
169 Dong Hu Lu
Wu Chang District
Wuhan 430071
Telephone: +86 (0) 27 87824212
地址：武汉武昌区东湖路169号

Xie He Hospital Affiliated to Tong Ji Medical University
同济医科大学附属协和医院
1095 Jie Fang Da Dao
Wuhan 430022

Telephone: +86 (0)27 85726114
地址：武汉汉口解放大道1277号

Yichang Center People's Hospital
宜昌中心人民医院
183 Yi Ling Da Dao
Yichang
Telephone: +86(0)717 6481969, +86(0)717 6483495
地址：宜昌市夷陵大道183号

XINJIANG UIGUR AUTONOMOUS REGION

Xinjiang People's Hospital
新疆人民医院
新疆乌鲁木齐市天池路91号
#91 Tianchi Lu, Urumqi, Xinjiang
Telephone: +86 (0)991-8564439, 0991-8564100 (outpatient services), +86 (0)991 8563120 emergency
English service available

No. 1 Hospital Affiliated to Xinjiang Medicine University
新疆医科大学附属第一医院
新疆乌鲁木齐市鲤鱼山路1号
#1 Liyushan Lu, Urumqi, Xinjiang
Telephone: +86 (0)991 4365663, 0991 4362930

YUNNAN PROVINCE

DALI

People's Hospital of Dali Prefecture
122 South Renmin Road
Xiaguan
Telephone: +86 (0)872 2125465

JINGHONG

Hospital of Xishuangbanna Prefecture
17 Central Galan Road
Jinghong City
Telephone: +86 (0)691 2123636 (office)
Fax: +86 (0)691 2123849

KUNMING

First Attached Hospital of Kunming Medical College
153 Xichang Road
Kunming
Telephone: +86 (0)871 5324888 (operator)
Emergency: +86 (0)871 5324590

First People's Hospital of Yunnan Province
172 Jinbi Road
Kunming
Telephone: +86 (0)871 3634031(operator)

LIJIANG

People's Hospital of Lijiang Prefecture
Fuhui Road, Dayan Town
Lijiang
Telephone: +86 (0)888 5121343 (office)

RUILI

Minzu Hospital of Ruili City
1 Biancheng Street
Ruili
Telephone: +86 (0)692 4141758

ZHONGDIAN

People's Hospital of Diqing Prefecture
28 Heping Road
Zhongdian County
Telephone: +86 (0)887 8222022

ZHEJIANG PROVINCE

Sir Run Run Show Hospital
3 Qing Chun Dong Rd
HangZhou City
Telephone: +86 (0)571 8609 0073

VETERINARIANS

Beijing Main Veterinary Hospital
96 Huizhong Temple
Yayuncun (Asian Games Village)
Datun Anwai
Telephone: +86 (0)10 64970591

Boai Small Animals Clinic
Building 11, 1st Floor
Wanquan Zhuangxiao
Haidian District Qu
Beijing, China
Telephone: +86 (0)10 82616151

China Agricultural University Animal Hospital
Yuanmingyuan Xi Lu 2
North Gate of the Agricultural University
Beijing, China
Telephone: +86 (0)10 6893036

Companion Animal Hospital
Dong Si Duo Fuxian
Yi Qu (Section B), Wanfujing (Prime Hotel—south side)
Beijing, China
Telephone: +86 (0)10 6449742

Guan Yuan Animal Hospital
Xicheng District
Siujie Hutong 4
(next to the Guanyuan Bird and Fish Market)
Beijing, China
Telephone: +86 (0)10 66162134

Guan Sang Pet Care Center
Bei Sanhuan Zhoug Lu 7
Beijing, China
Telephone: +86 (0)10 62371359

The Wuhan BeiBei Animal Hospital
Opposite Zhong Bei Cang Chu
187 Xing Hua Road
Jianghan District of Hankou
Wuhan City
Telephone: +86 (0)72 65651611

Babi Pet Hospital Suzhou
No. 27 Shidai Street, Heshan Road
Suzhou SND
Telephone: +86 (0)512 6809 0093

Cao Langfeng Pet Hospital Suzhou
No. 26 East Bai Ta Road
Suzhou
Telephone: +86 (0)512 6720 1761

CHAMBERS OF COMMERCE

BEIJING

American Chamber of Commerce in Beijing
The Office Park, Tower AB
6th Floor No. 10 Jintongxi Road
Beijing 100005
Telephone: +86 (0)10 8519-0800
Fax: +86 (0)10 8519-0899
Email: amcham@amcham-china.org.cn
Website: www.amcham-china.org.cn

Australian Chamber of Commerce in Beijing
E floor, Office Tower
Beijing Hong Kong Macau Center (Swissotel)
2 Chaoyangmenbei Dajie
Beijing 100027
Telephone: +86 (0)10 6595 9252

Fax: +86 (0)10 6595 9253
Email: info@austcham.org
Website: www.austcham.org

Benelux Chamber of Commerce in Beijing
1601 Zhongyu Plaza
A6 Gongtibei Road
Chaoyang District
Beijing 100027
Telephone: + 86 (0)10 8523 6101/05
Fax: +86 (0)10 8523 6305
Email: beijing@bencham.org
Website: www.bencham.org

British Chamber of Commerce in Beijing
The British Center
Room 1001
China Life Tower
16 Chaoyangmenwai Avenue
Beijing 100020
Telephone: +86 (0)10 85251111
Fax: +86 (0)10 85251100
Email: enquiries@britishchamber.cn
Website: www.britishchamber.cn

Canada China Business Council in Beijing
Suite 18-2, CITIC Building
19 Jianguomenwai Street
Beijing 100004
Telephone: +86 (0)10 8526 1820/21/22
Fax: +86 (0)10 6512 6125
Email: ccbcbj@ccbc.com.cn
Website: www.ccbc.com

China-Britain Business Council (CBBC)
The British Center
Room 1001, China Life Tower
16 Chaoyangmenwai Avenue
Beijing 100020
Telephone: +86 (0)10 8525 1111
Fax: +86 (0)10 8525 1001
Email: beijing@cbbc.org.cn
Website: www.cbbc.org

China Council for the Promotion of International Trade (CCPIT)
China Chamber of International Commerce (CCOIC)
1 Fuxingmenwai Street
Beijing 100860
Telephone: +86 (0)10 88075716
Fax: +86 (0)10 68030747
Website: http://english.ccpit.org/

Danish Chamber of Commerce in Beijing
9 Floor, Tower A, Global Trade Center,
No.36 North Third Ring Road East
Dong Cheng District, Beijing, 100013
P.R. China
Telephone: +86 (0)10 5825 6658
Fax: +86 (0)10 5825 6659
Email: mail@dccc.com.cn
Website: www.dccc.com.cn

European Chamber of Commerce
Lufthansa Center, Office C412
50 Liangmaqiao Road
Chaoyang District
Beijing 100016
Telephone: +86 (0)10 6462 2065/66
Fax: +86 (0)10 6462 2067
Email: euccc@euccc.com.cn
Website: www.europeanchamber.com.cn

Economic representation of Flanders in Beijing
San Li Tun Lu, 6
CN-100600 Beijing
Tel.: +86 (0)10 6532 4964
Fax: +86 (0)10 6532 6833
Email: beijing@fitagency.com

Economic Representation of Wallonia Region in Beijing
San Li Tun Lu, 6
CN-100600 Beijing
Tel.: +86 (0)10 6532 6695
Fax: +86 (0)10 6532 6696
Email: awexbrubeijing@188.com

French Chamber of Commerce in Beijing
Novotel Xinqiao Beijing, Area B, 6th Floor
2 Dongjiaominxiang
Dongcheng District
Beijing 100004
Telephone: +86 (0)10 65 12 17 40
Fax: +86 (0)10 65 12 14 96
E-Mail: ccifc-beijing@ccifc.org
Website: www.ccifc.org

Delegation of German Industry & Commerce (AHK)
German Industry & Commerce Beijing Branch (GIC)
Landmark Tower 2, Unit 0830
8 North Dongsanhuan Road
Chaoyang District
100004 Beijing
Telephone: +86 (0)10 6539 6688 (AHK)
Fax: +86 (0)10 6539 6689 (AHK)
Telephone: +86 (0)10 6539 6633 (GIC)
Fax: +86 (0)10 6539 6689 (GIC)
Email: info@bj.china.ahk.de
Website: http://china.ahk.de/home/

Italian Chamber of Commerce in Beijing
Unit 2606-2607, Full Tower
9, Dong San Huan Zhong Lu
Chaoyang District
Beijing 100020
Telephone: +86 (0)10 35910545
Fax: +86 (0)10 85910546
Email: info@cameraitacina.com
Website: www.cameraitacina.com

Singapore Chamber of Commerce in Beijing
SingCham Office
Block 5, Shidai Building
Room 302, 4th Floor
No.10 Dongbai Street
Chaoyang District Beijing 100022
Telephone: +86 (0)10 5200 6476, 5200 6478
Fax: +86 (0)10 5200 6374
Email: singcham@singcham.com.cn
Website: www.singcham.com.cn

Spanish Chamber of Commerce in Beijing
Room 304B, Great Rock Plaza
13 Xin Zhong Xi Li
Dongcheng District
100027 Beijing
Tel.: +86(0)10 6416 9774/7323
Fax: +86(0)10 6416 1534
Email: info@spanishchamber-ch.com
Website: www.spanishchamber-ch.com

Swedish Chamber of Commerce in Beijing
Room 313, Radisson SAS Hotel
(Beijing Huang Jia Da Fan Dian)
6A, East Beisanhuan Road
Chaoyang District
Beijing 100028
Telephone: +86 (0)10 5922 3388 ext. 313
Fax: +86 (0)10 6462 7454
Web site: www.swedishchamber.com.cn
Email: beijing@swedishchamber.com.cn

Swiss Chamber of Commerce in Beijing
Suite 100, CIS Tower
38 Liangmaqiao Lu
Chaoyang District
Beijing 100016
Telephone: +86 (0)8531 0015
Fax: +86 (0)6432 3030
Email: info@bei.swisscham.org
Website: www.swisscham.org

US-CHINA Business Council in Beijing
CITIC Building, Suite 10-01
19 Jianguomenwai Dajie
Beijing 100004
Telephone: +86 (0)10 6592 0727
Fax: +86 (0)10 6512 5854
Email: info@uschina.org.cn
Website: www.uschina.org

CHENGDU

The American Chamber of Commerce in Changdu
606 Hongchuan Mansion
Lingshiguan Rd. Section 4
South Renmin Rd.
Chengdu
Sichuan 610041
Telephone: +86 (0)28 8524 2405
Fax: +86 (0)28 8524 8577
Email: amcham@amcham-southwest.org

British Chamber of Commerce in Chengdu
1705B, 17/F
Times Plaza
2, Zongfu Road
Chengdu
Sichuan 610016
Telephone: +86 (0)28 86656917
Fax: +86 (0)28 86657296
Email: info@britchamswchina.org
Website: www.britchamswchina.org

Canada Business Development Office in Changdu
16/F, Chengdu Real Estate Mansion
No. 28, Section 1
Renminzhong Road
Chengdu
Sichuan 610015
Telephone: +86 (0)28 8627 9223
Fax: +86 (0)28 8627 9339
Email: bdochengdu@sina.com

China-Britain Business Council in Chengdu (CBBC)
1705B, 17/F, Block A
Times Plaza
2, Zongfu Road
Chengdu
Sichuan 610016
Telephone: +86 (0)28 86656302
Fax: +86 (0)28 86657296

Email: enquiries@cbbc.org
Website: www.cbbc.org

European Chamber of Commerce in Chengdu
Chengdu
Sichuan Province
Telephone: +86(0)28 8671 0577
Fax: +86(0)28 8666 5844
Email: chengdu@euccc.com.cn
Website: www.europeanchamber.com.cn

GUANGZHOU

The American Chamber of Commerce in
Guangzhou
Main Tower, 1603
Guangdong International Hotel
339 Huanshi Donglu
Guangzhou 510098
Telephone: +86 (0)20 8335 1476
Fax: +86 (0)20 8332 1642
Email: amcham@amcham-guangdong.org
Website: http://www.amcham-guangdong.org/

Association of British Commerce, Guangzhou
60 Taojin Rd
Guangzhou
Telephone: +86 (0)20 8359-8045

Australian Chamber of Commerce in Guangzhou
Suite E10, 2/F, Main Tower
Guangdong International Hotel
339 Huanshidong Rd.
Guangzhou 510098
Telephone: +86 (0)20 2237 2866, +86 (0)20 8330
2044
Fax: +86 (0)20 8319 0765
Email: mail@austcham-southchina.org
Website: www.austcham.org

Austrian Economic Chamber
Guangzhou

Telephone: +86 (0)20 8666 3388, +86 (0)20 8666
6401
Fax: +86 (0)20 8666 5312
Email: afecgz@163.net

British Chamber of Commerce in Guangzhou
Suite 1706, Main Tower
Guangdong International Hotel
339 Huanshi-dong Rd
Guangzhou, 510098
Telephone: +86 (0)20 8331 5013, +86 (0)20 8331
3120
Fax: +86 (0)20 8331 5016
Email: manager@britchamgd.com
Website: www.can.britcham.org/

Canadian Business Forum, Guangdong
Suite 801
China Hotel
Liuhua Rd.
Guangzhou
Telephone: +86 (0)20 8669 5148; +86 (0)20 8666
0569

Canada China Business Council
Suite 801, Office Tower China Hotel
Liu Hua Lu
Guangzhou, 510015
Telephone: +86 (0)20 8666 0569
Fax: +86 (0)20 8667 2401
Email: ccbcgz@ccbc.com.cn

Danish Chamber of Commerce in Guangzhou
c/o Royal Danish Consulate General
China Hotel Office Tower, Suite 1578 Liu Hua Lu
Guangzhou 510015
Telephone: +86 (0)20 8666 0795 ext.15
Fax: +86 (0)20 8667 0315
Email: dccsc@dccsc.net
Website: www.dccsc.net

Economic Representation of Flanders in
Guangzhou
c/o Consulate-General of Belgium in Guangzhou
Room 1601-1602A

Office Tower
Citic Plaza
233, Tian He Bei Lu
CN-510613 Guangzhou
Tel.: +86 (0)20 38770463, +86 (0)20 38770493
Fax: +86 (0)20 38770462
Email: guangzhou@fitagency.com

Economic Representation of Wallonia Region in Guangzhou
c/o Consulate-General of Belgium in Guangzhou
Room 1601
Office Tower
Citic Plaza
233 Tianhe Bei Lu
CN-510613 Guangzhou
Tel.: +86 (0)20 3877 1768
Fax: +86 (0)20 3877 1483
Email: awexgz@pub.guangzhou.gd.cn

European Chamber of Commerce in Guangzhou
Guangzhou 510000
Guangdong Province
Telephone: +86 (0)20 8758 0479
Fax: +86 (0)20 6121 1006
Email: prd@euccc.com.cn
Website: www.europeanchamber.com.cn

French Chamber of Commerce and Industry in Guangzhou
2/F, 64 Shamian St.
Guangzhou 510130
Telephone: +86 (0)20 8121 6818
Fax: +86 (0)20 8121 6228
Email: ccifc-guangzhou@ccifc.org
Website: www.ccifc.org

German Industry and Commerce Chamber (GIC) in Guangzhou
Suite 2915
Metro Plaza
Tianhe-bei Rd
Guangzhou, 510075
Telephone: +86 (0)20 8755 2353

Fax: +86 (0)20 8755 1889
Email: info@ahk.org.hk
Website: http://www.china.ahk.de/

China-Italy Chamber of Commerce, Guangzhou
CITIC Plaza, 233 Tianhe-Bei Rd
Guangzhou 510613
Telephone: +86 (0)20 3877 0892
Fax: +86 (0)20 3877 0893
Email: infoguangdong@cameraitacina.com
Website: www.cameraitacina.com

Italian Institute for Foreign Trade
Suite 1361, Office Tower China Hotel
Liuhua Rd
Guangzhou 510015
Telephone: +86 (0)20 8667 0013; +86 (0)20 8666 3566
Fax: +86 (0)20 8667 2573

Korea Trade Promotion Corporation
Suite 1010-11
Main Tower
Guangdong International Hotel
339 Huanshi-dong Rd.
Guangzhou 510098
Telephone: +86 (0)20 8334 0052, +86 (0)20 8334 0170
Fax: +86 (0)20 8335 1142

New Zealand Development Association
C950 Office Tower China Hotel
Liu Hua Road
Guangzhou 510015
Telephone: +86 (0)20 8667 0253
Fax: +86 (0)20 8666 6420

International Enterprise Singapore
Suite 2501
CITIC Plaza
233 Tianhe-Bei Rd
Guangzhou 510613
Telephone: +86 (0)20 3891 1911
Fax: +86 (0)20 3891 1772

Email: guangzhou@iesingapore.gov.sg
Website: www.iesingapore.com

Singapore Chamber of Commerce
Telephone: +86 (0)20 8850 8118
Email: chamber@singapore-club.org
Website: www.singcham.com.cn

Spanish Chamber of Commerce in Guangzhou
Room 30-D, A Tower
Guangdong International Hotel
339 Huan Shi Dong Rd.
Yue Xiu District
Guangzhou 510098
Tel.: +86(0)20 2237 2862
Fax: +86(0)20 2237 2864
Email: guangdong@spanishchamber-ch.com
Website: www.spanishchamber.ch.com

Swedish Trade Council
Suite 1306, Main Tower
Guangdong International Hotel
339 Huanshi-dong Rd.
510098
Telephone: +86 (0)20 8331 6019
Fax: +86 (0)20 8330 2939
Website: www.swedishchamber.com.cn

HANGZHOU

China-Britain Business Council in Hangzhou (CBBC)
A-809, Zhejiang World Trade Center
122 Shuguang Road
Hangzhou
Zhejiang 310007
Telephone: +86 (0)571 87631069
Fax: +86 (0)571 87630961
Email: hangzhou@cbbc.org.cn
Website: www.cbbc.org

NANJING

Canada Business Develo ment Office in Nanjing
Suite D, 24th Floor, Chun Feng Mansion
No. 37 Hua Qiao Road
Nanjing 210029
Telephone: +86 (0)25 847 1 2286
Fax: +86 (0)25 8471 228€

China-Britain Business Council in Nanjing (CBBC)
Rm 2514-2515
50 Zhong Hua Road
Nanjing 210001
Telephone: +86 (0)25 52 11740
Fax: +86 (0)25 52233773
Email: nanjing@cbbc.org. n
Website: www.cbbc.org

European Chamber of Commerce in Nanjing
C/o Xuanwu Hotel
4F 193 Zhong Yang Road
Nanjing 210009
Email: nanjing@euccc.com.cn
Website: www.europeanchamber.com.c

QINGDAO

China-Britain Business Council in Qingdao
Room 503, 5th Floor
121 Yan An San Road
Qingdao 266071
Telephone: +86 (0)532 83869772
Fax: +86 (0)532 8386932 9
Email: qingdao@cbbc.or .cn
Website: www.cbbc.org

SHANGHAI

American Chamber of Commerce in Shanghai
Shanghai Center, #568
1376 Nanjing Xilu

Shanghai 200040
Telephone: +86 (0)21 6279 7119
Fax: +86 (0)21 6279 7643
Email: info@amcham-shanghai.org
Website: www.amcham-shanghai.org

Australian Chamber of Commerce in Shanghai
Suite 6709, Apollo Building
1440 Yan 'An Middle Road
Shanghai 200040
Telephone: +86 (0)21 6248 8301/ 2496/ 5989
Fax: +86 (0)21 6248 5580
Email: admin@austchamshanghai.com
Website: www.austchamshanghai.com

Belgium Chamber of Commerce in Shanghai
Telephone: +86 (0)21 5403 8177 ext 118, 117
Fax: +86 (0)21 5403 8167
Email: office-sh@bencham.org
Website: www.bencham.org

British Chamber of Commerce in Shanghai
Suite 1703 Westgate Tower
1038 Nanjing Xi Lu
Shanghai 200041
Telephone: +86 (0)21 6218 5022
Fax: +86 (0)21 6218 5066
Website: www.sha.britcham.org

Canada China Business Council in Shanghai
Suite 912, Central Plaza
227 Huang Pi Bei Lu
Shanghai 200003
Telephone: +86 (0)21 6359 8908/09
Fax: +86 (0)10 6375 9361
Email: ccbcsh@ccbc.om.cn

China-Britain Business Council in Shanghai
Unit 1701-2, Westgate Tower
1038 Nanjing Road W
Shanghai 200041
Telephone: +86 (0)21 6218 5183
Fax: +86 (0)21 6218 5193
Email: shanghai@cbbc.org.cn
Website: www.cbbc.org

Danish Chamber of Commerce in Shanghai
Tian An Center
338 Nanjing Road West
Shanghai 200003
Telephone: +86 138 1811 4020
Fax: +86 (0)21 6359 3592
Email: mail@dccc-shanghai.com
Website: www.dccc-shanghai.com

European Chamber of Commerce in Shanghai
Unit 2204, Shui On Plaza
333 Huai Hai Zhong Road
Shanghai 200021
Telephone: +86 (21) 6385 2023
Fax: +86 (21) 6385 2381
Email: shanghai@euccc.com.cn
Website: www.europeanchamber.com.cn

Economic Representation of Flanders in Shanghai
Wu Yi Road, 127
CN-200050 Shanghai
Tel.: +86 (0)21 6437 8467
Fax: +86 (0)21 6437 7574
Email: shanghai@fitagency.com

French Chamber of Commerce in Shanghai
Mayfair Tower
83 Fu Min Road, 2e floor
Shanghai 200040
Telephone: +86 (0)21 6132 7100
Fax: +86 (0)21 6132 7101
E-Mail: ccifc-shanghai@ccifc.org
Website: www.ccifc.org

Delegation of German Industry & Commerce (AHK)
German Industry & Commerce Shanghai Branch (GIC)
29/F Pos Plaza
1600 Century Avenue
Pudong
Shanghai 200122
Tel.: +86 (0)21 50812266 (AHK)

Fax: +86 (0)21 50812009 (AHK)
Tel.: +86 (0)21 68758536 (GIC)
Fax: +86 (0)21 68758573 (GIC)
Email: office(at)sh.china.ahk.de
Website: http://china.ahk.de

Italian Chamber of Commerce in Shanghai
Suite 3605, The Center
989 Changle Road
Shanghai 200031
Telephone: +86 (0)21 54075181
Fax: +86 (0)21 54075182
Email: infoshanghai@cameraitacina.com
Website: www.cameraitacina.com

Spanish Chamber of Commerce in Shanghai
Room 514, No.885 Renmin Road
Huaihai Zhonghua Tower
Huangpu District
Shanghai 200010
Tel.: +86(0)21 6326 4177
Fax: +86(0)21 6326 4082
Email: shanghai@spanishchamber-ch.com
Website: www.spanishchamber.ch.com

Swedish Chamber of Commerce in Shanghai
c/o Beijing Scandinavian Furniture Co. Ltd
3908B, Nanzheng Building
580 Nanjing West Road
Shanghai 200041
Telephone: +86 (0)21 6217 0838
Fax: +86 (0)21 6217 0562
Web site: www.swedishchamber.com.cn
Email: shanghai@swedishchamber.com.cn

Swiss Chamber of Commerce in Shanghai
Room 1710-1711
1388 Shaan Xi North Road
Shanghai 200060
Telephone: +86 (0)21 6149 8207
Fax: +86 (0)21 6149 8132
Email: info@sha.swisscham.org
Website: www.swisscham.org

US-CHINA Business Council in Shanghai
1701 Beijing West Road, Room 1301
Shanghai 200040
Telephone: +86 (0)21 6288 3840
Fax: +86 (0)21 6288 3841
Email: info@uschina.org.cn
Website: www.uschina.org

SHENYANG

Canada Business Development Office in Shenyang
B-704, 21st Century Tower
Century Road, Hunan New District
Shenyang 110179
Telephone: +86 (0)24 2374 6008
Fax: +86 (0)24 2374 6009
Email: bdoshenyang@sina.com
Website: www.ccbc.com

China-Britain Business Council in Shenyang
Room 901, Tower 2, Shenyang City Plaza
206 Nanjing North Street
Heping District
Shenyang 110001
Telephone: +86 (0)24 23341600
Fax: +86 (0)24 23341858
Email: lisa.liu@cbbc.org.cn
Website: www.cbbc.org

European Chamber of Commerce in Shenyang
Shenyang
Telephone: +86 (24) 8681 1888
Fax: +86 (24) 81077521
Email: shenyang@eucc.com.cn
Website: www.europeanchamber.com.cn

SHENZHEN

Canada Business Development Office in Shenzhen
3/F, C-1
International Science and Technology Business Platform
Southern District of Shenzhen
High-Tech Industrial Park
Shenzhen 518057
Telephone: +86 (0)755) 2671 2368
Fax: +86 (0)755) 2671 2166
Email: bdoshenzhen@sina.com

China-Britain Business Council in Shenzhen
Room 1121, Tower A, International Chamber of Commerce
Fuhua Yi Lu, Futian District
Shenzhen 518048
Telephone: +86 (0)755 8219 8148
Fax: +86 (0)755 8219 3159
Email: shenzhen@cbbc.org.cn
Website: www.cbbc.org

Italian Chamber of Commerce in Shenzhen
Room 318, Comprehensive Building
South District
Shenzhen High Tech Park
Shenzhen 518057
Telephone: +86 (0)755 26017768
Fax: +86 (0)755 26017798
Email: infoguangdong@cameraitacina.com
Website: http://cameraitacina.com/

TIANJIN

The American Chamber of Commerce
Hyatt Regency, #402
Tianjin No.219 Jiefang North Road
Tianjin 300042
Telephone: +86 (0)22 2312 2517 ext.402
Fax: +86 (0)22 2312 2519

Email: secretary@amchamtianjin.org
Website: http://www.amchamtianjin.org/

European Chamber of Commerce in Tianjin
Telephone: +86(22) 23520011
Fax: +86(22) 23531011
Email: tianjin@euccc.com.cn
Website: www.europeanchamber.com.cn

WUHAN

China-Britain Business Council in Wuhan
Room 1203, Tower
New World International Trade Center
568 Jianshe Avenue
Wuhan 430022
Telephone: +86 (0)27 8577 0989
Fax: +86 (0)27 8577 0991
Email: wuhan@cbbc.org.cn
Website: www.cbbc.org

EMBASSIES AND CONSULATES

BEIJING

Embassy of the Islamic State of Afghanistan
8 Dong Zhi Men Wai Da Jie
Chao Yang District, Beijing
Telephone: +86 (0)10 6532 1582
Fax: +86 (0)10 65322269

Embassy of the Republic of Albania
28, Guang Hua Lu
Beijing
Telephone: +86 (0)10 6532 1120
Fax: +86 (0)10 6532 5451

Embassy of the Democratic People's Republic of Algeria
7, San Li Tun Lu
Beijing
Telephone: +86 (0)10 6532 1231

Embassy of the Republic of Angola
1-8-1 Ta Yuan Diplomatic Office Building
Beijing
Telephone: +86 (0)10 6532 6969
Fax: +86 (0)10 6532 6969

Embassy of the Republic of Argentina
11, Dong Wu Jie, San Li Tun
Beijing
Telephone: +86 (0)10 6532 2104
Fax: +86 (0)10 6532 2319

Embassy of Armenia
9, Tayuan Nanxiaojie Diplomatic Apartments
Beijing 100600
Telephone: +86 (0)10 65325677
Fax: +86 (0)10 65325654

Embassy of Australia
21 Dong Zhi Men Wai Da Jie
San Li Tun
Beijing
Telephone: +86 (0)10 5140 4111
Fax: +86 (0)10 5140 4230
Email: pubaff.beijing@dfat.gov.au
Website: www.china.embassy.gov.au

Embassy of the Republic of Austria
5, Dong Wu Jie
Xiu Shui Nan Jie
Jian Guo Men Wai
Beijing
Telephone: +86 (0)10 6532 2061/62
Website: www.aussenministerium.at/peking
Email: peking-ob@bmeia.gv.at

Embassy of the Republic of Azerbaijan
Qijiayuan Diplomatic Compound
Villa B-3

Beijing 100600
Telephone: +86 (0)10 6532 4614
Fax: +86 (0)10 6532 4615
Website: www.azerbembassy.org.cn
Email: mailbox@azerbembassy.org.cn

Embassy of the Commonwealth of the Bahamas in China
4th Floor, Tayuan Diplomatic Office Building
14 Liangmahe Nan Lu
Chaoyang District
Beijing, China, 100600
Telephone: +86 (0)10 6532 2922
Fax: +86 (0)10 6532 2304
Website: www.bahamasembassy.cn
Email: info@bahamasembassy.cn

Embassy of the State of Bahrain
312–313, Third Floor, Lufthansa Center (Office Building)
50 Chao Yang District
Beijing 100016
Telephone: +86 (0)10 64635574
Fax: +86 (0)10 64635504

Embassy of the People's Republic of Bangladesh
42, Guang Hua Lu
Beijing China
Telephone: +86 (0)10 6532 2521/3706
Fax: +86 (0)10 6532 4346
Website: www.bangladeshembassy.com.cn

Embassy of the Republic of Belarus
2-10-1, Ta Yuan Diplomatic Office Building
Beijing, China 100600
Telephone: +86 (0)10 6532 1691
Fax: +86 (0)10 6532 6417
Email: china@belembassy.org

Embassy of Belgium
6 San Li Tun
Beijing
Telephone: +86 (0)10 6532 1736
Fax: +86 (0)10 6532 5097

Email: Beijing@diplobel.fed.be
Website: www.diplomatie.be/beijing/

Embassy of the Republic of Benin
38, Guang Hua Lu
Beijing
Telephone: +86 (0)10 6532 2741
Fax: +86 (0)10 6532 5103

Embassy of the Republic of Bolivia
2-3-2, Ta Yuan Diplomatic Office Building
Beijing
Telephone: +86 (0)10 6532 3074/4370
Fax: +86 (0)10 6532 4686

Embassy of Bosnia in China
1-5-1 Ta Yuan Diplomatic Office Building
Bejing 100600
Telephone: +86 (0)10 6532 6587/+86 (0)10 6532 0185
Fax: +86 (0)10 6532 6418

Embassy of the Republic of Botswana
Chancery: Unit 811
IBM Tower Pacific Century Place
2A Gong Ti Beilu
Beijing P.R. China
Telephone: +86 (0)10 6539 1616
Fax: +86 (0)10 6539 1199

Embassy of the Federative Republic of Brazil
27, Guang Hua Lu
Beijing
Telephone: +86 (0)10 6532 2881
Fax: +86 (0)10 6532 2751
Email: info@brazil.org.cn
Website: www.brazil.org.cn

Embassy of the Brunei Darussalam
No. 1, Liangmaqiao Beijie
Chaoyang District, 1000600
China
Telephone: +86 (0)10 6532 9773/6
Fax: +86 (0)10 6532 4097

Embassy of the Republic of Bulgaria
4, Xiu Shui Bei Jie
Jian Guo Men Wai
Beijing
Telephone: +86 (0)10 6532 1946
Commercial Office: +86 (0)10 6532 4925

Embassy of Burkina Faso in China
9 Salitun Dongliujie
100600
Telephone: +86 (0)10 6532 2250 and/or + 86 (0)10 6532 2492

Embassy of the Republic of Burundi
25, Guang Hua Lu
Beijing
Telephone: +86 (0)10 6532 1801
Fax: +86 (0)10 6532 2381

Royal Embassy of Cambodia
9, Dong Zhi Men Wai Da Jie
Beijing 100600
Telephone: +86 (0)10 6532 1889
Fax: +86 (0)10 6532 3507
Email: camemb.chn@mfa.gov.kh

Embassy of the Republic of Cameroon
7, Dong Wu Jie, San Li Tun
Beijing
Telephone: +86 (0)10 6532 1771
Fax: +86 (0)10 6532 1761

Embassy of Canada
19, Dong Zhi Men Wai Da Jie
Beijing
Telephone: +86 (0)10 5139 4000
Fax: +86 (0)10 5139 4449
Email: beijing-immigration@international.gc.ca
Website: www.beijing.gc.ca

Embassy of Central African Republic in Beijing, China
1-1-132, Ta Yuan Diplomatic Office Building
1 Xin Dong Lu
Chaoyang District

Beijing, China
Telephone: +86 (0)10 6532 7353
Fax: +86 (0)10 6532 7354
Email: centra_chine@yahoo.fr

Embassy of the Republic of Chad
21, Guang Hua Lu
Beijing
Telephone: +86 (0)10 6532 1296/4830
Fax: +86 (0)10 6532 3638

Embassy of the Republic of Chile
1, Dong Si Jie, San Li Tun
Beijing
Telephone: +86 (0)10 6532 1591/1522
Fax: +86 (0)10 6532 3170

Embassy of the Republic of Colombia
No. 34, Guang Hua Lu
Beijing
Telephone: +86 (0)10 532 3367/77

Embassy of the Republic of the Congo
No.6, Dong Wu Jie
San Li Tun, Chaoyang District
Beijing, 10060
China
Telephone: +86 (0)10 6532 3224

Embassy of Costa Rica in Beijing, China
Jianguomenwai Waijiao Gongyu Yu 1-5-41 COP
Beijing 100600, China
Telephone: +86 (0)10 65324157
Fax: +86 (0)10 65324546

Embassy of the Republic of Croatia
2-2-2, San Li Tun Diplomatic Apartments
Beijing
Telephone: +86 (0)10 6532 6241
Fax: +86 (0)10 6532 6257

Embassy of the Republic of Cuba
1, Xiu Shui Nan Jie, Jian Guo Men Wai
Beijing

Telephone: +86 (0)10 6532 6656/1714
Fax: +86 (0)10 6532 2870/6532

Embassy of the Republic of Cyprus
2–13–2, Ta Yuan Diplomatic Office Bldg
14 Liang Ma He Nan Lu
Chao yang District
Beijing 100600
Telephone: +86 (0)10 6532 5057
Fax: +86 (0)10 6532 4244

Embassy of the Czech Republic
Ri Tan Lu, Jian Guo Men Wai
Beijing
Telephone: +86 (0)10 8532 9500
Fax: +86 (0)10 8532 5653

Embassy of the Democratic People's Republic of Korea
11, Ri Tan Bei Lu, Jian Guo Men Wai
Beijing 100600
Telephone: +86 (0)10 6532 1186
Commercial Office: +86 (0)10 6532 4308

Danish Embassy
1 Dong Wu Jie, San Li Tun
Beijing, China
Telephone: +86 (0)10 6532 9900
Fax: +86 (0)10 6532 2435/9999
Website: http://www.ambbeijing.um.dk
Email: bjsamb@um.dk

Embassy of the Republic of Djibouti in Beijing
1-1-122 Ta Yuan Diplomatic Compound
Chaoyang District
Beijing 100600
Telephone: +86 (0)10 65327857, 65329309
Fax: +86 (0)10 65327858

Embassy of the Dominican Republic
3-2-62 Tanyuan Gongyu Diplomatic Compund
Beijing 100600
Telephone: +86 (0)10 853 22423

Embassy of the Republic of Ecuador
2-62 San Li Tun Diplomatic Compound
Chaoyang District-Beijing
Telephone: +86 (0)10 6532 4371/3849
Fax: +86 (0)10 6532 9209

Embassy of Egypt
2, Ri Tan Dong Lu
Beijing
Telephone: +86 (0)10 6532 1825
Fax: +86 (0)10 6532 5365

Embassy of the Republic of Equatorial Guinea
No. 2, Dong Si Jie, San Li Tun
Beijing, China
Telephone: +86 (0)10 6532 3679
Fax: +86 (0)10 6532 3805/0438

Embassy of the State of Eritrea
2-10-1, Ta Yuan Diplomatic Office Building
Beijing
Telephone: +86 (0)10 6532 6534
Fax: +86 (0)10 6532 6532

Embassy of the Federal Democratic Republic of Ethiopia
No. 3, Xiu Shui Nan Jie
Beijing
Telephone: +86 (0)10 6532 5258/5318
Fax: +86 (0)10 6532 5591
Email: ethiochina@ethiopiaemb.org.cn
Website: www.ethiopiaemb.org.cn

Embassy of the Republic of Fiji
1-15-2 Ta Yuan Diplomatic Building
14 Liang Ma He Nan Lu
SanLiTun, Chaoyang District
Beijing 100600
Telephone: +86 (0)10 6532 7305
Fax: +86 (0)10 6532 7253
Email: info@fijiembassy.org.cn
Website: www.fijiembassy.org.cn

Embassy of the Republic of Finland
1-10-1 Ta Yuan Office Building

Beijing
Telephone: +86 (0)10 8519 8300
Fax: +86 (0)10 8519 8301

Embassy of the Republic of France
3 Dong San Jie, San Li Tun
Beijing
Telephone: +86 (0)10 8532 8080
Fax: +86 (0)10 8532 8009
Website: www.ambafrance-cn.org

Embassy of the Republic of Gabon
36, Guang Hua Lu
Beijing
Telephone: +86 (0)10 6532 2810
Fax: +86 (0)10 6532 2621

Embassy of Georgia
Embassy of Georgia in Beijing, China
Kings Garden Villa 17, Block D, Xiao Yun Road 18
Chaoyang District
Beijing, 100016
Telephone: +86 (0)10 6468 1203
Fax: +86 (0)10 6468 1202
Website: www.china.mfa.gov.ge

Embassy of the Federal Republic of Germany
17, Dong Zhi Men Wai Da Jie
Chaoyang District
Beijing
Telephone: +86 (0)10 85329000
Fax: +86 (0)10 65325336
Email: embassy@peki.diplo.de
Commercial Office: +86 (0)10 6532 5556/5560

Embassy of the Republic of Ghana
8, San Li Tun Lu
Beijing
Telephone: +86 (0)10 6532 1319/1544
Fax: +86 (0)10 6532 3602

Embassy of the Hellenic Republic of Greece
9, Guang Hua Lu
Beijing
Telephone: +86 (0)10 6587 2838

Fax: +86 (0)10 6587 2839
Email: gremb.pek@mfa.gr
Website: www.grpressbeijing.com

Embassy of Grenada in Beijing
T3-2-52, Ta Yuan Diplomatic Office Building
Telephone: +86 (0)10 65321208/1209
Fax: +86 (0)10 65321015

Embassy of the Republic of Guinea-Bissau in Beijing
2-2-101, Ta Yuan Diplomatic Compound
Telephone: +86 (0)10 65327393
Fax: +86 (0)10 65327106

Embassy of the Cooperative Republic of Guyana
1, Xiu Shui Dong Jie
Jian Guo Men Wai
Beijing
Telephone: +86 (0)10 6532 1431/1273

Embassy of the Republic of Hungary
10 Dong Zhi Men Wai Da Jie
Beijing
Telephone: +86 (0)10 6532 1431/1473
Fax: +86 (0)10 6532 2719
Email: consular_office@pek.kum.hu

Embassy of the Republic of Iceland
Landmark Tower 1
802, 8 Dongsanhuan Bei Lu
Beijing 100004
Telephone: +86 (0)10 6590 7795
Fax: +86 (0)10 6590 7801
Email: icemb.beijing@utn.stjr.is
Website: www.iceland.org/cn/english

Embassy of the Republic of India
1 Ri Tan Dong Lu
100600 Beijing, China
Telephone: +86 (0)10 6532 1908/1856
Fax: +86 (0)10 6532 4684
Email: webmaster@indianembassy.org.cn
Website: www.indianembassy.org.cn

Embassy of the Republic of Indonesia
No.4 Dongzhimen Wai Street
Chaoyang District
Beijing 100600
People's Republic of China
Telephone: +86 (0)10 6532 5489
Website: www.indonesianembassy-china.org
Email: webmaster@indonesianembassy-china.org

Embassy of the Islamic Republic of Iran
13, Dong Liu Jie
San Li Tun
Beijing 100600
Telephone: +86 (0)10 6532 2040/4871
Fax: +86 (0)10 65321403
Email: information@iranembassyinchina.org

Embassy of the Republic of Iraq
25, Xiu Shui Bei Jie
Jian Guo Men Wai
Beijing
Telephone: +86 (0)10 65323385, 65321873, 65320731
Fax: +86 (0)10 65321596, 65320733

Embassy of the Republic of Ireland
3, Ri Tan Dong Lu
Beijing
Telephone: +86 (0)10 65322691, 65322914
Fax: +86 (0)10 6532 6857
Email: beijing@dfa.ie
Website: www.embassyofireland.cn

Embassy of Israel
West Wing Office, CWT
No. 17, Tianzelu
Chaoyang District
Beijing 100600
Telephone: +86 (0)10 35320500, 85320662
Fax: +86 (0)10 85320555, 85320613
Website: http://beijing.mfa.gov.il

Embassy of the Republic of Italy
No. 2 Dong Er Jie
San Li Tun

Beijing
Telephone: +86 (0)10 65322131
Fax: +86 (0)10 65324676
Website: www.ambpechino.esteri.it

Mission of the Republic of Cote d'Ivoire in China
9 Beixiao Jie, Sanlitun
Beijing, 100600
Telephone: +86 (0)10 65321223/3192

Embassy of Jamaica in Beijing
Jian Guo Men Wai Diplomatic Compound
1 Xiu Shui Street, Room 6-2-72
Beijing 100600
Telephone: +86 (0)10 65326701
Fax: +86 (0)10 65320669
Email: embassy@jamaicagov.cn
Website: www.jamaicagov.cn

Embassy of Japan
7, Ri Tan Lu, Jian Guo Men Wai
Beijing
Telephone: +86 (0)10 6532 2361
Fax: +86 (0)10 65324625
Email: info@eoj.cn
Website: www.cn.emb-japan.go.jp/index_e.htm

Embassy of the Hashemite Kingdom of Jordan
5, Dong Liu Jie
San Li Tun
Beijing 100600
Telephone: +86 (0)10 6532 3906
Fax: +86 (0)10 6532 3283

Embassy of the Republic of Kazakhstan
9, Dong Liu Jie
San Li Tun
Beijing
Telephone: +86 (0)10 6532 6182
Fax: +86 (0)10 6532 6183
Email: doors@public3.bta.net.cn
Website: www.kazembchina.org

Embassy of the Republic of Kenya
4, Xi Liu Jie

San Li Tun
Beijing
Telephone: +86 (0)10 6532 3381
Fax: +86 (0)10 6532 1770
Email: kenrepbj@hotmail.com

Embassy of the State of Kuwait
23, Guang Hua Lu
Beijing
Telephone: +86 (0)10 6532 2216
Fax: +86 (0)10 65321607

Embassy of the Kyrgyz Republic
2-4-1, Ta Yuan Diplomatic Office Building
Beijing
Telephone: +86 (0)10 6532 6458
Fax: +86 (0)10 6532 6459

Embassy of the Laos People's Democratic Republic
11, Dong Si Jie, San Li Tun
Beijing
Telephone: +86 (0)10 6532 1224
Fax: +86 (0)10 6532 6748

Embassy of the Republic of Latvia in Beijing
71 Greenland Garden
Greenland Road 1A
Chaoyang District
Beijing 100016
Telephone: +86 (0)10 64333863
Fax: +86 (0)10 64333810
Email: embassy.china@mfa.gov.lv
Website: www.latvianembassy.org.cn/en/

Embassy of Lebanon
51, Dong Liu Jie, San Li Tun
Beijing
Telephone: +86 (0)10 6532 1560
Fax: +86 (0)10 6532 2770
Email: Lebanon@public.bta.net.cn

Embassy of the Kingdom of Lesotho
2-3-13, San Li Tun Diplomatic Compound
Beijing

Telephone: +86 (0)10 6532 6842/3
Fax: +86 (0)10 6532 6845

Embassy of the Republic of Liberia in Beijing
Room 013, Gold Island Diplomatic Compound
1 Xi Ba He Nan Lu
Beijing 100028
Telephone: +86 (0)10 64403007
Fax: +86 (0)10 64403918

Embassy of Libya
3, Dong Liu Jie, San Li Tun
Beijing 100600
Telephone: +86 (0)10 6532 3666
Fax: +86 (0)10 6532 3391

Embassy of the Republic of Lithuania
8-2-12, Ta Yuan Diplomatic Office Building
Beijing
Telephone: +86 (0)10 6532 4421/84518520
Fax: +86 (0)10 6532 4421/84514442

Embassy of the Grand-Duchy of Luxembourg
21, Nei Wu Bu Jie
Beijing
Telephone: +86 (0)10 6513 5937
Fax: +86 (0)10 6513 7268

Embassy of the Republic of Macedonia
5-2-22 San Li Tun Diplomatic Apartments
Beijing
Telephone: +86 (0)10 6532 6282/7846
Fax: +86 (0)10 6532 6756/7847
Website: www.macedonianembassy.com.cn

Embassy of the Republic of Madagascar
3, San Li Tun Dong Jie
Beijing
Telephone: +86 (0)10 6532 2571
Fax: +86 (0)10 6532 2102

Embassy of Malaysia
2, Liang Ma Qiao Bei Jie
Chaoyang District
Beijing 100600

Telephone: +86 (0)10 6532 2531/2/3
Fax: +986 (0)10 6532 5032
Email: mwbjing@kln.gov.my
Website: www.kln.gov.my/perwakilan/beijing

Embassy of the Republic of Mali
8, Dong Si Jie, San Li Tun
Beijing
Telephone: +86 (0)10 65321704, 65325530
Fax: +86 (0)10 6532 1618

Embassy of the Republic of Malta
1-51, Diplomatic Office Building
San Li Tun
Beijing
Telephone: +86 (0)10 6532 3114
Fax: +86 (0)10 6532 6125

Embassy of the Republic of the Marshall Islands
2-14-1, Ta Yuan Diplomatic Office Building
Beijing
Telephone: +86 (0)10 6532 5904
Fax: +86 (0)10 6532 4679

Embassy of the Islamic Republic of Mauritania
9, Dong San Jie
San Li Tun
Beijing
Telephone: +86 (0)10 6532 1346
Fax: +86 (0)10 6532 1685

Embassy of the Republic of Mauritius in Beijing
202 Dong Wai Diplomatic Office Building
23, Dong Zhi Men Wai Da Jie
Beijing 100600
Telephone: +86 (0)10 65325695/5696/5698
Fax: +86 (0)10 65325705

Embassy of Mexico
5, Dong Wu Jie
San Li Tun
Beijing
Telephone: +86 (0)10 65322574/2070/1947
Fax: +86 (0)10 65323744

Embassy of the Republic of Moldova in Beijing
2-9-1, Ta Yuan Office Building
14 Liang Ma He Nan Lu
Chaoyang District
Beijing 100600
Telephone: +86 (0)10 65325494
Fax: +86 (0)10 65325379

Embassy of Mongolia
2 Xiu Shui Bei Jie
Jian Guo Men Wai
Beijing
Telephone: +86 (0)10 6532 1203
Fax: +86 (0)10 6532 5045
Commercial Office: +86 (0)10 6532 1952
Email: mail@mongolembassychina.org
Website: www.mongolembassychina.org

Embassy of the Kingdom of Morocco
16, San Li Tun Lu
Beijing
Telephone: +86 (0)10 65321489, 65321796
Fax: +86 (0)10 6532 1453

Embassy of the Republic of Mozambique
1-71 Tayuan Office Building
San Lui Tun, L, 8th Floor
Beijing 100600
Telephone: +86 (0)10 6532 3664
Fax: +86 (0)10 6532 5189

Embassy of the Union of Myanmar in Beijing
6, Dong Zhi Men Wai Street
Chaoyang District
Beijing 100600
Telephone: +86 (0)10 65320351
Fax: +86 (0)10 65320408
Website: www.myanmarembassy.com

Embassy of the Republic of Namibia
1-13-2, Ta Yuan Diplomatic Office Building
Beijing
Telephone: +86 (0)10 6532 4810
Fax: +86 (0)10 6532 4549

Nauran Embassy in Peoples Republic of Beijing, China
Ta Yuan Diplomatic Compound Xin Dong Lu
Chaoyang Beijing PRC
Telephone: +86 (0)10 8532 2668
Fax: +86 (0)10 8532 636
Email: china@nauruembassy.org

Nepalese Embassy
1, Xi Liu Jie
San Li Tun Lu
Beijing
Telephone: +86 (0)10 6532 1795
Fax: +86 (0)10 65323251
Email: info@nepalembassy.org.cn
Website: www.nepalembassy.org.cn

Royal Netherlands Embassy
4, Liang Ma He Nan Lu
Beijing
Telephone: +86 (0)10 6532 1131
Fax: +86 (0)10 6532 4689
Email: pek@minbuza.nl
Website: www.hollandinchina.org/index_cn.htm

Embassy of New Zealand
1 Dong Er Jie, Ri Tan Lu
Beijing
Telephone: +86 (0)10 8532 7000
Fax: +86 (0)10 6532 4317
Email: enquiries@nzembassy.cn
Website: www.nzembassy.com/china

Embassy of the Republic of Niger in Beijing
1-21, San Li Tun Apartment
Beijing 100600
Telephone: +86 (0)10 65324279
Fax: +86 (0)10 65327041

Embassy of the Federal Republic of Nigeria
2, Dong Wu Jie, San Li Tun
Beijing
Telephone: +86 (0)10 6532 3631
Fax: +86 (0)10 6532 1650
Website: www.nigeriaembassy.cn

Royal Norwegian Embassy
1 Dong Yi Jie, San Li Tun
Beijing
Telephone: +86 (0)10 8532 9600
Fax: +86 (0)10 6532 2392
Website: www.norway.cn

Embassy of the Sultanate of Oman
6, Liang Ma He Nan Lu
Beijing
Telephone: +86 (0)10 6532 3692
Fax: +86 (0)10 6532 5030

Embassy of the Islamic Republic of Pakistan
1, Dong Zhi Men Wai Da Jie
Beijing
Telephone: +86 (0)10 6532 2504/2072
Fax: +86 (0)10 6532 2715

Embassy of the State of Palestine
2, Dong San Jie, San Li Tun
Beijing
Telephone: +86 (0)10 6532 3327
Fax: +86 (0)10 65323241

Embassy of Papua New Guinea
2-11-2, Ta Yuan Diplomatic Office Building
Beijing
Telephone: +86 (0)10 6532 4312
Fax: +86 (0)10 6532 5483
Website: http://en.pngembassy.org.cn/

Embassy of the Republic of Peru
2-82 San Li Tun Diplomatic Office Building
Beijing
Telephone: +86 (0)10 6532 3719
Fax: +86 (0)10 6532 2178

Embassy of the Republic of the Philippines
23, Xiu Shui Bei Jie, Jian Guo Men Wai
Beijing
Telephone: +86 (0)10 6532 2518/1872
Fax: +86 (0)10 65323761
Email: main@philembassy-china.org
Website: www.philippine-embassy.cn

Embassy of the Republic of Poland
1 Ri Tan Lu
Jian Guo Men Wai
Beijing
Telephone: +86 (0)10 6532 1235
Fax: +86 (0)10 6532 1745
Commercial Office: Tel. +86 (0)10 6532 1388
Fax: +86 (0)10 6532 4958
Website: www.polecom.com.cn

Embassy of the Republic of Portugal
2-15-1/2 Ta Yuan Diplomatic Office Building
Beijing
Telephone: +86 (0)10 6532 3242/3220
Fax: +86 (0)10 6532 4637
Commercial Office: +86 (C)10 6532 6745
Fax: +86 (0)10 6532 6746

Embassy of the State of Qatar
2-9-2, Ta Yuan Diplomatic Office Building
Beijing
Telephone: +86 (0)10 6532 2231/5
Fax: +86 (0)10 65325274.'5122

Embassy of the Republic of South Korea
4/f China World Tower
1 Jian Guo Men Wai Da Jie
Beijing
Telephone: +86 (0)10 6505 2608
Fax: +86 (0)10 6505 3067
Website: www.koreaemb.org.cn

Embassy of Romania
Ri Tan Lu Dong Er Jie
Beijing
Telephone: +86 (0)10 6532 3442
Fax: +86 (0)10 6532 5728

Embassy of the Russian Federation
4 Dong Zhi Men Bei Zhong Jie
Beijing
Telephone: +86 (0)10 6532 1267/1991
Fax: +86 (0)10 6532 4853
Website: www.russia.org.cn

Embassy of the Republic of Rwanda
30, Xiu Shui Bei Jie
Beijing
Telephone: +86 (0)10 6532 2193
Fax: +86 (0)10 6532 2006

Royal Embassy of Saudi Arabia
1, Bei Xiao Jie, San Li Tun
Beijing
Telephone: +86 (0)10 6532 4825
Fax: +86 (0)10 6532 5324

Embassy of the Republic of Senegal in Beijing
305, Dong Wai Diplomatic Office Buiding
23, Dong Zhi Men Wai Da Jie
Beijing 100600
Telephone: +86 (0)10 65322593
Fax: +86 (0)10 65322646

Embassy of the Republic of Serbia in Beijing
1, Dong Liu Jie
San Li Tun
Beijing 100600
Telephone: +86 (0)10 65323516/1693/5413/3016
Fax: +86 (0)10 65321207
Website: www.embserbia.cn

Embassy of the Republic of Seychelles in Beijing
Appt. D 25 B, Global Trade Mansion
No. 9 Guanghua Road, Chaoyang District
100020 Beijing
Telephone: +86 (0)10 5870 1192, +86(0)10 5870 1195
Fax: +86(0)10 5870 1219

Embassy of the Republic of Sierra Leone
7, Dong Zhi Men Wai Da Jie
Beijing
Telephone: +86 (0)10 6532 1222
Fax: +86 (0)10 6532 3752

Embassy of the Republic of Singapore
1, Xiu Shui Bei Jie
Jian Guo Men Wai
Beijing

Telephone:+86 (0)10 6532 1115
Fax: +86 (0)10 6532 9405
Website: www.mfa.gov.sg/beijing/

Embassy of the Slovak Republic
Ri Tan Lu, Jian Guo Men Wai
Beijing
Telephone: +86 (0)10 6532 1531
Fax: +86 (0)10 6532 4814

Embassy of the Republic of Slovenia
57, Block F
Ya Qu Yuan, King's Garden Villas
18, Xiao Yun Road
Chao Yang District
Beijing 100600
Telephone: +86 (0)10 64681030, 64681154
Fax: +86 (0)10 64681040

Embassy of the Republic of Somalia
2, San Li Tun Lu
Beijing
Telephone: +86 (0)10 65321651, 65320717
Fax: +82 (0)10 6532 1752

Embassy of South Africa
5, Dong Zhi Men Wai Da Jie
Beijing 100600
Telephone: +86 (0)10 65320171
Fax: +86 (0)10 65327139
Website: www.saembassy.org.cn

Embassy of Spain
9 San Li Tun Lu
Beijing
Telephone: 6532 3742
Fax: +86 (0)10 6532 3401
Commercial Section: +86 (0)10 6532 2072
Fax: +86 (0)10 6532 1128
Website: www.mae.es/embajadas/pekin

Embassy of the Democratic Socialist Republic of Sri Lanka
3, Jian Hua Lu
Jian Guo Men Wai

Beijing
Telephone: +86 (0)10 6532 1861
Fax: +86 (0)10 6532 5426
Website: www.slemb.com

Embassy of the Republic of Sudan
1, Don Er Jie
San Li Tun
Beijing
Telephone: +86 (0)10 6532 2205
Fax: +86 (0)10 65321280
Email: mail@sudanembassychina.com
Website: www.sudanembassychina.com

Embassy of the Republic of Suriname in Beijing
2-2-22, Jianguomenwai Diplomatic Compound
Beijing 100600
Telephone: +86 (0)10 65322939/2938
Fax: +86 (0)10 65322941

Embassy of Sweden
3, Dong Zhi Men Wai Da Jie
Beijing
Telephone: +86 (0)10 6532 9790
Fax: +86 (0)10 6532 5008
Commercial Section:
Fax: +86 (0)10 6532 3803
Email: ambassaden.peking@foreign.ministry.se
Website: www.swedemb-cn.org

Embassy of Switzerland
3, Dong Wu Jie
San Li Tun
Beijing
Telephone: +86 (0)10 6532 2736
Fax: +86 (0)10 6532 4353

Embassy of the Syrian Arab Republic
6, Dong Si Jie
San Li Tun
Beijing
Telephone: +86 (0)10 6532 1372
Fax: +86 (0)10 6532 1575
Email: sy@syria.org.cn
Website: www.syria.org.cn

Embassy of the Republic of Tajikistan in Beijing
1-4, Section A, Liangmaqiao Diplomatic Compound
Beijing 100600
Telephone: +86 (0)10 65322598
Fax: +86 (0)10 65323039

Embassy of the United Republic of Tanzania
8, Liang Ma He Nan Lu
San Li Tun
Beijing
Telephone: +86 (0)10 6532 1719
Fax: +86 (0)10 65324351/1695
Email: tanrep@tanzaniaembassy.org.cn
Website: www.tanzaniaembassy.org.cn/eindex.asp

Royal Thai Embassy
40, Guang Hua Lu
Beijing
Tel. +86 (0)10 65321749
Fax: +86 (0)10 65321748

Embassy of the Republic of Togo
11, Dong Zhi Men Wai Da Jie
Beijing
Telephone: +86 (0)10 6532 2202
Fax: +86 (0)10 6532 5884

Embassy of the Kingdom of Tonga in Beijing
Suite 3002, Embassy House
Dong Zhi Men Wai Xiac Jie
Beijing 100600
Telephone: +86 (0)10 34499757
Fax: +86 (0)10 84499758

Embassy of the Tunis an Republic
1, San Li Tun Dong Jie
Beijing
Telephone: +86 (0)10 6532 2435
Fax: +86 (0)10 65325818

Embassy of the Republic of Turkey
9, Dong Wu Jie, San Li Tun
Beijing
Telephone: +86 (0)10 65321715
Fax: +86 (0)10 6532 5480

Embassy of Turkmenistan
King's Garden Villa D-1
18 Xiaoyun Lu
Beijing
Telephone: +86 (0)10 6532 6975/6976
Fax: +86 (0)10 6532 2269

Embassy of the Republic of Uganda
5, San Li Tun Dong Jie
Beijing
Telephone: +86 (0)10 6532 2370
Fax: +86 (0)10 6532 2242
Email: info@ugandaembassycn.org

Embassy of Ukraine
11, Dong Liu Jie
San Li Tun
Beijing
Telephone: +86 (0)10 6532 6359
Fax: +86 (0)10 6532 6765
Commercial Section: +86 (0)10 6532 4013
Website: www.ukremb.cn/eng

Embassy of the United Arab Emirates
1-9-1, Ta Yuan Diplomatic Office Building
Beijing
Telephone: +86 (0)10 65325085
Fax: +86 (0)10 65323024
Email: info@uaeemb.com

Embassy of the United Kingdom of Great Britain and Northern Ireland
11, Guang Hua Lu
Beijing
Telephone: +86 (0)10 51924000
Fax: +86 (0)10 5192 4239
Email: commercialmail@peking.mail.fco.gov.uk
Website: www.uk.cn

Embassy of the United States of America
3, Xiu Shui Bei Jie, Jian Guo Men Wai
Beijing
Telephone: +86 (0)10 6532 3831 and +86 (0)10 6532 3431

Email: AmCitBeijing@state.gov
Website: http://beijing.usembassy-china.org.cn

Embassy of the Republic of Uruguay
2-7-2, Ta Yuan Diplomatic Office Building
Beijing
Telephone: +86 (0)10 6532 4445
Fax: +86 (0)10 6532 7375
Email: urubei@public.bta.net.cn

Embassy of the Republic of Uzbekistan
2-1-92, Ta Yuan Diplomatic Compound
Beijing
Telephone: +86 (0)10 65326305, 65322551
Fax: +86 (0)10 6532 6304
Email: Embassy@uzbekistan.cn
Website: www.uzbekistan.cn

Embassy of Vanuatu
3-1-11 San Li Tun
Diplomatic Compound
Beijing
Telephone: +86 (0)10 6532 0337
Fax: +86 (0)10 6532 0336

Embassy of the Republic of Venezuela
14, San Li Tun Lu
Beijing
Telephone: +86 (0)10 6532 1295
Fax: +86 (0)10 6532 3817
Email: embvenez@public.bta.net.cn
Website: www.venezuela.org.cn

Embassy of the Socialist Republic of Vietnam
32, Guang Hua Lu
Jian Guo Men Wai
Beijing
Telephone: +86 (0)10 6532 1155
Fax: +86 (0)10 6532 5720

Embassy of the Republic of Yemen
5, Dong San Jie
San Li Tun
Beijing
Telephone: +86 (0)10 6532 1558

Fax: +86 (0)10 65324305
Email: info@embassyofyemen.net
Website: www.embassyofyemen.net

Embassy of the Republic of Zaire
6, Dong Wu Jie
San Li Tun
Beijing
Telephone: +86 (0)10 6532 2713

Embassy of the Republic of Zambia
5, Dong Si Jie
San Li Tun
Beijing
Telephone: +86 (0)10 6532 1554
Fax: +86 (0)10 6532 1891

Embassy of the Republic of Zimbabwe
7, Dong San Jie
San Li Tun
Beijing
Telephone: +86 (0)10 6532 3397
Fax: +86 (0)10 6532 5383

CHENGDU

France Consulate-General Chengdu
30th Floor
Tianfu Time Square
2, Zong Fu Lu
Chengdu
Sichuan Province 610016
Telephone: +86 (0)28 66666060, 66666103
Website: www.consulfrance-chengdu.org

Consulate General of the Federal Republic of Germany in Chengdu
6th Floor, Western Tower
19, 4th Section
Renmin Nan Lu
Chengdu
Sichuan Province 610000

Telephone: +86 (0)28 85280800
Fax: +86 (0)28 85268308

Pakistan Consulate General Chengdu
8th Floor, Western Tower
19, 4th Section, Renmin Nan Lu
Chengdu
Sichuan Province 610041

Republic of South Korea Consulate General Chengdu
19F Paradise Oasis Mansion
2, Xia Nan Da Jie
Chengdu
Sichuan Province 610000
Telephone: +86 (0)28 86165800
Fax: +86 (0)28 86165789
Email: schong95@mofat.go.kr

Singapore Consulate General Chengdu
1st Floor, Guancheng Square
308, Shuncheng Da Jie
Chengdu
Sichuan Province 610000

Royal Thai Consulate-General in Chengdu
Kempinski Hotel, 2nd Floor, Office Building
42 Renmin Nan Lu, 4th Section
Chengdu
Sichuan Province 610000
Telephone: +86 (0)28 85180688, 85192668
Fax: +86 (0)28 85125923

Consulate General of the United States of America in Chengdu
Ling Shi Guan Lu
Chengdu
Sichuan Province 610041
Telephone: +86 (0)28 85583992, 85589642
Fax: +86 (0)28 85583520
Email: consularchengdu@state.gov
Website: http://chengdu.usconsulate.gov/

CHONGQING

Consulate General of the Kingdom of Cambodia in Chongqing
1902, Building A
9 Yanghe Lu, JiangBei District
Chongqing 401120
Telephone: +86 (0)23 89116415
Fax: +86 (0)23 89111369

Canada Consulate General Chongqing
Chongqing Suite 1705
Metropolitan Tower
Wu Yi Road
Yu Zhong District
Chongqing
Telephone: +86 (0)23 6373 8007
Fax: +86 (0)23 6373 8026
Email: chong@international.gc.ca

Denmark Consulate General Chongqing
1 Metropolitan Tower, 31/F
68 Zou Rong Lu, Yuzhong District
Chongqing 400010
Telephone: +86 (0)23 63726600, 63725280
Fax: +86 (0)23 63725160
Email: chongqing@dtcchina.dk

Japan Consulate General Chongqing
37 F, Metropolitan Tower
68 Zou Rong Lu, Yuzhong District
Chongqing 400010
Telephone: +86 (0)23 63733585
Fax: +86 (0)23 63733589

Consulate General of the United Kingdom of Great Britain and Northern Ireland in Chongqing
28F, Metropolitan Tower, Zou Rong Lu
Yuzhong District
Chongqing 400010
Telephone: +86 (0)23 63691500
Fax: +86 (0)23 63691525
Email: chongqing.consular@fco.gov.uk

DALIAN

Consulate General of Japan in Shenyang (Dalian Office)
3F, Senmao Building
147 Zhongshan Lu
Xigang District, Dalian
Liaoning Province 116011
Telephone: +86 (0)411 83704077
Fax: +86 (0)411 83704066
Email: ryojikan@dljapan.com

GUANGXI

Consulate General of the Kingdom of Cambodia in Nanning
2F, Nanfeng Tower
85, Minzu Avenue, Nanning
Guangxi Province 530000
Telephone: +86 (0)771 5889892, 5889893
Fax: +86 (0)771 5888522

Consulate Office of the Kingdom of Thailand in Nanning
Room 2212, Guilin Tower
1, Wen Xin Lu, Nanning
Guangxi Province 530000
Telephone: +86 (0)771 5506698
Fax: +86 (0)771 5506628
Email: thainng@mf.go.th

Consulate General of Socialist Republic of Vietnam in Nanning
1F, Investment Plaza
109 Minzu Dadao, Nanning
Guangxi Province 530000
Telephone: +86 (0)771 5510561
Fax: +86 (0)771 5534738

GUANGZHOU

Australian Consulate General in Guangzhou
12/F, Development Center
3 Linjiang Road, Zhujiang New City, Guangzhou
Telephone: +86 (0)20 3814 0111
Fax: +86 (0)20 3814 0112
Email: guangzhou.consular@dfat.gov.au
Website: www.guangzhou.china.embassy.gov.au

Belgian Consulate General in Guangzhou
Room 1601-02A, CITIC Plaza
233, Tianhe North Rd
Guangzhou 510613
Telephone: +86 (0)20 38770188
Fax: +86 (0)20 38770288

Cambodia Consulate General in Guangzhou
Suite 8114, Garden Tower, Garden Hotel
Huanshi-dong Rd.
Guangzhou 510064
Telephone: +86 (0)20 8387 9005, 8333 8999
Fax: +86 (0)20 8387 9006
Email: Cambodia@public.guangzhou.gd.cn

Canada Consulate General in Guangzhou
Suite 801, Office Tower
China Hotel, Liuhua Rd
Guangzhou 510015
Telephone: +86 (0)20 8666 0569
Fax: +86 (0)20 8667 2401
Email: ganzu.consular-consulaire@international.gc.ca
Website: www.beijing.gc.ca/guangzhou/en/

Cuba Consulate General in Guangzhou
Room 1004, East Tower
Huapu Plaza
13, Huaming Rd
Zhu Jiang New City
Guangzhou 510635
Telephone: +86 (0)20 22382603/04
Fax: +86 (0)20 22382605

Email: cgeneral@cubacon=uladogz.com
Website: http://embacuba.cubaminrex.cu/Default.aspx?tabid=1378

Danish Consulate General in Guangzhou
Suite 1578, Office Tower
China Hotel, Liuhua Rd
Guangzhou 510015
Telephone: +86 (0)20 8666 0795
Fax: +86 (0)20 8667 0315
Email: cangkl@um.dk
Website: www.gkguangzhou.um.dk/da

Finland Consulate General in Guangzhou
Suites 3309-3312
CITIC Plaza
233 Tianhe-Bei Rd
Guangzhou 510613
Telephone: +86 (0)20 3877 0188
Fax: +86 (0)20 3877 0288
Email: sanomat.kan@formin.fi
Website: www.finland.cr/

French Consulate General in Guangzhou
Suite I801, Main Tower
Guangdong Internationa Hotel
339 Huanshi-dong Rd
Guangzhou 510098
Telephone: +86 (0)20 8330 3405, 8331 0909
（Economic）
Fax: +86 (0)20 8331 3437
Email: info@consulfrance-canton.org
Website: www.ambafrance-cn.org

German Consulate General in Guangzhou
19/F, Main Tower
Guangdong International Hotel
339 Huanshi-dong Rd
Guangzhou 510098
Telephone: +86 (0)20 8330 6533
Fax: +86 (0)20 8331 7033
Email: info@kanton.diplo.de
Website: www.kanton.diplo.de

Indonesia Consulate General in Guangzhou
Suites 1201-1223 West Wing
Dongfang Hotel
Guangzhou 510016
Telephone: +86 (0)20 8601 8772 / 8790 / 8850 / 8870
Fax: +86 (0)20 8601 8773
Email: kjriguangzhou@yahoo.com
Website: www.indonesianembassy-china.com/EN/guangzhou.htm

Italy Consulate General in Guangzhou
Suite 5207, CITIC Plaza
233 Tianhe-Bei Rd
Guangzhou 510613
Telephone: +86 (0)20 3877 0556 Ext. 7/8/9
Fax: +86 (0)20 3877 0270
Email: itconsgz@gitic.com.cn
Website: www.itconsgz.org.cn

Japan Consulate General in Guangzhou
1/F Garden Tower
Garden Hotel, Huanshi-dong Rd
Guangzhou 510064
Telephone: +86 (0)20 8334 3009, 8399 2345 (visa appointments)
Fax: +86 (0)20 8333 8972
Email: ryojikan@public.guangzhou.gd.cn
Website: www.guangzhou.cn.emb-japan.go.jp/cgjp_cn/

Malaysian Consulate General
Suite 1915-1918
CITIC Plaza
233 Tianhe-Bei Rd
Guangzhou 510613
Telephone: +86 (0)20 8739 5660, 3877 0766/0763
Fax: +86 (0)20 8739 5669
Email: mwgzhou@public.guangzhou.gd.cn

Mexican Consulate General
Room 02-03, 14 Floor
Metro Plaza, Tianhe North Rd
Guangzhou 510620

Tel.: +86 (0)20 22220981
Fax: +86 (0)20 22221006

Consulate General of the Kingdom of Nepal in Guangzhou
Room 905, 9/F
Third Building of Dongjun Square
836, Dongfeng Dong Lu
Guangzhou, 510080
Telephone: +86 (0)20 87672448, 87662197, 87664560
Fax: +86 (0)20 87672523

Netherlands Consulate General in Guangzhou
Suite 705 Main Tower
Guangdong International Hotel
339 Huanshi-dong Rd
Guangzhou 510098
Telephone: +86 (0)20 8330 2067
Fax: +86 (0)20 8330 3601
Email: nedcons@gitic.com.cn
Website: www.hollandinchina.org/cn/cg/guangzhou.htm

Consulate General of New Zealand in Guangzhou
Room 1160, Commercial Mansion
China Hotel
Guangzhou 510015
Telephone: +86 (0)20 86670253
Fax: +86 (0)20 86666420

Philippine Consulate General in Guangzhou
Suites 709-711, Main Tower
Guangdong International Hotel
339 Huanshi-dong Rd
Guangzhou 510098
Telephone: +86 (0)20 81886968
Fax: +86 (0)20 81862041
Email: gzphcggz@public1.guangzhou.gd.cn

Poland Consulate General in Guangzhou
63 Shamian St.
Guangzhou 510130
Telephone: +86 (0)20 8121 9993, 8121 8991

Fax: +86 (0)20 8121 9995
Email: plcogeca@public.guangzhou.gd.cn (General)

Consulate General of Republic of Korea in Guangzhou
18/F West Tower
Yangcheng International Trade Center
Tiyu-dong Rd.
Guangzhou
Telephone: +86 (0)20 3887 0555 Ext. 102
Fax: +86 (0)20 3887 0923
Email: guangzhou@mofat.go.kr

Singapore Consulate General in Guangzhou
Suite 3318, CITIC Plaza
233 Tianhe-Bei Rd
Guangzhou 510613
Telephone: +86 (0)20 38912345
Fax: +86 (0)20 38912933, 38912131 (for visa)
Website: www.mfa.gov.sg/xiamenchi/

Swedish Consulate General in Guangzhou
1002B-1003 CITIC Plaza
233 Tianhe-Bei Rd
Guangzhou 510098
Telephone: +86 (0)20 3891 2383
Fax: +86 (0)20 3891 2100
Email: generalkonsulat.kanton@foreign.ministry.se
Website: www.swedenabroad.com/guangzhou

Consulate General of Switzerland in Guangzhou
Room 811–812
Commercial Mansion
Garden Hotel
Guangzhou 510133
Telephone: +86 (0)20 83338999-811,
8338999—812
Fax: +86 (0)20 83877447

Thai Consulate General in Guangzhou
M07, Garden Hotel
368 Huanshi Dong Lu
Guangzhou 510064

Telephone: +86 (0)20 83804277, 83849937,
83338989—10-19
Fax: +86 (0)20 83889959, 83889567

Consulate General of the UK of Great Britain and Northern Ireland in Guangzhou
7/F (Trade & Investment and Public Affairs Sections)
2/F (Consular and Visa Sections)
Main Tower, Guangdong International Hotel
339 Huanshi-dong Rd
Guangzhou 510098
Telephone: +86 (0)20 8314 3000, 8335 1354/1316
(Cultural & Education)
Fax: +86 (0)20 8333 6485, 8331 2799 (Consular Enquiries)
Consular Enquiries: guangzhou.consular@fco.gov.uk
Visa Enquiries: guangzhou.visas@fco.gov.uk
Website: www.uk.cn/cz/english/index.asp

USA Consulate General in Guangzhou
1 Shamian-Nan St
Guangzhou 510133
Telephone: +86 (0)20 3121 8000, 81218418
(American Citizen Services)
Fax: +86(0)20 8121 9001
Website: http://guangzhou.usembassy-china.org.cn/

Vietnam Consulate-General in Guangzhou
North Section
2/F Tower B
Landmark Hotel
Qiaoguang Rd
Guangzhou 510115
Telephone: +86 (0)20 8330 5911/ 5910
Fax: +86 (0)20 8330 5915

HOHHOT

Consulate General of Mongolia in Hohhot
Unit 1, Building 5
Wulan Residential Area
Saihan District

Hohhot 010020
Telephone: +86 (0)471 4923819, 4303266/254
Fax: +86 (0)471 4303250

KUNMING

Royal Consulate General of Cambodia in Kunming
20/F, Jinquan Hotel
93 Renmin Dong Lu
Kunming
Telephone: +86 (0)871 3317320
Fax: +86 (0)871 3316220

Consulate General of Lao People's Democratic Republic in Kunming
1/F Main Tower
Camellia Hotel
96 Dong Feng Dong Lu
Kunming
Telephone: +86 (0)871 3176623/4
Fax: +86 (0)871 3178556

Consulate General of Malaysia in Kunming
Room 401-405
Sakura Hotel
29 Dongfeng Lu
Kunming
Telephone: +86 (0)871 3165888/6241/6242
Fax: +86 (0)871 3113503

Consulate General of the Union of Myanmar in Kunming
2/F, Main Tower
Camellia Hotel
96 Dong Feng Road, E.
Kunming
Telephone: +86 (0)871 3163000/6215
Fax: +86 (0)871 3176309

Royal Thai Consulate General in Kunming
1/F, South Building
Kunming Hotel

145 Dong Feng Dong Lu
Kunming
Telephone: +86 (0)871 3168916/3149296
Fax: +86 (0)871 3166891

Consulate General of Socialist Republic of Vietnam in Kunming
1/F, Jiaxing Hotel
529 Beijing Lu
Kunming
Telephone: +86 (0)871 3183092
Fax: +86 (0)871 3183085

LHASA

Royal Nepalese Consulate General in Lhasa
Chancery: No.13 Norbulingka Lu
Lhasa
Telephone: +86 (0)891 6830609
Fax: +86 (0)891 6836890

QINGDAO

Consulate General of the Republic of South Korea in Qingdao
Chancery: No.17, Hong Kong Dong Lu
Laoshan District
Qingdao
Telephone: +86 (0)532 88976001
Fax: +86 (0)532 88976005
Email: qdconsul@mofat.go.kr
Website: www.qdcon.org.cn

SHANGHAI

Argentina Consulate-General in Shanghai
4F West Tower
Sun Plaza
88 Xianxia Lu
Shanghai

Telephone: +86 (0)21 62780300
Fax: +86 (0)21 62958539
Email: consuargensh@online.sh.cn
Website: www.consuargensh.com/chinese/

Australian Consulate-General Shanghai
Level 22
CITIC Square
1168 Nanjing Xi Lu
Shanghai 200041
Telephone: +86 (0)21 52925500
Fax: +86 (0)21 52925511
E-Mail: acgshang@public.sta.net.cn
Website: www.shanghai.china.embassy.gov.au

Austrian Consulate-General in Shanghai
3A, Qihua Tower
1375 Huaihai Zhong Lu
Shanghai
Telephone: +86 (0)21 64740268
Fax: +86 (0)21 64741554

Consulate General of the Kingdom of Belgium in Shanghai
127 Wuyi Lu
Shanghai
Telephone: +86 (0)21 64376579
Fax: +86 (0)21 64377041
Email: shanghai@diplobel.org
Website: www.diplobel.org/shanghai/

The Consulate General of the Republic of Bulgaria in Shanghai
7K Hongqiao Business Center
2272 Hongqiao Lu
Shanghai 200336
Telephone: +86 (0)21 62376183
Fax: +86 (0)21 62376189

Consulate General of the Federative Republic of Brazil in Shanghai
10F, Qihua Tower
1375 Huaihai Zhong Lu
Shanghai
Telephone: +86 (0)21 64370110

Fax: +86 (0)21 6437016C
Email: consbrasxangai@consbrasxangai.com
Website: http://consbrasxangai.com/

British Consulate General in Shanghai
Suite 301, Shanghai Center
1376 Nanjing Xi Lu
Shanghai
Telephone: +86 (0)21 62798103
Fax: +86 (0)21 62798254
Email: britishconsulate.shanghai@fco.gov.uk
Website: www.uk.cn/bj/ndex.asp?city=4

Royal Consulate General of Cambodia in Shanghai
Room 901-902
Hua Sheng Building
400 Hankou Lu
Shanghai
Telephone: +86 (0)21 63600949
Fax: +86 (0)21 63611437
Email: tangjx@online.sh.cn

Consulate General of Canada in Shanghai
Suite 604
Shanghai Center
1376 Nanjing Xi Lu
Shanghai
Telephone: +86 (0)21 62798400
Fax: +86 (0)21 62798401
Email: shngi@international.gc.ca
Website: www.shanghai.gc.ca

Consulate General of the Republic of Chile in Shanghai
Room 305, Equatorial Hotel Shanghai
65 Yan'an Xi Lu
Shanghai
Telephone: +86 (0)21 62498000
Fax: +86 (0)21 62498333

Consulate General of the Republic of Cuba in Shanghai
5F, New Town Mansion
55 Loushanguan Lu

Shanghai
Telephone: +86 (0)21 62753078
Fax: +86 (0)21 62753147

Consulate General of the Czech Republic in Shanghai
Room 808, New Town Center
83 Loushanguan Lu
Shanghai
Telephone: +86 (0)21 62369925/62369926
Fax: +86 (0)21 62369920
Email: shanghai@embassy.mvz.cz

Consulate General of the Kingdom of Denmark in Shanghai
Room 701, Shanghai International Trade Center
2201 Yan'an Xi Lu
Shanghai
Telephone: +86 (021 62090500
Fax: +86 (0)21 62090504
Email: shagk@um.dk
Website: www.gkshanghai.um.dk/da

Consulate General of the Arab Republic of Egypt in Shanghai
19A/B, Qihua Tower
1375 Huaihai Zhong Lu
Shanghai
Telephone: +86 (0)21 64331020/64330622/64330502
Fax: +86 (0)21 64330049

Consulate General of the Republic of Finland in Shanghai
2501-05, CITIC Square
1168 Nanjing Xi Lu
Shanghai
Telephone: +86 (0)21 52929900
Fax: +86 (0)21 52929880
Email: sanomat.sng@formin.fi
Web page: www.finland.cn

Consulate General of the Republic of France in Shanghai
2 F, Hai Tong Securities Tower

689 Guang Dong Lu
Shanghai
Telephone: +86 (0)21 61032200
Fax: +86 (0)21 63411055
Email: info@consulfrance-shanghai.org
Website: www.consulfrance-shanghai.org

Consulate General of the Federal Republic of Germany in Shanghai
118 Yongfu Lu
Shanghai
Telephone: +86 (0)21 34010106
Fax: +86 (0)21 64714448

Greece Consulate-General in Shanghai
Suite 3501-02
Shanghai Center
989 Changle Lu
Shanghai
Telephone: +86 (0)21 54670505
Fax: +86 (0)21 54670202

Consulate General of the Republic of Hungary
Room 2811, Haitong Securities Tower
689 Guangdong Lu
Shanghai
Telephone: +86 (0)21 63410564/63410764
Fax: +86 (0)21 62410574

Consulate General of the Republic of India in Shanghai
Room 1008, Shanghai International Trade Center
2201 Yan'an Xi Lu
Shanghai
Telephone: +86 (0)21 62758882/62758885/62758886
Fax: +86 (0)21 62758881
Email: cgisha@public.sta.net.cn
Website: www.indianconsulate.org.cn/

Consulate General of the Islamic Republic of Iran in Shanghai
17 Fuxing Rd. (W)
Shanghai 200030

Telephone: +86 (0)21 64332997
Fax: +86 (0)21 64336826

Consulate General of Ireland in Shanghai
Room 700A, Shanghai Center
1376 Nanjing Xi Lu
Shanghai
Telephone: +86 (0)2162798729
Fax: +86 (0)21 62798739

Israel Consulate-General in Shanghai
Room 703, New Town Mansion
55 Loushanguan Lu
Shanghai
Telephone: +86 (0)21 62098008
Fax: +86 (0)21 62098010

Consulate General of the Republic of Italy in Shanghai
11A, 11B, Qihua Tower
1375 Huaihai Zhong Lu
Shanghai
Telephone: +86 (0)21 64716980
Fax: +86 (0)21 64716977

Honorary Consul of Jamaica to Shanghai
16F, Zhongda Square
989 Dongfang Lu
Shanghai
Telephone: +86 (0)21 58313553
Fax: +98 (0)21 68763299
Email: gs_intl@163.net

Consulate General of Japan in Shanghai
8 Wanshan Lu
Shanghai
Telephone: +86 (0)21 52574766
Fax: +86 (0)21 62788988

General Consulate of Luxembourg in Shanghai
4th Floor
12 Zhongshan Dong Yi Lu
Shanghai 200002
Telephone: + 86 (0)21 6339 0400

Fax: +86 (0)21 6339 0433
Email: shanghai.cg@mae.etat.lu

Consulate General of Malaysia in Shanghai
Room 1101, CITIC Square
1168 Nanjing Xi Lu
Shanghai
Telephone: +86 (0)21 52925424
Fax: +86 (0)21 52925951

Consulate General of the United States of Mexico in Shanghai
9A, 9B, Qihua Tower
1375 Huaihai Zhong Lu
Shanghai
Telephone: +86 (0)21 64373451
Fax: +86 (0)21 64370336

Honorary Consul of Monaco to Shanghai
1 Longdong Ave.
Pudong New District
Shanghai
Telephone: +86 (0)21 58332199
Fax: +86 (0)21 58331577

Royal Nepalese Honorary Consul to Shanghai
28F, No.2 Lane
1040 Caoyang Lu
Shanghai
Telephone: +86 (0)21 52661811
Fax: +86 (0)21 52661819

Consulate General of the Kingdom of the Netherlands in Shanghai
4F, East Tower, Sun Plaza
88 Xianxia Lu
Shanghai
Telephone: +86 (0)21 62099076
Fax: +86 (0)21 62099079

Consulate General of New Zealand in Shanghai
15F, Qihua Tower
Huaihai Zhong Lu
Shanghai

Telephone: +86 (0)21 64711127
Fax: +86 (0)21 64310226

Royal Norwegian Consulate General in Shanghai
Room 321
Zhongshan Dong Yi Lu
Shanghai
Telephone: +86 (0)21 63239988
Fax: +86 (0)21 63233938

Consulate General of the Islamic Republic of Pakistan
Suite 0
7F Hongqiao Business Center
2272 Hongqiao Lu
Shanghai
Telephone: +86 (0)21 62377000
Fax: +86 (0)21 62377066

Consulate General of the Republic of Peru in Shanghai
Suite 2705, Kerry Center
1515 Nanjing Xi Lu
Shanghai
Telephone: +86 (0)21 52985900
Fax: +86 (0)21 52985905
Website: www.conpersh.com

Consulate General of the Republic of Philippines in Shanghai
Suite 368, Shanghai Center
1376 Nanjing Xi Lu
Shanghai
Telephone: +86 (0)21 62798337
Fax: +86 (0)21 62798332
Email: pcg@philcongenshanghai.org

Consulate General of the Republic of Poland in Shanghai
618 Jianguo Xi Lu
Xuhui District
Shanghai
Telephone: +86 (0)21 64339288
Fax: +86 (0)21 64330417

Consulate General of the Republic of Korea in Shanghai
Room 402, Shanghai International Trade Center
2200 Yan'an Xi Lu
Shanghai
Telephone: +86 (0)21 62196420
Fax: +86 (0)21 62196918

Consulate General of Romania in Shanghai
Room 305, West Tower, Sun Plaza
Xianxia Lu
Shanghai
Telephone: +86 (0)21 62701146
Fax: +86 (0)21 62085105

Consulate General of the Russian Federation in Shanghai
20 Huangpu Lu
Shanghai
Telephone: +86 (0)21 63248383/63242628
Fax: +86 (0)21 63069982
Email: gkshanghai@mail.ru
Website: www.russia.org.cn/eng/

Consulate General of the Republic of Singapore in Shanghai
89 Wanshan Lu
Shanghai
Telephone: +86 (0)21 62785566
Fax: +86 (0)21 62956038
Email: singcg_sha@sgmfa.gov.sg
Website: www.mfa.gov.sg/shanghai/

Consulate General of Slovak Republic in Shanghai
4B Qihua Tower
Huaihai Zhong Lu
Shanghai
Telephone: +86 (0)21 64314205
Fax: +86 (0)21 64713604

Consulate General of Republic of South Africa in Shanghai
Room 2706, the Bund Center
220 Yan'an Zhong Lu

Shanghai
Telephone: +86 (0)21 53594977
Fax: +86 (0)21 63352980

Consulate General of Spain in Shanghai
12 Zhongshan Dong Yi Lu
Shanghai
Telephone: +86 (0)21 63213543
Fax: +86 (0)21 63211396

Consulate General of the Kingdom of Sweden in Shanghai
Room 1530-1541, Shanghai Central Plaza
381 Huaihai Zhong Lu
Shanghai
Telephone: +86 (0)21 63916767
Fax: +86 (0)21 63915067

Consulate General of the Swiss Confederation in Shanghai
Room 302, 22F, Building A
Far East International Plaza
88 Xianxia Lu
Shanghai
Telephone: +86 (0)21 62700519-21
Fax: +86 (0)21 62700522

Royal Thai Consulate General in Shanghai
3F, No.7 Zhongshan Dong Yi Lu
Shanghai
Telephone: +86 (0)21
63234095/63219371/63219406
Fax: +86 (0)21 63234140

Consulate General of the Republic of Turkey in Shanghai
13F, Qihua Tower
1375 Huaihai Zhong Lu
Shanghai
Telephone: +86 (0)21 64746838
Fax: +86 (0)21 62785272
Email: tcsanghaybsk@163.com

Consulate General of Ukraine in Shanghai
Room 502, Sun Plaza West Tower

88 Xianxia Lu
Shanghai
Telephone: +86 (0)21 62953195/62953196
Fax: +86 (0)21 62953171
Email: ukrconsh@sh163.net

Consulate General of the United States of America in Shanghai
1469 Huaihai Zhong Lu
Shanghai
Telephone: +86 (0)21 64336880
Fax: +86 (0)21 64334122

Consulate General of the Oriental Republic of Uruguay
Room 2403, Hong Kong New World Tower
300 Huaihai Zhong Lu
Shanghai
Telephone: +86 (0)21 63353927
Fax: +86 (0)21 63353741

SHENYANG

Consulate General of the Democratic People's Republic of Korea in Shenyang
1 Huanghe Ave
Huanggu District
Shenyang
Telephone: +86 (0)24 86852742
Fax: +86 (0)24 86855432

Consulate General of Japan in Shenyang
50 14th Wei Lu
Heping District
Shenyang
Telephone: +86 (0)24 23227490
Fax: +86 (0)24 23222394
Email: sykohou@mail.sy.ln.cn
Website: www.shenyang.cn.emb-japan.go.jp/cn/

Consulate General of the Republic of Korea in Shenyang
37 South 13th Wei Lu

Heping District

Shenyang

Telephone: +86 (0)24 23853388

Fax: +86 (0)21 23855170

Consulate General of the Russia Federation in Shenyang

31 South 13th Wei Lu

Heping District

Shenyang

Telephone: +86 (0)24 23223927

Fax: +86 (0)24 23223907

Email: ruscons@mail.sy.ln.cn

Website: www.russia.org.cn/eng/

US Consulate General in Shenyang

Consulate General of the United States of America

52 14th Wei Lu

Heping District

Shenyang

Telephone: +86 (0)24 23220804

Fax: +86 (0)24 23222374

Website: http://shenyang.usembassy-china.org.cn/

WUHAN

Consulate General of the Republic of France in Wuhan

Room 809, Wuhan International Trade Center

566 Jianshe Dadao

Hankou

Wuhan

Telephone: +86 (0)27 85778403/85778405/85778 406/85778423

Fax: +86 (0)27 85778426

Email: chancellerie@consulfrance-wuhan.org

Website: www.ambafrance-cn.org

XIAMEN

Consulate General of the Republic of the Philippines in Xiamen

Lingxiang Li, Lianhua Xincun

Xiamen

Telephone: +86 (0)592 5130355/51303662

Consulate General of the Republic of Singapore in Xiamen

Unit 05-07/08

The Bank Center

189 Xiahe Lu

Xiamen

Telephone: +86 (0)592 2684691

Fax: +86 (0)592 2684694

Email: singcg_xmn@sgmfa.gov.sg

Website: www.mfa.gov.sg/xiamenchi

XI'AN

Royal Thailand Consulate Office in Xi'an

4th Floor, Yu Lang International Building

77, Jie Fang Lu

Xi'an

INTERNATIONAL SCHOOLS

BEIJING

Australian International School Beijing

7 Louzizhuang Road

Chaoyang District;

Beijing 100018

Tel.: +86 (0)10 84394315-6

Fax: +86 (0)10 84391842

Email: enquiries@aisb.cn

Website: www.aisb.cn

Beanstalk International Bilingual School (3 branches)
38, Nanshiliju, Chaoyang District, Beijing, 100016
Telephone: +86 (0)10 84566019/5130 7951/6466 9255
Fax: +86 (0)10 8456 2808/5130 7946/6466 9255
Email: office@bibs.com.cn
Website: www.bibs.com.cn

Beijing City International School
77 Baiziwan Nan Er Road
Beijing 100022
Telephone: +86 (0)10 8771 7171
Fax: +86 (0)10 8771 7778
Email: info@bcis.cn
Website: www.bcis.cn

Beijing New Talaent Academy
9 Anhua Street, Shunyi District
Beijing 101300, China⊠
Telephone: +86 (0)10 8041 3036
Fax: +86 (0)10 8041 3009
Email: hyzx@bjnewtalent.com
Website: www.bjnewtalent.com

Beijing Rego British School
15 Liyuan Street, Tianzhu County
Shunyi District, Beijing, China 101312
China
Telephone: +86 (0)10 6465 4487
Fax: +86 (0)10 6465 7783
Email: info@bjrego.org
Website: www.bjrego.org

British World Youth Academy
No. 18 Huajiadi Beili
Chaoyang District
100102 Beijing, P.R. China
Telephone: +86 (0)10 6461 7787
Fax: +86 (0)10 6461 7717
Website: www.ibwya.net

British International School in Beijing
17, Area 4
An Zhen Xi Li

Chaoyang District
Beijing 100029
Telephone: +86 (0)10 6443 3151
Fax: +86 (0)10 6443 3155
Email: admissions@biss.com.cn
Website: www.biss.com.cn

British School of Beijing
Email: info@britishschool.org.cn
Website: www.britishschool.org.cn
Shunyi Campus
No.9 An Hua Street,
Shunyi District
Beijing 101300
Telephone: +86 (0)10 8047 3588
Fax: +86 (0)10 8047 3598/99

Sanlitun Campus
5 Xiliujie, Sanlitun Road
Chaoyang District
Beijing 100027
Telephone: +86 (0)10 8532 3088
Fax: +86 (0)10 8532 3089

Canadian Internationa School of Beijing
38 Liangmaqiao Lu, Chaoyang District
Beijing, 100125, P.R. China
Telephone: +86 (0)10 6465 7788
Fax: +86 (0)10 6465 7789
Email: admissions@cis-beijing.com
Website: www.cisb.com.cn

Dulwich College International Beijing
Dulwich College Beijing is a franchise of the famous English public school that has its main site in Dulwich, London. There is a Dulwich College in Shanghai and plans exist for possible branches in Suzhou and south China. Famous students include many prominent figures including Anand Panyarachun (twice Prime Minster of Thailand), Peter Lilly (Former British Shadow Chancellor).
Dulwich College Legend Garden Campus
89 Capital Airport Road

Shunyi District
Beijing 101300 PRC

Dulwich College Beijing Riviera Campus
1 Xiang Jiang Bei Lu
Jing Shun Lu
Chao Yang District
Beijing 100103 PRC

Dulwich College River Garden Campus
River Garden Villas
Hou Shai Yu Bai Xin Zhuang
Shunyi District
Beijing 101300 PRC
Telephone: +86 (0)10 6454 9000
Fax: +86 (0)10 6454 9001
Email: info@dulwich-beijing.cn
Website: www.dulwich-beijing.cn

Eton International School
(Not related to the famous Eton College in the UK)
Palm Springs International Apartments
8 Chaoyang Park South Road
Chaoyang District
Beijing 100026
Telephone: +86 (0)10 6539 7171
Fax: +86 (0)10 6539 8817
Email: info@etonkids.com
Website: www.etonkids.com

Harrow School International Beijing
Harrow School Beijing is a franchise of the famous
English public school that has its original site at
Harrow-on-the-hill, in the UK. Former students
have included former British Prime Minister Winston
Churchill, inventor of photography Fox Talbot, and
the first Prime Minister of India, Pundit Nehru,
among many renowned politicians and leaders of
industry.
5, 4th Block
Anzhenxili
Chao Yang District
Beijing 100029
Telephone: +86 (0)10 6444 8900/8951 6680

Fax: +86 (0)10 6445 3870/8951 6681
Email: enquiries@harrowbeijing.cn
Website: www.harrowbeijing.cn

International Academy of Beijing
Olympic Forest Park East
2 Yangshan Road
Chaoyang District, Beijing, 100107
Telephone: +86 (0)10 8493 8680/6430 1600
Fax: +86 (0)10 6430 1208/8493 1506
Website: www.iabchina.net
Email: admission@iabchina.net

International School of Beijing—Shunyi
10 An Hua Street
Shunyi District
Beijing 101318
Telephone: +86 (0)10 8149 2345
Fax: +86 (0)10 8046 2001/2
Email: isb-info@isb.bj.edu.cn
Website: www.isb.bj.edu.cn

**The International Children's House English
Montessori Kindergarten**
(There are 4 campuses in Beijing)
China World Trade Center
North Lodge
1 Jian Guo Men Wai Avenue
Beijing 100004
Phone: +86 (0)10 65053869/65052288 Ext.81299
Fax: +86 (0)10 6505 1237
Email: info@montessoribeijing.com
Website: www.montessoribeijing.com

Western Academy of Beijing
PO Box 8547
10 Lai Guang Ying Dong Lu
Chao Yang District
Beijing 100103
Telephone: +86 (0)10 5986 5588
Fax: +86 (0)10 6433 3974
Email: wabinfo@wab.edu
Website: www.wab.edu

Yew Chung International School
Honglingjin Park, No 5 Houbalizhuang
Chaoyang District
Beijing 100025
Telephone: +86 (0)10 8583 3731
Fax: +86 (0)10 8583 2734
Email: enquiry@bj.ycef.com
Website: www.ycef.com

CHANGSHA

Changsha WES Acacdmy
8, Dongyi Road, Xingsha, Changsha
Hunan Province, China 410100
Telephone: +86 (0)731 8275 8900
Fax: +86 (0)731 8275 8901
Website: www.cwa-changsha.com

CHANGZHOU

Changzhou International School
1 Nenjiang Road, Xinbei District, Changzhou City
Jiangsu Province, China 213032
Telephone: +86 (0)519 85165088
Fax: +86 (0)519 81660212
Website: www.czis.com.cn

CHENGDU

Chengdu International School
399 Shuxi Lu
Zhong Hai International Community
Chengdu
Sichuan 611731
P.R. China
Telephone: +86 (0)28 8608 1162
Fax: +86 (0)28 8759 2265
Website: www.cdischina.com

Chengdu Meishi International School
1340 Middle Section of Tianfu Avenue
Chengdu 610042, P.R. Chira
610042
Telephone: +86 (0)28 8533 0653
Fax: +86 (0)28 8533 0880
Website: www.miscd.com

Leman International School
G213 National Road, Da'an Village
Zhengxing County, Shuangliu Township
Chengdu, 610218, China
Telephone: +86 (0)28 67C3 8650
Fax: +86 (0)28 6703 6830
Website: www.lis-chengdu.com

Oxford International School of Chengdu
No. 1 South Shuangjian Lane
Bali Complex
Chenghua District, Chengdu
China, 610051
Telephone: +86 (0)28 8351 7000
Website: www.chengduo c.com

QSI International Schoo of Chengdu
American Garden
188 South 3rd Ring Road
Chengdu
Sichuan 610000
Fax: +86 (0)28 8519 8393
Telephone: +86 (0)28 8519 8393
Email: chengdu@qsi.org

CHONGQING

Chongqing Maple Leaf International School
Xuefu Avenue, Yongchuan District, Chongqing,
402160
Telephone: +86 (0)23 4950 7000
Fax: +86 (0)23 4956 6111
Website: www.mapleleafschools.com

QSI International School in ChongQing
Chongqing University West Road
University Town, Shapingba
Chongqing 401331
Telephone: +86 (0)23 65620109
Fax: +86 (0)23 65620105
Email: chongqing@qsi.org

Yew Chung International School of Chongqing
No. 2, Huxia Street, Yuan Yang Town
New Northern Zone, Chongqing 401122, P.R.C.
Telephone: +86 (0)23 6763 8482
Fax: +86 (0)23 6763 8483
Email: enquiry@cq.ycef.com
Website: www.ycis-cq.com

DALIAN

Dalian American International School
No. 2 Dianchi Road
Golden Pebble Beach National Resort
Dalian Development Area
P.R. China, 116650
Telephone: +86 (0)411 8757 2000
Fax: +86 (0)411 8791 5656
Email: admissions@daischina.org
Website: www.daischina.org

Dalian Maple Leaf International School
(13 campus branches in Dalian)
No. 9 Central Street, Jinshitan National Holiday Resort
Dalian, China 116650
Telephone: +86 (0)411 8790 6822
Fax: +86 (0)411 8790 6811
Email: esl@mapleleaf.net.cn
Website: www.mapleleafschools.com

DONGGUAN (GUANGDONG)

Dongguan HSKAMA International School
HSKAMA International School
Chashan Dongguan City
Guangdong Province
Telephone: +86 (0)769 8686 2669/8686 2648
Fax: +86 (0)769 8686 2881
Email: hkkama@126.com
Website: www.hskama.com

QSI International School in Dongguan
Block A2 Dongcheng Center
Dongguan, Guangdong
Fax: +86 (0)769 2230 0130, +86 (0)769 8507 7978
Telephone: +86 (0)769 2230 0131, +86 (0)769 8535 4999
Email: dongguang@qsi.org

GUANGZHOU

American International School of Guangzhou
Box 212, Ti Yu Dong Post Office
Guangzhou 5106(0)20
Telephone: +86 (0)20 8735 3393
Fax: +86 (0)20 8735 3339
Email: inquiries@aisgz.org
Website: www.aisgz.org

British School of Guangzhou
983-3 Tonghe Road
Nanhu, Guangzhou
Guangdong Province, 510515
Telephone: +86 (0)20 8709 4788/3725 9376
Fax: +86 (0)20 8709 8248/3725 9377
Email: info@bsg.org.cn
Website: www.bsg.org.cn

Guangzhou Grace Academy
Riverside Garden, Guangzhou
Guangdong

Telephone: +86 (0)20 8450 0180
Fax: +86 (0)20 8450 0190
Email: grace@ggagga.net
Website: www.ggagga.net

Guangzhou Nanhu International School
55, Huayang Street
Tiyu Dong Road
TianHe District
Guangzhou 510620
Telephone: +86 (0)20 38866952/38863606
Fax: +86 (0)20 38863680
Email: admissions@gnischina.com
Website: www.gnischina.com

Utahloy International School
800 Sha Tai Bei Road
Baiyun District
Guangzhou 510515
Telephone: +86 (0)20 8720 2019/0517
Fax: +86 (0)20 8704 4296
Email: uis@utahloy.com
Website: www.utahloy.com

NANJING
AND
NINGBO

British School of Nanjing
Building One, Jingling Resort
Jiahe Dong Lu
Jiangsu Province
Nanjing 211100
Telephone: +86 (0)25 5210 8987
Fax: +86 (0)25 5210 2385
Email: info@bsn.org.cn
Website: www.bsn.org.cn

Nanjing International School
Xue Heng Lu 8
Xi'an Lin College and University Town
Nanjing 210046

Telephone: +86 (0)25 8589 9111
Fax: +86 (0)25 8589 9222
Email: enquiries@nanjing-school.com
Website: www.nanjing-school.com

Ningbo International School
No 151 Lamei Road
Ningbo, Zhejiang Province
China
Telephone: +86 (0)574 8761 1005
Website: www.nbis.net.cn

SHANGHAI

British International School of Shanghai
(Two Campuses, Pudong and Puxi)
600 Cambridge Forest New Town
2729 Hunan Road
Pudong
Shanghai 201315
Telephone: +86 (0)21 5812 7455
Fax: +86 (0)21 5812 7465
Email: principal@bisshanghai.com
Website: www.bisshanghai.com
Pudong Campus: www.bisspudong.com
Puxi Campus: www.bisspuxi.com

Concordia International School (PK-12)
999 Ming Yue Road
JinQiao
Pudong
Shanghai 201206
US-style teaching curriculum with a Christian emphasis
Telephone: +86 (0)21 5899 0380
Fax: +86 (0)21 5899 1685
Website: www.concordiashanghai.org

Dulwich College International—Shanghai
(Nursery–Year 9)
Recently opened new Main Campus which currently admits students up to Year 9. The school will eventually provide a complete Secondary Education.

The Early Years students attend the DUCKS Campus just across the street from the new Main Campus. Dulwich College Shanghai is a franchise of the famous English public school with its main site in Dulwich, London. Former students include the famous author P.G. Wodehouse, Former Governor of the Bank of England Sir Eddie George, and many British actors (including Chiwetel Ejiofor) and politicians (Including Rt Hon Peter Lilley MP and Anand Panyarachun, who was twice Prime Minister of Thailand).
266 LanAn Road
JinQiao, Pudong
Shanghai 201206
Telephone: +86 (0)21 5899 9910
Website: www.dulwich-shanghai.cn
Email: info@dulwich-shanghai.cn

French School of Shanghai
(One location in Puxi and one location in Pudong)
1555 Jufeng Lu, Pudong District
Shanghai, 201208, China
Telephone: +86 (0)21 6897 6589/3976 0555
Fax: +86 (0)21 6897 6576/3976 0577
Website: www.lyceeshanghai.org

German School of Shanghai
1100 Jufeng Lu
201206, Shanghai, China
Telephone: +86 (0)21 6897 5508/3976 5508
Fax: +86 (0)21 6897 9596/3976 0566
Email: pudongcampus@ds-shanghai.de
Website: www.ds-shanghai.de

Shanghai American School
(two campuses)
258 Jin Feng Road, Huacao Town
Minhang Dist., Shanghai
China 201107
Telephone: +86 (0)21 6221 1445
Email: info@saschina.org
Website: www.saschina.org

Shanghai Community International Schools
(three campuses)
1161 Hongqiao Road
Shanghai 200051
Telephone: +86 (0)21 6261 4338/6295 1222
Fax: +86 (0)21 6261 4639
Website: www.scischina.org
Email: info@scischina.org

Shanghai Japanese School
3185 Hongmei Road, Hong Qiao
Japanese nationals only
Telephone: +86 (0)21 6401 2747
Fax: +86 (0)21 6401 2747

Shanghai Korean School
2999 Qi Xin Road
Korean nationals only
Email: admin@skoschool.com
Website: www.skoschool.com

Shanghai Livingston American School
Curriculum and instruction are modeled on the California public school system.
580 GanXi Rd
ChangNing District
Shanghai 200336
Telephone: +86 (0)21 6238 3511/5218 8372
Fax: +86 (0)21 5218 0390
Website: www.laschina.org

Shanghai Rego International School
189 Dongzha Road
Minhang District
Shanghai 201100
Telephone: +86 (0)21 5488 3431/8320
Email: enquiries@srisrego.com
Website: www.srisrego.com

Shanghai Singapore International School
301, Zhujian Road
MinHang District
Shanghai 201107
Telephone: +86 (0)21 62219288

Fax: +86 (0)21 62219188

Website: www.ssis.asia

Western International School of Shanghai—International School (American Curriculum)
555 Lian Min Road
Xujing Town, Qing Pu District
Shanghai 201702
Telephone: +86 (0)21 6976 6388, 6976 6969
Fax: +86 (0)21 6976 6833
Email: admission@wiss.cn
Website: www.wiss.cn

SHENZHEN

Shekou International School
Jing Shan Villas, Nan Hai Road
Shekou, Shenzhen
Guangdong Province 518067
Telephone: +86 (0)755 2669 3669
Fax: +86 (0)755 2667 4099
Email: sis@sis.org.cn
Email: admissions@sis.org.cn
Website: www.sis.org.cn

QSI International School of Shenzhen (Shekou)
2nd Floor, Bitao Building
8 Tai Zi Road, Shekou
Shenzhen, Guangdong, 518069
Telephone: +86 (0)755 2667 6030/ +86 (0)755 2667 6031
Email: Shenzhen@qsi.org
Email: Shekou@qsi.org

SUZHOU

Dulwich College International Suzhou
Opened in August 2007 with a registered 200 students, Dulwich College Suzhou is a franchise of the famous English public school with its main site in Dulwich, London. Former students include the

famous author P.G. Wodehouse, Former Governor of the Bank of England Sir Eddie George, and many British actors (including Chiwetel Ejiofor) and politicians.
360 Gangtian Road
Suzhou Industrial Park
Suzhou, Jiangsu Province
215021
Telephone: +86 (0)512 62959500
Fax: +86 (0)512 62957540
Email: info@dulwich-suzhou.cn
Website: www.dulwich-suzhou.cn

QSI International School
Yangcheng Lake East Road 98
Xiang Cheng District
Suzhou, SIP
Telephone: +86 (0)512 6618 1009

Sino-Canada High School
1 Liannan Rd
Luxu Town Wujiang
Suzhou, Jiangsu Province
215211
Telephone: +86 (0)512 63261000
Email: info@sinocanada.cn
Website: www.sinocanada.cn

Suzhou Eton House International School
102 Kefa Road
Suzhou Science and Technology Town
Suzhou New District
P.R China 215011
Telephone: +86 (0)512 68255666
Email: enquiry-sz@etonhouse.com.cn
Website: http://suzhou.etonhouse.com.cn

Suzhou Singapore International School
208 ZhongNan Street,
Suzhou Industrial Park
Jiangsu 215021
Telephone: +86 (0)512 62580388
Fax: +86 (0)512 62586388

Email: information@ssis-suzhou.net
Website: www.ssis-suzhou.com

Suzhou Japanese School
83, Jinshan Road
Telephone: +86 (0)512 6807 0080

TIANJIN

Teda International School
No. 72, Third Avenue, Teda
Tianjin, China 300457
Telephone: +86 (0)22 66226158
Fax: +86 (0)22 62001818
Website: www.tedais.org

Tianjin International School
No. 4-1 Sishui Dao, Hexi District
Tianjin, China, 300222
Telephone: +86 (0)22 8371 0900
Fax: +86 (0)22 8371 0300
Website: www.tiseagles.com

The International School in Tianjin
Wei Shan Nan Lu
Jin Nan Economic Development Zone
Jin Nan District
Tianjin 300350
Telephone: +86 (0)22 2859 2001
Fax: +86 (0)22 2859 2007
Website: www.istianjin.org

Tianjin Rego International School
38 Huandao Xi Lu, Meijiangnan Residence Zone
Tianjin
Telephone: +86 (0)22 8816 1180/81/82/83
Fax: +86 (0)22 8816 1190
Email: info@regoschool.org
Website: www.regoschool.org

WUXI

EtonHouse International School Wuxi
Regent International Garden
Xing Chuang, 4th Road
Wuxi New District
Telephone: +86 (0)510 8522 5333

International School of Wuxi
No. 300 Xing Chuang Si Road
New District, Wuxi
Telephone: +86 (0)510 8101 9012

Taihu International School
Jin Shi Road
Bin Hu District
Wuxi
Telephone: +86 (0)510 8507 0333

ZHUHAI

Dulwich College Zhuhai
Dulwich College International
High School Programme
Huafa International Training School
1, Zhuhai Avenue, Zhuhai, 519060
Guangdong Province
Telephone: +86 (0)756 8693133
Fax: +86 (0)756 8693053
Email: info@dulwich-zhuhai.cn
Website: www.dulwich-zhuhai.cn

QSI International School of Zhuhai
2 Longxing St.105 Gongbei
Zhuhai 51902
Telephone: +86 (0)756 8156134
Fax: +86 (0)756 8189021
Email: Zhuhai@qsi.org

OTHER INTERNATIONAL SCHOOLS

Qingdao MTI International School
Children's Club
3rd Floor Children's Activity Center
6 Dong Hai Xi Road
Qingdao 266071
Email: qmis@qmischina.com
Website: www.qmischina.com

Xiamen International School
262 Xingbei San Lu
Xingling, Jimei
Xiamen, Fujian
China
Telephone: +86 (0)592 6256581/6256583
Fax: +86 (0)592 6256584
Email: askxis@xischina.com.cn
Website: www.xischina.com

LAW FIRMS

BEIJING

Allen & Overy
Suite 522, China World Tower 2
1 Jian Guo Men Wai Avenue
Beijing 100004
Telephone: +86 (0)10 6505 8800
Fax: +86 (0)10 6505 6677
Website: www.allenovery.com

Anderson & Anderson LLP
Suite 15158, 15th Floor
Yintai Office Tower Two
Jianguomenwai Avenue
Chaoyang District, Beijing 100022
Telephone: +86 (0)10 6563 7087

Fax: +86 (0)10 6563 7999
Website: www.anallp.net

Andrews Kurth LLP
Room 2007, Capital Mansion
6 Xinyuan Nanlu
Chaoyang District
100004 Beijing
Telephone: +86 (0)10 8486 2699
Fax: +86 (0)10 8486 8565
Website: www.andrewskurth.com

Baker Botts L.L.P.
702 Beijing International Club Office Tower
21 Jianguomenwai Dajie
Beijing 100020
People's Republic of China
Telephone: +86 (0)10 8532 7900
Fax: +86 (0)10 8532 7999
Website: www.bakerbotts.com

Beiten Burkhardt
Suite 3130, 31st Floor, South Office Tower
Beijing Kerry Center
1 Guang Hua Road
Chao Yang District
Beijing 100020
Telephone: +86 (0)10 8529 8110
Fax: +86 (0)10 8529 8123
Website: www.bblaw.com

Blake, Cassels & Graydon LLP
7 Dong Sanhuan Zhonglu
Suite 901, Office Tower A
Beijing Fortune Plaza
Chaoyang District
Beijing 100020
Telephone: +86 (0)10 6530 9010
Fax: +86 (0)10 6530 9008
Website: www.blakes.com

Chadbourne & Parke LLP
Beijing Fortune Center
Room 902
Tower A, 7 Dongsanhuan Zhonglu

Chayoyang District
100020 Beijing
Telephone: +86 (0)10 6530 8846
Fax: +86 (0)10 6530 8849
Website: www.chadbourne.com

Chang Tsi & Partners
Attorneys at Law and IP Attorneys
8th Floor Tower A
Hundred Island Park
Bei Zhan Bei Jie Street
Xicheng District
Beijing 100044
(Main Office)
Telephone: +86 (0)10 8836 9999
Fax: +86 (0)10 8836 9996
Website: www.ctw.com.cn

Cleary Gottlieb Steen & Hamilton LLP
Twin Towers—West
12 B Jianguomen Wai Da Jie
Chaoyang District
100022 Beijing
Telephone: +86 (0)10 5920 1000
Website: www.clearygottlieb.com

Clifford Chance LLP
3326 China World Tower 1
1 Jianguomenwai Dajie
Beijing 100004
Telephone: +86 (0)10 65352288
Fax: +86 (0)10 65059028
Website: www.cliffordchance.com

C&M (China) Law Offices
CTS Tower, Suite 1610
2 Bei Sanhuan East Road
Beijing 100028
(Main Office)
Telephone: +86 (0)10 64685454
Fax: +86 (0)10 64612507; 64571392
Email: cmlo@cmlo.com.cn
Website: www.sinosino.com

Dewey and LeBoeuf
Beijing Kerry Center, South Tower
Suite 1429
No. 1 Guanghua Road
Beijing, 100020
People's Republic of China
Telephone: +86 (0)10 6583 9500
Fax: +86 (0)10 6583 9600
Website: www.deweyleboeuf.com

DLA Piper UK LLP
20th Floor, South Tower
Beijing Kerry Center
1 Guanghua Road
Chaoyang District
Beijing 100020
Telephone: +86 (0)10 6561 1788
Fax: +86 (0)10 6561 5158
Website: www.dlapiper.com

Duan & Duan Lawyers
Suite 3506
Beijing Fortune Center
Middle Road East 3rd Ring
Beijing

Faegre, Baker & Daniels LLP
Suite 1919, Tower 2
China World Trade Center
1 JianGuoMenWai Avenue
Beijing 100004
Telephone: +86 (0)10 6505 7733
Fax: +86 (0)10 6505 8730
Website: www.faegrebd.com

Frederick W. Hong Law Offices
Suite 11-D, Buidling1
Majestic Towers (baifu guoji)
No.20 Gongti Donglu
Chaoyang Beijing, 100020
Telephone: +86 (0)10 6506 1180
Fax: +86 (0)10 6506 1720
Email: beijing@fwhonglaw.com
Website: www.fwhonglaw.com

Garvey Schubert Barer
820 South Tower
Beijing Kerry Center
1 Guang Hua Road
Chaoyang District
Beijing 100020
Telephone: +86 (0)10 8529 9880
Fax: +86 (0)10 8529 9881
Website: www.GSBlaw.com

Gide Loyrette Nouel (French speaking)
Suite 3501, Jingguang Center
Hu Jia Lou, Chaoyang District
Beijing 100020
Telephone: +86 (0)10 6597 4511
Fax: +86 (0)10 6597 4551
Website: www.gide.com

Herbert Smith LLP
28th Floor Office Tower
Beijing Yintai Center
2 Jianguomenwai Avenue
Chaoyang District
Beijing 100022
Telephone: +86 (0)10 6535 5000
Fax: + 86 (0)10 6535 5505
Website: www.herbertsmith.com

Hogan Lovells International LLP
31st Floor, Tower 3
China Central Place
No. 77 Jianguo Road
Chaoyang District
Beijing 100025
China
Telephone: +86 (0)10 6582 9488
Fax: +86 (0)10 6582 9499
Website: www.hoganlovells.com

Holland & Knight LLP
1206, 12th Floor, West Tower
Twin Towers
B-12 Jianguomenwai Avenue
Chaoyang District

Beijing 100022
Telephone: +86 (0)10 65661968; +86 (0)10 656
61278
Fax: +86 (0)10 656 61258
Website: www.hklaw.com

Hunton & Williams LLP
517-520 South Office Tower
Beijing Kerry Center
1 Guanghua Road
Chaoyang District
Beijing 100020
Telephone: +86 (0)10 5863 7500
Fax: +86 (0)10 5863 7591
Website: www.hunton.com

Jones Day
3201 China World Tower 1
1 Jianguomenwai Avenue
Beijing 100004
Telephone: +86 (0)10 5866 1111
Fax: +86 (0)10 5866 1122
Website: www.jonesday.com

Jun He Law Offices
China Resources Building
20th Floor
8 Jianguomenbei Avenue
Beijing 100005
(Main Office)
Telephone: +86 (0)10 8519 1300
Fax: +86 (0)10 8519 1350
Website: www.junhe.com

KingSound & Partners
11/Fl., Block B
KingSound International Center
116 Zizhuyuan Road
Haidian District
Beijing 100089
(Main Office)
Telephone: +86 (0)10 5893 0011
Fax: +86 (0)10 5893 0022
Website: www.kingsound-ip.com.cn

King & Wood
40th Floor, Office Tower A
Beijing Fortune Plaza
7 Dongsanhuan Zhonglu
Chaoyang District
Beijing 100020
(Main Office)
Telephone: +86 (0)10 5878 5588
Fax: +86 (0)10 5878 5599
Website: www.kingandwood.com

Kirkpatrick & Lockhart Preston Gates Ellis LLP
Suite 1009-1011, Tower C1, Oriental Plaza
No.1 East Chang An Avenue
Dongcheng District
Beijing 100738
Telephone: +86 (0)10 5817 6000
Fax: +86 (0)10 8518 9299
Website: www.klgates.com

Kun Lun Law Firm
Suite A508, Nanxincang International Tower
A22 Dongsi Shitiao
Dongcheng, Beijing
Telephone: +86 (0)10 64096455
Fax: +86 (0)10 64096437
Email: beijing@kunlunlaw.com
Website: www.kunlunlaw.com

Lehman, Lee & Xu
(International Law & Practice Group)
China Lawyers, Patent & Trademark Agents
10-2 Liangmaqiao Diplomatic Compound
22 Dongfang East Road
Chaoyang District
Beijing 100600
(Main Office)
Telephone: +86 (0)10 8532 1919
Fax: +86 (0)10 8532 1999
Website: www.lehmanlaw.com

Liu, Shen & Associates
Hanhai Plaza (1+1 Plaza)
10th Floor, 10 Caihefang Road

Haidian District
Beijing 100080
(Main Office)
Telephone: +86 (0)10 6268 0066
Fax: +86 (0)10 6268 1818
Website: www.liu-shen.com

Mayer Brown
Suite 1102, Tower 2, China Central Place
79 Jianguo Road
Chaoyang District, Beijing 100025
Telephone: +86 (0)10 6599 9200
Fax: +86 (0)10 6598 9277
Website: www.mayerbrown.com

Milbank, Tweed, Hadley & McCloy LLP
79 Jianguo Road, Chaoyang District
Units 05-06, 15th Fl., Tower 2
Beijing
Telephone: +86 (0)10 5969 2700
Fax: +86 (0)10 5969 2707
Website: www.milbank.com

Morgan, Lewis & Bockius LLP
Beijing Kerry Center North Tower
Suite 823, 20th Floor
1 Guang Hua Road
Chaoyang District
Beijing 100020
Telephone: +86 (0)10 5876 3500
Fax: +86 (0)10 5876 3501
Website: www.morganlewis.com

Morrison & Foerster LLP
22nd Floor, Tower 3
China Central Place
No. 77, Jianguo Road
Chaoyang District
Beijing 100025 China
Telephone: +86 (0)10) 5909 3399
Fax: +86 (0)10 5909 3355
Website: www.mofo.com; www.mofo.com.cn

O'Melveny & Myers LLP
37th Floor, Yin Tai Center

2 Jianguomenwai Avenue
Beijing 100004
Telephone: +86 (0)10 6535 4200
Fax: +86 (0)10 6535 4201
Website: www.omm.com

Paul, Weiss, Rifkind, Wharton & Garrison LLP
Unit 3601, Fortune Plaza Office
Tower A, No. 7 Dong Sanhuan Zhonglu
Chao Yang District
Beijing 100020
Telephone: +86 (0)10 5828 6300
Fax: +86 (0)10 6530 9070/9080
Website: www.paulweiss.com

Shearman & Sterling LLP
12th Floor East Tower, Twin Towers
B-12 Jianguomenwai Dajie
Beijing 100022
Telephone: +86 (0)10 5922 8000
Fax: +86 (0)10 6563 6000
Website: www.shearman.com

Sidley Austin LLP Beijing
Suite 608, Tower C2, Oriental Plaza
No.1 East Chang An Ave.
Beijing 100738
Telephone: +86 (0)10 5905 5588
Fax: +86 (0)10 6505 5360
Website: www.sidley.com

Simpson Thacher & Bartlett LLP
29/F China Merchants Tower
118, Jianguo Road
Chaoyang District
Beijing 100022
Telephone: +86 (0)10 8567 2999
Fax: +86 (0)10 8567 2988

Skadden, Arps, Slate, Meagher & Flom LLP
30th Floor, Tower 2
China World Trade Center
1 Jianguomenwai Avenue
Beijing 100004
Telephone: +86 (0)10 6535 5500

Fax: +86 (0)10 6535 5577
Website: www.skadden.com

Squire, Sanders & Dempsey L.L.P.
25th Floor, North Tower
Suite 2501
Beijing Kerry Center
1 Guang Hua Road
Chaoyang District
Beijing 100020
Telephone: +86 (0)10 8529 6998
Fax: +86 (0)10 8529 8088
Website: www.ssd.com

Sullivan & Cromwell LLP
Suite 501, China World Trade Center
1 Jianguo Menwei Avenue
Beijing 100004
Telephone: +86 (0)10 5923 5900
Fax: +86 (0)10 5923 5950
Website: www.sullcrom.com

TransAsia Lawyers
Suite 2218, China World Tower 1
1 Jianguomenwai Avenue
Beijing 100004
(Main Office)
Telephone: +86 (0)10 6505 8188
Fax: +86 (0)10 6505 8138
Website: www.transasialawyers.com

Vinson & Elkins LLP
20/F, Beijing Silver Tower
2, Dong San Huan Bei Lu
Chaoyang District
Beijing 100027
Telephone: +86 (0)10 6410 6300
Fax: +86 (0)10 6410 6360
Website: www.velaw.com

Vivien Chan & Co.
Solicitors & Notaries
Agents for Trade Marks & Patents
China-Appointed Attesting Officer
Changan Tower

Suite 508
10 East Changan Street
Beijing 100006
Telephone: +86 (0)10 6522 7069
Fax: +86 (0)10 6522 6967
Website: www.vcclawservices.com

Wang & Wang
A Limited Liability Partnership
B1207, Huixin Plaza
8 Beishihuan Zhong Road
Chaoyang District
Beijing 100101
Telephone: +86 (0)10 6493 3139
Fax: +86 (0)10 6499 3036
Website: www.wangandwang.com

White & Case
19th Floor, Tower 1 of China Central Place
81 Jianguo Lu, Chaoyang District
Beijing 100025
China
Telephone: +86 (0)10 5912 9600
Fax: +86 (0)10 5969 5760
Website: www.whitecase.com

Wilmer Cutler Pickering Hale and Dorr LLP
1206 North Tower
Beijing Kerry Center
1 Guanghua Road
Beijing 100020
Telephone: +86 (0)10 8529 7588
Fax: +86 (0)10 8529 7566
Website: www.wilmerhale.com

CHENGDU

Chengdu Public Notary office
35 Dong Cheng Gen Xia St
Chengdu, Sichuan
Telephone: +86 (0)28 86696320

King and Wood Lawyers
22/F, City Tower
86 Section One
Renminnanlu
Chengdu 610016
Telephone: +86 (0)28 8620 3818
Fax: +86 (0)28 8620 3819/3820

CHONGQING

King & Wood Lawyers
Room 2, 18th Floor
Metropolitan Tower
68 Zourong Road
Chongqing 400010
Telephone: +86 (0)23 6371 5199
Fax: +86 (0)23 6371 5399

DALIAN

Jun He Lawyers
International Finance Tower
Suite F, 16th Floor
15 Remin Road
Dalian 116001
Telephone: +86 (0)411 8250 7578
Fax: +86 (0)411 8250 7579
Email: junhedl@junhe.com

HAINAN

Jun He Lawyers
Nanyang Building
Suite 1107
Binhai Avenue
Haikou
Hainan 570105
Telephone: +86 (0)898 6851 2544
Fax: +86 (0)898 6851 3514
Email: junhehn@junhe.com

HANGZHOU

King & Wood
Room 810-812
Jiahua International Business Center
15 Hangda Road Hangzhou
Zhejiang Province 310007
Telephone: +86 (0)571 8993 5988
Fax: +86 (0)571 8993 5989

SHANGHAI

Adamas Law Firm
Suite 608 Dynasty Business Center
457 Urumqi Road North
Jing An District
Shanghai 200040
Telephone: +86 (0)21 6249 0302
Fax: +86 (0)21 6249 0501
Email: shanghai@adamas-asia.com

Allen & Overy, Shanghai Office
15F, Phase II, Shanghai IFC
8 Century Avenue
Pudong, Shanghai 200120
Telephone: +86 (0)21 2036 7000
Fax: +86 (0)21 2036 7100
Website: www.allenovery.com

Anderson & Anderson LLP
Suite 1621, 16th Floor
Tower one, Zhonghuan Binjiang
2742 Pudong Avenue
Pudong New District, Shanghai 200136
Telephone: +86 (0)21 5846 0290
Fax: +86 (0)21 5846 0329
Website: www.anallp.net

Beiten Burkhardt
Rechtsanwälte (German Attorneys-at-Law)
Suite 1001-1002, 10th Floor
Chong Hing Finance Center

288 Nan Jing Road West
Huang Pu District
200003 Shanghai
Telephone: +86 (0)21 6141 7888
Website: www.bblaw.com

Clifford Chance LLP
40/F Bund Center
222 Yan An East Road
Shanghai 200002
Telephone: +86 (0)21 2320 7288
Fax: +86 (0)21 2320 7256
Website: www.CliffordChance.com

DLA Piper UK LLP
36/F, Shanghai World Financial Center
100 Century Avenue, Pudong
Shanghai 200120
Telephone: +86 (0)21 3852 2111
Fax: +86 (0)21 3852 2000
Website: www.dlapiper.com

Duan & Duan
Shartex Plaza
Suite 1700
88 Zun Yi Nan Road
200336 Shanghai
(Main Office)
Telephone: +86 (0)21 6219 1103
Fax: +86 (0)21 6275 2273
Website: www.duanduan.com

Herbert Smith LLP
Herbert has a formal alliance with the leading
German firm Gleiss Lutz and the leading Dutch and
Belgian firm Stibbe.
38/F Bund Center, 222 Yan An Road East
Shanghai 200002
Telephone: +86 (0)21 2322 2000
Fax: +86 (0)21 2322 2322
Website: www.herbertsmith.com

Hogan Lovells
Park Place, 18th Floor
1601 Nanjing Road West

Shanghai 200040
Telephone: +86 (0)21 6122 3800
Fax +86 (0)21 6122 3899
Website: www.hoganlovells.com

Jin Mao Law Firm
19th Floor, Sail Tower
266 Hankou Road
Website: www.jinmao.com.cn

Jones Day
30th Floor
Shanghai Kerry Center
1515 Nanjing Road West
Shanghai 200040
Telephone: +86 (0)21 2201 8000
Fax: +86 (0)21 5298 6569
Website: www.jonesday.com

King & Wood Lawyers
28-29/F, Huai Hai Plaza
1045 Huai Hai Road (M)
Shanghai 200031
Telephone: +86 (0)21 2412 6000
Fax: +86 20 2412 6150

Kun Lun Law Firm
Suite F, 13th Floor
Hua Min Empire Plaza
728 Yan An Xi Road
Shanghai
Telephone: +86 (0)21 62113098
Fax: +86 (0)21 62112108

Lehman, Lee & Xu
(International Law & Practice Group)
Room 1506-1507, Floor 15, Tower 2, Plaza 66
No. 1266, West Nanjing Road, Jing'an District
Shanghai
Telephone: +86 (0)21 5877 9296
Fax: +86 (0)21 5877 9196
Website: www.lehmanlaw.com

Mayer Brown
JSM Shanghai Representative Office

Suite 2301, Tower II, Plaza 66
1366 Nan Jing Road West
Shanghai 200040
Telephone: +86 (0)21 6120 1066 x518
Fax: +86 (0)21 6120 1068/9
Website: www.mayerbrown.com

O'Melveny & Myers LLP
Plaza 66, Tower 1
37th Floor
1266 Nanjing Road West
Shanghai 200040
Telephone: +86 (0)21 2307 7000
Fax: +86 (0)21 2307 7300
Website: www.omm.com

Squire, Sanders & Dempsey L.L.P.
Suite 1207, 12th Floor
Shanghai Kerry Center
1515 Nanjing Road West
Shanghai 200040
Telephone: +86 (0)21 6103 6300
Fax: +86 (0)21 6103 6363
Website: www.ssd.com

TransAsia Lawyers
Unit 1101 Platinum
233 Tai Cang Road
Shanghai 200020
Telephone: +86 (0)21 6141 0998
Fax: +86 (0)21 6141 0995
Website: www.transasialawyers.com

Vivien Chan & Co.
The Headquarters Building
Suite 1002
168 Central Tibet Road
Shanghai 200001
Telephone: +86 (0)21 6387 9222
Fax: +86 (0)21 6387 9111
Website: www.vcclawservices.com

Wang & Wang
A Limited Liability Partnership
580 Nan Jing West Road 2308

Shanghai 200041
Telephone: +86 (0)21 523 40739
Fax: +86 (0)21 523 40672
Website: www.wangandwang.com

White & Case
Citic Square, 39th Fl.
1168 Nanjing Road (West)
Shanghai 200041
Telephone: +86 (0)21 6132 5900
Fax: +86 (0)21 6323 9252
Website: www.whitecase.com

SHANXI

Shanxi Kebei Law Firm
20F High-Tech Dongli Tower
High-Tech Developing Zone
No. 226 Changzhi Rd.
Taiyuan City, Shanxi
Telephone: +86 (0)351 8330241; 8330242
Telephone: +86 (0)351 8330243; 8330244
Fax: +86 (0)351 8330240
Website: www.kebeilaw.com

XINJIANG

Xinjiang Tianyang Law Firm
(English-speaking)
24&25F Tower A Shiji Baisheng Plaza
No. 36 Xinhua S Rd.
Urumqi City, Xinjiang
Telephone: +86 (0)991 2842887; 2818102
Fax: +86 (0)991 2825559
Email: bgsxj@tianyanglaw.com
Website: www.tianyanglaw.com

Xinjiang Zhengjia Law Firm
(English-speaking)
12F Xiangcheng Plaza
No. 527 Kezi Duwei Rd.

Kashi City, Xinjiang, China
Telephone: +86 (0)998 2879696; 2879715

RELOCATION COMPANIES

AGS FOUR WINDS
Corporate website: www.agsfourwincs.com
(Has offices in major cities on the mainland
including Wuhan, Chengdu, Chongqing, Tianjin)

AGS Beijing Office
Tayuan Diplomatic Compound
Building 5, Entrance 2, and Suite 51
Beijing, China
Telephone: +86 (0)10 8532 5288
Fax: +86 (0)10 6566 3406

AGS Guangzhou Office
Room 6, 51/F, Jinan
Building No. 300
Dongfengzhong Road
Guangzhou, 513000, China
Telephone: +86 (0)20 8363 4629
Fax: +86 (0)20 8363 4356

AGS Hong Kong Office
5/F Len Shing Industrial Center
4, A Kung Ngam Village Road
Shaukeiwan
Hong Kong
Telephone: +852 2 865 9666
Fax: +852 2 567 7594

AGS Shanghai Office
Room 217, Jingan Modern
Industry Tower, No. 68 Changping Rcad
200041, Shanghai, China
Telephone: +86 (0)2" 3126 2221
Fax: +86 (0)21 6288 9837

ALLIED PICKFORDS (Sirva Relocation)
China Corporate website: www.alliedpickfords.com.cn

Allied Pickfords Beijing
The Spaces International Center
Suite 812, Building A No. 8 Dongdaqiao Road
Beijing, China 100020
Tel + 86 (0)10 5870 0866

Allied Pickfords Guangzhou
Room 1801A, Unit 2
CTS Center No. 219. Zhong Shan Wu Road
Guangzhou, 510095
Telephone: +86 (0)20 8730 6001
Fax:+ 86 (0)20 8730 6005

Allied Pickfords Hong Kong
Suites 602-608, 6th Floor
248 Queen's Road East
Wanchai
Hong Kong
Telephone: +852 2104 6668

Allied Pickfords Shanghai
Unit 801, 268 Zhongshan Nan Road
New Resources Plaza,
Shanghai China 200010
Telephone: +86 (0)21 6332 3322

ASIAN EXPRESS
Corporate website: www.aemovers.com.hk
Have offices in all major cities on the mainland.

Asian Express (Beijing) Ltd.
Room-1612, Tower-D, SOHO New Town
88 Jianguo Road, Chaoyang District
Beijing 100022, PR China
Telephone: +86 (0)10 8580 1471
Fax: +86 (0)10 8580 1475
Email: beijing@aemovers.com.hk

Asian Express (Guangzhou) Ltd.
Room-1002, Block-2, Dong-Jun Plaza
836 Dongfengdong Road, Yuexiu District

Guangzhou 510080, PR China
Telephone: +86 (0)20 8767 8023
Fax: +86 (0)20 8767 8091
Email: guangzhou@aemovers.com.hk

Asian Express Hong Kong (China HQ)
26th Floor Two Chinachem Plaza
68 Connaught Road Central
Two Chinachem Plaza
Hong Kong
Telephone: +852 2893-1000
Fax: +852 2311-3036
Email: hongkong@aemovers.com.hk

Asian Express International Movers Ltd.
Room-1105, Hua Sheng Tower
399 Jiujiang Road, Huangpu District
Shanghai 200001, PR China
Telephone: +86 (0)21 6258 2244
Fax: +86 (0)21 6258 4242
Email: shanghai@aemovers.com.hk

ASIA PACIFIC ACCESS
Beijing Ancient Observatory
Jianguomen Nei Dajie
Dongcheng District
Beijing 100005 China
Telephone: +86 (0)10 6512 9996
Website: www.apachina.com

ASIAN PACIFIC PROPERTIES
Website: www.asiapacificproperties.com

Beijing
Suite 703A The Exchange Beijing
No. 118B Jian Guo Lu, Chao Yang District
Beijing 100022 P.R. China
Telephone: +86 (0)10 6567 8177
Fax: +86 (0)10 6567 8171

Guangzhou
Unit 841 The Garden Tower
368 Huanshi Dong Lu
Guangzhou 510064 P.R. China

Telephone: +86 (0)20 8365 2922
Fax: +86 (0)20 8365 2923

Hong Kong
14/F Wilson House
19-27 Wyndham Street
Central, Hong Kong
Telephone: +852 2281 7800
Fax: +852 2810 6981

Shanghai
Suite 601 Plaza 66 Tower 2
1366 Nanjing Xi Road
Shanghai 200040 P.R. China
Telephone: +86 (0)21 6288 7333
Fax: +86 (0)21 6288 7371

ASIAN TIGERS K.C. DAT (CHINA) LTD
Corporate website: www.asiantigersgroup.com

CHINA HQ (Shanghai)
8F Asionics Technology Building
6, Lane 1279 Zhong Shan
West Road
Shanghai 200051, China
Telephone: +86 (0)21 3209 5561
Fax: +86 (0)21 3209 5560

Asian Tiger Beijing
19 Shunchi Road
Beijing Airport Logistics Zone
Shunyi District, 101300
Beijing, China
Telephone: +86 (0)10 6415 1188
Fax: +86 (0)10 6417 9579

Asian Tiger Guangzhou
Room 1707 NewPoly Tower
No.2 Zhong Shan Liu Lu
Guangzhou 510180, China
Telephone: +86 (0)20 8666 2655
Telephone: +86 (0)20 8326 6751

BALTRANS INTERNATIONAL MOVING
Corporate website: www.bim.com.hk

BALtrans International Cargo Ltd (Beijing Office)
B11, 16/F., Han Wei Plaza
7 Guang Hua Road
Chao Yang District
Beijing 100004
Telephone: +86 (0)10 65614131
Fax: +86 (0)10 65616202

BALtrans International Moving Hong *Kong Office*
Unit 1510, 15/F
Ocean Center
5 Canton Road
Tsim Sha Tsui
Kowloon, Hong Kong
Telephone: +852 2756 2382
Fax: +852 2759 9772/ 2 48 6712
Email: contact@bim.com.hk

BALtrans International Moving (Shanghai Office)
Block A, 3/F
C & E Building
1898 Tian Shan Road
Shanghai, 200051
Telephone: +86 (0)21 62737669
Fax: +86 (0)21 62727667
Email: infor@belrelo.com

CARTUS CHINA (formerly Primacy Relocation)
Website: www.cartus.com

Cartus Beijing
Unit 34
16/F Gemdale Plaza Tower A
91 Jian Guo Road
Beijing
100022, China

Cartus Chengdu
Unit 1705-1706, Hua Min Empire Plaza
1 Fu Xing Street,
Chengdu 610016, China

Cartus Hong Kong
9th Floor, W Square

314-324 Hennessy Road
Wan Chai, Hong Kong

Cartus Shanghai
Room 2339-2341
23/F, Central Plaza
381 Huai Hai Zhong Road
Shanghai, China 200020
Telephone: +86 (0)21 6133 1333

Cartus Shanghai
Room 1128, 1129, 1130 and 1153
Level 11, Regency One—The Pacific Center
889 West YanAn Road
Shanghai 200050, China

COLUMBIA INTERNATIONAL REMOVALS
Corporate website: www.columbia-removals.com.hk
Specializes in international & local household removals, fine art services, office relocation, household items & documents storage, total logistics solutions
Room 2213 Hong Kong Plaza
188 Connaught Road West
Hong Kong
Telephone: +852 2547-6228
Fax: +852 2858-2418
Email: info@columbia-removals.com.hk

CROWN RELOCATIONS
Corporate website: www.crownrelo.com
Have warehouses and offices in 12 cities in China (and Hong Kong), all of which have connections to any city or town within Greater China.

Crown Relocations Beijing Office
No. 16 Xingmao 1st Street
Tongzhou Logistics Park, Majuqiao Town
Tongzhou District
Beijing, 101102, China
Telephone:+86 (0)10 5801 8088
Fax:+86 (0)10 5801 8099

Crown Relocations Guangzhou
Room 1202, YueLiang Plaza

222 Yuexiu Bei Road,Guangzhou
Guangzhou, 510050, China
Telephone: +86 (0)20 8364 2852
Fax: +86 (0)20 8364 2865
Email: guangzhou@crownrelo.com

Crown Relocations Shanghai
Crown Worldwide Building, No. 59 Lane
729-75 Sui De Road, Shanghai, 200331, China
Telephone: +86 (0)21 6250 8820
Fax: +86 (0)21 6250 8978
Email: shanghai@crownrelo.com

HELMA RELOCATIONS
Rm 212 A, 16 Henan Rd (South)
Shanghai
Telephone: +86 (0)21 6355 3022
Fax: +86 (0)21 6355 3066

KING'S MOVER INTERNATIONAL (KMI)
Corporate website: www.kingsmoverintl.com

King's Mover International (CHINA HQ)
Sinotrans Beijing Logistics Area
No.1 Louzizhuang Village, Jinzhan Township,
Chaoyang District,
Beijing, 100018, P.R. China
Toll Free: 800 810 0898
Telephone: + 86 (0)10 8432 7267
Fax: + 86 (0)10 8432 7263
Email: kmi@kingsmoverintl.com

King's Mover International (Shanghai Branch)
Room 1615, Building 1, Tianbaohuating
775, Siping Road
Hongkou District
Shanghai 200092
Toll Free: 800 810 0898
Telephone: +86 (0)21 65756707
Fax: +86 (0)21 65083425
Email: shanghai@kingsmoverintl.com

KUEHNE & NAGEL GLOBAL RELOCATION
Corporate website: www.kuehne-nagel.com
The Kuehne + Nagel network in China comprises 21 strategically located office and warehouse locations, offering comprehensive supply chain solutions to a fast-growing local and international customer base. Kuehne + Nagel in China is part of the worldwide Kuehne + Nagel Group, which has 830 offices in more than 100 countries.

Kuehne & Nagel Beijing Office
26 Xiaoyun Road
Beijing, Chaoyang District
Beijing 100016
Telephone: +86 (0)10 84580908
Fax: +86 (0)10 84585315
info.beijing@kuehne-nagel.com

Kuehne + Nagel Hong Kong (Asia Pacific HQ)
38 Gloucester Road
Wanchai
Hong Kong
Telephone: +852 2823 7688
Fax: +852 2527 8396
Email: info.hongkong@kuehne-nagel.com

LINKS RELOCATIONS
Corporate website: www.linksrelo.com

Links Relocation Hong Kong Office
Rm. A-C, 11/F, Champion Building
287-291 Des Voeux Road
Central, Hong Kong
Telephone: +852 2366 6700
Fax: +852 2366 6400
Email: links@linksrelo.com (this email address is being protected from spam bots; you need Javascript enabled to view it)

Links Relocation Shanghai Office
Rm. 3309, 3rd Floor, East Wing
Harbour Building
1 Feng He Road
Pudong, Shanghai
China 200120

Telephone: +86 (0)21 5882 2282
Fax: +86 (0)21 5882 2810
Email: shanghai@linksrelo.com

PARAGON RELOCATION
Website: www.paragonrelocation.com

Paragon China (Beijing)
1701 Hyundai Motor Tower
38 Xiaoyun Road, Chaoyang District
Beijing 100027
China

Paragon Hong Kong
Suite 1802
88 Gloucester Road
Global Relocation Services
Wanchai, Hong Kong, SAR China
Telephone: +852 2907 5880

RELOCASIA
Corporate website: www.relocasia.com

Relocasia Hong Kong Office
F2, 13F
Gee Tung Cheong Ind Building
4 Fung Yip Street
Chai Wan
Hong Kong
Telephone: +852 2976 9369
Fax: +852 2976 9947

Relocasia Shanghai Office
No. 158 Zahngyang Road
Block C, Room 717
Shanghai 200040
China
Telephone: +86 (0)21 5877 8318
Fax: +86 (0)21 5877 2808

SANTA FE RELOCATION SERVICES CO. LTD.
Corporate website: www.santaferelo.com
(Santa Fe Relocation has offices in 16 Chinese cities including Hong Kong)

Santa Fe Relocation Beijing Office
2, Street No. 8
Beijing Airport Logistics Zone
Beijing 101300
Telephone: +86 (0)10 6947 0688
Fax: +86 (0)10 6947 0699
Email: beijing@santafe.com.cn

Santa Fe Relocation Guangzhou Office
Room 1307-9
West Tower
Guangzhou International Commercial Center
Ti Yu Dong Road
Guangzhou 510620
Telephone: +86 (0)20 3887 0630/12
Fax: +86 (0)20 3887 0629
Email: guangzhou@santafe.com.cn

Santa Fe Relocation Hong Kong Office
18/F, C.C. Wu Building
302-8 Hennessy Road
Wanchai, Hong Kong
Telephone: +852 2574 6204
Fax: +852 2575 1907
Email: sales@santafe.com.hk

Santa Fe Relocation Shanghai Office
5th Floor
Tian Hong Building
80 Xi'an Xia Road
Shanghai 200336
Telephone: +86 (0)21 6233 9700
Fax: +86 (0)21 6233 9005
Email: shanghai@santafe.com.cn

SINOTRANS GLOBAL FREIGHT
Corporate website: www.sinotrans.com
Sinotrans Beijing Head Office
Sinotrans Plaza
Xizhimen North St.
Beijing 100044
Telephone: +86 (0)10 62296666
Fax: +86 (0) 62296600

STERLING RELOCATION
45/F The Lee Gardens
33 Hysan Avenue
Causeway Bay
Hong Kong
Telephone: +852 3180 2345
Fax: +852 3180 2299
Email: hongkong@sterlingrelocation.com

THE MI GROUP
Hong Kong Office
Unit 1201-04, 12th Floor, Tai Yau Building
181 Johnston Road
Wanchai, Hong Kong
Telephone: +852 2810 1812
Website: www.themigroup.com

WEICHERT RELOCATION RESOURCES INC.
#602, Devon House
979 King's Road, Taikooplace
Hong Kong, SAR
Telephone: +852 2545-5885
Fax: +852 2545-2022
Website: www.wrri.com

DOMESTIC AIRLINES – PASSENGER

Air China
IATA Code: CA
Corporate website: www.airchina.com.cn
Corporate HQ (Beijing)
Capital International Airport
Beijing 100621
CHINA
Global Sales Hotline: +86 4008 100 999
China Sales hotline: 95583
Telephone: +86 10 59281588
Fax: +86 10 8449 2550

AIR MACAU
IATA Code: NX
Corporate website: www.airmacau.com.mo

Air Macau Beijing Office
8/F, 22 Jian Guo Men Wai Da Jie
CVIK
Beijing
Telephone: +86 (0)10 6515 8988
Telephone: +86 (0)10 6515 9398
Fax: +86 (0)10 6515 9979

Air Macau Shanghai Office
Rm 806, Shanghai International Equatorial Hotel
65 Yan An Road West Shanghai PRC
Telephone: +86 (0)21 6248 1110
Fax: +86 (0)21 6248 7870

Air Macau Shenzhen Office
Room 1101, Hualian Bldg.
2008 Shennan Middle Road, Futian
Shenzhen 51828
Telephone: +86 (0)755 2777-3728/3738
Fax: +86 (0)755 2777 0787

CATHAY PACIFIC AIRWAYS
(IATA Code: CX)/Dragonair (IATA Code: KA)
(Dragon is a subsidiary of Cathay Pacific Airways)
Cathay Pacific Airways Corporate website: www.cathaypacific.com
Dragonair Corporate website: www.dragonair.com

Cathay Pacific Airways/Dragonair—Beijing Office
28/F, East Tower, Twin Towers
B-12 Jianguomenwai Avenue
Chaoyang District
Beijing 100022
Telephone: 400-888-6628 (within China only)
Fax: +86 (0)10 5905 7730

Cathay Pacific Airways/Dragonair—Guangzhou Office
2520-2521, Tower A, China Shine Plaza
9 Linhe Xilu

Tianhe District
Guangzhou China 510610
Telephone: 400 888 6628 (opening hours: 0700—2300) (within China only)

Cathay Pacific Airways/Dragonair—Shanghai Office
Room 1605-1608, 1788 Nanjing Xi Road
Shanghai, China
Telephone: 400 888 6628 (opening hours: 0700—2300) (within China only)

CHENGDU AIRLINES
IATA Code: EU
Corporate website: www.chengduair.cc
Floor 6, South West China
Aeronautical Devices Company
Shuang Liu International Airport
Cheng Du
Telephone: +86 (0)28 6666 8888
Telephone: +86 (0)28 6600 6333
Fax +86 (0)28 8570 6 99

CHINA EASTERN AIRLINES
IATA Code: MU
Corporate website: www.ce-air.com
Shanghai International Airport Co., Ltd.
900 Qihang Road
Pudong Airport
Shanghai 201202

CHINA SOUTHERN AIRLINES
IATA Code: CZ
Corporate website: www.cs-air.com
Bai Yun Airport
International Affairs Dept.
Guangzhou City
510406
Telephone: +86 (0)20 8668 2000
China United Airlines
IATA Code: KN
Corporate website: www.cu-air.com, www.cu-air.com.cn

Beijing Fengtai Area, Garrison East Road 6, 1st West Area
北京市丰台区警备东路 6 号西区一号院
Beijing
100076
Sales Booking: 67978899
24 Hour customer Service: 95530

HAINAN AIRLINES
IATA Code: HU
Corporate website: www.hnair.com
HNA Development Building
29 Hixiu Road
Hainan
570206, P.R. China
Telephone: +86 (0)898 66739684/ 66739224
Fax: +86 (0) 898 66739634

HELI EXPRESS LTD
Room 1603
16/F China Merchants Tower
Shun Tak Center
200 Connaught Road Central
Hong Kong
Telephone: +852 2108 9988
Fax: +852 2108 9938

HONG KONG AIRLINES/ HONG KONG EXPRESS AIRWAYS
IATA Code: HX/ IATA Code: UO
Corporate website: www.hkairlines.com

Hong Kong Office
L2 CNAC House
12 Tung Fai Road
Hong Kong International Airport
Lantau
HONG KONG
Telephone: +852 2559 1966
Fax: +852 2215 3028

Beijing Office
3/F, Grand China Building
B-2, East 3rd Ring, Road North Road

Chaoyang District, Beijing, CHINA
Telephone: +86 (0)10 5915 7528
Fax: +86 (0)10 5915 7524

Shanghai Office
Room H-I, 28/F
Pu Fa Mansion
588 Pudong South Road, Shanghai, CHINA
Telephone: +86 (0)21 3251 2768/2769/2770
Fax: +86 (0)21 3251 2728

JUNEYAO AIRLINES
IATA Code: HO
Corporate website: www.juneyaoairlines.com
Telephone: +86 (0)21 51116511
24 Hour hotline: 4007006000 (within China only)

LUCKY AIR
IATA Code: 8L
Corporate website: www.luckyair.net
Kunming, Yunan

OKAY AIRWAYS
IATA Code: BK
Corporate website: www.okair.net
Tianjin Binhai International Airport
Tianjin 300300
Telephone: +86 (0)22 6032 5500/+86 (0)10 5175 0000
Fax: +86 (0)22 6032 5575/+86 (0)10 5175 0022

SHANDONG AIRLINES
IATA Code: SC
Corporate website: www.shangdongair.com.cn
11th floor, Shandong Aviation Mansion
5746 Er Huan East Road
Lixia District
Jinan Shandong 250014
Telephone: +86 (0)531 96777

SHANGHAI AIRLINES
IATA Code: FM
Corporate website: www.shanghai-air.com
212 Jiangning Road

Shanghai 200041

Telephone: +86 (0)21 6835 5528

INTERNATIONAL AIRLINES

SHENZHEN AIRLINES

IATA Code: ZH

Corporate website: www.shenzhenair.com

Baoan International Airport

Shenzhen 518128

24 Hour Service Hotline: +86-(0)755-95080 or

4008895080

(+86-(0)755-88814023 for outside of China)

SICHUAN AIRLINES

IATA Code: 3U

Corporate website: www.scal.com.cn

Number 11 Sector

2 Renmin Nan Lu

Chengdu, Sichuan

Telephone: +86 4008 300 999/+86 (0)28 88888888

SPRING AIRLINES

IATA Code: 9S

Corporate website: www.china-sss.com

Spring Airlines Customer Service Center

4th Floor, Building No. 3, Homeyo Hotel

No.2550 Hongqiao Road

Shanghai 200335

Email: cs@air-spring.com

24 hour service line: +86 400-820-6222

Fax: +86 (0) 21 6252 3734

Business Office: +86 (0)21 62692626

Service Quality Hotline: +86 (0)21 62515444

XIAMEN AIRLINES

IATA Code: MF

Corporate website: www.xiamenair.com.cn

22 Dailao Road

Xiamen, 361006

AEROFLOT RUSSIAN AIRLINES

IATA Code: SU

Corporate website: www.aeroflot.ru

Aeroflot—Beijing Office

2 Chao Yang Men Bei Da Jie

Beijing 100027

Telephone: +86 (0)10 6501 2563

Fax: +86 (0)10 6594 1869

Email: bjstosu@aeroflot.ru

Aeroflot—Hong Kong Office

Suite 2918, 29 Floor, Shui on Center

6-8 Harbour Road

Wanchai, Hong Kong

Telephone: +852 2537 2611

Fax: +852 2537 2614

Email: sures@aeroflot.com.hk

Aeroflot—Shanghai Office

SUITE 522, Shanghai Center

1376, Nanjing Xi Road

Shanghai, 200040

Telephone: +86 (0)21 62798033

Fax: +86 (0)21 62798035

Email: shatosu@aeroflot.ru

AEROSVIT—UKRAINIAN AIRLINES

IATA Code: VV

Corporate website: www.aerosvit.ua

Aerosvit Beijing Office

Room 1305, Office Building

Guangming Hotel, Chaoyang District

Beijing 100016, P.R. China

Telephone: +86 (0)10 84580909

Fax: +86 (0)10 84580910

AEROMEXICO

IATA Code: AM

Corporate website: www.aeromexico.com

Unit 8B, Zhaofeng Universal Building

No.1800 West Zhongshan Road, Xuhui District
Shanghai, China 200235
Telephone: +86 (0)21 6089 9985
Fax: +86 (0)21 6089 9385
Email: ampax@megacap.com.cn

AIR ALGERIE
IATA Code: AH
Corporate website: www.airalgerie.dz
Tower 1, Kunsha center, 16 Xinyuanli
Beijing, 100027, China
Telephone: +86 (0)10 846 834 70

AIR ASTANA
IATA Code: KC
Corporate website: www.airastana.com
Air Astana Beijing Office
Office C517, 50 Liangmaqiao Road, Chaoyang
District
Beijing, 100125 RPC (Kempinski Hotel, Beijing
Lufthansa Center)
Tel.: +86 (0)10 64651030, +86 (0)10 64665067
Fax: +86 (0)10 64569178
Email: pek@airastana.com

AIR BUSAN
IATA Code: BX
Corporate website: www.airbusan.com
Telephone: +852 3489-6320/3489 6321

AIR CANADA
IATA Code: AC
Corporate website: www.aircanada.com
China: +86 400 811 2001

Air Canada Beijing Office
C201 Beijing Lufthansa Center
50 Liangmaqiao Road
Beijing 100016
Fax: +86 (0)10 6463 0576

Air Canada Hong Kong
Room 1612, Tower One
New World Tower
18 Queens Road, Central

Hong Kong
Telephone: +852 2112 9697 (24 hours a day)
Fax: +852 2523 5633

Air Canada Shanghai Office
Room 3901, United Plaza
1468 Nan Jing Rd West
Shanghai 200040
Fax: +86 (0)21 6247 2982

AIR FRANCE
IATA Code: AF
Air France China—General/Reservations
Telephone: 4008 808 808 (within China)
Fax: +86 (0)20 3878 5225
Corporate website (China): www.airfrance.com.cn

Air France—Beijing Office
Kuntai International Mansion
Building 1, 16/F Room 1606-1611
12A Chao Yang Men Wai Dajie
Beijing 100020

Air France—Guangzhou Office
13F Gao Sheng Building
109 Ti Yu West Road
Tian He District
Guangzhou 510620

Air France—Hong Kong Office
18/F Vicwood Plaza
199 Des Voeux Road
Central, Hong Kong

Air France—Shanghai Office
Ciro's Plaza Room 3901B
No. 388 Nanjing Xi Lu
Shanghai 200003

AIR INDIA
IATA Code: AI
Corporate website: www.airindia.in

Air India –Shanghai Office
1002, OOCL Plaza
841, Yanan (M) road

Shanghai 200040 China
Telephone: +86 (0)21 5298 5698
Fax: +86 (0)21 5298 6798

Air India—Hong Kong Office
Unit No 4401 Hope Well Center,
183 Queen's Rd Wanchai
Hong Kong
Telephone: +852 25224779/25221176/25229257

AIR MADAGASCAR
IATA code: MD
Corporate website: www.airmadagascar.com
Room 709, China Life Tower, No 16 Chaowai Street
Chaoyang District
100020 Beijing
Fax: +86 (0)10 8569 9606
Fax :+86 (0)10 8569 9618
Email: beijing@airmadagascar.com.hk

Guangzhou Office
Room 1508
Main Tower G.D. International Hotel
339 Huanshi Dong Lu
510098 Guangzhou, CHINA
Telephone: +86 (0)20 8336 4995
Fax:+86 (0)20 8336 5105
Email: guangzhou@airmadagascar.com.cn

AIR MAURITIUS
IATA Code: MK
Corporate website: www.airmauritius.com

Air Mauritius Beijing Office
Room 509A, 5/F, Kelun Building
12 Guanghua Street
Chaoyang District
Beijing 100020
Telephone: +86 (0)10 6581 2968
Fax: +86 (0)10 6581 5908
Email: bjsmkpax@tam.com.hk

Air Mauritius Hong Kong office
Room 1901A
19/F Far East Finance Center

16 Harcourt Road
Admiralty
Hong Kong
Telephone: +852 2523 1114
Fax: +852 2525 0910
Email: mkhongkong@airmauritius.com.hk

AIR NEW ZEALAND LIMITED
IATA Code: NZ
Corporate website: www.airnewzealand.com

Air New Zealand Hong Kong Office
Unit 5111-12, 51/F
The Center
99 Queen's Road Central
Hong Kong
Telephone: +852 2862 8988
Fax: +852 2862 8989
Email: hkgreservations@airnz.co.nz

Beijing Office
Room 1121-1122, South Tower
Beijing Kerry Center
No. 1 Guang Hua Road
Chao Yang District
Beijing 100020
P.R. China
Telephone: +86 (0)10 6587 0000
Fax: +86 (0)10 6587 0100
Email: resbjs@airnz.co.nz

Shanghai Office
Unit 1208-1209, Floor 12
Citic Square
No. 1168 Nanjing Road West
Shanghai, 200041
P.R. China
Telephone: +86 (0)21 2325 3333
Fax: +86 (0)21 2325 3330
Email: ressha@airnz.co.nz

AIR NIUGINI LTD
IATA Code: PX
Corporate website: www.airniugini.com.pg
Room 1901, 19/F

16 Harcourt Road
Admiralty
Hong Kong
Telephone: +852 2527 7098
Fax: +852 2527 7026

AIR PACIFIC
IATA Code: FJ
Corporate website: www.airpacific.com
Suites 805-806
8th floor
World Finance Center
South Tower
Harbour City
Tsimshatsui
Kowloon
Hong Kong
Telephone: +852 2737 6755
Fax: +852 2737 6789
Email: airpacific-hkg@toureast.net

AIRASIA
IATA Code: AK
Corporate website: www.airasia.com
No.0163A Floor of Yi No.6
Chaowai Street of Chaoyang District
Beijing, China

AirAsia Guangzhou
First floor, No 8 Zhong Shan 3 Road,
Guang Zhou, 510000, China
Call AirAsia's China Call Center Number: +86 20
2281 7666
Operating Hours: 8 a.m.—9 p.m. (GMT+8)
Monday to Sunday

AIRPHIL EXPRESS
IATA Code: 2P
Corporate website: www.airphilexpress.com

ALITALIA
IATA Code: AZ
Corporate website: www.alitalia.com

Alitalia Beijing Office
B 1602, TYG Center
No. 2 Dong San Huan Bei Lu
Chaoyang District, Beijing
100027 PRC
Telephone: +86 (0)10 8446 4070
Fax: +86 (0)10 8446 4729

ALL NIPPON AIRWAYS
IATA Code: NH
Corporate website: www.anaskyweb.com
China Number: 4008-82-8888
National Reservation number: +86 (0)10 8559 9292

ANA Hong Kong Office
Suite 1908, Tower 6
The Gateway
9 Canton Road, Harbour City
Kowloon, Hong Kong
Telephone: +852 2810 7100

AMERICAN AIRLINES
IATA Code: AA
Corporate website: www.aa.com

American Airlines Beijing Office
Suite 1109A, Twin Towers (East)
B12 Jian Guo Men Wai Avenue
Beijing, China
Telephone: 400 815 0800 (within China)

American Airlines Guangzhou Office
1313 China Shine Plaza
No 3-15 Lin He West Road
Tian He District
Guangzhou
Telephone: 400 815 0800 (within China)

American Airlines Shanghai Office
Suite 701, Huaihai Plaza
No. 1045 Middle Huaihai Road
Shanghai, China
Telephone: 400 815 0800 (within China)

ASIANA AIRLINES

IATA Code: OZ
Corporate website: www.flyasiana.com
China nationwide Telephone: 400-650-8000 (within China)

Asiana Airlines—Beijing Office
12th Floor A/F Tower GATEWAY
18 XiaGuangLi North Road East Ring
Chaoyang District, 100027
Beijing, China
Telephone: +86 (0)10 8451 0101 (Operation Hours: 7:00 a.m.–9:00 p.m.)
Fax: +86 (0)10 8460 9588

Asiana Airlines—Guangzhou Office
Room 906, South Tower, World Trade Center
371-375, Huanshi East Road
Guangzhou, China
Telephone: +86 (0)10 8451 0101
Fax: +86 (0)20 8760 4108

Asiana Airlines Hong Kong Office
Suites1210-11,12/F, Tower2
The Gateway, 25 Canton Road
Harbour City, Tsimshatsui
Hong Kong
Telephone: +852 2523 8585
Fax: +852 2524 6152

Asiana Airlines Shanghai Office
Unit 05, 3F, Tower A
SOHO Zhongshan Plaza
No.1055 West Zhongshan Road
Shanghai, China
Telephone: +86 (0)10 8451 0101
Fax: +86 (0)21 6270 3167

AUSTRIAN AIRLINES

IATA Code: OS
Corporate website: www.austrian.com
Austrian Airlines Beijing
S101 Beijing Lufthansa Center
50 Liangmaqiao Road
Beijing, China 100125

Telephone: +86 4008 810 770
Fax: +86 (0) 21 63 40 6100

AZERBAIJAN AIRLINES

IATA Code: J2
Corporate website: www.azal.az
Room 413
Hotel "Silk Road"
9A Jianguomennei Avenue
Tel/Fax: +86 (0)991 258 14 13

BANGKOK AIRWAYS

IATA Code: PG
Corporate website: www.bangkokair.com

Bangkok Airways Beijing Office
Room 412, Lido Office Tower
No 6, Jiangtai Road
Beijing, China 10004
Telephone: +86 (0)10 64301517
Telephone: +86 (0)10 64301206
Fax: +86 (0)10 64301519

Bangkok Airways Guangzhou Office
Travel Link Marketing Co., Ltd.
Room 2412, South Tower
World Trade Center
375 Huan Shi Dong Road
Guangzhou, China 510095
Telephone: +86 (0)20 8760 7805
Fax: +86 (0)20 8760 7895

Bangkok Airways Hong Kong Office
Suite 912, 9th Floor, Ocean Center
Harbour City, Tsim Sha Tsui
Kowloon, Hong Kong
Telephone: +852 2899 2597 (RSVN)
Telephone: +852 2899 2634 (RSVN)
Telephone: +852 2840 1302 (Sales)
Telephone: +852 2899 2607 (Sales)
Fax: +852 2537 4567

BATAVIA AIRLINES

IATA Code: Y6
Corporate website: www.batavia-air.com

Huanshi Dong Road
No. 326 Room 1109
Asia International Hotel
Guangzhou 510060
Telephone: +86 (0)20 6120 6350
Fax: +86 (0)20 6120 6354

BIMAN BANGLADESH AIRLINES
IATA Code: BG
Corporate website: www.biman-airlines.com
Huston Center Suite 216/217
63 Mody Road
Tshim-Sha-Tsui, Kowloon
Hongkong
Telephone: +852 27248464
Fax: +852 27246284

BRITISH AIRWAYS
IATA Code: BA
Corporate website: www.ba.com
Telephone: 400 650 0073 (within China only)

BA Travel shop—Beijing
Room 2112, Building 1
Kun Tai International
Mansion Yi
12 Chao Yang
Men Wai Street
Beijing 100020
Telephone: +86 (0)10 6459 0081
Telephone: +86 (0)10 6459 0082
Telephone: +86 (0)10 6459 0083

BA Travel Shop—Hong Kong
24 Floor
Jardine House
One Connaught Place
Central, Hong Kong
Telephone: +852 2822 9000

BA Travel Shop—Shanghai
Suite 703
Central Plaza, 227 Huang Pi
North Road

Shanghai 200003
Telephone: +86 (0)21 6835 5633

CEBU PACIFIC AIR
IATA Code: 5J
Corporate website: www.cebupacificair.com
Unit 407 Mirror Tower
61 Mody Road, Tsimshatsui East
Kowloon, Hong Kong
Telephone: +852 2722 0609

CHINA AIRLINES
IATA Code: CI
Corporate website: www.china-airlines.com

China Airlines Beijing Office
Tower 1, Room 1111
No 7, Jian Guo Men Nei Avenue
Beijing 100005, P.R. China
Telephone: +86 (0)10 65102671
Fax: +86 (0)10 65102677

China Airlines Guangzhou Office
Room 1210, 12F
TeemTower, No. 208 Tianhe Road
Tianhe District, Guangzhou, P.R. China
Telephone: +86 (0)20 8527 2950
Fax: +86 (0)20 8516 8144
Fax: +86 (0)10 65102677

China Airlines Hong Kong Office
Suites 2701-2705 Devon House
Tai Koo Place
979 King's Road, Quarry Bay
Hong Kong
Telephone: +852 2843 9800
Fax: +852 2845 0155

China Airlines Shanghai Office
HuaMin Empire Plaza Suite 22A
726 West Yanan Road
Shanghai 200050
Telephone: +86 (0)21 52375269/70/71/72
Fax: +86 (0)21 52375322

DELTA AIRLINES
IATA Code: DL
Corporate website: www.delta.com

Delta Airlines Beijing Ticketing Office
Room 1308, China World Office 1
No.1 Jian Guo Men Wai Avenue
Beijing 100004, China
Telephone: +86 40081 40081
Fax: +86 (0)10 800 650 0472

Delta Airlines Guangzhou Ticketing Office
C509 China Hotel
Liu Hua Road
Guangzhou 510015, China
Telephone: +86 40081 40081
Fax: +86 (0)10 800 265 0488

Delta Airlines Shanghai Ticketing office
Suite 1007, Kerry Center
No.1515 Nanjing Road West
Shanghai 200040, China
Telephone: +86 40081 40081

EGYPTAIR
IATA Code: MS
Corporate website: www.egyptair.com.eg
Suite 2260, Sunflower Tower Building
37 Maizidan Street
Beijing 100026
Telephone: +86 (10) 85275000
Fax: +86 (10) 85275940

Egyptair Guangzhou Office
Oriental Sky Aviation Services
C/6f n.611-13, China Hotel
Liuhua Road Guangzhou 510015
China
Telephone: +86 (0)20 862 66969/8626 6900

EL AL ISRAEL AIRLINES
IATA Code: LY
Corporate website: www.elal.com

El Al Israel Airlines—Beijing Office
Room 1812B, Kuntai International Mansion
Yi No.12 Chaowai Street
Chao Yang District
Beijing 100020
Telephone: +86 (0)10 5879 7361
Telephone: +86 (0)10 5879 7358
Fax: +86 (0)10 5879 7359

EL AL Israel Airlines—Hong Kong Office
Room 2205, Tower One, Lippo Center
89 Queensway
Hong Kong
Telephone: +852 2380 3362
Fax: +852 2536 4968

EMIRATES AIRLINES
IATA Code: EK
Corporate website: www.emirates.com

Emirates Beijing Office
Room 1003, Tower A
Eagle Run Plaza
26, Xiao Yun Road
Chao Yang District
Beijing 100016, CHINA
Telephone: +86 400 8822380 or +86 (0)20 8510
3232 (if calling from outside China)

Emirates Guangzhou Office
Room 3001-3003, 30/F
Teem Tower, 208 Tianhe Road
Tianhe District, Guangzhou, 510620, CHINA
Telephone: +86 400 8822380 or +86 (0)20 8510
3232 (if calling from outside China)

Emirates Hong Kong Office
11/F, Henley Building
5 Queen's Road Central
Hong Kong
Telephone: +852 2801 8777

Emirates Shanghai Office
Room 1905-1907, United Plaza
1468, Nan Jing Road West

Shanghai 200040, CHINA
Telephone: +86 400 8822380 or +86 (0)20 8510
3232 (if calling from outside China)

ETHIOPIAN AIRLINES
IATA Code: ET
Corporate website: www.ethiopianairlines.com

Ethiopian Airlines Beijing Office
L203 China World Tower
Tower 2 /L203
No1 JianGuomenWai Ave.
Beijing (100004)
Telephone: +86 (0)10 6505 0314/5
Fax: +86 (0)10 6505 4120

Ethiopian Airlines Guangzhou Office
Rm. 1303-1305, 13F, South Tower
World Trade Center
Huan Shi Dong Rd. Guangzhou
Telephone: +86 (0)20 87621101/87620120/87620
836/87318765
Fax: +86 (0)20 8762 0837

Ethiopian Airlines Hong Kong Office
1102 Lippo Sun Plaza
28 Canton Road
Tsim Sha Tsui
Kowloon, Hong Kong
Telephone: + 852 2117 0233/2117 1863
Fax: +852 2117 1811

ETIHAD AIRWAYS
IATA Code: EY
Corporate website: www.etihadairways.com
Twins Tower
30th Floor of East Tower
No B12, Jianguomenwai Avenue
Chaoyang District, Beijing, China
Telephone: +86 (0)10 8521 7988
Fax: +86 (0)10 6567 6883

Etihad Airways Shanghai Office
12/F Platinum Building
233 Taicang Road

Shanghai, China
Telephone: +86 (0)21 5175 1523/24
Fax: +86 (0)21 5175 1521

EVA AIRWAYS CORP.
IATA Code: BR
Corporate website: www.evaair.com

EVA Airways Beijing Office
22/F Block C
Central International Trade Center
6A Jianguomenwai Avenue
Chaoyang District
Beijing, China
Telephone: +86 (0)10 6563 5000
Fax: +86 (0)10 6563 0068

EVA Airways Hong Kong Office
11F, Luk Kwok Center
72 Gloucester Road
Wan Chai
Hong Kong
Telephone: +852 28109251
Fax: +852 25250025

FINNAIR
IATA Code: AY
Corporate website: www.finnair.com

Finnair Beijing Office
Scitech Tower, Room 204
22 Jian Guo Men Wai Dajie
Beijing
Tel. +86 (0)10 6512 7180

Finnair Hong Kong Office
Room 2312, 23/F, Cosco Tower
183 Queen's Road, Central
Telephone: +852 2117 1238
Email: finnair.hkg@finnair.com

Finnair Shanghai Call Center
Telephone: +86 (0)21 6335 3999
Fax: +86 (0)21 3366 2650
Email: finnair.shanghai@finnair.com

GARUDA INDONESIA
IATA Code: GA
Corporate website: www.garuda-indonesia.com

Garuda—Beijing Office
RM 1902:19F: Kuntai
International Mansion Y112
Chaowei Avenue
Chaoyang District
Beijing
Telephone: +86 (0)10 58797699
Fax: +86 (0)10 58790784

Garuda Hong Kong Office
Unit 01, Level 10
68 Yee Woo Street
Causeway Bay, Hong Kong
Telephone: +852 28400000
Fax: +852 28455021

Garuda Shanghai Office
Unit G-H, level 17
Huamin Empire Plaza
No.726 Yan'an Road (West)
Shanghai, China
Telephone: +86 (0)21 52391000
Fax: +86 (0)21 52398126

IRANAIR
IATA Code: IR
Corporate website: www.iranair.com
No.19 Jianguomenwai Dajie
Beijing, Citic Building 701, CHINA
Telephone: +86 (0)10 65124940
Telephone: +86 (0)10 65124945
Telephone: +86 (0)10 65120047

JAL (JAPAN AIRLINES)
IATA Code: JL
Corporate website: www.jal.com
Telephone: 4008-88-0808 (within China)
Telephone: +86 (0)21 5467 4530 (from overseas)

JAL Beijing Office
Room No. 1516

Beijing Fortune Building
5 Dong San Huan Bei-Lu
Chao Yang District
Beijing, CHINA 100004

JAL Guangzhou Office
Room 3011 Tower B
China Shine Plaza
No. 9 Lin He Xi Road
Guangzhou, Guangdong, 510610, China

JAL Hong Kong Office
30th Floor, Tower 6
The Gateway, Harbour City
9 Canton Road
Tsim Sha Tsui, Kowloon
Hong Kong

JAL Shanghai Office
7th Floor, Huaihai Plaza
1045, Huaihai Zhong Road
Shanghai, 200031

JEJU AIR
IATACode: 7C
Corporate website: www.jejuair.com
Hong Kong International Airport
Lantau, Hong Kong (Terminal 2)
1st Floor, Room #3PC009
Telephone: +852 2185 6499
Fax: +852 3170 5399

JET AIRWAYS
IATA Code: 9W
Corporate website: www.jetairways.com
Jet Airways Hong Kong
Tower 2, 10th Floor
33 Canton Road
Tsim Sha Tsui, Kowloon
Hong Kong
Telephone: +852 3966 5008
Email: hkgreservations@jetairways.com

JETSTAR AIRWAYS
IATA Code: 3K
Corporate website: www.jetstar.com

JIN AIR
IATA Code: LJ
Corporate website: www.jinair.com
Room 122-123
1st Floor, Airport World Trade Center
One Sky Plaza Road
Lantau Island, Hong Kong
Telephone: +852 3756 3512

Shanghai office
14-324 3rd Floor, Terminal 1
Pudong International Airport
Shanghai 201207
Telephone: +86 (0)21 6836 5136

KENYA AIRWAYS
IATA Code: KQ
Corporate website: www.kenya-airways.com

Kenya Airways Guangzhou Office
12A, Goldsun Building
No.109 Ti Yu Xi Road
Guangzhou, 510620
Telephone: +86 (0)20 3866 3221
Telephone: +86 (0)20 3866 3119
Fax: +86 (0)20 3866 2330

Kenya Airways Hong Kong Office
Pacific Aviation Marketing (Kenya) Ltd.
Room 2505A Caroline Center
28 Yun Ping Road
Causeway Bay
Hong Kong
Telephone: +852 3678 2000
Fax; +852 3579 0808

KLM ROYAL DUTCH AIRLINES
IATA Code: KL
For calls from China: 4008 808 222
For all other countries: +852 2808 2168
Corporate website: www.klm.com

KLM Beijing Office
1609-1611, 16/F
Kuntai International Mansion Building
12, Chaoyangmenwai Avenue
Beijing
KLM Hong Kong Office
18/F, Vicwood Plaza
199 Des Voeux Road, Central
Hong Kong

KLM Shanghai Office
3901A, Ciro's Plaza
388 Nan Jing Xi Lu
Shanghai, CHINA

KOREAN AIRLINES
IATA Code: KL
Corporate website: www.koreanair.com
Sales China: 40065-88888

KAL Beijing Office
901-3, Hyundai Motor Towers
38 Xiao Yun Road
Chao Yang District
Beijing, CHINA
Telephone: +86 (0)10 8468 5288
Fax: +86 (0)10 8453 8124

KAL Guangzhou Office
Citic Plaza 5306
233 Tianhebei Road
Guangzhou, CHINA
Telephone: +86 (0)20 3877 3878

KAL Hong Kong Office
11/F, Tower 2, South Seas Center
75 Mody Road
Tsimshatsui East, Kowloon
Hong Kong
Telephone: +852 2733 7110

KAL Shanghai Branch
1009 Maxdo Center 10F
8 Xing Yi Road

Shanghai
Telephone: +86 (0)21 5208 2080

LOT POLISH AIRLINES
IATA Code: LO
Corporate website: www.lot.com
Oriental Sky Aviation
9, Fuqianer Street, Tianzhu
Shunyi District, Beijing
Telephone: +86 (0)10 84580325
Fax: +86 (0)10 84584991

LUFTHANSA GERMAN AIRLINES
IATA Code: LH
Corporate website: www.lufthansa.com

Lufthansa Beijing Office
Beijing Lufthansa Center
50 Liangmaqiao Road
Unit S101
Beijing 100016
Telephone: +86 (0)10 6468 8838
Fax: +86 (0)10 6465 3223

Lufthansa Hong Kong Office
Lufthansa City Center/Schenker Travel
Unit 2001-4
20/F The Broadway
54-62 Lockhart Road
Wanchai
Hong Kong
Telephone: +852 2868 2313

Lufthansa Shanghai office
8th Floor, Henderson Metropolitan
300 Nanjing Road East
Huangpu District, Shanghai
Telephone: +86 (0)21 5352 4999
Fax: +86 (0)21 6340 6899

MALAYSIA AIRLINES
IATA Code: MH
Corporate website: www.malaysiaairlines.com

MAS Beijing Office
Unit 1008B, 10th Floor, Tower B
Pacific Century Place
2A Gong Ti Bei Lu, Chaoyang District
Beijing 100027
People's Republic of China
Telephone: +86 (0)10 6505 2681 Ext. 613

MAS Guangzhou Office
Shop M04-05 Garden Hotel
368 Huanshi Dong Lu Road
Guangzhou, 510064
Telephone: +86 (0)20 8335 8868
Telephone: +86 (0)20 8333 8989 Ext. 3286
Telephone: +86 (0)20 8333 8999 Ext. 226

MAS Hong Kong Office
23/F, AIA Plaza, 18 Hysan Avenue
Causeway Bay, HongKong
People's Republic of China
Telephone: +852 2916 0066
Fax: +852 2868 4080

MAS Shanghai Office
Unit 2508, 25th Floor, Tian An Center
No.338 West NanJing Road
200003 Shanghai
People's Republic of China
Telephone: +86 (0)21 2329 3999/2329 3988

MAHAN AIR
IATA Code: W5
Corporate website: www.mahan.aero
30 ShanXi Road (S)
Moller Villa, Shanghai, China
Telephone: +86 (0)21 62473300
Fax: +86 (0)21 62475595

MANDARIN AIRLINES
IATA Code: AE
Corporate website: www.mandarin-airlines.com
Beijing: +86 (0)10 6510 2671
Guangzhou: +86 (0)20 8550 1410/11/1213
Hong Kong: +852 2868 2299
Shanghai: +86 (0)21 5237 5269/70/71/72

MEGA MALDIVES
IATA Code: 5M
Corporate website: www.megamaldivesair.com

MIAT MONGOLIAN AIRLINES
IATA Code: OM
Corporate website: www.miat.com
Room #705, 7th floor
Sunjoy Mansion Jianguomenwai
Ritan Lu #6 100020 Beijing, China
Telephone: +86 (0)10 650 79297/61231
Fax: +86 (0)10 650 77397
Email: beijing@miat.com

MYANMAR AIRWAYS INTERNATIONAL
IATA Code: 8M
Corporate website: www.maiair.com
Rm3218, Tower China Shine Plaza
No.3-15 Lin He Xi Road
Guangzhou 510610 China.
Telephone: +86 (0)20 8523 7335, +86 (0)20 8523 7136
Fax: +86 (0)20 8523 7495

NEPAL AIRLINES
IATA Code: RA
Corporate website: www.nepalairlines.com.np

Nepal Airlines Hong Kong Office
Room No.704, Lippo Sun Plaza Building
28 Canton Road, Tsimshatsui
Kowloon, Hong Kong
Telephone: +852 23 752180/756094
Fax: +852 23 757069

ORIENT THAI AIRWAYS
IATA Code: OX
Corporate website: www.flyorientthai.com
6/F., China Hong Kong Center, No. 122-126,
Canton Rd., Tsim Sha Tsui, Kowloon,Hong Kong.
Telephone: +852 2366 6869
Fax: +852 2366 8646

PAKISTAN INTERNATIONAL AIRLINES (PIA)
IATA Code: PK
Corporate website: www.piac.com.pk

PIA Beijing Office
617, Level 6
China World Tower
Beijing
Telephone: +86 (0)10
65051681/65051682/65051683
Fax: +86 (0)10 65052257

PIA Hong Kong Office
Room 607, Tsim Sha Tsui Center
66 Mody Road, Tsim Sha Tsui East
Kowloon, Hong Kong
Telephone: +852 23664747
Fax: +852 27211739

PHILIPPINE AIRLINES
IATA Code: PR
Corporate website: www.philippineairlines.com

Philippine Airlines Beijing Office
Unit 1621, Tower 2,
Bright China Chang An Building
No. 7 JianGuoMenNei Ave.
Dong Cheng District
Beijing 100005
Telephone: +86 (0)10 6510 2991 to 2993
Fax: +86 (0)10 6518 0882

Philippine Airlines Shanghai Office
Shanghai Center
1376 Nanjing West Road
Suite 735A, East Wing
Shanghai 200040
Telephone: +86 (0)21 627 98765
Fax: +86 (0)21 627 98762

QANTAS
IATA Code: QF
Corporate website: www.qantas.com
Unit 510, 5th Floor East Ocean Center
A24 Jianguomenwai Avenue

Chaoyang District, Beijing, CHINA
Telephone: 800 819 0089
Telephone: 400 888 0089

Qantas Hong Kong Office
24/F, Jardine House
One Connaught Place
Central, Hong Kong
Telephone: +852 2822 9000
Fax: +852 2822 9095

Qantas Shanghai Office
Room 3202, 32F
K Wah Center
1010 Huai Hai Middle Road
Shanghai
Telephone: 800 819 0089 (within China only)
Telephone: +86 (0)21 6145 0188

QATAR AIRWAYS
IATA Code: QR
Corporate website: www.qatarairways.com

Qatar Airways Beijing Office
Unit A+F1, 16th Floor
Building A, Gateway Plaza
18, Xiaguangli
North Road East Third Ring
Chaoyang District
Beijing 100027
Telephone: +86 (0)10 5923 5100
Fax: +86 (0)10 5923 5200

Qatar Airways Chongqing office
Unit 15, 5th Floor, JW Marriott Hotel Chongqing
No. 77 Qing Nian Road Yuzhong District
Chongqing, China
Telephone: +86 (0)23 6379 6001
Fax: +86 (0)23 6379 6007

Qatar Airways Guangzhou Office
Unit 1404, 14th Floor, R&F Center
No.10 Huaxia Road, Zhujiang New Town
Tianhe District, Guangzhou 510623, China

Telephone: +86 (0)20 3£14 3000
Fax: +86 (0)20 3814 3030

Qatar Airways Hong Kong Office
Unit B, 20/F, No. 9 Queer's Road Central
Hong Kong, Hong Kong
Telephone: +852 2868 9833
Fax: +852 2868 9081

Qatar Airways Shanghai Office
Room 3703-04 Raffles C ty
268 Xi Zang Road (M)
Shanghai, 200001
Telephone: +86 (0)21 2320 7555
Fax: +86 (0)21 2320 7588/7566

ROYAL BRUNEI AIRLINES
IATA Code: BI
Corporate website: www.bruneiair.com
Room 0, 22nd Floor, Xhiyuan Building
No.768 Xietu Road, Luwan District
Shanghai, China 200023
Telephone: +86 (0)21 53027288
Fax: +86 (0)21 63047686

ROYAL JORDANIAN AIRLINES
IATA Code: RJ
Corporate website: www.rj.com
Room 1101, Jubilee Center
18 Fenwick Street
Wanchai, Hong Kong
Telephone: +852 2804 1203

S7 AIRLINES
IATA Code: S7
Corporate website: www.s7.ru
Beijing Asia Hotel offic= 202
8 Xinzhong Xijie, Gongti Beilu
Beijing, China
Telephone: +86 (0)10 655 296 72, 655 296 73
Fax: +86 (0)10 655 295 43

SAS SCANDINAVIAN AIRLINES
IATA Code: SK
Corporate website: www.flysas.com

SAS Hong Kong Office
3607, China Resource Building
26 Harbour Road
Wanchai, Hong Kong
Telephone: +852 2865 1370
Fax: +852 2865 1448

SAT AIRLINES
IATA Code: HZ
Corporate website: www.satairlines.ru
No. 1808, Zhonganshengye Tower
No. 168 Beiyuan Road
Chaoyang District, Beijing, CHINA, 100101
Telephone: +86 (0)10 582 470 28, +86 (0)10 582 47029

SAUDI ARABIAN AIRLINES
IATA Code: SV
Corporate website: www.saudiairlines.com
Intergulf Express H.K. LTD, Room 1902-3
Tower A, Zhongtai International Plaza
161 Lin He Xi Road, Tianhe District, Guangzhou
Telephone: +86 (0)20 38319771/2/3
Fax: +86 (0)20 38319775
Intergulf Express H.K. Ltd, Unit 1902, 19/F
Far East Finance Center, 16 Harcourt Road
Admiralty, Hong Kong, S.A.R
Telephone: +852 2377 2070

SILKAIR
IATA Code: MI
Corporate website: www.silkair.com

Silkair Chengdu Office
36C First City Plaza
308 Shuncheng Street
Chengdu, Sichuan 610017
Telephone: +86 (0)28 8652 8626 / 8652 8636
Fax: +86 (0)28 8652 8656

Silkair Shenzhen Office
Rm 3007 Kerry Center
2008 Ren Min Nan Road
Shenzhen 518001

Telephone: +86 (0)755 8236 6106
Fax: +86 (0)755 8230 0032

SILKAIR XIAMEN OFFICE
International Plaza
11th floor unit G
8 Lujiang Road
Xiamen 361001
Telephone: +86 (0)592 205 3257 /205 3280
Fax: +86 (0)592 205 3273
Email: xmnmi@public.xm.fj.cn

SINGAPORE AIRLINES
IATA Code: SQ
Corporate website: www.singaporeair.com

Singapore Airlines Beijing Office
8th Floor China World Tower 2
1 Jian Guo Men Wai Avenue
Beijing 100004, China
Telephone: +86 (0)10 65052233 (Reservations & Ticketing)
Fax: +86 (0)10 65051178 (Reservations & Ticketing)

Singapore Airlines Guangzhou office
Room 2701-04, Metro Plaza
183-187 Tian He Bei Road
Guangzhou 510620, China
Telephone: +86 (0)20 87556300 (Reservations & Ticketing)
Fax: +86 (0)20 87555518 (Reservations & Ticketing)

Singapore Airlines Hong Kong Office
17th Floor United Center
95 Queensway
Admiralty
Hong Kong, China
Telephone: +852 25202233
Telephone: +852 25296821

Singapore Airlines Shanghai Office
Rm 1106-1110
Plaza 66 Tower 1
1266 Nanjing Xilu
Shanghai 200040, China

Telephone: +86 (0)21 6288 7999 (Reservations & Ticketing)

Fax: +86 (0)21 6288 7667 (Reservations & Ticketing)

SOUTH AFRICAN AIRWAYS
IATA Code: SA
Corporate website: www.flysaa.com

BEIJING BEALL GSA BUSINESS
Consulting Services Ltd.
Room 1703
Richen International Center
No. 13 Nong Zhan Guan Nan Lu
Chaoyang District
Beijing 100125, China.
Telephone: +86 (0)10 6595 0066

Beijing BEALL GSA Business
Consulting Services Ltd.
Room 1906
World Trade Plaza
No. 500 Guangdong Road
Huangpu District
Shanghai 200001
China
Telephone: +86 (0)21 6362 1461

General Office (Incl. Administration & Finance)
6th Floor
Club Lusitano
16 Ice House Street
Central
Hong Kong
Telephone: +852 2722 5768
Fax: +852 2311 1174

SOUTH EAST ASIAN AIRLINES
IATA Code: DG
Corporate website: www.flyseair.com

SRI LANKAN AIRLINES
IATA Code: UL
Corporate website: www.srilankan.aero

SriLankan Airlines Ltd. Beijing Office
Unit S119, Lufthansa Center
50, Liangmaqiao Road
Chaoyang District
Beijing 100016
Telephone: +86 (0)10 6461 7208
Fax: +86 (0)10 6461 608
Email:bjs.res@srilankan.aero

SriLankan Airlines Ltd. Guangzhou Office
SriLankan Airlines Ltd.,
C710-711, China Hotel Office Tower,
No 122, Liu Hua Lu,
Guangzhou 510015.
People's Republic of China
Telephone: +86 (0)20 8626 6786

SriLankan Airlines Ltd. Hong Kong office
Room 2703, 27th Floor
Tower 1, Lippo Center
89 Queensway
Admiralty
Hong Kong
Telephone: +852 25210812 / 825 / 852 (Sales)
Fax: +852 28015600
Email: res_hkg@srilankan.aero

SriLankan Airlines Ltd. Shanghai Office
SriLankan Airlines Ltd.,
Unit G 4th floor Hongqiao Business Center,
No 2272 Hong Qiao Road,
Shanghai 200336,
People's Republic of China
Telephone: +86 (0)21 6237 6887
Toll Free number 4006 120 887

SWISS AIR
IATA: LX
Corporate website: www.swiss.com

Swiss Air Beijing Office
S101, Beijing Lufthansa Center
50 Liangmaqiao Road
Beijing, China
Telephone: +4008820880

Fax: +86 (0)21 63406678
Email: team.china@swiss.com

Swiss Air Hong Kong Office
Airport Ticket Office
c/o Cathay Pacific Airways
Hong Kong Intl. Airport
Departure Level / Area E
Telephone: +852 30 021330
Fax: +852 23 627513

Swiss Air Shanghai Office
801-803 Henderson Metropolitan,
300 East Nanjing Rd.
Shanghai 200001 PRC
Telephone: +4008820880
Fax: +86 (0)21 63406678
Email: team.china@swiss.com

TAAG ANGOLAN AIRLINES
IATA Code: DT
Corporate website: www.taag.com
Oriental Sky Aviation service Co., Ltd.
A2601, Eagle Run Plaza, No 26
Xiaoyun Road
Chayoanga District, Beijing, 100016
Telephone: +86 (0)10 84580327
Fax: +86 (0)10 84584991

THAI AIRWAYS
IATA Code: TH
Corporate website: www.thaiair.com

Thai Airways Beijing Office
Units 303-4, Level 3 Office Tower W3
Oriental Plaza
1 East Chang An Ave
Dong Cheng District
Beijing 100738
Telephone: +86 (0)10 8515 0088
Fax: +86 (0)10 8515 1134

Thai Airways Guangzhou Branch
G3, West Wing
The Garden Hotel

368 Huanshi Dong Lu
Guangzhou 510064
Telephone: +86 (0)20 8365 2333 Ext. 12
Fax: +86 (0)20 8365 2300

Thai Airways Hong Kong Office
Unit A24/F
United Center
95 Queensway
Hong Kong
Telephone: +852 2179 7700
Fax: +852 2179 7600

Thai Airways Shanghai Office
Unit 2302, Chong Hing Finance Center,
288 Nan Jing Rd West Shanghai 200003, China
Telephone: +86 (0)21 3366 4111
Fax: +86 (0)21 3366 4020

TIGER AIRWAYS
IATA Code: TR
Corporate website: www.tigerairways.com
China: +86 40 0120 2090

TONLESAP AIRLINES
IATA Code: K9
Corporate website: www.tonlesapairlines.com

TRANSASIA AIRWAYS
IATA Code: GE
Corporate website: www.tna.com.tw
Beijing: +86 (0)10 5923 1012
Shanghai: +86 (0)21 6196 0999/6196 0988
Macau: +853 2870 1777

TRANSAERO
IATA Code: UN
Corporate website: www.transaero.ru
No.8 Yong'andongli, Jianguomen,
Chaoyang District, Beijing
Telephone: +86 85289529
Fax: +86 85289528

TURKISH AIRLINES

IATA Code: TK

Corporate website: www.thy.com

Turkish Airlines Beijing Office
C810, Beijing Lufthansa Center
50 Liang Ma Qiao Road
Chaoyang District 100016
Beijing, China
Telephone: +86 (0)10 6465 1867/ 68/69/70
Fax: +86 (0)10 6465 1865

Turkish Airlines Guangzhou Office
Room 6107, Citic Plaza
Tianhebei Road No. 233
Guangzhou, China
Telephone: +86 (0)20 38771690-93 (4 LINE)

Turkish Airlines Hong Kong Office
Turkish Airlines Inc.
Room 1703
Jubilee Center
18 Fenwick Street
Wanchai
Hong Kong
Telephone: +852 28613111
Fax: +852 3101 0596

Turkish Airlines Shanghai Office
Room 320, Shanghai Center
1376 West Nanjing Road
Shanghai, China 200040
Telephone: +86 (0)21 3222 0022

TURKMENISTAN AIRLINES

IATA Code: T5

Corporate website: www.turkmenairlines.com
17 Floor, Room 1717. Hanwei Plaza
Guanchua Roa
Beijing, China
100004
Telephone: +86 (0)10 6561 4240/6561 4230
Fax: +86 (0)10 6561 4231/6561 4238

UNI AIR

IATA Code: B7

Corporate website: www.uniair.com.tw

UNITED AIRLINES

IATA Code: UA

Corporate website: www.unitedairlines.com

United Airlines Beijing Office
Room 1708, Richen International Center
13 Nong Zhan Guan Nan Lu,
Chaoyang District
Beijing, 100125 China
Telephone: +86 (0)10 8468 6666 ext. 1

United Airlines Shanghai Office
Room 1905, World Trade Tower
No. 500 Guang Dong Road
Shanghai, 200001 China
Telephone: +86 (0)21 3311 4567

URAL AIRLINES

IATA Code: U6

Corporate website: www.uralairlines.ru

UZBEKISTAN AIRWAYS

IATA Code: HY

Corporate website: www.uzairways.com
Jian Guo Men Wai
19 Citic Building
2-01B, 100004
Beijing
Telephone: +86 (0)10 6500 6442
Fax: +86 (0)10 6525 3867
Email: bjs@uzairways.com

VLADIVOSTOK AIRLINES

IATA Code: XF

Corporate website: www.vladivostokavia.ru
15, 1503, Jianway SCHO, Chaoyang district
Beijing, China
Telephone: +86 (0)10 5869 8771

VIETNAM AIRLINES
IATA Code: VN
Corporate website: www.vietnamairlines.com

Vietnam Airlines Beijing Office
S121, Kempinski Hotel
Beijing Lufthansa Center
50 Liangmaqiao Road
Chaoyang District
Beijing 100016
Telephone: +86 (0)10 84541196 / 64638448
Fax: +86 (0)10 84541287

Vietnam Airlines Guangzhou Office
M04
368 Huanshi Dong Lu
Guangzhou 510064
Telephone: +86 (0)20 83765568; 83867093;
83846664 ext 13, 14
Fax: +86 (0)20 83827187

Vietnam Airlines Hong Kong Office
Unit 1004, 10th Floor
Tower One, Lippo Center
No 89 Queensway, Hong Kong
Telephone: +852 28104896
Fax: +852 28698856

Vietnam Airlines Shanghai Office
Room 1203, United Plaza
1468 Nanjing Rd (W)—Jing An district
200040 Shanghai
Telephone: +86 (0)21 6289 3306
Fax: +86 (0)21 6289 3316

VIRGIN ATLANTIC AIRWAYS
IATA Code: VS
Corporate website: www.virgin-atlantic.com

Virgin Atlantic Hong Kong Office
8th Floor, Alexandra House
18 Chater Road
Central
Hong Kong
Telephone: +852 2532 3030

Fax: +852 2537 4544
Email: customer.relations.hk@fly.virgin.com

Virgin Atlantic Shanghai Office
Unit 3221-3234
Shanghai Central Plaza
No.381 Huai Hai Middle Road
Shanghai 200020
China
Telephone: +86 (0)21 5353 4600
Fax: +86 (0)21 5353 4601

ZEST AIRWAYS
IATA Code: Z2
Corporate website: www.zestair.com.ph

CARGO OPERATORS

AIR BRIDGE CARGO
IATA Code: RU
Corporate website: www.airbridgecargo.com

Air Bridge Cargo Beijing Office
Room 2006B, Air China Plaza, No 36 Xiaoyun Road
Chaoyang District, Beijing 100027
Telephone: + 86 (0)10 8447 5936/37/38
Fax: + 86 (0)10 8447 5935
Email: service.pek@airbridgecargo.com

Air Bridge Cargo Hong Kong Office
Room 536A, 5/F
South Office Block
Super Terminal One
Chek lap Kok, HK Intl Airport
Telephone: + 852 2215 3928
Fax: + 852 2215 3878
Email: service.hkg@airbridgecargo.com

Air Bridge Cargo Shanghai Office
Room 3104-3105
Shanghai Maxdo Center
8 Xingyi Road
Shanghai 200336
Telephone: + 86 21 52080011

Fax: + 86 21 52080508

Email: service.sha@airbridgecargo.com

AIR CHINA CARGO

IATA Code: CA

Corporate website: www.airchina.com.cn

Corporate HQ (Beijing)

BeiJing international post office

PO BOX: 100600-6606

Beijing 100600

Global Sales Hotline: +86 4008 100 999

Telephone: +86 (0)10 6459 5912

Fax: +86 (0)10 8479 8686

CARGOLUX AIRLINES

IATA Code: CV

Corporate website: www.cargolux.com

Cargolux Airlines International S.A.

Room 341-343 BGS Cargo Terminal

Beijing Capital International Airport

Chao Yang District

Beijing 100621

Telephone: +86 (0) 10 6459 0572

Fax: +86 (0) 10 6459 0571

Email: asiapacific@cargolux.com

Cargolux Airlines Hong Kong Office

Units 615-616, North Tower, Concordia Plaza

1 Science Museum Road

Tsimshatsui East

Kowloon

Hong Kong

Telephone: +852 2736 7832

Fax: +852 2730 5137

Email: hkg@cargolux.com

Cargolux Airlines International S.A.

Room 3704, Bund Center

222 Yan An road (E)

Shanghai 200002

Telephone: +86 (0)21 63350012/13/14/15

Fax: +86 (0)21 63350016

Email: sha@cargolux.com

Cargolux Airlines Interr ational S.A.

Room 210, Xiamen International Airpor:

Air Cargo Terminal

Xiamen City

Fujian 361006

P.R. China

Tel+86 (592) 570 8531

Fax+86 (592) 570 8533

E-Mail: xmn@cargolux.cɔm

CHINA CARGO AIRLINES

IATA Code: CK

Corporate website: www.cc-air.com

Domestic Space Control ;SHA)

Shanghai Pudong Int. Airport

Shanghai

Telephone: +86 (0)21 62682821/ 68331005

Fax: +86 (0)21 626871<1

CHINA POSTAL AIRLINES

IATA Code: 8Y

Corporate website: www.cnpostair.com

Unit 11-14

Beijing Capital Internat onal Airport

Beijing 100037

Telephone: +86 (0)10 €845 8899

Fax: +86 (0)10 6847 7555

Email: cpa@cnpostair.cɔm

DHL CHINA

Corporate website: www.cn.dhl.com

DHL-Sinotrans International Air Courier Ltd

No. 18 Ronghua Nanlu,

BDA Beijing 100176

P.R. China

Telephone: +8610 87852000

Fax: +8610 67805799

JADE CARGO INTERNATIONAL

IATA Code: JI

Corporate website: www.jadecargo.com

Jade Cargo Internatioral Company Limited

Shenzhen Airlines Flig1t Operations Euilding, 6/F

Baoan International A rport

518128 Shenzhen
Guangdong
Customer Service (SZX): +86 (0)755 6188 6288

POLAR AIR CARGO
IATA Code: PO
Corporate website: www.polaraircargo.com

Polar Air Cargo Hong Kong Office
Polar Air Cargo
Suite 605-607
One Citygate
20 Tat Tung Road
Tung Chung, Lantau
Hong Kong
Telephone: + 852 2769 6110
Fax: + 852 2756 4085

Polar Air Cargo Shanghai Office
Room 4331-4333
Jun Ling Building
Jin Jiang Hotel
59 Mao Ming Rd (S), Luwan District
Shanghai 200020
China
Telephone: + 86 21 5111 9548
Fax: + 86 21 5466 3063

SF EXPRESS
China 24-hour hotline: 4008 111 111
Website: http://en.sf-express.com/cn/sc/

**SINOTRANS AIR TRANSPORTATION
DEVELOPMENT CO., LTD.**
Corporate website: www.sinoair.com
Head Office of Sinotrans Air Transportation
Development Co., Ltd.
5th floor, Office Building of Tianzhu Logistics Park of
Sinotrans Development
No.20 Tianzhu Road
Area A of Tianzhu Airport Industrial Park
Shunyi District, Beijing City 101312
Tel: +86 (0) 10-80418808
Fax: +86 (0) 10-80418933

TRANSMILE AIR SERVICES
IATA Code: TH
Corporate website: www.transmile.com
Transmile Beijing Office
Transmile Air Services Sdn Bhd
Hang'anbei Road Capital Airport
Beijing International Airport
P.R. CHINA
Zip Code 100621

Transmile Hong Kong Office
Transmile Air Services Sdn Bhd
Room 502, Asia Airfreight Terminal Building
Hong Kong International Airport,
HONG KONG
Telephone: +852 2215 3525
Fax: +852 2215 3719

Transmile Shenzhen Office
Transmile Air Services Sdn Bhd
No. 217, 2nd Floor of Terminal 2
Shenzhen Bao'an Airport,
P.R. CHINA

ULS AIR CARGO
IATA Code: GO
Corporate website: www.uls-global.com

Beijing Office (China HQ)
Office No .2004, Building"A"
Chaowaimen Business Center
Chaowai St. No 26, Chaoyang Dist.
Beijing
Telephone: +86 (0)10 8565 6559
Fax: +86 (0)10 8565 5992

Guangzhou Office
NO.306 South Tower
JINBIN DRAGON-FL Y Building.
NO.49 Huaxia Road, Tianhe District
Guangzhou, Guangdong
Telephone: +86 (0)20 3809 2916, 38092917
Fax: +86 (0)20 38092704

Shenzhen Office
Sanda Yayuan 1S17(near Mingtong Digital)
Huafa North Road 48, Futian District, Shenzhen
Contacts:
Telephone: +86 (0) 755 83244025
Fax: +86 (0) 755 82585036

UNI TOP AIRLINES
IATA Code: UW
Corporate website: www.uni-top.com.cn
Telephone: +86 (0)755 8367 2632
Fax: +86 (0)755 8367 2673

UPS CHINA
IATA Code: 5X
Corporate website: www.ups.com
UPS Customer Service Center (Call Center)
People's Republic of China
Nationwide Toll Free No: 800-820-8388 / 400-820-8388 (For cell phone users)
Overseas Dial-In: +86 (0)21 3896 5555
Fax: +86 (0)21 5831 0314

UPS Beijing
Room 1818, China World Tower 1
1, Jianguomenwai Avenue
Chaoyang District
Beijing 100004

UPS Guangzhou
Room 1801-1805/2705, Jianlibao Tower
410-412 Dongfeng Road Central
Guangzhou 510030

UPS Shanghai
23/F, China Insurance Building
166 Lujiazui East Road, Pudong District
Shanghai 200120

VOLGA DNEPR AIRLINES
IATA Code: VI
Corporate website: www.volga-dnepr.com
Volga-Dnepr China
2108 Air China Building
36 Xiaoyun Road

Chaoyang District 100027
Telephone: +86 (0)10 84₵7 5502
Fax: +86 (0)10 8447 5501

YANGTZE RIVER EXPRESS AIRLINES
IATA Code: Y8
Shanghai Office
2nd Konggang Street
2550 Hongqiao Road, Shanghai 200335
Telephone: +86 (0)21 5115
1372, +86 (0)21 5115 13J8
Fax: +86 (0)21 6269 7680

CORPORATE EXECUTIVE TRAVEL

DEER JET EXECUTIVE/CHARTER SERVICES
Corporate website: www.deerjet.com

Beijing Headquarters
24-hour Customer Service Center
10F, Grand China Air Building
B-2 East Third Ring Road
Chaoyang District
Beijing 100027
Tel: +86 (0)10 6506 8300
Fax: +86 (0)10 6506 8221
Email: deerjet@deerjet.com

HELISERVICES
Corporate website: www.heliservices.com
The Peninsula Hong Kong
Salisbury Road
Kowloon
Hong Kong
Telephone: +852 2802 0200
Fax: +852 2824 2033

HELI EXPRESS LTD
Corporate website: www.heliexpress.com
Room 1603
16/F China Merchants Tower
Shun Tak Center
200 Connaught Road Central

Hong Kong
Telephone: +852 2108 9988
Fax: +852 2108 9938

METROJET EXECUTIVE TRAVEL
Hong Kong Aviation Group
Corporate website: www.metrojet.com
Suite 1303-1306
One Citygate
20 Tat Tung Road
Tung Chung
Hong Kong
Telephone: +852 2523 6407
Fax: +852 2596 0359

Ministry of Education for the People's Republic of China
37 Damucang Hutong
Xidan
Beijing 100816
Telephone: +86 (0)10 6609 6114
Website: www.moe.edu.cn

The Office of Chinese Language Council International
17th Floor
Fangyuan Mansion
B56
Zhongguancun South Street
Beijing 100044
Telephone: +86 (0)10 88026121
Website: http://english.hanban.edu.cn

USEFUL WEBSITES AND ADDRESSES

- www.chinatoday.com—General Information about China

- www.gov.cn—The Chinese Central Government Web Portal

- www.china.org.cn—China's official gateway to news and information.

- www.alibaba.com—Trade directory for import/export of goods fro China

- www.asiaexpat.com—Expat website for major cities in Asia

- www.yp.com.cn/english—Mainland China Yellow Pages Website

- www.britishexpat.com—Expat website for Brits around the world

- www.fmprc.gov.cn/eng—Ministry of Foreign Affairs of the People's Republic of China

INDEX

H

Hainan xiv, 41, 83, 164, 204, 302, 303, 360, 370
Han Dynasty 4, 125
Hangzhou (section on) 62
Health Care 204
Hebei 303
Heilongjiang xvi, 298, 303
Henan 304, 366
History 1, 2, 18, 51, 59
    Timeline 1
Hobbies 251
Hong Kong (section on) 127
Hospitals 204, 205, 230, 294
Hotels 151
Hotpot 33
Housing 131, 144
Hubei 39, 42, 43, 304, 312
Humor, Sense of 287
Hunan 39, 42, 43, 78, 304, 321, 349, 351

I

India xvi, 4, 10, 11, 12, 43, 116, 150, 183, 188, 286, 327, 342, 348, 372, 373
Inner Mongolia 220, 305
Insurance 199
International Airlines 371, 382
International Calls 259
International Schools 200, 346, 352, 355
Internet Access 258
Internet Cafés 259
Invitations 286

J

Japan xi, xvi, 12, 13, 43, 44, 47, 49, 79, 80, 113, 123, 150, 256, 328, 336, 338, 343, 345, 379
Jiangsu 17, 42, 43, 62, 72, 75, 88, 104, 124, 160, 220, 292, 305, 307, 349, 351, 353
Jiangxi 43, 255, 306
Jilin 298, 306
Job Hunting 169

K

Kindergartens 202
KTV (Karaoke) Bars 255

L

Language 162, 184, 278, 285, 392

Law Firms 355
Learning Chinese 263, 266, 288
Liaoning 298, 336
Libraries 203
Light Railway 115
Links 29, 61, 96, 103, 128, 130
Little Emperors/Empresses 253

M

Macau (section on) 28
Maglev 91, 96
Mah-Jong 132, 252
Maids 134
Management Consultancies 291
Mao Zedong 3, 6, 7, 239
Marriage 224, 226, 276
May Day Holiday 248
Media 261
Metro 21, 31, 39, 41 45, 54, 55, 64, 73, 89, 100, 103, 106, 113, 158, 164, 216, 318, 338, 384
Midday Sun 286
Ming Dynasty 4, 5, 25, 26, 59, 75 76, 77, 93, 96, 109, 116
Miracle Cures 212
Mobile Doctors 212
Modems 260
Money Transfer 196
Moving to China
    What to Pack 273

N

Nanjing (section on) 72
Networking 176, 187
Newspapers 261
Ningxia 306
Noise 137, 138, 152

O

October Mid-Autumn Festival 247
One-child Policy 253
Opening Bank Accounts
    for Foreigners 194
Opera 24, 36, 59, 72, 77, 92, 125, 255
Opium Wars 5, 13, 44
Opticians 213

P

Pagodas 59, 66, 68, 107, 108, 110

ACKNOWLEDGMENTS

WITH THANKS TO THE FOLLOWING FOR THEIR GREAT SUPPORT AND advice:

Staff members at the British Embassy in Beijing.

Staff members at the American Embassy in Beijing.

Mr James A.C. Sinclair—Senior Consultant at Interchina Consulting in Shanghai

Mr. Tim Scharf—Dulwich College Management, Shanghai, China

Ms. Priscilla Wu—Editor of the Xinmin Evening News (Shanghai)

Mr. Roger Houghton, Hong Kong

ABOUT THE AUTHOR

NAVJOT SINGH IS A BRITISH WRITER AND PHOTOGRAPHER. NAVJOT HAS traveled to more than thirty-seven countries; and has lived and worked in four of them as an expat, including China where he has resided for over nine years, and where he continues to spend time.

Navjot contributes to various media applications on China, South-East Asia and Asia Pacific regions travel and business advice for expats. Alt hough China, SE Asia and the Asia Pacific Regions remain special subjects close to Navjot's heart, he is actively engaged in writing projects throughout the world.

Navjot was educated at Dulwich College; and later at Loughborough University. He is fluent in spoken Mandarin.

"I would like to dedicate this book to all my friends, with whom I shared many great and unforgettable memories during my time in China. Life is a wonderful and amazing gift from God, so enjoy every moment of it. Navjot."

CPSIA information can be obtained
at www.ICGtesting.com
Printed in the USA
LVOW13s0635200618

581356LV00019B/485/P